Anonymous

Transactions of the Royal Historical Society

Anonymous

Transactions of the Royal Historical Society

ISBN/EAN: 9783337417840

Printed in Europe, USA, Canada, Australia, Japan

Cover: Foto ©ninafisch / pixelio.de

More available books at **www.hansebooks.com**

TRANSACTIONS

OF THE

ROYAL HISTORICAL SOCIETY.

New Series.

Vol. VII.

LONDON :
LONGMANS, GREEN, AND CO.
AND NEW YORK : 15 EAST 16th STREET.
1893.

CONTENTS

	PAGE
PRESIDENTIAL ADDRESS. By the RIGHT HON. SIR MOUNT-STUART E. GRANT DUFF, G.C.S.I., PRESIDENT	1
NOTES ON THE FAMILY OF BETOUN IN CONNECTION WITH SOME ROYAL LETTERS OF JAMES VI. By HENRY ELLIOT MALDEN, M.A., F.R.Hist.S.	21
THE MAGYAR COUNTY: A STUDY IN THE COMPARATIVE HISTORY OF MUNICIPAL INSTITUTIONS. By EMIL REICH, Dr. Juris, F.R.Hist.S.	37
THE DRUIDS OF IRELAND. By PROFESSOR VON PFLUGK-HARTTUNG (Translated from the German).	55
ON THE INSTITUTA CNUTI ALIORUMQUE REGUM ANGLORUM. By F. LIEBERMANN, Corresponding Member of the R.Hist.S.	77
THE LAWS OF THE MERCERS COMPANY OF LICHFIELD. Communicated and Transcribed from the Original MS. by W. H. RUSSELL. With an Introduction by the REV. PROFESSOR CUNNINGHAM, D.D.	109
THE INQUISITION OF 1517. INCLOSURES AND EVICTIONS. Edited from the Lansdowne MS. I. 153. By I. S. LEADAM, M.A. Part II.	
PREFACE	127
NORFOLK	134
YORKSHIRE	219
HEREFORDSHIRE	254
STAFFORDSHIRE	270
HAMPSHIRE AND THE ISLE OF WIGHT	277
THE PROGRESS OF HISTORICAL RESEARCH DURING THE SESSION 1892-93	293
INDEX	307

REPORT OF COUNCIL.

LIST OF FELLOWS

FACSIMILE LETTER OF JAMES THE SIXTH . *to face p.* 27

TRANSACTIONS
OF THE
ROYAL HISTORICAL SOCIETY

PRESIDENTIAL ADDRESS

BY THE RIGHT HON. SIR MOUNTSTUART E. GRANT DUFF,
G.C.S.I., President.

SOME fifteen years ago, before Mr. Lowe had developed into Viscount Sherbrooke, we were sitting next each other, one afternoon, on the front Opposition Bench. The House was in the possession of an orator of the kind to whom it pays 'the genuine tribute of undissembled horror' by reducing itself to a handful of members, but we, for some reason or other, could not escape, and fell accordingly to talking in self-defence. The conversation found its way to Thucydides, and I asked my companion whether it had ever struck him to write an article on the uses of that author to the modern statesman. He said, 'No,' but the idea pleased him; he dallied with it for some time, and had even, I believe, some correspondence on the subject with the editor of one of the monthly reviews. Nothing, however, came of his good intentions, and I am not aware that anyone else has done what he did not do. It seems to me, accordingly, that it might not be wholly uninteresting to this Society if I were to try to answer the question whether the study of Thucydides is useful at all to the modern statesman, and, if so, to what extent?

Before these questions can be profitably asked or answered we must clear the way and clear our apprehensions by separating them from certain other important questions which are apt in common talk to get confused with them. We are not asking whether Thucydides was a great genius. That question has been answered by the admiration of the ages which have ratified his own proud words: 'My history is an everlasting possession, not a prize composition which is heard and forgotten.'

Again, we are not asking whether Thucydides had historical powers of a very high order. It is clear to every eye that he had the first great requisite of an historian: the readiness to take pains, and a great deal of pains, to search out truth. Many men, it has been wisely said, accept the very first version of any story they hear, and live with it ever afterwards as with a wife or a mistress. That was not the course pursued by Thucydides, who was, I suppose, the first person in the world to comment upon the little trouble which men take in the search after truth, and in their ready acceptance of whatever first comes to hand.[1] He wrote, too, *ad narrandum*, not *ad probandum*. He who writes a history to prove any thesis is insensibly tempted to strain facts to his purpose. He wrote to give a true picture of the events which had happened, and of the like events which might be expected to happen under similar circumstances in the order of human things.[2]

Yet further, we are not inquiring whether Thucydides had the mind of a statesman: who can read his speeches without seeing that he had? His speeches, I say, for although there may be here and there, as surely in the Funeral Oration, echoes of what he himself heard, or of what the speakers were reported to him to have said, they are evolved almost entirely out of the mind of the historian. It is his criticism of life which we obtain from them, and by no means any great insight into the minds of Archidamus, or Alcibiades, or Hermocrates, or Nicias. As far as the speeches are concerned, the history, so careful in its narrative portions, must be treated as an historical novel, and a novel in which the personality of the writer shines through his characters.

Lastly, we are not inquiring whether the work of Thucy-

[1] Book i. chap. xx.   [2] *Ibid.* chap. xxii.

dides was likely to be useful to Greek statesmen, nor even to statesmen who lived in a world not wholly unlike the Greece of the Peloponnesian War—say, in that of the Italian Republics.

The questions I intend to ask have to do simply with the modern statesman—the statesman of the year 1893, and, more especially, with the English statesman.

First, then, let us look at the narrative portions of the history. Of course there are endless passages in Thucydides which everyone would read with great interest on the spots described, and there are many which everyone would wish to have read from their literary merit; but I am not considering at present either the pleasure of the traveller or that of the man of taste. To Thucydides, the war which filled up so large a portion of his life seemed from the first likely to be the most important ever waged, but we can see now that, in its consequences, it was nothing like so important as the shorter struggles with which we chiefly associate the names of Marathon and Salamis.

Mr. Ruskin has picturesquely described the Peloponnesian War as 'the central tragedy of all the world; the suicide of Greece.' The phrase, however, is a good deal more picturesque than accurate. The Peloponnesian War was not the suicide of Greece. The idea that it was came from the pestilent habit of confining the attention of boys at school and young men at college far too much to a brief, though no doubt remarkable, period of Greek history. For many purposes it may be said that the political importance of Greece only began with Alexander. If she committed suicide in the Peloponnesian War, she assuredly rose to life again when he invaded Asia.

The modern statesman who wishes to be thoroughly furnished for his work ought to have a good foundation of historical knowledge; ought to have present to his mind the outlines of Greek history, and of that history the events of the Peloponnesian War are a part, but a large portion of its details are for his purposes really of no importance whatever. Many of us learnt them at Oxford only to forget them in no long space of time, and I do not think we had much to regret.

Then, the circumstances of Greece during the period of the Peloponnesian War are so utterly unlike anything now existing, that I do not see how any of its incidents can bear upon a single one of the countless problems which are now demanding solution. The word Democracy is constantly on our lips, but the Greek democracies of those days were entirely different from anything we know under that name. The Institution of Slavery of itself vitiates all comparisons.

I think, then, it is not to the narrative of Thucydides, but to the speeches and other reflections interspersed through it, that we must look for anything likely to be of much use to the modern statesman, and the simplest course will probably be to go straight through the whole work, noticing those sayings which seem to show most statesmanlike insight and to be most worthy of being treasured in the memory. The first, to which I alluded a few moments ago, is to be found in chapter xxi. of book i. The author is speaking of the greatness of the Peloponnesian War: 'Men will always judge,' he says, 'any war in which they are actually fighting to be the greatest at the time, but, after it is over, revert to their admiration of some other which has preceded it.'

The next is in the speech of the Corcyræans, in chapter xxxiv.: 'All colonies honour their mother-city when she treats them well, but are estranged from her by injustice. For colonists are not meant to be the servants but the equals of those who remain at home.'

That is a maxim which, duly pondered, might have saved England a very serious calamity, though it must be admitted that Mr. Lecky has shown that the amount of injustice done by George Grenville's proposals to our American colonists was a good deal less than is usually supposed. Not equally wise, perhaps, is the dictum a little further on in the same speech: 'For he passes through life most securely who has least reason to reproach himself with complaisance to his enemies.' There is a good deal to be said for the Persian adage, ' The peace of the two worlds depends on these two maxims—Be kind to your friends and be merciful to your enemies.'

The speech of the Corinthians is conceived in a higher tone. The two following sentences, in chapter xlii, are both worthy of the best kind of statesman: ' Do not say to yourselves that this is just, but that in the event of war something else is expedient; for the true path of expediency is the path of right.' And again: ' Do not be attracted by their offer of a great naval alliance; for to do no wrong to a neighbour is a surer source of strength than to gain a perilous advantage under the influence of a momentary illusion.'

Then in the speech of the Athenian envoys in chapter lxxvii, comes a very shrewd observation: ' The ruler of the day is always detested by his subjects. And should your empire supplant ours, may not you lose the goodwill which you owe to the fear of us?'

That is a maxim which might well be remembered by the not very wise people who talk about British rule in India not being ' sympathetic.' I wonder when a ruler belonging to another nation was really felt to be ' sympathetic' by the ruled.

Mountstuart Elphinstone used to say that if you asked any native of India belonging to one of the more powerful races whether he would like to be rid of British rule, he would, if he spoke the truth, say, 'Most assuredly.' If, however, you went through every possible alternative, suggesting that he should be ruled by any one of the peoples of India save that to which he himself belonged, he would shriek with horror and say that he infinitely preferred the British Raj to that.

Excellent, too, is the following in the same chapter: ' Realise while there is time the inscrutable nature of war, and how, when protracted, it generally ends in becoming a mere matter of chance over which neither of us can have any control, the event being equally unknown and equally hazardous to both.'

The next passage I have marked is in chapter lxxxiii., when the wise Archidamus is made to tell the Spartans : 'War is not an affair of arms but of money, which gives to arms their use.'

And again, near the end in chapter lxxxv. : 'We can afford to wait when others cannot, because we are strong.'

That has seemed to me very often to be our own wisest policy in dealing with the Central Asian question. I remember sitting down one day in 1873, after making a speech upon that subject as Under-Secretary for India, with almost these very words on my lips, only I put them in their Spanish form : 'Let him attack who wills : the strong man waits.'

We may pass on now to the speech of the Corinthians when the Lacedæmonians had summoned their allies to confer with them at Sparta, and to the words in chapter cxxii. : 'For war least of all things conforms to prescribed rules ; it strikes out a path for itself when the moment comes.'

With this passage we may compare the words of Pericles to the Athenians in chapter cxl. : 'The movement of events is often as wayward and incomprehensible as the course of human thought ; and this is why we ascribe to chance whatever belies our calculation.'

We may next turn to chapter viii. of book ii., in which occurs the remark : 'On neither side were there any mean thoughts ; they were both full of enthusiasm, and no wonder, for all men are energetic when they are making a beginning.'

In the same chapter is the memorable sentence describing the general excitement at the outset of the war—an excitement to be repeated in so many countries on so many similar occasions : 'Cities and individuals were eager to assist them, and where a man could not hope to be present, there it seemed to him that all things were at a stand.'

A little later in chapter ii. we have the dictum of Archidamus : 'The general and the soldier of every State should be always expecting that his own division of the army will be the one first in danger.'

In the Funeral Oration, so full of striking things which

do not bear upon my present subject, are four passages which more or less do : ' Mankind are tolerant of the praises of others so long as each thinks that he can do as well or nearly as well himself, but when the speaker rises above him jealousy is aroused, and he begins to be incredulous.'

'The whole earth is a sepulchre of famous men.'

'A man's counsel cannot have equal weight or worth when he has no children to risk in the general danger.'

'For a woman it is a great glory not to be talked about for good or for evil among men.'

Later in the same book comes the speech of Pericles on his defence. He says in the course of it : 'He judges well who accepts unpopularity in a great cause. Hatred does not last long.'

In book iii. the first thing I have noticed is a passage in the speech of Cleon : 'Dulness and modesty are a more useful combination than cleverness and licence, and the more simple sort generally make better citizens than the more astute. For the latter desire to be thought wiser than the laws ; they want to be always taking a lead in the discussions of the Assembly.' Although Cleon was the speaker, the same thought has occurred to a good many people who were not demagogues. We have all heard the story of a Whip who, talking of his steady supporters, remarked with enthusiasm to a friend : ' They are the best brute votes in Christendom ;' and some of us have heard of the old Scotch member who, at the end of a long Parliamentary life, remarked : 'I have heard a great many speeches which have changed my opinion, but never one which has changed my vote.' His politics were by no means demagogic or even democratic, but Cleon would, I am sure, have approved the sentiment, and would have no less approved his one speech ; for it was the shortest ever made in the House of Commons, and consisted of six words only—words which in this grave assembly I will not quote. That gentleman was, however, surpassed by another, whom Lord Palmerston used to call the best member whom Ireland ever sent to Parliament, for he sat thirty years in the House and never once opened his lips.'

An observation not very unlike Cleon's is to be found in the 'Testament de Richelieu,' and really, put in the form in which it occurs in that work, there is a great deal of truth in it:

'Les plus grands esprits sont plus dangereux qu'utiles au maniement des affaires ; s'ils n'ont beaucoup plus de plomb que de vif argent ils ne valent rien pour l'Etat.

'Il y en a qui sont fertiles en inventions et abondans en pensées, mais si variables en leurs desseins, que ceux du soir et du matin sont toujours différens, et qui ont si peu de suite et de choix en leurs résolutions, qu'ils changent les bonnes aussi bien que les mauvaises, et ne demeurent jamais constans en aucune.'

In the speech of Diodotus in reply to Cleon, we have the words : ' In my opinion the two things most adverse to good counsel are haste and passion.' The whole of the reflections on the Corcyræan sedition, beginning with the words at the end of chapter lxxxi. down to the end of chapter lxxxiv., are well worth the study of all statesmen in all times.

' This seemed to be the worst of revolutions, because it was the first.

' For not long afterwards the whole Hellenic world was in commotion ; in every city the chiefs of the democracy and of the oligarchy were struggling, the one to bring in the Athenians, the other the Lacedæmonians. Now, in time of peace, men would have had no excuse for introducing either, and no desire to do so, but when they were at war, and both sides could easily obtain allies to the hurt of their enemies and the advantage of themselves, the dissatisfied party were only too ready to invoke foreign aid. And revolution brought upon the cities of Hellas many terrible calamities, such as have been, and always will be, while human nature remains the same, but which are more or less aggravated and differ in character with every new combination of circumstances. In peace and prosperity both States and individuals are actuated by higher motives, because they do not fall under the dominion of imperious necessities; but war, which takes away the comfortable provision of daily life, is a hard master, and tends to assimilate men's characters to their conditions.

'When troubles had once begun in the cities, those who followed carried the revolutionary spirit further and further, and determined to outdo the report of all who had preceded them by the ingenuity of their enterprises and the atrocity of their revenges. The meaning of words had no longer the same relation to things, but was changed by them as they thought proper. Reckless daring was held to be loyal courage; prudent delay was the excuse of a coward; moderation was the disguise of unmanly weakness; to know everything was to do nothing. Frantic energy was the true quality of a man. A conspirator who wanted to be safe was a recreant in disguise. The lover of violence was always trusted, and his opponent suspected. He who succeeded in a plot was deemed knowing, but a still greater master in craft was he who detected one. On the other hand, he who plotted from the first to have nothing to do with plots was a breaker up of parties and a poltroon who was afraid of the enemy. In a word, he who could outstrip another in a bad action was applauded, and so was he who encouraged to evil one who had no idea of it. The tie of party was stronger than the tie of blood, because a partisan was more ready to dare without asking why. (For party associations are not based upon any established law, nor do they seek the public good; they are formed in defiance of the laws and from self-interest.) The seal of good faith was not divine law, but fellowship in crime. If an enemy, when he was in the ascendant, offered fair words, the opposite party received them not in a generous spirit, but by a jealous watchfulness of his actions. Revenge was dearer than self-preservation. Any agreements sworn to by either party, when they could do nothing else, were binding as long as both were powerless. But he who, on a favourable opportunity, first took courage and struck at his enemy when he saw him off his guard, had greater pleasure in a perfidious, than he would have had in an open, act of revenge; he congratulated himself that he had taken the safer course and also that he had overreached his enemy and gained the prize of superior ability. In general, the dishonest more easily gain credit for cleverness than the simple for goodness; men take a pride in the one, but are ashamed of the other.

'The cause of all these evils was the love of power, originating in avarice and ambition, and the party-spirit which is engendered by them when men are fairly embarked in a contest. For the leaders on either side used specious names, the one party professing to uphold the constitutional equality of the many, the other the wisdom of an aristocracy; while they made the public interests, to which in name they were devoted, in reality their prize. Striving in every way to overcome each other, they committed the most monstrous crimes; yet even these were surpassed by the magnitude of their revenges, which they pursued to the very utmost; neither party observing any definite limits either of justice or public expediency, but both alike making the caprice of the moment their law.

'Either by the help of an unrighteous sentence or grasping power with the strong hand, they were eager to satiate the impatience of party-spirit. Neither faction cared for religion; but any fair pretence which succeeded in effecting some odious purpose was greatly lauded. And the citizens who were of neither party fell a prey to both: either they were disliked because they held aloof, or men were jealous of their surviving.

'Thus revolution gave birth to every form of wickedness in Hellas. The simplicity which is so large an element in a noble nature was laughed to scorn and disappeared. An attitude of perfidious antagonism everywhere prevailed, for there was no word binding enough, nor oath terrible enough to reconcile enemies. Each man was strong only in the conviction that nothing was secure; he must look to his own safety, and could not afford to trust others. Inferior intellects generally succeeded best. For, aware of their own deficiencies, and fearing the capacity of their opponents, for whom they were no match in powers of speech, and whose subtle wits were likely to anticipate them in contriving evil, they struck boldly and at once. But the cleverer sort, presuming in their arrogance that they would be aware in time, and disdaining to act when they could think, were taken off their guard and easily destroyed.

'Now, in Corcyra most of these deeds were perpetrated, and for the first time. There was every crime which men might be supposed to perpetrate in revenge who had been governed not wisely, but tyrannically, and now had the oppressor at their mercy. There were the dishonest designs of others, who were longing to be relieved from their habitual poverty, and were naturally animated by a passionate desire for their neighbour's goods ; and there were crimes of another class which men commit, not from covetousness, but from the enmity which equals foster towards one another, until they are carried away by their blind rage into the extremes of pitiless cruelty. At such a time the life of the city was all in disorder, and human nature, which is always ready to transgress the laws, having now trampled them under foot, delighted to show that her passions were ungovernable ; that she was stronger than justice, and the enemy of everything above her. If malignity had not exercised a fatal power, how could anyone have preferred revenge to piety, and gain to innocence ? But, when men are retaliating upon others, they are reckless of the future, and do not hesitate to annul those common laws of humanity to which every individual trusts for his own hope of deliverance should he ever be overtaken by calamity ; they forget that in their own hour of need they will look for them in vain.'

In book iv., chapter xvii., in the speech of the Lacedæmonians at Athens, when so large a portion of their force was shut up in Sphacteria, you have a sentence, the recollection of which might well have prevented the widespread calamities which have recently thrown so many private fortunes into confusion: 'You will then escape the reverse which is apt to be experienced by men who attain any unusual good fortune; for, having already succeeded beyond all expectation, they see no reason why they should set any limit to their hopes and desires.'

In chapter lv. there is the happy phrase: 'A power like the Athenians, in whose eyes to miss an opportunity was to lose a victory.'

In chapter lxii. we have this remark of Hermocrates: 'The revenge of a wrong is not always successful merely because it is just; nor is strength most assured of victory when it is most full of hope. The inscrutable future is the controller of events, and, being the most treacherous of all things, is also the most beneficent; for when there is mutual fear, men think twice before they make aggressions upon one another.'

In chapter cviii. is the judicious reflection: 'For such is the manner of men; what they like is always seen by them in the light of unreflecting hope; what they dislike they peremptorily set aside by an arbitrary conclusion.'

The speech of Brasidas when he was attacked by the Illyrians, to be found in chapter cxxvi., contains the whole philosophy of civilised campaigning amongst barbarians. Many an Indian officer might have addressed his troops in almost the very same words.

The fifth book helps us very little. There is the saying of Brasidas in chapter ix. which may be pressed into the service: 'Reinforcements are always more formidable to an enemy than the troops with which they are already engaged.'

There is also the reflection in chapter lxix., when, speaking of the Spartans, Thucydides says: 'They had learnt that true safety was to be found in long previous training, and not in eloquent exhortations uttered when they were going into action.'

In the Melian controversy we have, in chapter ciii., the following: 'Avoid the error of which so many are guilty, who, although they might still be saved if they would take the natural means, when visible grounds of confidence forsake them have recourse to the invisible, to prophecies and oracles, and the like, which ruin men by the hopes which they inspire in them.'

And in chapter cv.: 'Of gods we think, and of men we know, that by a law of their nature wherever they can rule they will.' The words in chapter cx. are not without a bearing on English naval policy, and might have been quoted, not inappropriately, against those who were opposed to the American proposals of 1856 with regard to belligerent rights at sea, because they thought it was to the advantage of England, as the greatest naval power, to keep up the old rule, and by no means to enlarge the Declaration of Paris: 'The masters of the sea will have more difficulty in overtaking vessels which want to escape than the pursued in escaping.' There is wisdom, too, in the Athenian remark in chapter cxi., a remark, by-the-by, much belied by their conduct: 'To maintain our rights against equals, to be politic with superiors, and to be moderate towards inferiors, is the path of safety.'

I do not think there is anything bearing on my present subject in book vi., unless it be the sentence in chapter xv. about Athens having been ruined because she had attached more importance to the private vices of Alcibiades than to his powers of being useful to the State. One can conceive circumstances under which such a reflection as that might occur to a modern mind, though, of course, it has more bearing on the affairs of a small City State, where men are few, than it could have in France or other large countries. Note, too, the curious passage in chapter lxxxix., in which Alcibiades says: 'Of course, like all sensible men, we know only too well what democracy is, and I better than any one, who have so good a reason for abusing it. The follies of democracy are universally admitted, and there is nothing new to be said about them.'

In book vii., which is, as we all know, much the most remarkable portion of the whole history, the portion which has done most to conduce to the belief that Thucydides had great tragic, as Herodotus had great epic, genius, we look in vain, as might have been expected from the character of the narrative, for almost anything of which I can make use in the present connection. The memorable phrase of Nicias, which concludes chapter lxxvii.—'For men, and not walls nor ships in which are no men, constitute a State'—perhaps comes nearest to doing so.

No one would expect the unfinished eighth book to contribute very much. Possibly the first chapter, describing the consternation at Athens when the news of the annihilation of the Sicilian expedition was received, is the part of it which contains the most instruction for our times. It is in it that occurs the observation: 'After the manner of a democracy they were very amenable to discipline while their fright lasted.' Then, in chapter xxiv., there is the implied recommendation of moderation in prosperity contained in the words: 'No people, as far as I know, except the Chians and Lacedæmonians (but the Chians not equally with the Lacedæmonians), have preserved moderation in prosperity, and in proportion as their city has gained in power they have gained also in the stability of their government.'

In chapter lxxvi. is the not unreasonable question of the mutinous soldiery, who, speaking of the authorities at Athens, said : 'They cannot aid us by good counsel ; and yet for what other reason do States exercise authority over armies ? '

I may call attention, also, to the sentence in chapter xcvii. about the government of the five thousand : 'This government, during its early days, was the best which the Athenians ever enjoyed within my memory. Oligarchy and democracy were duly attempered.'

If anyone will go through Thucydides again and bring up more political pearls from his depths, I am sure I shall be delighted. Almost every scholar who reads what I am now saying will feel quite certain, at first, that I have overlooked a great many treasures. Perhaps it is so ; but all I can say is that these are all the passages which, after a very careful and conscientious search, I have been able to find, and it cannot be denied that a certain number of them, although containing observations which were probably new when they were written down, belong now to the commonplace of politics. One is tempted to ask whether a natural sentiment of gratitude to a writer who has preserved for us many important facts, and who was the pioneer of political history, has not led scholars a little astray?

What sane person nowadays, who was not making a voyage in the Ægean, would care to retain in his mind even for a day the details of all those petty conflicts on the shores of Asia Minor and amongst the Turkish islands? Is there anything, I wonder, in Thucydides which, having regard to the number of great books that have now to be read and great subjects that ought to be more or less understood, should be read in the original even by a young man who wishes to have all the chances, and who carries on his general education to two-and-twenty, save the first twenty-three chapters of the first book, the Funeral Oration in the second book, and perhaps the whole of book vii.? I do not know what is the case now, but certainly when I was at Oxford, some two- or three-and-forty years ago, the attention of young men was far too much fixed upon the difficulties of the language, and the result was that most men could not see the wood for the trees, or form any reasonable view of the merits of the book as a whole, or what the study of it was doing for their minds. And it is not as if the involved language so common in Thucydides had been deliberately selected by him, as was that of Tacitus, for the purpose of producing what some one has very well called Rembrandtesque effects. It was nothing of the kind. Thucydides had to deal with an instrument which had not yet been used for the purpose to which he put it, and he used it as well as he could.

That he used it quite successfully either in political reflections or in speeches cannot be reasonably asserted. With regard to the latter I may remark, a modern statesman may be, and constantly is, tolerably indifferent to the impression he produces upon the minds of the two or three hundred people who hear him, because he knows that what he is saying will be read within twelve hours by hundreds of thousands; but a speaker at Athens or at Sparta had no press to multiply his utterances. He was dependent on the impression produced, and the impression produced by most of the speeches in Thucydides, even upon the most quick-witted audience, would have been but slight.

An able man and excellent scholar complained to me the other day that the Master of Balliol's translation, from which I have taken the extracts I have read to-day, was too smooth and flowing; did not sufficiently reflect the struggle of the writer to express his thoughts. I cannot think that that is a defect. Surely, except in cases where obscurity is intentional, the business of a translator is to arrive at the meaning of his author, and to make it as clear as he knows how. When obscurity is intentional, the translator had better pass by on the other side, and find some fitter occupation, unless his object is merely the Bohnian one of enabling the student to read the original. On this subject the whole of the preface to the Master of Balliol's translation is extremely well worthy of study, and, not least, the following remarks:

'He who considers that Thucydides was a great genius writing in an ante-grammatical age, when logic was just beginning to be cultivated; who had thoughts far beyond his contemporaries, and who had great difficulty in the arrangement and expression of them; who is anxious, but not always able, to escape tautology, will not be surprised at his personifications; at his confusion of negatives and affirmatives, of consequents and antecedents; at his imperfect antithesis and involved parentheses; at his employment of the participle to express abstract ideas in the making; at his substitution of one construction for another; at his repetition of a word, or unmeaning alteration of it, for the sake of variety; at his over-logical form; at his forgetfulness of the beginning of a sentence before he arrives at the end of it. The solecisms or barbarisms of which he is supposed to be guilty are the natural phenomena of a language in a time of transition; and though not always, as Poppo maintains, common to other Greek writers, yet having some analogy by which they may be defended. They are also to be ascribed to a strong individuality which subtilises, which rationalises, which concentrates, which crowds the use of words, which thinks more than it can express (ψελλιζομένῳ γὰρ ἔοικε).'

This seems to me the only true account that can be given of the involved diction of Thucydides; unless, indeed, we are prepared to accept the extraordinary one which the late Mr. Robert Browning told me he once heard suggested in perfect good faith by a young man. 'Perhaps,' said the ingenious critic, 'he was out of his mind!'

When, however, putting aside all question of the difficulties of every kind which beset his path, we reread the history of Thucydides merely for the purpose for which I have been rereading it—that is, to form an opinion as to its uses to the modern statesman—I am afraid we shall be apt to think that we have been accustomed to overrate it. It is so easy to overrate the importance of any study which has given us a great amount of trouble. Of course the history of the Peloponnesian War teaches some lessons. The importance of sea power is brought home to us by the whole narrative; the folly of Chauvinism, or Jingoism, or Spread-eagleism is admirably illustrated by the story of the Sicilian expedition; but then both lessons are equally well illustrated by other histories which are forced by circumstances on the attention of our generation. The student may amuse himself by finding parallels to many of the personages of Thucydidean times. The supremely successful municipal statesman, rising to play a part and a brilliant part on a far wider stage, has not been unknown in days a good deal nearer to us than the age of Pericles, and a walk of less than two miles from the place where we are assembled would enable us to interview several personages who form excellent *pendants* to the least scrupulous politicians of whom Thucydides has left any record. Such parallels, however, are merely amusements, and they are always liable to fail in some essential particular.

I do not know whether any of my hearers remember the personal appearance of the late Mr. Serjeant Dowse, a very able and brilliant man, who was a member for too short a time of Mr. Gladstone's first Administration, and later an Irish judge of high repute. If they do, they will not be surprised to learn that someone said to Mr. Disraeli : ' Don't you think that Dowse is very like Socrates ? ' Disraeli put up his eyeglass and, looking across to the Treasury Bench, said : ' Yes, about as like as —— is to Alcibiades,' mentioning the name of another member of the Government who is still alive, and who had nothing in common with Alcibiades except his charm. That is an illustration of the kind of defect which is found in most ' historical parallels.'

I wonder whether very much is to be learnt from the details of Greek politics or war. Did the whole Peloponnesian struggle bring forward one considerable commander with the exception of Brasidas ? Gylippus was evidently an able officer, and Hermocrates a sensible politician. Were they more ? Is there any evidence that Pericles had that aptness to be right which is the first merit of a statesman ? Mr. Evelyn Abbott, the last eminent scholar in this country who has devoted himself to the subject, would say not, while regarding him as a very great benefactor to the world. That leads me to the question, whether we approach Greek history for teaching purposes in the right way. I hope there will for a long time be students who will work at the details of Greek history ; who will turn Greek into English classics like the Master of Balliol ; who will dig up ancient remains, survey battlefields, and gather every fragment of information that can be accumulated, from inscriptions, from Egyptian papyri, from every imaginable source. When it has been all done, however, will Greek politics or Greek history ever be worth the study, not of the scholar, but of the mere highly-educated man of the world, except in their outlines ? Do not we want a history of Greece, the central idea of which shall be that what made Greece important was its art, science, and literature, not its practical politics ? Renan used to say that the man whom he most envied was he who, after studying the history of Greece for sixty years, should sit down lovingly to write it ; adding, that if a second life could be granted to him he would employ it in that way. . . . Well, we know how he would have written it. He would have written it on the principle on which he wrote the history of Israel. He thought that if there was one miraculous history there were certainly three miraculous histories— that of Israel, the people who created and developed religion as we understand the term ; of Greece, which invented art and began to apply right reason to the study of all things ; of Rome, which by its force and its administration made it possible for the other two to combine and gradually to conquer the world. . . . Is there no one who will produce a work a third part of the size of Grote, and as unlike the history of that eminent and excellent man as a speech on the Ballot is to a chorus of Sophocles ? We shall hardly arrive at such a result until people come to recognise where Greece was strong and where she was weak. Just think of the astounding fact to which Mr. Abbott calls our attention, that in 479 Athens was a heap of blackened ruins, and that fifty years afterwards all the great works of the Periclean age, except the Erechtheum, had been finished. Remember that Thucydides was the contemporary of, amongst others, Ictinus, the architect of the Parthenon ; of Menacles, the architect of the Propylæa ; of Phidias and Myron and Polycleitus, of Sophocles, of Euripides, of Anaxagoras, of Aristophanes. How many details of petty and inconclusive skirmishes we could willingly have spared, if we could have known instead a little more about these men. That is past praying for ; but we at least do know, thanks to the labours of ten thousand scholars, a great deal more than we did about the persons and the things which made Greece really great. Will no one bring them into relief in a history of Greece which shall give proper prominence to important political and military events, but pass over everything that is not essential to the work which Greece, and especially Attica, had to do in the world, which was to raise the human intellect and ' to open windows for it in every direction ' ?

NOTES ON THE FAMILY OF BETOUN IN CONNECTION WITH SOME ROYAL LETTERS OF JAMES VI.

By HENRY ELLIOT MALDEN, M.A., F.R.Hist.S.

THE following paper has for its *raison d'être* certain letters, three of James VI. of Scotland, and one of Francis Stewart, Earl of Bothwell, which have never before been made public, I believe, and the originals of which I can submit to the inspection of the Society. They are of no great historical importance, but with the circumstances amid which they were written they will help to throw some light upon the state of society in Scotland during the latter part of the sixteenth century, when James VI. was endeavouring to hold his own and support the dignity of the crown among the contending religious and family parties in Scotland, and was so serving an apprenticeship in kingcraft which ill fitted him for his subsequent place at the head of a peaceful, well-ordered kingdom like England. The letters are addressed to members of the family of Betoun, James Betoun of Creich, and his third cousin, Robert Betoun of Balfour.

The family of Betoun, Beton, Betun, Bethune (for the English spelling, *Beaton*, there is no Scotch authority), sprang from a younger line of the family who became Counts of Flanders, and were named from the town of Béthune in Artois. Various members of the family won more or less distinction in the early histories of France and England. One, Baldwin de Betun, commanded part of the crusading fleet of Richard I., and became in right of his wife Earl of Albemarle. The head of the house in his native country accompanied the Count of Flanders upon the Fourth Crusade, when Constantinople was taken in 1204, and the Latin Empire of the East was founded. He became Lord of Adrianople. A branch of the family settled in France. Their most distinguished descendant was Maximilian Béthune de Sully, Seigneur de Rosni, the famous minister of Henri IV. Marie Casimire de la Grange, the Queen of John Sobieski, was descended from the same family. With the foreign branch, however, we have nothing to do at present. A descendant of Baldwin, Richard I.'s mercenary leader, sought his fortune in Scotland, and his descendant marrying (A.D. 1360) the heiress of the Balfours of that ilk in Fife, founded the Scotch family of Bethune, or Betoun, of Balfour, with some of whom we are immediately concerned.

The heads of the family appear in Parliament among the lesser barons of Scotland at various dates, but they became of greater influence in the early sixteenth century.

James, Archbishop of Glasgow in 1508, Archbishop of St. Andrews in 1522, Lord Treasurer 1505-1507, Chancellor of Scotland in 1513-1526, was the second son of a laird of Balfour. His younger brother, Sir David Betoun of Creich, was Treasurer of Scotland 1507-1509.[1] James Betoun found himself as Chancellor at once called upon to cope with the misfortunes which threatened to overwhelm Scotland after the disastrous defeat of Flodden, 1513. The result of that battle, leaving a child upon the throne, had been to nearly extinguish the power of the central government. It had also almost destroyed the independence of the country. The Scotch kings had, by the aid of France, laboriously established a national independence of England, and during the weakness of the English Government in the fifteenth century, had become free from the need of French help and had attained a really independent position. Flodden changed all this. It was felt generally that the country must depend

[1] It is recorded of the Archbishop in a MS. family history that: 'He was a good, godly, wise, and charitable man, who promoted his brethren all to honourable estates and offices of the kingdom.'—*Family MS.* 1690. (This MS. was rescued when about to be applied to the singeing of chickens).

upon either France or England. Alliance with France meant political subservience: alliance with England might mean national subjection. The widow of James IV., slain at Flodden, married Archibald Douglas, the Earl of Angus. She was the sister of Henry VIII., and through her and her husband the English Government were hoping to control Scotland. The Douglasses were at the head of the turbulent nobility who constantly defied the Crown; they had a particular quarrel with the House of Stewart, whose original right by blood to the throne was, perhaps, worse than their own, and their enmity never ceased till James Douglas, Earl of Morton, still in alliance with England, helped to compass the final ruin of Mary Stewart. In necessary opposition to the Douglasses were the Hamiltons, descended from King James II., and heirs to the House of Stewart, if the one life of the young king, James V., should become extinct.

Naturally, therefore, the Hamiltons were found acting against the Douglasses and the English, and in favour of the French alliance. With them Betoun the Chancellor threw in all his influence and genius. In the famous skirmish in the streets of Edinburgh in 1520, called 'Cleanse the Causeway,' when the Douglasses drove the Hamiltons out of the High Street, the Chancellor was acting with the party defeated on that occasion. In 1526 Betoun was deprived of the Chancellorship by the Douglas interest. But in 1528 the young king, James V., escaping from the custody of the Douglasses, restored the royal power. James Betoun, however, though he continued to take an active part in the government, was not restored to the chancellorship. His more famous nephew, David Betoun, Abbot of Aberbrothwick, became Keeper of the Privy Seal. James was glad to use in his government ecclesiastics like the Betouns, who by birth and profession were separated from any of the too great nobles who had continually overshadowed the Crown.

The history of Scotland is largely made up of family feuds. They are not unimportant. When the great issues of the Reformation and Civil Wars are to be settled, the strength of the opposing parties is largely influenced by that of the families who embrace either side. Because one house is French or Spanish and Catholic in its sympathies, another will be found English and Reforming, till in the very last of the Scotch civil wars, the strength of the Jacobites is found to depend less upon any attachment to the House of Stewart than upon the hostility of certain other clans and families to the Campbells of Argyle.

But to return to the affairs of the sixteenth century. When James Betoun died in 1538, he had an immediate successor in his see in his nephew David Betoun, sometime Abbot of Aberbrothwick, now Archbishop of St. Andrews, and shortly Cardinal and *Legatus a Latere*, and Chancellor of Scotland, 1543. David Betoun pursued the policy of his uncle, and steadily resisted the attempts of Henry VIII. to obtain influence in Scotland. He has been the subject of much obloquy, owing chiefly to his persecution of the Reforming preachers and his execution of Wishart at St. Andrews. As Wishart had been privy to a plot against the Cardinal's life, the story has another side to it. Those who know most, however, of the state of Scotland will be the least inclined to look for tenderness or aversion to shed blood in those who had the task of maintaining order and national independence. Betoun was no worse than his neighbours, and was at all events a victim to the same spirit which he had displayed. He was barbarously murdered in his own house by Norman Leslie, not without the connivance of the English Government, which recognised in him the ablest champion of Scotch independence.

By the action of these two great statesmen of their line his family seems to have been committed to their policy and party. The Cardinal's nephew James became Archbishop of Glasgow (restored to his estates 1598 ; ob. 1603). This Archbishop of Glasgow's younger brothers, John and Andrew Betoun, were instrumental in the escape of Mary from Lochleven Castle. John Betoun was sent by her into France immediately after the defeat of Langside, and returning remained in attendance upon the Queen in England, till he died in 1570. He was buried at Edensor near Chatsworth, where a Latin epitaph, on a tomb erected by his brothers, commemorated the part he took in the rescue of the Queen *e manibus truculentissimi tyranni.*[1] The then head of the family however, the Cardinal's eldest nephew, also named John, pursued a safer line of policy, and remained quietly at home, dying in 1579. His eldest son John died without children 1591, and was succeeded as Laird of Balfour by his brother Robert, the recipient of three of the letters now before us. Robert had plunged into the support of the Queen's party as heartily as his cousin had done. He fought on the losing side at Langside; and his father became surety for his appearance at Edinburgh, if called upon, to answer for having 'committit slaucteris' in the civil war. He suffered no punishment, however, for this, nor for a subsequent adventure, so far as I can learn. In 1592, at a period when the King was seeking some support among the friends of his mother, he appears as a Privy Councillor, but is lax in his attendance. The letters of the King are addressed to this Robert. The letter from Bothwell is addressed to James Betoun of Creich, great-grandson of David Betoun of Creich, the Lord Treasurer and brother to the first Chancellor.

Having thus, at more length than I intended, but as briefly as I can, introduced the family, we may turn to the letters and their circumstances.

The letter from Bothwell to James Betoun is as follows:

Traist Freind, Eftar our maist hairttie commendationis, be kingis majesteis directioun brocht be the Maister of Werk, he hes commandit his greit hors that he laitlie gat out of Flanderis, as also for his hunting hors and quhat sumever uther greit hors his majestie left behind him in any handis to be send for and reterit altogeder to his hienes stablis at Halyruidhous; and thair to be weill provydit of

---

[1] His brothers there call him son of *John* B. of Auchmuty; there were two brothers John in the same family. The *Dict. of National Biogr.*, art. 'James B.,' is wrong in calling the Archbishop of Glasgow son to Betoun of Balfour. As the original brass reads *truculentiss: tyrann:* we may take the tyrant to be either the Regent or his mother, Lady Douglas of Lochleven.

several furniture and in full redines agains his majesteis arryvell. Querfore we will requeist yow, and in his hienes name command yow, the ye faill not all excuses set apairt to have the broun cusseur deliverid to yow be George Hume at Halyruidhous, to be deliverit to Mr. Williame Leslie or uther ye resident Maister Stabular thair, upon ye aucht day of Aprill; as ye will do his hienes gude service and plesure. And swa luking that this salbe obeit, committis yow to God. At Edinburgh the last day of Marche 1590.

BOTHWELL.

Endorsed : To our Ryght traist freind the laird of Creich.

The writer, Francis Stewart, Earl of Bothwell, was the son of a natural son of James V. His father married the sister of the notorious James Hepburn, Earl of Bothwell, and the forfeited dignity was revived for Francis Stewart, with the hereditary post of Lord High Admiral which had belonged to the Hepburns. He was perhaps the most turbulent person of a turbulent age. His rebellions and raids were so ill concerted and aimless that it is charitable to suppose that he was a little out of his mind. At this period, however (1590), he was in favour with his cousin the King—who was away on his matrimonial expedition to Denmark—and had been appointed with the Duke of Lennox to preside over the Council during the King's absence. James had sailed for Denmark November 23, 1589, and returned early in May, 1590. The royal stud had evidently been quartered upon his lieges during his absence, and now the *avant courier* of the King, the Master of Werk, had brought word that they should be collected prior to the King's return with his bride. James Betoun had no doubt become custodian of the 'broun cusseur,' from the fact that he was Keeper of the Palace of Falkland, where was a park in which the King's horses were kept. James Betoun had occasion to rue the King's marriage. For in the Register of the Privy Council held at Stirling, March 14, 1593 (o.s.), we find James Betoun of Creich, possessor of the office and keeping of his Highness' Castle and Palace of Falkland, called to show his titles to that office, which are pronounced insufficient to justify his possession thereof, so that he is forced to give up the palace to the King's 'darrest

Receipt kept hand from his mates gross rent. The players
bought of for funn sale of the Rutland May 6 th Rec: bi-
the Nobleman becomes and partaining to gentm: from m: Bristles
to commen according to the other appoyntment bi not of
Imbolement made ffynement
kept afterwards for that in respect going now from
forme of oth. was obey'd for the going of m: Arthure
merfield And takeing fine in furnace and sent im: Sir Walter
of m: Bunch and 6,000m: to send too the first coo o
Rogeall Littur andmorecombe ffynement bi 2 peeces Cond bi
May of 20 twinfales And that In racept of greate in Londen
to pot ffome not Abutive notfall — 30 rma workemens ffynement
... made tonfied As you will ffnd, the moneyes of the
fyme of 1660 tyll, 97 funde good, wch, with m: ffm, ii. xi ffnd our vt paid
ffyom st Crisler: unntzme and ttt: followinge i paid the

from Oure in January. 1595

                                            James

bedfelowe' the Queen, who subsequently resided there. James Betoun had in fact received the office from his father Sir Robert, Comptroller of Queen Mary's household, husband to one of the Queen's French ladies, Jeannette de Renville, and father to Mary Betoun, one of the Queen's Maries. Sir Robert had gone with the Queen to France, and had married Mlle. de Renville there.

Falkland, I suspect, was a sore trouble to the family, for the next letter to the following effect from the King to Robert Betoun of Balfour is as follows:

Richt traist freind, We greit yow hairtlie weill : The last sommer resolveing to plenische our Parkis, we directed our trustie counsulor the laird of Halhill to yow and sum utheris our guid subjectis affecting our thrift and weill to se quhat guidis we myght have of benevolence for that effect. To quhome ye offering sum for your pairt, the same hes notwithstanding restit unsenttit for in defalt of not voiding of our Parkes to ressave thame. Quhilk being now done, be a decreit of removeing obteint agains the Keiperis and possessoris thairof, we have directed this barar our sirvand, and eirand, to crave ye number of guidis that ye will bestow for help of our guid intentioun and to signifie to yow ye tyme and place quher and quhan thai salbe send : As alsua to desyre yow effectuouslie to have the same in reddines upoun our next adverteisment As ye will kyth affected toward our weill and furtherance of that gude turne and will do us speciall and thankfull pleassur to be rememberit as occasioun sall present. Sua we commit yow to God. From Halyruidhous ye xvij day of Februar 1595
JAMES R.

Endorsement covered by mount but catalogued as to Robert Betun of Balfour.

The removing of the keepers and possessors of the royal parks, must include the removing of James Betoun from Falkland, and now his cousin Robert is called upon to plenish the park by way of benevolence, presumably with deer, for the sport of which both James and his Queen were extremely fond. Robert had a deer park at Kilrenny.

With the next letter we come into a long story illustrating most markedly the lawlessness of the country.

Richt traist freind, we grete yow weill. The plegeis brocht in for the gude rule of the borders mon be kepit be the noblemen barronis and gentlemen to quhom they are direct to remaine according to the order appointit be the act of Parliament maid thairanent. Thairfore we require yow rycht effectuuslie that ye ressave young Will. Johnnstoun of Auldwais plege for the gaing of Mylnebank and Myreheid; and keip him in fre ward, and caus him be assurit of meit, drink and bedding, ay and tyll he be fred be our speciall lettre and warrand subscrivit be our hand and be sevin of our counsale. And that yow nawyse grant him licence to pair hame nor libertie without our said warrand subscrivit in manner foresaid as ye will eschew the incurring of the pane of twa thowsand pundes prescrivit be the said act of Parliament. Thus we commit you to God. At Halyrudhous the last day of Januar. 1595.

JAMES R.

Endorsed : To oure richt traist freind the laird of Balfoure.

Now hereby hangs a long tale.

Among the standing feuds of Scotland, none were more bitter than that between the families of Johnstone in Annandale and Maxwell in Nithsdale. In 1593, Lord Maxwell, though a Catholic and formerly a Queen's man, was Warden of the West Marches. Sir James Johnstone of that ilk and of Dunskellie, fearing perhaps the official dignity of his hereditary enemy, made a formal peace with him. The Johnstones and Maxwell seem to have considered that this implied an overlooking by the Warden of any trifling delinquencies on the part of his ally, and on the strength of it the Johnstones harried part of Nithsdale, and drove off the cattle of some gentlemen of the name of Douglas of Torthorrald and of Drumlanrig, Crichton, Kirkpatrick of Closeburn, and Grierson of Lag. The injured parties applied to the Warden for help in vain, and the Crichtons, who tried to right themselves, were severely handled by the Johnstones. Then they bethought them of another way. They went to Maxwell and offered to enter into bonds of *Man-rent* with him, by which they would become bound to 'ride and gang' with him in any quarrel, provided he would help them in their need now.[1]

---

[1] Man-rent bonds were one of the worst causes of disorder in Scotland. By their means great men gathered a following by which they could defy the Government, and lesser men committed violence with impunity, secure in the protection of those to whom they could offer service in return.

What he would not do as Warden he agreed to do for the private advantage of acquiring useful followers. The bonds of man-rent were made, and Maxwell called upon Johnstone to surrender his booty. The rival chief, with all the formality of a diplomatist confronted by a foreign enemy, expressed surprise at this breach of his late understanding with Maxwell, and summoned his allies in turn. Who they were indicates the fellow-feeling of the Border riders against a Warden who was too interfering. The Scotts of Teviotdale and Eskdale, the Elliots and Armstrongs of Liddesdale, the Graemes of the Debateable Land, all came to help the Johnstones. A pitched battle was fought on Dryffe Sands, the Johnstones won the victory; Lord Maxwell was left desperately wounded on the ground, and was killed by one of the women of the Johnstones who was searching the field after the battle.

The most characteristic point of the story follows. The Government, who had the Northern Catholic Earls Huntly and Errol, aided by Bothwell, on their hands at the time, were powerless to interfere; so after a brief space they appointed Johnstone Warden of the Marches in succession to Maxwell. Hostages, however, were demanded for the future peacefulness of the contending parties. In the Privy Council Register, January 2, 1595 (o. s.), we find: 'Cautions in 10,000*l.* by Sir James Johnstone that he shall appear before the King and Council when required, and underlie such order as shall be given him.' Then Johnstone 'gaif up and nemmyt' the persons underwritten to be entered before his Majesty and his Secret Council as pledges for the good rule of the gangs undermentioned. A list of names of such hostages follows, including 'for the gang of Mylnebank and Myreheid young Will Johnstone of Auldwais.' Accordingly we find in the Register: 'Cautions by Sir James Johnstone and James Douglas of Torthorrald that the persons underwritten, presently entered by the same Sir J. J. as pledges for the good rule of their gangs undermentioned, shall immediately enter and keep ward with the Barons and others following, and that they shall in nowise escape till they be freed by the King's warrant, subscribed by him and seven of his Pr. Co. under the pain of 1,000£ for each pledge that so escapes, in case Douglas and Johnstone both or either of them enter not such escaped pledge again, or another pledge of the same gang or branch and as sufficient before the K. and Co. within 10 days of the said escape. To wit &c. and young Will J. of Auldwais pledge with the Laird of Balfour.' The Register of the Pr. Co. is full of such instances of surety being given for the good behaviour of troublesome persons. In 1593 Robert Betoun, the custodian of young Will Johnstone, the same who was at Langside and ' committit slaucteris,' was surety in 1,000 merks for James Tweedie of Drummelzear ' that he shall not invade nor trouble Lord Fleming, Sir James Douglas of Drumlanrig, Charles Geddes of Raucleane or any other person of the name of Geddes.'

In 1594, Robert Betoun was surety in 5,000 merks for George Gordoun apparent of Gight, that he shall remain south of the Tay when freed of his ward. This was at the time of the rebellion of the Gordons under Huntly in the north, and the Master of Gight had to be kept out of the way of bad example. One wonders how far it was possible to really control those for whom these men became sureties, or how much of the bail the sureties could have paid had their charges escaped. We must remember, though, that the pounds are pounds Scots.

Persons who were so freely trusted as bail for others might be presumed to be of exemplary behaviour themselves. The Privy Council Registers tell a different story. In 1593, James Scott of Balwearie was surety for Robert Betoun and his son David that they shall not harm George Seytoun of Errelstoun. Worse remains to be told. In 1594, January 26 (o.s.), John Fermour of Kingsbarns, in Fife, complained to the Council that whereas Sir John Melville of Carnbie had built a mill upon the lands of the King's tenants of Kingsbarns, and they had begun an action at law against him, Sir John with James Melville and Robert Betoun of Balfour (who was Sir John's cousin) and his servants, fell upon the said John Fermour

when going from St. Andrews to his house, and being
'missilit' and armed with hackbuts, pistolets, and other un-
lawful weapons, they cruelly beat and wounded him, shot him
in the head with a pistolet, and left him for dead. We do
not now look to Scotland for examples of this sort of thing,
nor elsewhere at present are such actions committed by landowners and privy councillors. For this, so far as appears,
only Sir John Melville was bound over to keep the peace.
Robert Betoun got off as scot free as he had apparently got
off from his other 'slaucteris.' Young Will Johnstone from
the Borders may, in comparatively peaceful Fife, have felt
quite at home in such a household; and even south of
the Tay the Gordoun from Buchan may have found life
worth living with Robert Betoun as his surety.

If the last letter, and all that hangs upon it, illustrates the
weakness of the Scottish crown, the last which I will read
illustrates perhaps its poverty. The third child of James VI.
and Anne of Denmark was born on Christmas Eve, 1598.
Her name was Margaret. She died as quite a young child.
Her baptism was delayed till the April following her birth,
perhaps to give time for celebrating it with becoming splen-
dour.

Richt traist freind We greit you hertlie wele Having appoynted
the Baptisme of our dearest Dochter to be heir at Halyruidhous
upoun Sonday the fyftene day of Aprile nixt, in sic honorable maner
as yat actioun craveth, We have therfore thoght guid richt effectuusly
to request and desire you to send us sic propynis and presentis agane
that day as is best then in seasoun and convenient for that actioun,
as ye regard o^r honno^r and will mereit o^r speciall thankes. Sua not
doutinge to find yor grete willingnes to pleasur us herin, sen ye ar
to be envyted be o^r uther letter to tak therof your awne guid cheir :
We commit you to God. From Halyruidhous, this tent day of
Februar 1598

JAMES R.

Endorsed : To o^r richt traist freind, The laird of Balfour, Betoun, &c. D.D.
(Signet)

The royal christening feast was apparently to be a sort of
picnic, to which the guests were to bring each their quota of

'guid cheir.' For we cannot suppose that this letter was singular, and that Balfour alone was asked for 'propynis and presentis.' Mr. Tytler, in his 'History of Scotland,' relates— I do not know on what authority—that the King's means of action against the Catholic lords had been hampered by the expenses of the christening of his son Henry in 1594; such a contingency was to be avoided, perhaps, by this economical arrangement. The King was often obliged to come upon the charity of his lieges. Once, when expecting the Spanish ambassador to demand an audience, he wrote to Boswell of Balmuto, asking for the loan of a pair of silk stockings, adding the pathetic argument, 'Ye would na wish your king to appear a scrub on sic an occasion.' It would be interesting to know what 'guid cheir' was provided by the different guests. I can make a reasonable conjecture that Robert Betoun brought herrings, cod, and lobsters to the feast.

He enjoyed extensive feudal rights over the town of Kilrenny in Fife, with its port of Cellardyke on the Firth of Forth. From the fishermen of Cellardyke he had certain dues of fish, the fish teinds they were called. I have a note of what these were, written in 1779, but evidently a record of the ancient dues. 'The teinds due to Mr. Bethune are the fourteenth white fish, that is, lobsters, cod, ling, haddocks, and these fish, except lobsters, are fished during the whole year; the seventeenth herring—both Lammas and winter herrings; the thirty-fourth fish from a Cellardyke boat going to another harbour than Cellardyke; and, likewise, a thirty-fourth part from each stranger boat coming into Cellardyke.' From thirteen to eighteen boats fished from Cellardyke about that time. If the teinds were duly exacted, and there was anything like a good haul of fish, Robert Betoun must certainly have had plenty of probably stale fish on his hands, ready for the King's necessities. It is at least a plausible surmise that the little Lady Margaret's christening feast was furnished forth with red herrings.

No doubt the feudal lord had originally built the harbour from which these dues were drawn, but we can readily see what an engine of annoyance they might have become to the fishermen. The privileges granted to the townsmen of Kilrenny, with the somewhat extensive return which they were expected to make to the laird, appear in the following charter, granted after 1543 (see *supra*).

We have wandered from the graver regions of history, and even in the story of Border faction fights and Fife 'moonlighting,' a vein of comedy exists for us at this distance of time, when we contemplate the struggles of an embarrassed government. There is a good deal of truth in

> Suave mari magno turbantibus æquora ventis
> E terra magnum alterius spectare laborem.

But in all seriousness the state of Scotland is illustrated by what I have related. The state of Scotland at a time when in England the law was really all powerful, when men lived in unfortified houses, and private war was as impossible as it is now. It is no great wonder that, after living for thirty-seven years in such a chaos of crime and treason, James was not fitted to rule at the head of a parliamentary government.

APPENDIX A

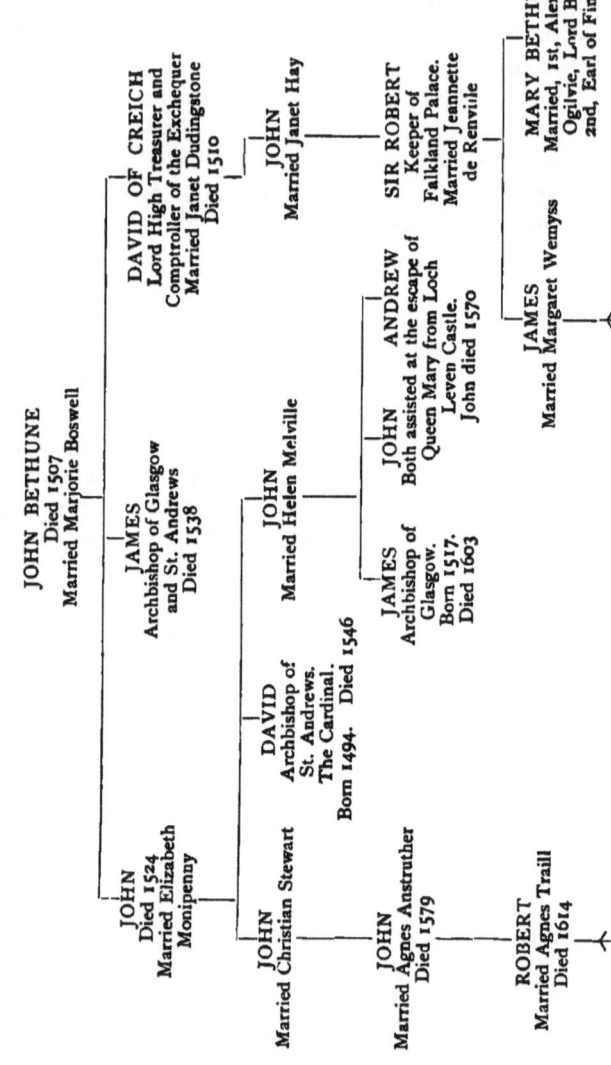

APPENDIX B

Coppy of the Priviledges and Services contained in the Charters and precepts of Clareconstat, granted by the Laird of Balfour to his vassalls at Kilrenny.[1]

After the dispositive clause in the charters follow these words : And with liberty to the said (here Vassalls name) for exerciseing all lawfull merchandize trafique and trade allowed by acts of parliament within the haill bounds of the said Burgh of Kilrenny Harbour and priviledges thereof AND inbringing and forthcarrieing in and from the said harbour ships boats and crears full or empty but any stop or impediment to be made by ME or any others in my name therin sette WITH priviledge also to them with the rest of the neighbours tennants Inhabitants and Freemen within the said Burgh of Kilrenny Once in the year as use is To elect Create and Choise one or more Baillies of the said Burgh haveing house and ffamily therein AND residing continualy or for the most part within the same for good rule and government of the said Burgh and administering Justice to the Inhabitants Burgesses and others repairing to and from the said Burgh AND to elect and choise the Council serjeants and others necessear for good rule and government of the said Burgh WITH this provision always that the names of all such persons to be nominate and chosen in the offices foresaide within the said Burgh before they be chosen be first yearly shewen to ME my heirs and successors and we consent thereto AND if any of these persons be seen or appear to be not loving and obedient to ME and my foresaids Then that person or persons shall be discharged and removed from bearing all office and charge within the said Burgh AND I and my foresaids shall imputt and place others in their room more favourable loveing and obedient to us AND THAT how oft as occasion shall present AND ALSO with priviledge to them to make Acts Statutes and Ordinances as use is within Burghs for keeping order and good neighbourhood, so that the said Acts be made with consent of ME and my foresaids and to be noways predjudicial to our priviledge utility and profite and to convicte the unlaws of Ryots and other unlaws to be convicted in their courts to the welfare of the said Burgh and Harbour thereof as shall please the Baillies of the said Burgh for the Time.

Follows a coppy of the Reddends and services : Paying therefore yearly the said —— and his heirs and successors to ME my

[1] No date, but after 1543.

heirs and successors Immediate Lawfull Superiors thereof the sum of —— of old feu duty with —— money foresaid in augmentation of my Rentall in name of feuduty at two Terms in the year Whitsunday and Martinmas by equal portions AND doubling the same the first year of the entry of each heir or heirs thereto AND GIVEING their sute and presence yearly to MY Three head Courts to be holden within the town of Kilrenny And to all other our particular Courts so oft as they shall be cited thereto AND OBEYING the Acts Statutes and Decreets thereof And bearing Scott and Lott with the rest of the Inhabitants AND shall be astruted to come with all kind of their Corns and Especially Malt to my Milne called Kilrenny Milne or Wind milne thereof And to grind their haill cornes at the said Milnes and none others And paying the moutures and other Dutys therefore used and wont, The said milne having water and wind milne wind and going able to serve them And likeways carrying from our harbour called Skinfasthaven fire coalls, Lime, Sclates and Timbers to our place of Kilrenny for maintaining and upholding thereof, AND FURTHER they shall be obliged to take and receive Cognetts of all (of us our heirs and successors and none others) their ships and boats and crears And sailling with us betwixt any part betwixt St. Abbs Head Montrose and Stirling Bridge upon our reasonable expences AND shall ride and gang with us upon our cost and charges And if they shall be charged to his Majesty's warrs and fall under the proclomation they shall be obligded to wait on ME and my foresaids and none others during the proclomation AND ALSO they shall be obligded to assist and concur with our officers in executing of our Acts and Decreets or if they shall Deforce our officers or break arriestments laid on in their hands by order of us or our Baillies THEN and in that case they shall be punished in their person and estate conform to the Acts of Parl[t] laws and practize of this kingdom and Acts of our Court made or to be made thereanent AND ALSO they shall take plain part with and maintain and defend Us and our foresaids against all pursuers and invaders of our person (The King's Majesty Excepted) WHEREIN if they faillie or come in the contrair or yet shall faillie in timeous and thankfull payment of the foresaid feuduty so that two terms thereof run together in the Third unpaid or yet shall annailzie or Dispone the feu and heritage above written or greatest part thereof to any person or persons without our consent or confirmation or Resignation made in Our hands THEN and in either of these cases they shall ipso facto lose and forfault the feu and heritage above written without any process of Law or Declarator to be moved or obtained thereanent.

THE MAGYAR COUNTY: A STUDY IN THE COMPARATIVE HISTORY OF MUNICIPAL INSTITUTIONS

By EMIL REICH, Dr.Juris, F.R.Hist.S.

Brief description of Hungary—General characteristics of Hungary in the Middle Ages—Statistical comparison of the territorial development of Prussia and Hungary—Hungary a 'national state'—Standpoint wherefrom to appreciate the Magyar County—History of the Magyar County—Comparison of Magyar and English counties—Sovereignty of the Magyar County—Comparison with Slav counties—Salutary effect of the Hungarian County—The privileges of noblemen in the administration of Hungarian counties—Recriminations of the non-Magyar nationalities of Hungary.

HUNGARY is an independent kingdom of its own ruling, more than one-half the size of France, and consists of Hungary proper (including Transylvania), and, moreover, Croatia, Slavonia, and the district of Fiume. In the present study we shall treat of Hungary proper only.

The territory of St. Stephen's crown proper is now divided into sixty-three counties (in Magyar, *vármegyék*), each of which is subdivided into districts (in Magyar, *járások*), the number of which is 407.[1] In addition to the counties, and partly independent of them from an administrative point of view, are nineteen 'free royal towns' (*szabad királyi város*), six towns with independent municipal institutions (*önálló törvényhatósági joggal felruházott város*), and other towns and smaller *communes*.[2] The population is, in round numbers, 15,000,000.

The Hungarian county is and always has been one of the vital organs of the Hungarian kingdom. In sharp

[1] George Fésüs, *Magy. Közigazg. Jog* (1887), p. 31. [2] G. Fésüs, *ib.*

contrast to the territorial divisions and subdivisions of Austria, Germany, and even France, the territorial unit in Hungary has always been, not a mere mechanical delimitation of space forced upon the people from without, but an organic element and constituent part of the very body of the Hungarian nation. He, and he alone, who fully grasps the significance and purport of the Hungarian county will also fully grasp the main features of Hungarian history.

Even a quick glance at the map of Europe in the eleventh, twelfth, and thirteenth centuries respectively, will suffice to impress upon us the cardinal divergence in the constitution of nations such as the Hungarians, the Bohemians, the Poles on the one hand, and the Germans, the French, and the Italians on the other. In the course of those centuries the present boundaries of Hungary and Bohemia are already clearly discernible, and, while occasionally advancing or retreating, they mark off in broad and well-defined lines a large expanse of territory united into one homogeneous realm. In Austria, Germany, or France, on the other hand, there are no such homogeneous territories of large extent; during the middle ages Austria, Germany, and France were broken up, and, as it were, atomised into ever-changing small and petty territories, the boundaries of which were constantly advancing or retreating, so that even the most learned despair of ever obtaining a clear and positive knowledge of the history of the territorial development of modern Germany, for instance. This general fact of mediæval history forces itself upon us at every turn. If, for instance, we compare the territorial development of modern Prussia with that of modern Hungary, the general fact just mentioned will stand out in most instructive plasticity. Modern Prussia was in 1797 about the size of modern Hungary. Its territorial development is well known in all its details,[1] and may be summed up in the following way :—When in 1415 Elector Frederick I. was given the dignity of the Electorate, he possessed 445

[1] See W. Fix, *Die Territorialgeschichte des preussischen Staates* (Berlin, 1869, 2nd ed.).

German square miles [1] of territory; at his death he left 535 square miles;[2] up to 1797 his successors increased the territory in four different ways. They either purchased whole districts, or obtained them by barter, inheritance, or cession. This constitutes their first method of increasing their territory; and since it is exactly identical with the methods employed by private people or civilians in increasing their private property, we may properly call it the civilian method. Their second method consisted in obtaining the vast territories owned and ruled by the dignitaries and orders of the Catholic church. To this effect they proceeded on lines running parallel to the direction, if not to the ethics, of the civilian method; this second procedure may be called the secularising method. Thirdly, they obtained considerable territory by apt diplomacy, availing themselves as they did of the unparalleled misfortune of the Poles. And fourthly, they secured a portion of their territory by right of war or conquest. By the first, or civilian method, no less than 650 square miles of modern Prussia were acquired; by the second, or secularising method, no less than 1,153 square miles; by the third, or diplomatic method, or, to speak properly, by the laceration of unfortunate Poland (and a few minor 'acquisitions'), 2,612 square miles; and finally, by direct conquest, only 782 square miles.[3]

If now we compare this territorial development of Prussia, the typical state of central Europe, with that of Hungary, we shall easily find that of the four methods employed by the rulers of Brandenburg and Prussia only one obtained with the kings of Hungary, and that is the last method, or acquisition of territory by conquest. In fact, the use of the first, or civilian method, is so utterly alien to the constitution of the Hungarian state from its very beginnings; the manner of securing state property after the fashion of private goods is so fundamentally opposed to the character of St. Stephen's realm, that there is scarcely an instance in the

[1] W. Fix, *op. cit.* p. 260. [2] *Id. ib.*
[3] *Id. ib.* pp. 260 *sq.* By 'miles' German miles are meant.

whole of Hungarian history—that is, for fully one thousand years—of one square mile of territory having been permanently added by purchase, barter, contract, or inheritance through and in the person of the king.¹ The territory of Hungary has been seized and appropriated by the Hungarian nation by means of victorious battles. As to the second, or secularising method, it could never take place in Hungary, for the simple reason that the Catholic Church has never exercised any civil sovereignty whatever over any one portion of the Hungarian kingdom.² Catholic bishops, archbishops, and abbots of Germany and Austria ruled at times over more than one-fifth of the Holy Roman Empire,³ and to their sovereignty an end was put in this century only. In Hungary, ecclesiastical sovereigns having been unknown, their territories could not have been appropriated by the method of secularisation. The third, or diplomatic method, has no doubt been employed by the rulers of Hungary, but only as the rational sequence and on the basis of wars.

It will thus be seen that Hungary has from the very outset formed the most modern type of states—namely, the *national state.* In European history we can discern four types of states, and four only. First, the Græco-Roman city-state; second, the Catholic Church; third, the German territorial state, which, from its being closely bound up with the person and dynasty of the ruler, and from its partaking more of the nature of private undertakings than public functions, may be called an estate rather than a state; and fourthly, the modern national state. Hungary is the oldest

[1] The Kingdom of Poland, of which Lewis the Great, King of Hungary, became King in 1370, on the strength of a contract with Kasimir the Great of Poland, had no organic relation whatever to the state of Hungary. Moreover, that union of Poland and Hungary, although again revived subsequently, never lasted longer than a few years.

[2] Compare F. A. Staudenmaier, *Geschichte der Bischofswahlen* (Tübingen, 1830), p. 249; J. E. T. Wiltsch, *Handbook of the Geography and Statistics of the Church* (Lond. 1859), i. p. 428 *sq.*; and Sugenheim's *Staatsleben des Klerus im M.A.*, passim.

[3] On the beginnings of the territorial sovereignty of German bishops see especially F. Merkel, *De Republica Alemannorum* (1849), note 27 to § xii.

and most distinctly developed type of a national state, and its only worthy rival in Europe at present is England. One single illustration will set forth the real character of a national state as distinct from a territorial state. The latter—as, for instance, the states of the German Empire, or France anterior to the Revolution—is so intimately settled, as it were, on and in the dynasty of its ruler, that the people of such a state would never so much as think of offering their crown to any other than a near relation of the late sovereign, just as if a case of private inheritance were at issue. National states, on the other hand, such as England, Hungary, or Poland, will occasionally offer the crown to utter strangers, a nation as such not standing in any relation of blood-kinship to any individual person or dynasty. Thus, the Electors of Hanover became kings of England in exactly the same way as the Arch Dukes of Austria became kings of Hungary. In France, on the other hand, the only pretenders to the crown are, to the present day, such persons as can found their claims on the right of inheritance.

Hungary being a national state, and nothing but a national state—that is, the nation itself constituting the state—it has always been a self-evident necessity in Hungary that the nation as such should be given the means of transacting its own business, or, in other words, of administering the affairs of the country. The most natural and direct way of doing this is the institution of meetings, or parliaments, where the nation assembled shall pronounce on current affairs, or advise on measures for the future. Such meetings the Hungarians have always had, the trysting place being the *Rákosmező*, near Budapest. For reasons, however, the discussion of which may be reserved for a subsequent part of this essay,[1] the Hungarian nation, while by no means neglecting their national or general assemblies, have, from the very outset, preferred to assemble in local meetings severally, and the territorial substratum of these local parliaments is the counties.

We have thus reached the proper standpoint wherefrom

[1] See p. 48 *sq*.

to view and appreciate the historical and constitutional value of the Hungarian county. It is, together with the Hungarian parliament proper (*országgyülés*), the exponent of the very nature of the Hungarian state. With the exception of England, Poland, Aragon, and to some extent Bohemia, and a few minor Slav states, no European state has, prior to this century, developed a municipal or ' local ' institution similar to the Hungarian county; and since even England, Aragon, and Poland, not to speak of Bohemia, have preferred to concentrate their public national life in their general parliaments rather than in their local assemblies—the essential difference between Hungary and England, for instance, being the fact that many of the functions performed in Hungary by the county have been vested in the English parliament—the Magyar *megye*, or county, may rightly claim a significance far beyond the value attached to it by the patriotism of such Magyars as, in the parlance of some painfully enlightened progress-fiends in Hungary, are contemptuously styled *laudatores temporis acti*.[1]

We shall now turn our attention to the history or development of the Magyar *megye*. Leaving the philological derivation of the Magyar and Latin term for the Hungarian county to a foot-note,[2] we may feel confident that our evolution-ridden contemporaries will at once desire us to tell in clear words at what hour of the day, in what year, from what inferior institutions, at whose hands, and in what locality did the Magyar county arise or evolve first. To this one of the most authoritative Magyar historians says, '*Ignoramus*.'[3] We

[1] There is an immense li'erature on the German institution of the Mark, but scarcely any on the Hungarian county. However, the typical importance of the latter is considerably greater than that of the former, and modern Hungarian scholars are only far too ' liberalism '-bitten to devote the requisite studies to this their cardinal institution.

[2] The various etymological theories are discussed in Emerich v. Krajner's *Die ursprüngliche Staatsverfassung Ungarns . . . bis zum Jahre* 1382 (Vienna, 1872), p. 167, n. 1.

[3] Theodor Botka, ' Jogtörténelmi tanulmányok a magyar vármegyék szervezeteről ' (in *Budapesti Suemle*, 1865, Kötet I, p. 306). Of Mr. Botka, Fred. Pesty, one of the best known Magyar historians, says (in *A Várispánságok története*, Budapest, 1882, p. 2) that he is the greatest authority on the history of the Magyar county.

may properly add, '*Ignorabimus*'; not because of the inadequacy of our material or our mind, but because of the inadequacy of the question itself. Hungary having from the very outset been a national state of considerable extent, it must, like all national states, have needs given rise to an institution similar to or identical with the Slav *zupan*, or the English shire. Moreover, there were two powerful causes, one negative, the other positive, by dint of which the growth of the Magyar county proceeded at once more rapidly and more intensely than that of either the Slav or English county. The negative cause was the absence of feudalism in Hungary. This cannot astonish you; for, since we have learnt at the very opening of this essay that Hungary has always been a state of the modern or national type, and since the modern state is palpably inconsistent with the hierarchy of feudal institutions, it becomes at once clear that Hungary, having always been a state grafted on and consisting in the nation itself, could by no means be made to embrace feudalism in its *political* aspects. In fact, during the whole course of Hungarian history all political power or tenure was derived either from the nation or its personal representative, the king. And thus Hungary affords us a less mixed specimen of a national state than does England; and to this circumstance—that is, to the partial inoculation of feudalism into the body of the English nation—we owe many differences in the history of England and Hungary, although both are essentially national states.

The total absence of the feudal hierarchy in mediæval Hungary is an additional proof of the statement of the earliest Hungarian chroniclers, to the effect that the Hungarian nation on settling in Hungary distributed the country according to tribes (*nemzetségek*), the number of which was 108.[1]

The second potent cause for the establishment of counties endowed with exceptional vitality was the small number of the conquerors compared with the overwhelming numbers of the nations conquered. Unless the Magyars proper, who even nowadays do not form more than a little above one-

[1] L. Szalay, *Magyarország története*, i. p. 11 (1st ed.).

third of the entire population, had a ready grip upon every portion of the country, they could not have maintained a conquest of nations opposed to them in language, race, law, and mode of life. These considerations are so cogent as to make it more than probable that King St. Stephen (end of tenth century) completed, if he did not originate, the establishment of counties. For the analogy of England, where thirty-two of the modern counties have been proved to have existed in the latter part of the Anglo-Saxon period,[1] entitles us to assume that the county system is, partially at least, of a date older than the reign of St. Stephen. Together with the counties, whose function was more of a political and administrative character, the first kings of Hungary founded numerous military posts all over the country, which have frequently been held to represent the germ or incipient stage of the county proper.[2] The most recent researches, however, have clearly pointed out the difference between these military bulwarks and the *megye*, or county proper.[3]

The original number of the early counties cannot be fixed for every reign severally. By the middle of the thirteenth century, or under King Béla IV., there were seventy-two counties.[4] Regarding the constitution of those early counties we are furnished with no, or very unsatisfactory, contemporary reports; and it is not before the time of King Charles Robert, or the first half of the fourteenth century, that we are permitted to get an insight into their inner structure. That king issued an order reforming the county system, and although the original order has been lost, the industry of one of the most meritorious of Hungarian historians has been requited with the discovery of a document, termed '*Ars notarialis*,' which to some extent makes up for the loss of King Charles Robert's ordinance.[5] According to

[1] R. Gneist, *Self-Government* (3rd ed. Berlin, 1871), p. 8.
[2] E. v. Krajner, *Ursprgl. Vfassg. Ungarns*, pp. 176 *sq.* ; and the literature quoted in F. Pesty's *Várispánságok*, Preface.
[3] Argum. F. Pesty's work quoted in note 2.
[4] Th. Botka, *l.c.* 318, quoting the 'Carmen miserabile' of Rogerius.
[5] Th. Botka, *l.c.* p. 318.

this document the constitution of the Hungarian county by the middle of the fourteenth century was as follows. At the head of the county stood the *főispán*, or what in English we might call the lord-lieutenant, remarking, however, that, although in later times the position and influence of the *főispán* corresponded and still corresponds pretty closely to that of the mainly honorary lord-lieutenant of an English county, in former times, and especially up to the beginning of the sixteenth century, the *főispán* wielded an influence considerably greater than in the last three centuries. Thus it was the *főispán* who nominated and appointed the *alispán*, who in course of time grew to represent the important office held in England by the sheriff. It need hardly be said that the *főispán* was invariably appointed by the Crown.[1] In passing we may remark that while, with temporary exceptions, sheriffs in England were always appointed by the Crown,[2] sheriffs in Hungary were first appointed by the Crown through the *főispán*, and subsequently (since 1504) elected by the people. King Charles Robert's county had moreover four justices of the peace, and four only, for every county; their Magyar title to the present day has been and is *szolgabiró*. Their office corresponds very closely to that of the English justice of the peace, and as the latter has, in Glasson's words, nothing in common with the French *juge de paix*,[3] neither has the Hungarian *szolgabiró* much in common with French or German district officials. Originally there were eight sworn assessors, or *eskütt*, in every county.[4]

These officials, however, in most conspicuous contrast to the local officials in most of the continental countries during

[1] In fact, he has always been considered the representative of the king in the county. Compare Statute 16 of 1222, and other Hungarian laws.

[2] The statement, current in older treatises on English law (e.g. in John Impley's *The Office of Sheriff*, London, 1800, p. 9), that sheriffs, previous to 9 Edw. II., St. 2, were elected by the people, has been corrected by Bishop Stubbs. See *Constit. Hist.* ii. pp. 225, 226.

[3] Ernest Glasson, *Hist. du Droit et des Institutions polit. civ. et judic. de l'Angleterre* (Par. 1883), tome vi. p. 486: '*Les juges de paix anglais n'ont de commun avec les nôtres que le nom.*' The French *juge de paix* is part of a bureaucracy which in times anterior to 1848 was entirely unknown in Hungary.

[4] 1486, 8 tcz. (statute 8 of the year 1486); 1498, 15 tcz., 1514, 4 tcz.

the latter part of the middle ages, did by no means absorb the county. For, true to and consistent with the national character of the Hungarian state, the people itself, or the *populus* of each county were not only entitled, but also forced by law, to attend personally or, in exceptional cases, by proxy, the bi-monthly, or even more frequent meetings of the county.[1] And just as the real character of these local assemblies cannot be brought home to modern readers more appropriately than by calling them so many local parliaments, the subjects there discussed and decided being of the most multifarious and incisive nature, even so did the members of those county parliaments view it, passing and enforcing extremely rigorous ' statutes ' (as they were called) against such as should in the slightest way infringe upon the dignity of the *szék*, or county meeting.[2]

The officials just enumerated, together with a few others of whom due mention will be made, have existed and still exist to the present day, and a few remarks will sufficiently outline their history. Regarding the *főispánok*, or lord-lieutenants of the counties, many of them had in course of time acquired an hereditary right in the tenure of that office, although a law passed as early as 1504 had abolished all hereditary claims to the highest office of the shire.[3] However, the influence of the lord-lieutenant waning away rapidly before that of the sheriff, or *alispán*, and the dignity of the former getting to be more and more of an academical character, hereditary claims on the tenure of the lord-lieutenancy were tacitly admitted, so that by the commencement of the eighteenth century we find twenty-eight hereditary lord-lieutenants in so many counties. Up to the end of the sixteenth century the *főispánok* had regular and considerable fees ;[4] but subsequently those fees came into desuetude, and by the end of the seventeenth century it was generally considered a matter of course that the office was

---

[1] Th. Botka, *l.c.* (*Budapesti Szemle*, 1865, 2ᵏ Kötet), pp. 173–176.
[2] *Id. l.c.* pp. 184–186.   [3] 1504, 3 tcz.
[4] Botka (in *Bud. Szemle*, 1865, 1 Köt.), p. 436 *sq.*

purely honorary. This, however, did not prevent lord-lieutenants, as well as other high dignitaries of the then states, from being open to 'substantial insinuations' of all kinds, the acceptance of such gifts not being deemed dishonourable. At the present day Hungarian lord-lieutenants hold pretty much the same position as of old, the only remarkable novel feature being the custom according to which lord-lieutenants will, on the fall of the ministry that had appointed them, forthwith tender their resignation. This much about the *főispánok*.

The *sheriff*, or *alispán*, is, together with the *szolgabiró*, or justice of the peace, the most important official of the shire. Their practical influence ever since 1504, when they were first elected by the people, became so great that the Arch Dukes of Austria, on their accession to the throne of Hungary, well-nigh neglected the lord-lieutenants altogether, so that under Ferdinand I. eleven shires were suffered to be without any *főispán* at all. In the political as well as the administrative life of the county, and the country, the sheriffs played a most incisive *rôle*. It was generally from amongst them that the members for the royal parliament were elected;[1] from amongst them deputations to the *nádor*, or palatine, to the king, or to the enemy were sent;[2] and within the shire, although their tenure of office was only of short duration,[3] they have to the present day been of paramount importance.

The *szolgabiró*, or justice of the peace, is to the district, or *járás*, what the *alispán*, or sheriff, is to the shire. He was and is in constant and immediate touch with the people, and his office, at once that of an administrative, judicial, and police magistracy, has always required infinite tact, prompt sagacity, and rich experience. He is by no means the bureaucratic subordinate of the sheriff in the French or German sense; but enjoys a broad independence of action, such as to endear the office of the *szolgabiró*, if not always to the people under his sway, yet certainly to the incumbent. This office, having scarcely ever changed, has no history.

[1] Botka, *l.c.* p. 450, and *Budapesti Szemle*, 1866, pp. 229-33.
[2] *Id. ib.*   [3] Generally for one year.

There is one more office of which mention should be made—the clerk, or *jegyző*, of the shire. That office was established by King Charles Robert in the first half of the fourteenth century, and it is said that there were itinerant scribes, or clerks, who drew up the minutes of the county meetings, and were strictly enjoined to write out the deeds at their own homes, and not in wine-shops : for, said the wise patriots, *ebrietas frangit quidquid sapientia tangit*.[1] Even as late as 1613, the *jegyző* of the shire was not considered as being member of the county magistracy ; subsequently, however, his office became one of great importance and dignity.[2] There were, and are, various other offices, such as taxgatherers, who, ever since Leopold I.,[3] collect both county and general rates and taxes ; the county prosecutor (*ügyész*) for criminal matters ; the county physician ; the county board for orphans (*árvaszék*), &c., &c.

In thus sketching the constituent magistracies of the Hungarian county I have, in the attempt to find English terms for Magyar offices, taken great liberties with the terminology current in either country. For, as a matter of fact, the term 'lord-lieutenant' or 'sheriff' does not cover the Magyar *főispán* or *alispán* ; and although in the law books and statutes of the Middle Ages both the Magyar *alispán* and the English 'sheriff' are called *vice-comes*, it would be decidedly incorrect to conclude an identity of function from the identity of name. However, convinced as most of us are that the study of mediæval institutions can be brought to really prosperous issues only when the comparative study of analogous institutions is pursued with greater zeal and more minute care than heretofore, we shall risk little by using historical terms somewhat inappropriately, until the identity and discrepancy of analogous institutions has been finally determined. For, although many of the features or functions of an English sheriff may not apply to the Magyar

---

[1] Botka, *ib.* p. 454.
[2] Up to the first half of the seventeenth century they did not form members of the magistracy of the county. Botka, *ib.* p. 455. [3] *Id. ib.*

alispán, and although the very corporate nature of the Magyar county is considerably more organised, or differentiated, than is that of the English shire, yet it still remains true that both Hungary and England are and always have been strictly national states, whose government consisted of a central parliament and local self-government. In England the tendency to concentrate the political life of the nation in the parliament proper was stronger, and became manifest at an earlier time, than in Hungary, where the political life of the nation had a tendency of centring in local parliaments or county meetings. This general fact alone suffices to account for many a divergence in the functions of county officials in the two countries. Thus, in England elections of members of parliament soon assumed their modern form of elections by districts ; whereas in Hungary, where the political unit was the county as such, members of parliament were elected by the county corporate, and they were, in fact, the mere messengers of the counties. For no member of the Hungarian parliament could, up to modern times, overstep or vote against the strict injunctions he had received from the county.[1] The slightest neglect of its expressed will was resented most severely by the county,[2] and thus parliamentary parties could hardly arise, and consequently parliamentary life was reduced and stinted ; so that while English constitutional history of the last three centuries is mainly a history of parliament, Hungarian constitutional history of the same period, with the exception of the last thirty years, is so to a much less degree. The Magyar county, fully conscious of its sovereignty, not only guided and controlled its deputies to the national parliament, but also exercised, and most frequently and obstinately too, the right of contesting and even ignoring laws or royal ordinances passed or given against the desire of the county. This right had been vouchsafed them repeatedly, both in the *Arany Bulla*, or Magna Charta of Hungary (1222),

[1] *Budap. Szemle*, 1866, p. 223 (Botka).
[2] *Ib.* 1865, II. Köt. pp. 184-186.

and in subsequent laws.¹ They practised it by sending their written protestations, either to parliament or the king; furthermore, by special envoys to the court, and by what in Magyar constitutional law is termed *passiva resistentia*—in other words, by quietly shelving the laws, decrees, or ordinances sent down to them from Pesth or Presburg.²

But what will still more clearly set forth the sovereign character of the Magyar county is the fact that there existed, previous to the eighteenth century, so-called provincial councils (*tartományi gyűlések*), that is, assemblies of two or more counties, just after the fashion of confederate states. Of such councils there are numerous traces both in the Hungarian *Corpus juris* and in the minutes of the various counties.³

All this will, no doubt, impress you as pointing to an essential difference between Hungarian and English counties. And it need scarcely be said that the counties in other national states of Europe, especially those of Poland and Bohemia, were still more different from the Magyar *megye*. Regarding the counties of Poland little need be said. In the old treatises on Polish constitutional law the constitution and function of counties is despatched very briefly,⁴ and what we can gather from the better histories of Poland indicates that the part played by the *supan* was very poor indeed, the whole of the political life of the Polish nation being absorbed by their provincial and national assemblies.⁵ The same applies to the *supans* of the Bohemians and Servians.⁶

If it be true, as very probably it is, that nations decay, not by this or that blunder of any one or two individuals, kings or generals—considering that the life of nearly every individual is little better than a serio-comic sequel of blun-

---

¹ 1291, 17; 1298, 7, 20, 21, 23, 41; 1444, 33; 1471, 12; &c.
² The last case of that powerful, if passive, resistance happened in 1859–1860.
³ *Budap. Szemle*, 1865, II. Köt. p. 167.
⁴ See the treatises of Lengnich, Hartknoch, Hüppe, and others on the constitutional law of Poland.
⁵ The well-known diets where each noble had the full *veto*.
⁶ W. A. Macieiowsky, *Slav. Rechtsgeschichte* (1835), i. p. 54 *sq.*

ders—but that they decay by the diseased or feeble frame of their institutions; if this be true, it can admit of little doubt that Hungary—that is, the only continental national state of considerable size that has maintained its independence these thousand years—has been enabled to do so in consequence of the thorough political schooling every Hungarian was obliged to undergo in the lobbies, meeting-halls, election campaigns, and court-rooms of his county. National states must necessarily draw very much more heavily on the political activity and public-spiritedness of every citizen than do states where people are governed from above; the governing bureauracy furnishing order, law, and administration pretty much as do gas-companies furnish gas to the householders. One of the main reasons, therefore, of the fact that Hungary has escaped the fate of Poland must be found in the institution of the Hungarian county.

It is thus evident that, while there is an undeniable analogy between the Hungarian county and the English shire, there are also very essential discrepancies. This remark, however, applies more to the Magyar county previous to 1848; for in modern and particularly in very recent times the Magyar counties have been more or less levelled down to the indistinctness of a hybrid institution, a cross of the old English shire and the German *Bezirk*.

The greatest and most incisive discrepancy, however, between the old Hungarian *megye* and the English shire I have not yet mentioned, although it was, in the opinion of all liberalism-smitten journalists and adolescent sages of modern Hungary, the most momentous feature and most crying evil of the old Hungarian county. It consisted in this, that the institution of the Magyar *megye*, with all its glory,' advantages, and privileges, embraced the Hungarian noblemen, the small gentry, and the great magnates only. The numerous peasantry, whether Slowak, Servian, Roumanian or Ruthenian, and the small but industrious German *bourgeoisie*, were all outside the pale of the county, inasmuch as during no period of Hungarian history, anterior to 1848, could the peasants or *bourgeois*, the yeomen or burghers, actively participate in the county-halls or courts.[1] They were mere denizens, and no citizens; and while the *Bürger* in Germany developed into a powerful class—the one that gave Germany not only her artisans and merchants, but her poets, thinkers, artists, scholars, and bureaucrats—the few cities in Hungary led the somnolent life of embryos, leaving scarcely any mark whatsoever on the course or contents of Hungarian history.[2]

The expression *people*, repeatedly used in the course of the present essay, applies, therefore, to Hungarian noblemen only. They, and they alone, formed that national state that has weathered all the storms and hurricanes of over one thousand years; and if at present their privileges are no longer existent, this is owing, not to a revolution on the part of the *tiers état*, as was the case in France, but to their own good-will and independent resolution. It was in 1848 that the Hungarian nobility, pressed or urged by none, spontaneously divested themselves of their ancient privileges, thus opening the council-halls of the counties to citizens of non-noble origin. And so strong is the impress imparted to the Hungarian mind by the past generations of noblemen, that even at the present moment only such non-noble persons can hope to hold office in any one of the sixty-three counties as are in language, habits and convictions true representatives of the Magyar nobleman. Thus, of nearly two and a half million Roumanians in Hungary, there is not a single sheriff or *alispán*. The same applies to most of the government offices.

This utter neglect of the Slav and Daco-Roman population has of late given rise to most tragic recriminations against the Hungarians; and no doubt such state-philosophers (to imitate the German phrase) as base their theory of the state on the territory of the country, and not on the

---

[1] This right was accorded to some classes of non-nobles after and in consequence of the events of 1848.

[2] Nearly all towns were built and inhabited by Germans and non-nobles.

nation inhabiting the territory, cannot but fail to see why the Magyars should wield more power in Hungary than any of the numerous other nationalities of that country. The answer to this is simple—because the Magyars, and they only, have succeeded in establishing a real state in Hungary, whereas the other nationalities, although nearly twice as numerous as the Magyars, have never so much as attempted to form or found any state whatsoever. Their very protestations show that they do not know the ABC of statecraft; for states and state rights are not founded on or obtained by printed petitions and rhetorical declamations in out-of-the-way daily papers, but by concerted actions of unanimous masses, that dread neither death nor financial ruin. It was thus that the Roundheads in England founded the Commonwealth of England; it was thus that the Magyar noblemen maintained the independence of the Hungarian state for thirty generations. But if from this striking picture of sustained energy during ten centuries we turn to the cool groves of historical research, trying to trace that marvellous energy to its sources, we shall scarcely go astray in asserting that it was the Magyar county that nurtured and matured the upholders of the Hungarian national state.

THE DRUIDS OF IRELAND

BY PROFESSOR JULIUS VON PFLUGK-HARTTUNG

(Translated from the German)

BYZANTINES, Romans, Kelts, Germans, and Sclavs form the five civilising peoples of mediæval Europe. Three of them inhabited, and still inhabit, the actual body of the Continent, whereas the Byzantines were driven into the extreme south-east, and the Kelts into the extreme north-west, even farther than suited their capacities and pursuits, owing to the continued onward march of the others. It was also unfortunate for the Kelts that they were, so to say, a distinctly unhistorical and unsettled people; that they had no history of any importance; did not keep any record even of such events as occurred around them; and that other communities, distinct from themselves as regards place and speech, took but little notice of them. Hence, of the earlier history of the mediæval Kelts, and especially of their chief branch, the Irish, we know practically nothing; and this although there is yet extant concerning them a literature which compares favourably in extent with that of any other early people. Imagination and the works of scholars, especially after the tenth century, supplied that which was painfully wanting in actuality.

This general outline is also applicable to the subject which is now to occupy our attention—that of the far-famed Druids, whose powerful priesthood ruled over all the Keltic peoples of historic times. Latin and Greek writers have furnished good accounts respecting the Druids in Gaul, and these again throw side-lights upon those of Britain. Of the Irish they have given us no information; but the later native writers, both sacred and secular, contribute something about them, although, unfortunately, in the most obscure and insufficient manner—partly because they no longer knew anything of the Druids of former times, and partly because they had no wish to make known much about them. In literature it is striking how the Druids disappear: in the so-called 'Hymn of St. Patrick' they are only once mentioned; in Fiacc's 'Life of St. Patrick,' in Dallan Forgaill's 'Amra,' in the 'Felire' of Ængus, and in other old works, they are not mentioned at all. On the other hand, they figure largely in the 'Book of Armagh,' but merely in order to exalt their overthrower, Patrick. In the place of venerable priests, we have their degenerate soothsayers and sorcerers. Druids and Filé, the representatives of spiritual and secular education, were confounded or classed together. And the prehistoric finds which were especially abundant in Ireland served to obscure the picture still further, since conspicuous sepulchral monuments were thought to be Druidical places of worship. In addition to this, modern writers were greatly wanting in critical discrimination. Todd in his writings, and O'Beirne Crowe ('Journal,' 69, 320 sq.), were the first to rise above this practice. Quite recently D'Arbois de Jubainville took up surer ground in his excellent and exhaustive memoir in the 'Cours de Littérature Celtique,' i.

Let us now, so far as original material and preliminary works enable us, endeavour to obtain some insight into the Druidism of Ireland. In doing this we need not entirely lose sight of the Gallic and British Druids. The Irish, British, and Gallic Kelts constitute branches of the same stock, which were evidently very nearly related in culture, politically and socially, and, as can be proved, also stood in fairly close intercommunication.

Even the very signification of the word 'Druid' has led to controversy. Formerly the favourite way of interpreting the word was as 'Tree-man,' after the sacred trees connected with their worship. But this interpretation has latterly come to be regarded as doubtful, without any satisfactory explanation being given in its stead.

Still more doubtful, naturally, is the period of the first origin of Druidism. Rhys ('Early Britain,' p. 68 and fol.) assumed that they had established themselves among the non-Keltic inhabitants of Britain, and passed from them to the Kelts, in which case they must be of primæval antiquity. D'Arbois de Jubainville and other investigators are of opinion that Druidism came over to Gaul from Britain shortly before Cæsar's time. O'Beirne Crowe supposes it not to have been introduced till the second century after Christ; but of proofs there are none. Like sun-worship, like the priesthood of Greeks, Romans, and Germans, this of the Kelts will carry us back to one of early Aryan origin, which in the course of time assumed the special form of Druidism. Among the Persians 'Dara' signifies priest, savant. The elaboration of Druidism clearly did not happen until the Kelts had separated themselves from the rest of the Aryan peoples. Hence the latter show no Druids. And Druidism developed variously among the different Keltic nations. To judge from their grade of culture, from their contact with the outer world, and their consequent increase of wealth, one would be inclined to suppose that Druidism originated and took shape in Gaul. But Cæsar says that their *disciplina* was considered to have been devised in Britain, and thence transferred to Gaul. He does not know with certainty—*existimatur*. It seems almost as if this opinion rested upon the fact that in his time many Gauls went to Britain in order carefully to study Druidism. This at any rate seems to prove that Druidism flourished peculiarly well in Britain.

One chief seat of the British Druids was the island of Mona (Anglesey), not far from the Irish coast—an island occupied from time to time by victorious nomads from Ireland; and thus communication would be kept up on all sides. It is perhaps worthy of notice that, in a communication of Avienus from the best Carthaginian period, Ireland is termed 'Insula Sacra;' and it is also stated that it had been called 'sacred' from time immemorial.

In Gaul the Druids occupied the forefront of social rank, like the Indian Brahmins. They formed a powerful order: influenced and decided the choice of magistrates; performed divine service; brought offerings and explained oracles; were doctors and teachers; and acted as arbitrators in the absence of state jurisdiction, enforcing their decision by a kind of civil outlawry. They possessed privileges and revenues, were rich and despotic, and held the people in subjection.

The Druids of Ireland seem never to have attained to similar power, probably for two chief reasons: (1) because here, side by side with the spiritual hierarchy, existed the secular one of the Filé in poetry, learning, and jurisprudence.[1] When O'Beirne Crowe assumes that the Filé were considerably older than the Druids, his assumption is doubtful, and cannot be proved. Altogether arbitrary is his supposition that the Filé were the original administrators of religion, and that they lost their authority after the introduction of Druidism. Both functions, that of Filé and that of Druid might obviously have been united in one and the same person—a circumstance, of course, of rare occurrence. (2) Gallic Druidism rose to a national power with communal assemblies; Irish Druidism remained stationary in cliques of race and kindred, just as was later the case with the clergy, and hence it became involved in all the endless struggles and changes of its immediate surroundings. It is possible that Irish Druidism absorbed much from the contemporary Roman priesthood. Their priestly functions and their position with regard to the government were very similar. Whereas Lucan represents the Gallic Druids leading a retired life in the woods, the Irish resided in the towns and at court. Indeed, some influence from Christianity is probable, in view of the manifold relations of Christianised Britons and Gauls with Ireland and Scotland.

---

[1] Some investigators (*e.g. Encycl. Brit.* v. 302) consider the Druids as a higher order of the Filé—hence, as poets with priestly duties; this is certainly not correct.

'The Irish Druids were revered and worthy men; they formed no caste, but only a class, the distinction being attained by knowledge and worth. In the legends we meet with kings and noblemen among the Druids. Their outward appearance seems to have been distinguished by white robes of office and a peculiar tonsure.[1] The Druids of Gaul, according to Strabo, wore gold necklaces and bracelets, and coloured raiments embroidered with gold. If one may apply to them the orders of Irish society, of which indeed we know nothing certain till Christian times, they fell into various classes—Chief Druids, Druids, and Disciples of Druids—a gradual progression which they seem to have transmitted to their successors, the Irish clergy.

Probably every tribe and, if they existed as early, every province possessed its Chief Druid, who, after the manner of princes, was probably distinguished by some head ornament ('Cours. de Litt. Celt.' v. 221). Obviously these were flat crescents of gold (Mind, Minn), of which a fair number have been preserved (Wilde, 'Catalogue,' 10). The most powerful Chief Druid was attached to the chief king of Tara. Whether he enjoyed any privileges outside the kingdom of Meath, and if so to what extent, does not appear. The periodical gathering of Uisnech secured him the chief seat, and therefore honourable precedence. The 'Tripartite Life of St. Patrick' calls Tara the chief seat of the worship of the gods and of the Druidism of Erin. When Patrick visited the chief king there, he is said to have found him celebrating the high festival, surrounded by Druids and great men. Not far from the hill of assembly in Tara stood three stones, which marked the tombs of three Druids, and seem to have played a part at coronations. Close beside these stood a house in which King Laogaire's Druid Lucad was burnt. There may also at times have been two or three men who took to themselves the office

---

[1] According to a canon ascribed to St. Gildas, the Druids tonsured the front of the head from ear to ear, while they let the hair on the back of the head grow. This is the same tonsure as that of the early Irish ecclesiastics. The canon can hardly date from Gildas, but shows the opinion of a somewhat later time.

of Chief Druids; tradition at least gives us these numbers. In Gaul the Chief Druid was elected; probably also in Ireland, although in the latter case the office never attained the same distinction. We get most information about the province of Ulster from the Cuchulinn tradition. The position occupied by the Druid Cathbad of Ulster was one of exceeding importance. He lived at the king's court; his authority was pretty much the same as that of the king; his retinue was formed by a circle of disciples, precisely as was the case later among the chief Filé. On one occasion we read: 'The people of Ulster did not answer to Sualtan's call of alarm, because it was their custom not to speak before the king, and the latter not before the Druid. Sualtan therefore hastens forth and cries to the Druid; when the latter has answered him, the king speaks; and finally the people of Ulster lift up their voice.' On other occasions also Cathbad speaks before the king. Perhaps some considerations connected with kindred, or with a curse which at that time rested upon Ulster, may have been the cause. Owing to the position occupied by the Druids, they became the counsellors of the rulers; they accompanied the latter on journeys and into battle. According to tradition, the last heathen king, Laogaire, had Druids in his suite, among them Dubhtach as Chief Druid. The latter is said to be buried with three sons; a bilingual inscription on a pillar stone near Killeen Cormac names them the four true Druids ('Journ.' iii. 24). A word from a Druid was sufficient to prevent the departure of an army for weeks; before Queen Medb took the field against Ulster, she consulted her Druids and a prophetess. Hence they were entitled to act as judges in important cases, even in cases pertaining to warfare. The right to a species of outlawing which Druids seem to have possessed in Ireland, too, offered them a powerful weapon against their detractors: it was a kind of discipline, which exalted them above the laity. Yet it remains doubtful how far the procedure of the Druids was permitted and their authority exercised.

The chief activity of the Druids was their priestly function, religious services which consisted in prayers, invocations, and especially in public and private sacrifices. The chief places of worship were on hills, the favourite sites being probably by the graves of the dead. By virtue of their office, the Druids took part in all matters which required sacrifices, particularly in assemblies of the people and burials. All the various tribes of Ireland, or separate groups of them, met in consecrated places, sometimes in royal Tara, where they took counsel with one another, held games, and besought the blessing of their gods by sacrifices. When King Mog-Neid of Munster was interred, the Druid Dergdamsa bewailed the fate of the dead, buried the king in full armour in a large tomb, and ended with a dirge.

The sacrifices were accompanied generally with bloodshed. The favourite offering was a white bull; part of the flesh was offered to the gods. Opinions are divided as to whether human sacrifices were made. Burton ('History of Scotland,' i. chap. vi.) and others do not believe in them. Rhys ('Celtic Britain,' p. 69) thinks they are not of Indo-Germanic origin, but instituted by the aborigines of the islands—a proposition quite incapable of proof. That human sacrifices with bloodshed were held in Gaul, a custom which afterwards yielded to the softening influence of Massilia and the power of Rome, can be as little doubted as that the British Druids long adhered to the custom. When Pliny (xxx. 13) speaks of the suppression of human sacrifices in the Roman Empire, he expressly remarks that the Druidical worship continued undisturbed in the independent parts of Brittany. The somewhat rhetorical description of the Druids of Mona in the 'Annals' of Tacitus (xiv. 30) also records sacrifices with bloodshed. He relates that they sacrificed prisoners on the altars, and besought God through human entrails. Nennius makes the Druids reply to the British King Gortigern: 'Seek out a youth, whose father is unknown, and let his blood bespatter the castle court, for thereby can it be built.' As regards Ireland, we must not omit to remark that in the Lives of the saints and in the legends we have no direct information concerning human sacrifices. Yet this evidence is not so conclusive as it at first appears, owing to the late date of the writings in question, and to altered views. Besides this, two instances of such sacrifices have been pointed out in them—one from the Life of St. Patrick (Todd, 'Life of St. Patrick,' 452 *sq.*) and one from that of St. Columba (Leabhar Breac, in Skene, 'Celtic Scotland,' ii. app. 499, 2). The Book of Leinster informs us frankly that the Irish offered children to Crom-Cruach (Cenn-Cruaich). There are traces that human sacrifices were considered efficacious in securing stability in building, perhaps also as a means of acquiring land. Possibly an echo of these sacrifices still lurks in the belief of the peasantry that every seven years the fairies have to offer up a child to the Evil One; and to save themselves they endeavour to decoy a fair earth-maiden to deliver her up to the Prince of Darkness (L. Wilde, 'Ancient Legends,' i. 11). In a Life of St. Columba we read that a monk, Odhran by name, sought voluntary death in order to deliver the island of Hy from the influence of the Druids: a legend conceived in a thoroughly heathen spirit.

The tombs speak the most distinctly; in them many discoveries have been made which can hardly be otherwise explained than by human sacrifices and great sacrificial feasts. Tradition tells of a burial where the grave was first made, then the wailing commenced, and finally animals were slain. Burial-mounds have been found with a large chief grave in the centre, and around it small graves of the same period, carelessly formed. Among a wild, warlike people, to whom the cutting off a head was a simple usage, the slaughter of prisoners and slaves can hardly be wondered at. St. Patrick insisted that all sacrifices should be abolished. The most important seats of culture were situated upon hills, near the graves of the dead. Undoubtedly the gigantic cromlechs on commanding heights not uncommonly served as sacrificial altars; they were ringed round with stately circles of stones. Near Rath Archaill in Sligo, for instance, there is said to have been a Druids' hill with altars and idols. Even St. Boniface is acquainted with the fact that the heathens of his time employed single stones (menhirs) for sacrificial purposes, and held them to be the dwelling-places of spirits.

It appears characteristic that the Druids took part in warfare. According to Tacitus, the Druids of Anglesey implored victory for their own people with loud prayers and uplifted hands. Otherwise also they exercised their miraculous powers in this behalf. When the men of Tara retreated, the people of Munster pursued them, led by their blind Druid in a waggon drawn by oxen. A passive attitude could hardly be always maintained; still less so when, at a later date, Irish priests and women were drawn into warlike service. Legends tell of Druids fighting and falling in the tumult of battle. And famous Cathbad is said in his youth to have been both Druid and warrior. Leabhar Gabhala asserts that King Lughaidh of Ireland was killed by a Druid. As they were bound up with the very existence of the tribe, they also found themselves involved in their fights and conflicts.

The knowledge possessed by the Druids was remarkable for their time. It consisted probably of secret teachings, and of that which they imparted openly. To the former belonged hymns, rules for prophecy, formulæ for charms, the knowledge of ancient hieroglyphics, and, later, of the Ogham writing. On the whole, their education was formal and a matter of memory.

The Gallic Druids are designated by Cæsar and Lucan as revered philosophers and theologians. Even Aristotle is said to have been acquainted with Druid philosophers; but the work of Diogenes Laertius which mentions this is spurious. The Druids seem to have developed a sort of natural philosophy and theology out of their worship of nature, and, in accordance with this, they held that man owed his origin to an earth-god, and believed in the immortality of the soul and universe, and the triumph of fire and water. Greek influences from Massilia and fundamental ideas of ancient Indo-Germanic origin probably worked together: the deluge and the conflagration of the universe, transmigration of souls and immortality. The idea of immortality produced so great a contempt for death that it induced individuals to mount the funeral pile of friends in order to live for ever with them, or rather till the day of 'Erdathe,' the meaning of which is unknown. One Christian writer translated it as 'Day of Judgment.' Perhaps the whole idea is of Christian origin. That the Gallic Druids believed in the transmigration of souls Cæsar relates, and Lucan likewise. This will also apply to the Irish Druids; for, according to tradition, Cairill became successively a man, a stag, a boar, a vulture, a salmon, and again a man; hence moved upon earth, in air, and in water.

With regard to the course of the stars, the size of the earth, and religious-philosophical questions, the Gallic Druids entered upon learned expositions. They had a thirty-year cycle of lunar years, in which the month began at the sixth day. Pomponius Mela says, 'The Druids profess to know the size and shape of the earth, the movement of the heavens, with the stars, and the will of the gods.' The Irish even maintained that they had created heaven, earth and sea, sun moon and stars; according to which the world had its first origin in the priesthood. But already at an early date these and other such assertions did not remain without contradiction.

The secret teachings were imparted within a circle of students, by means of verbal tradition. Yet written information was not entirely wanting to the Druids; pious tradition even tells that they possessed books, which Patrick burnt. The Gallic Druids used Greek letters; the Irish, on the other hand, those curious signs which are so frequently found on stones: deeply cut scoops, spirals, circles, straight and crooked strokes, and the like. From these, especially from the strokes, the Ogham writing was then formed. They scratched these signs on wooden tablets, but they certainly would not suffice to express consecutive philosophical ideas.

The various kinds of knowledge possessed by the Druids augmented their influence as regarded the outer world, and thus a public system of teaching was added to the mysteries.

In Gaul the Druids kept large schools for the sons of the nobility; in Ireland we seem to possess in the later monastic schools a reflection of the old Druidical schools, their characteristic feature being a difference in the education of clergy and laity—in other words, of those within and of those without the community. Tradition speaks of the Druid Cathbad being surrounded by one hundred disciples. The 'Tripartite Life of St. Patrick' relates that two Druids together educated two princesses, from which it may be assumed that attention was paid to the education of girls of the higher classes of society. According to the legends, the Druids are said to have imparted their secret practices.

It may be assumed that Druidical learning extended over the whole domain of contemporary Keltic knowledge, even in some degree to artistic handiwork, as was the case with the monks of later times. Tradition speaks of a Druid who made a valuable shield; the Druid Simon (Magus) in the legend of the 'Great Cattle Raid' makes a coat for Darius, King of the Romans; and the celebrated Castle Almain was built by a Druid. The course of time and of the stars was calculated by them, and they used instruments for the observation of the latter. In matters of law, they probably originally possessed powers of arbitration similar to those of their Gallic brethren; but this cannot be altogether satisfactorily gathered from the original sources, because the Filé are there already met with in their stead. A reflex of their office of arbitration seems to have survived, for example, in the narrative of Cuchulainn, Conall, and Laogaire, with the giant and Druid named Terrible (D'Arbois, 'Cours de Litt.' v. 133). According to the Introduction of the most noteworthy lawbook (the Senchus Mor), the Commission of Nine, to which was entrusted its compilation, did not include any Druid. Druids were also doctors, as we shall presently see.

It was natural to ascribe to the priestly and learned caste, to the professional communicators with the gods, powers of a higher order, and especially the art of prophecy, which was not far removed from magic. Later traditions represent them, therefore, as thoroughly versed in both. Magic even became to a certain extent the essence of Druidism, so that Druid and sorcerer were almost identical; for which reason in traditions 'Druidical' might be substituted for 'magical,' and in the older Latin authors 'magus,' 'magicus' be replaced by 'Druid.' As magicians they were so identified with those of the Nile, that the writer of a glossary of the ninth century described Jannes and Jambres as two Egyptian Druids. In a hymn put into the mouth of St. Columba, it is said, 'Christ, the Son of God, is my Druid.'

The Druids prophesied the outbreak of war, births and deaths, indicated lucky and unlucky days, and knew the means with which to encounter threatened danger. The whole life of the ancient Irish seems to have been under the influence of such soothsayings; it was considered impossible to undertake anything important without them.

The Druids seem to have carried on their investigations into the future especially at night and at the beginning of a battle. These investigations sometimes took place without any outward preparation, sometimes on occasion of sacrifices, dreams, the course of the clouds, and other such omens, even the roaring of the sea. In a poem ascribed to St. Columba he mentions the chief heathen form of prophecy as obtained from sneezing, the flight of birds, tree-roots, and the clapping of hands (Todd, 'St. Patrick,' p. 122). With a certain kind of tree they made a heap of faggots, and set fire to it amid incantations; the direction of the smoke then indicated what was to be done. When Queen Medb caused Fedelm to prophesy, the latter at first saw obscure pictures of general battle, which then gradually took a more clear and distinct form. The wren was called the 'Druids' bird.' It was said that those who understood its chirpings could thereby foretell what would happen in the future. Druidical soothsaying consisted probably in short, often obscure verses, the explanation of which was not always easy; they could even be so ambiguous that a clever person might turn them against their authors —as, for instance, Aife, the wife of Trad. Specially important seem the 'Gesa,' or things which betokened ill to the tribe and ruler. The legend of Finn is permeated with sorcery. It cannot be wondered at that Druids are said to have foreseen the coming of St. Patrick and the conversion of the island ; that one of them foretold the birth of St. Bridget, another that of St. Ciaran, while a third pointed out the omens of the crucifixion of Christ. There exists a so-called Druid prophecy (Todd, p. 411) which runs thus:

> He comes, he comes, with shaven crown, from off the storm-toss'd sea;
> His garment pierced at the neck, with crook-like staff comes he.
> Far in his house, at its east end, his cups and patens lie;
> His people answer to his voice: Amen, Amen, they cry.
> Amen, Amen.

Christian interference is here unmistakable; and yet the verses are very old, even as regards language, and they show in what manner such Druidical sayings were conceived. When Patrick, contrary to custom, lighted his paschal fire at night, and the king questioned his Druids about it, they replied: 'This fire which we see shall never be extinguished to all eternity, unless it is put out to-night.' We see here the activity of the Christian imagination of later times.

The Druids, while prophesying themselves, had also the power of enabling others to prophesy. The Druid Bresal, for example, communicated his chief devices to a rival of Etain. Once, when an extraordinary choice of a king was to take place, a man had part of a sacrificed bull given him to eat, and was then allowed to fall asleep. Four Druids sang incantations over him, till the sleeping man saw the future king in his dream and pointed him out on awakening. One Druidical oracle is said to have been obtained by someone rubbing his tongue on a glowing adze of bronze, or by putting it into molten lead (!) which had been heated at a fire of blackthorn or mountain-ash. The 'Teinm laegda' (loida) and the 'Imbas forosmai,' whose nature is variously explained, were held in the highest respect. The 'Teinm laegda' probably consisted in the throwing of staves. The 'Imbas forosmai' is, on the one hand, explained as an animal sacrifice, two incantations, two invocations of the gods, and a magnetic sleep during which the thing desired was seen; on the other hand, it is thought to have consisted in the eating of something special or touching it with the tongue, putting the thumb in the mouth or under the wisdom-tooth, whereupon the hitherto unknown thing revealed itself. According to Cormac's glossary, the Imbas showed the poet what he wished to know. The poet chews a mouthful of raw meat, and betakes himself therewith to the bed behind the door, where he says a prayer over it, offers it to his gods, and invokes them. And should he receive no revelation till the following day, he says a charm over the palms of both his hands, and takes the gods with him to bed, that he may not be disturbed in his sleep; then he lays his hands on both cheeks and falls asleep, till all that he desired reveals itself to him at the end of one or more days, according as he continues his gifts. Zimmer regards the Teinm and Imbas as borrowed from the German, and classes the latter with Sigurd, to whom the speech of birds becomes intelligible by Fafnir's blood coming upon his tongue. There seems to us no forcible reason for borrowing a foreign custom in this manner; the inclination to such things was deep-rooted in the very nature of the Irish. They have from time immemorial been inclined to superstition, as is proved by amulets which have been preserved, some made of stone with circles and discs scratched on them.

In the legends the prophesyings of the Druids is often exceeded by their magic arts. According to the Book of Leinster the most effectual means of destruction consisted, for Druids, in charms, for poets, in satire, and for warriors, in murder and burning. Glam Dichinn contains a solemn invocation, with a lengthy appendix. Among their magic implements, at a later date, mention is made of the magic wand, the dark grey skin of a hornless bull, the head of a white-spangled bird with fluttering wings, various kinds of trees and shrubs, etc.

Numerous accounts exist of their sorceries; imagination here found ample scope for all manner of vagaries. By conjuration (*geis*) they could force a man to appointed actions, or make certain actions impossible to him. The Druid Bresal, by means of spells, separated Mider from his wife Etain. To Cuchulainn the Druids gave a potion to produce ardent love; to a woman they gave another to enable her to get the better of consuming jealousy. The Druid Dalan even succeeded in discovering a beautiful woman who had been abducted by a god, and in restoring her to her rightful husband. In the war between Diarmait and his rebellious vassals, which led to the battle of Culdreimne (presumably in the sixth century), a Druid conjured up a magic hedge, which he placed before the army as a hindrance to the enemy. They could kindle magic fires, transform themselves into the form of animals, turn day into night, produce famines and a state of defencelessness, cause snow to fall and floods to appear, and many other such things. The battle of Magh-Tuireadh is utterly enveloped in magic. The Druids here caused magic clouds to appear, and showers of blood and fire. The Druid Mogh-Ruith sent his breath up to heaven, and immediately it became a threatening black cloud, which poured down in a shower of blood. By means of such things they appeared the most formidable persons in the hostile army, and efforts were made to kill them. On the other hand, the Druids of the different tribes wrought charms against one another, and thus rendered their own doings ineffectual, or else the stronger out-conjured the weaker. Mogh-Ruith, for example, kindled a mighty fire, which overcame that of the hostile Druid. He blew upon three hostile Druids and thus transformed them into stones, and in later times they were pointed out as the stones of Raighne. This knowledge he had acquired in the far East from Simon Magus, who was himself of Irish descent. Adamnan reports of the Scotch Druids that one of them endeavoured to raise a storm to oppose St. Columba, and that others tried to render the voices of the missionaries inaudible to the heathens ('Vita Columbae,' ii. 34, i. 37). As with the Catholic

Church of the Middle Ages, it was by fear especially that the Druids effected the overthrow of their antagonists ; and, again like the Catholic Church, the Druids knew how to represent unusual events as the result of their work. King Cormac MacAirt is said not to have believed their teachings ; so a Druid killed him by causing him to choke over a fish-bone. Any violation of their rules, even when quite trifling, led to the wreck of projected undertakings, and other mischief. Cuchulainn lost power, and even his life, because he had partaken of dog's flesh against a magician's command. Considering all this, it cannot be wondered at that St. Patrick, in his prayer, implores to be protected from the magic of the Druids. He is said to have forbidden sorcery ; but, on the other hand, this did not prevent him from raising the dead, shaking the earth, and causing the sun to obscure itself.

There is something naïve in the fact that sacred tradition has made Patrick an arch-magician. King Laogaire of Tara drives with his two Chief Druids to meet the saint, and there summon him to appear before some assembly. He comes and disputes with the Druids after the fashion of Moses and the magicians of Pharaoh. When one of the magicians curses the Christian faith, Patrick fixes his eyes upon him and prays for his destruction. Immediately the scoffer is raised into the air, and then falls, shattering his skull against a stone. The king, furious, commands that Patrick be seized. He, however, again appeals to God ; a thick mist descends, the earth quakes, the heathen slay one another, till the last flee into the mountains, and the king and queen alone remain before Patrick. But the king still broods on revenge ; whereupon the saint transforms himself and his followers into deer. The following day things proceed in the same manner in Tara. Patrick causes poison to become harmless, snow and night to vanish, and other things of a similar kind. Hence he is nothing more or less than a most mighty Druid, only that he always exercises his magic in the name of God. In genuine heathen fashion, the sacred tradition reports that during the battle of Culdrimne St. Columba prayed against St. Finnian of Maghbile until the latter ceased, and thus left the victory to St. Columba's party; a piece of Christian poetry ('Lorica') being considered a safeguard against demons and danger.

All kinds of customs were connected with these magic arts of the Druids and their worship of nature. With the Gallic Druids snake-eggs played a great part; they likewise knew and valued a plant to which the absolute power of healing was ascribed; honoured the oak, and the mistletoe which grew upon it, and which blossomed in winter. This, when solemnly gathered, made all animals prolific, and destroyed every kind of poison. Originally the mistletoe was probably a deeply significant image of life in death, but this idea became alienated, and was used superstitiously.

In Ireland, also, plants of various sorts were connected with Druidism. In the tradition of King Eachaidh the Druids, to reveal hidden things, cut boards from a yew-tree and inscribed Ogham writing on them. Similar tablets are mentioned elsewhere also. The yew, oak, blackthorn, and mountain-ash served as magic trees.

Lady Wilde ('Legends,' ii. 116) designates the yew-tree, ash, and elder as sacred trees. In fairy tales a branch of ivy at times plays the part of a magic shrub. The fairies' favourite resting-place was beneath a hawthorn-tree.

In Ireland five famous trees were held to be sacred—they were yews. One magic custom, evidently of much later date, was to charm a heap of straw, hay, or grass by means of incantations, and to throw a handful in the face of the victim. The person thereby became lunatic, restless, and insane. The so-called 'cursing-stones' also deserve mention—larger and smaller round stones (pebbles), which were turned over when maledictions were uttered against anyone. Some of these are still found in various places, especially among the ruins of the monastery of Inismurray.

In very early times the supernatural powers of the Druids

were connected with their skill in the medical arts. Hence they are met with in the Irish traditions as doctors and assistants at childbirth : for instance, Cathbad and Fedelmid. In the combat between Cuchulainn and Ferdiad in the 'Great Cattle Raid,' magic and incantations seem to have been among the means of healing ; hence it is unnecessary to assume that this was borrowed from the Germans. As a safeguard against the poisonous weapons of the Bretons, the Druid Drostan recommended the milk of 140 (2 x 70) white, hornless cows to be placed in a hole dug on the field of battle. Any wounded men who bathed themselves within it would be healed ; and so it came to pass. The fate of Prince Connle is poetically conceived. In the form of a beautiful woman, the goddess of death seeks to lead him hence ; the father thereupon takes refuge with a Druid, whose wisdom holds the terrible seducer in check for a month. Among the successors of the Druids, the Christian saints, miracles of healing again flourished luxuriantly. Later on, doctors belonged to the laity.

Taking the activity of the Irish Druids as a whole, we perceive that it was full of vigour. It is a mistake to believe them to have been gloomy fanatics or monks who withdrew from the world ; on the contrary, in tradition they are often described as endowed with the pleasure-loving character of their race, for which reason they played a by no means subordinate part in the love affairs of persons of rank. It may likewise be assumed that they might marry: tradition often speaks of married Druids. Their children were accounted legitimate. Cathbad, by the Princess Ness, became the father of Conchobar, King of Ulster, and his daughter Dechtire was mother of the hero Cuchulainn, so that the chief figures of northern Irish tradition are descendants of a Druid. Finn, also in Fenian tradition, was descended on the mother's side from the Druid Tadg: the latter was son of the Druid Nuadu, and his successor in office. Here, again, the later Irish Church shows points of agreement.

According to Pomponius Mela there were female Druids.

Upon a British island famed for its oracles they lived in perpetual virginity. This does not often appear to have been the case with the Irish Druidesses. Dubh was married, and killed her rival in her husband's affections by drowning her in a flood which she invoked. In fact, the prophetesses and witches of these traditions are by no means old and decayed women, but in most cases lovely maidens, the explanation being that soothsaying did not creep in the dark, but was accounted a most respectable profession. The Princess Fedelm had studied it beyond the seas in Alban.

Druidism, like so many other things among the Kelts, never attained full maturity, never succeeded in rising above opposition. On the one hand we find among them profound thought, the endeavour to tame wild, excited natures, the solemn dignity of a God-favoured class; on the other hand, hollow superstition, cruel human sacrifices, an inclination to warfare, adventure, and levity. The greater the influence they attained, the more strongly did the darker sides of their nature assert themselves; hence their decay. In Gaul this took place as early as Pliny's time, during the sixth decade of the first century. Strabo already reproaches the Druids with roughness, stupidity, and vanity. The prayer of Ninnian speaks of their pride and hardness of heart.

The Roman conquest, with its entire transformation of life, gave the death-blow to Gallic Druidism. The new rulers forbad its sanguinary customs, and broke its social position. The office of Chief Druid and the regular Druidical assemblies ceased; their judicial powers were taken over by Roman officials; Roman doctors and teachers appeared in their place. They gradually lost their vitality: with their power their influence vanished; their teachings deteriorated and died out; they became charlatans, magicians, and dealers in secrets, withdrawing into woods and caves. What remained of them was suppressed in the third century by Christianity.[1]

[1] Ammianus Marcellinus certainly still speaks of the Druids with great praise, but quotes Timagenes, who lived under Augustus. In his time the Druids seem to have been hardly known in wider circles. (Cf. Fustel de Coulanges in *Revue Celtique*, iv. 56.)

The Druids held their ground longest in remote and but little Romanised Brittany. If the later Lives of the saints are to be trusted, as Roman influence decreased this country again quickly fell into Druidical heathenism. It was reserved to British 'saints,' who were driven out by the Anglo-Saxons and fled to Brittany, to put an end to Druidism in the fifth and sixth centuries, though only after obstinate opposition. By the beginning of the seventh century, Christianity held sway over the peninsula. (For particulars, see De la Borderie, 'Etudes historiques Bretonnes,' i. p. 129 *sq.*)

The circumstances of Gaul reacted upon Britain, which was now likewise under Roman rule. A chief seat of Druidism, that of Anglesey, was conquered in the year 61 by Suetonius Paulinus; seventeen years later Agricola appeared there, slew the Druids, and destroyed their groves and temples. Things were different in the remote highlands of Scotland. There the Druids maintained themselves till the sixth and the beginning of the seventh century. Adamnan, in his 'Life of St. Columba,' still speaks of Druids disturbing the evening devotions of the saints.

In Ireland the flourishing period of the Druids seems to have coincided more or less with the Bronze age. The Roman successes may at first have driven many Druids to the Keltic islands that remained independent, and this may have given rise to a period of Druidical prosperity there. It is probable that it fell into decay towards the fourth century. They were left isolated by British Christianity and Anglo-Saxon heathenism. Rottenness within and foreign influences from without together wrought their destruction.[1] When Christianity was introduced into Ireland, the Druids certainly opposed it with all their might. Patrick's activity consisted in great part in spiritual combat with them, and he is said to have repeatedly been waylaid by them. His success

---

[1] Conlavin of Connaught is said to have written a treatise against the Druids, and King Cormac to have had a theological dispute with them (cf. *Trans.* xvi. 89). Even though this evidence is legendary and worthless, still it is no bad manifestation of internal disruption.

must have been unsatisfactory. A heathen reaction took place, led, as it seems, mainly by the chief kings of Tara, who remained true to the old faith, and with it to the Druids. In the second half of the sixth century a bloody battle took place at Culdrimne, in which Christianity was in league with the rebellious lesser kings against Diarmaid of Tara (544-65), and defeated him. With the death of Diarmaid and the overthrow of magnificent Tara, official Druidism also fell to the ground, and gradually vanished like a phantom that had been conjured up. It came to an end at about the same time everywhere—in Ireland, Scotland, and Brittany—but latest of all in Scotland.

A list of the seats according to rank in the palace of Tara, compiled at a later date, indicates the place of the Druids as being as much as six or seven degrees lower than the man of letters; but this list appears to us of little value. It is worth notice that here Druids were generally ranked with augurs, *i.e.* were already essentially accounted as fortune-tellers.[1]

In the remote parts of the island, especially in the rocky west, heathenism long asserted itself by outward manifestations, and does so to this day. An inscription on a stone from the Isle of Man, dating from Christian times, runs: 'Dovaido, son of the Druid.' On that island even now Druidical survivals are to be found in the hereditary and socially not unimportant exorcists and herb-doctors. Tighernach in 1067 mentions the death of Morrough O'Carty, Arch-Druid (Ard-draoi) and chief Filé. In this case the term 'Druid' had probably become the mere title of a savant. But the clearest echo of Druidism comes from the early Irish Church.

[1] D'Arbois, *Cours*, i. 198, says: 'La quatrième case est affectée au savant en lettres, c'est-à-dire au prêtre chrétien.' We believe this is erroneous. Had the author of the list meant the priest, he would have named him, above all abbot and bishop. The man of letters appears as a layman like the rest. That the Ollam Filé sat two steps lower cannot be accepted.

ON THE INSTITUTA CNUTI ALIORUMQUE REGUM ANGLORUM

By F. LIEBERMANN

CORRESPONDING MEMBER OF THE ROYAL HISTORICAL SOCIETY

1. Importance of the work—2. Former editions—3. The title—4. All the three parts the work of one author—5. Their contents—6. Their Anglo-Saxon sources—7. The author wrote about A.D. 1110.—8. He was not a native of England and used Franco-Norman words—9. His knowledge of English—10. He seems to have lived in or near the Mercian Denalagu—11. He belonged to the secular clergy—12. Completeness, language, and corrections—13. Traces of systematic treatment. No forgery—14. Stylistic explanations and contemporary allusions—15. Monarchy—16. Feudality; private jurisdiction; local government; ranks—17. Criminal law—18. Procedure—19. Ecclesiastical and matrimonial law—20. The Anglo-Saxon source of two pieces is lost, viz. (21) the royal prerogative and (22) the dignity of earl and bishop—23. Circulation of the 'Instituta.' 24. Two classes of MSS. : H ; Rl ; T—25. Cb—26. Shorter MSS. : Di and the Interpolator of Henry of Huntingdon—27. Were William's *Hic intimatur*, Leges Edwardi Confessoris and Genealogia Normannica found in the autograph of the 'Instituta'?

1. THE short[1] Latin treatise to which I give the above title claims the attention of all who study the mediæval history of England, in several respects. It is one of the earliest Latin compilations of English law written by a jurist; it serves to explain some Anglo-Saxon ordinances and to reconstruct their text; it contains the only trace, though hidden under a foreign form, of some Anglo-Saxon legal articles; and it sheds some light on the English constitution about A.D. 1100, especially on the remnants and traditions of an earlier policy.

2. The work as a whole has only once been published, viz. in the 'Anniversaria Universitatis Havniensis' of 1826, a quarto

[1] It would fill about twenty octavo pages of small print.

volume which bears at the foot of the title-page the following inscription: 'Antiquam legum Canuti versionem ed. J. L. A. Kolderup-Rosenvinge.' [The manuscript used by the Danish lawyer begins, however, with a prologue and closes with two sentences which belong to another contemporary law-book, viz. the 'Consiliatio Cnuti.'[1]] While Price and Thorpe[2] and the majority of English historians ignored that edition almost entirely, Schmid,[3] on the other hand, used it freely. In his annotations to Cnut's law he gave characteristic extracts from the first two parts, called by him 'Versio Cnuti Colbertina'; also he printed in full the last part, which, however, he relegated to his 'XX. Appendix' under the misleading inscription 'Pseudo-Cnut.' This continuation had already been published a century before by Thomas Hearne,[4] who rightly recognised Chapters III. 1–45 to be 'tanquam appendices' to Cnut's law; but for parts I. and II. this writer has referred to Lambarde's[5] edition of Cnut's original, as if they were merely literal translations. Moreover he makes an erroneous distinction[6] in the middle of the third part of our tract, as he treats its concluding portion (III. 46-64) as though it were a separate work.

3. All the former methods of naming the tract will have to be abandoned, since the title of the Copenhagen edition covers only half the contents and might easily lead to confusion with the 'Consiliatio' or with the 'Quadripartitus,'[7] both of which contain other old Latin versions of Cnut's laws.

As to the two titles invented by Schmid, one depends merely on the fact that Kolderup's text was indirectly based on a manuscript once belonging to the great Colbert, which, however, contains neither the earliest nor the best text, while the other, 'Pseudo-Cnut,' conveys the misleading impression

---

[1] Ed. F. Liebermann, Halle, 1893, cf. below, n. 25.
[2] *Ancient Laws and Institutes of England*, 1840.
[3] *Gesetze der Angelsachsen*, 1858.
[4] *Textus Roffensis* (1720), p. 38, which does not follow the Rochester codex, but its transcript, MS. Harley 6323.
[5] *Archaionomia* (1568), f. 93.   [6] P. 44.   [7] Ed. by me, Halle, 1892.

that the anonymous author had been trying to smuggle a harmless collection of early English enactments under great Cnut's flag, and moreover that he was a different person from the translator of the first two parts.

The author himself seems to have named his work [1] 'Instituta de legibus secundum Cnud regem Anglorum.' But in order to avoid any possible confusion either with the other two translations or with the Anglo-Saxon original,[2] and at the same time to indicate the whole contents, I propose henceforth to call the tract 'Instituta Cnuti aliorumque regum Anglorum.' This long title may be conveniently abbreviated by the symbol 'In. Cn.'

4. The work consists of three parts,[3] the beginnings of which are distinctly marked.[4] Its end is not so clearly indicated ; and after the termination of some codices with III. 44 eighteen further chapters are added in another class of manuscripts. As the oldest of these exhibits a change of ink after III. 44, this break must have been caused by some peculiarity of the autograph or archetype.

Now, judging from the title he probably selected, the author may have planned at first to translate only Cnut and may have added fresh matter by and by. This being so, may not the group of shorter manuscripts represent his own first edition ? I think not. The small enactment 'Ath' is his source for the sentences before and after III. 44, while, after III. 45, he indicates by a rubric that he is going to draw from a fresh source. It seems unlikely that he would intentionally have paused in the middle of a slight paragraph. I prefer to assume that either a page of the autograph ended in III. 44,

---

[1] Both the earliest MSS., H and Di, begin with the words *Incipiunt quaedam instituta de legibus*, to which Di adds *sec. Cn. r. An.*, and H : *regum Anglorum*. As one class of the MSS. ends with the words *Expliciunt* [*-cit* Pl.] *hic institutiones* [*-cio* Pl. ; *const*. S.] *Cnut regis*, Di's reading seems more original.

[2] Ed. Schmid, p. 250.

[3] The prooemium in Cb belongs to *Consiliatio* ; see below, 25.

[4] In MS. H the prooemium of part ii. is written in red ink, and part iii. begins after two blank lines with a large initial.

which the first copyist forgot to turn over or mistook for the conclusion of the work; or the author's fair copy may have fallen by chance into some antiquary's hands who eagerly had it copied before it was finished.

At any rate the whole of the third part belongs to the same author as parts I. and II. The above heading might indeed raise a suspicion, as it mentions Cnut alone, whilst the third part contains hardly anything of Cnut. But it is inaccurate even for parts I. and II., which contain some laws of other kings as well. This objection [1] therefore may be dismissed. The authorship of one man rests on the external argument that no manuscript contains either part I. and II. or part III. separately. Besides, one style, characterised by several unusual terms, pervades the whole work. Again Alfred-Ine's lawbook, translated in part III. (the concluding chapters of which are moreover wanting in the class of shorter manuscripts) serves also to supply interpolations in part II. Lastly the concluding portion refers to the former parts in the following words: ' quod supra nominavimus—sicut superius diximus.' [2]

The rubrics found only in a few codices [3] must not be ascribed to the author.

5. The first and second parts are in the main translations of Cnut's ecclesiastical and secular [4] laws respectively. In four places, however, the author inserts some chapters of Alfred's, Eadgar's, and probably of the Northumbrian priests' laws.[5] Once he quotes a ' Liber poenitentialis.'[6] He some-

---

[1] Which, by the way, is untenable, if H's heading (see above, p. 79, *note* 1) is more authentic than Di's.

[2] *In. Cn.* iii. 6 sq. (quoting ii. 59, 1) and iii. 6, 1 (quoting ii. 22, 1 sq.).

[3] All the rubrics in S differ from Cb.

[4] Though both these parts constitute but one statute, I still prefer to divide it into i. and ii., in order to make our chapter-numbers parallel to those of Cnut in Schmid's edition, so that *In. Cn.* ii. 54 translates Cnut's secular article 54. I shall mark the interpolations by letters. For instance, *In. Cn.* i. 12 c. means the third interpolation after Cnut's ecclesiastical article 12.

[5] After i. Cnut 5, 2: Alfred 20; after i. 9: ii. Eadgar 4; after ii. 59: Alfred 15 sqq. 38. 39; after i. 11, 1 and ii. 15, 1: Northumbrians 59. 51.

[6] ii. 50.

times inverts[1] the order of Cnut's statutes and omits a great many articles[2] apparently without any principle of selection.

The third part contains, besides a dozen chapters[3] of which no Anglo-Saxon original exists, a variegated patchwork of Latinised excerpts from Alfred-Ine, Merce, Ath, Had, Grith, Northleod, and Gethingth.[4]

6. Among the nine Anglo-Saxon legal collections[5] which have come down to us from the century after Cnut, not one contains all the pieces collected by our author. He may have used either one Anglo-Saxon compilation which is lost, without the slighest trace of it surviving, or, more probably, several books. In the latter case, however, he must not claim the whole merit of collecting single materials. Partly at least this labour had been performed before him, as the group Merce-Ath-Had exists in three other manuscripts.[6] This group, as well as Grith[7] and II. Eadgar,[8] he may have translated from manuscripts still extant; while he must have read Gethingth,[9] Alfred-Ine,[10] and Cnut[11] in a book, or in several codices, no longer traceable. His version, therefore, represents at least for three, and perhaps for ten, pieces of English law the only trace of an Anglo-Saxon manuscript, written about A.D.

[1] i. 2. 1. 2, 1; 12. 11. 10. 13; ii. 52, 1. 52; 71, 3. 71, 2. Into i. 5 the author inserts ii. 43.

[2] i. 2, 4. 14. 18. 19, 1. 20. 21. 23-26. ii. 10. 11. 29, 1. 38. 51. 67. 68. 71, 1. 81. 84.   [3] iii. 46-55. 58 sq.

[4] 1 : Ine 9; 2-4 : Ine 13, 1-15; 5-8 : Alfr. 29-31, 1; 9-39 : Alfr. 44-77; 40 : Alfr. 19; 41 : Alfr. 23; 42 sq. : Merce Pr. 4; 44 sq. : Ath 1 sq.; 45, 1-3 : Had 1-9 a; 56 sq. : Grith 6 sqq.; 11 sq.; 56 sq. : Northleod 2 sq.; 60-63, 1 : Gethingth 1-8; 64 : Ine 58 sq.

[5] MSS. A B D G H O., the sources of Quadripartitus (p. 45), Consiliatio (p. vi), and Ld, i.e. Lambarde's edition.

[6] In Merce 3 and Ath 2 our author offers better readings than H, Ld, or the Quadr. source; in Had 1. 9 better ones than D and H; but he may have followed O.

[7] From G or D?   [8] From G or D or A?

[9] He agrees oftener (c. 1) with H than with D; see, however, c. 7.

[10] He surpasses E (39, 2), B (38, 1), H (Ine 13, 1), and agrees with B : Af. 23, 2.

[11] He translates words left out by G D (Pr.; ii. 75, 1. 82. iii. 21). B (i. 15. ii. 18). A (i. 12). L (ii. 18); generally he agrees with class A-L (i. 3, 2. 4. 5, 3, ii. 73, 1), and especially with L (ii. 30, 7).

1030-1100. His merit for the reconstruction of the original text must, however, not be overrated, as we are able to base this text upon several Anglo-Saxon manuscripts. Besides another Latin version exists for eight of the ten pieces; only for Grith and Northumbre is this translation unique.

7. The author of the 'Instituta' wrote some time after the Norman Conquest. He misunderstands or confuses Anglo-Saxon legal terms and employs Franco-Norman ones; he constantly reckons according to the Norman shilling of twelve pence [1]; and he explains St. Peter's day as the first of August,[2] in order to distinguish it from the *Cathedra Petri* introduced by the Normans. From late Anglo-Saxon sources he notices the secular equality of bishop and ealdorman as something obsolete; and he distinguishes the canonical jurisdiction from the bishop's seignorial court in the hundreds and manors of his barony.[3] Among the articles our author has to translate there occurs this famous line: 'There was once in the laws of the English [the custom] that people and law went by ranks'; he perverts it into a sentence apparently written after the English nation and English law had been trodden down for a long time, *i.e.* not before A.D. 1100: 'Antiqua lex Anglorum fuit quod gens illorum et consuetudines in honore tenebantur.'[4]

On the other hand, he seems to consider the celibacy of the priesthood, which he lays great stress on, as an institution not yet fully established. He does not quote the canonical law of the twelfth century but the old Penitential. We hear nothing of *miles, baro, vavassor, relevium,* or trial by battle, while the author explains at length the institutions of thanes, heriots, and ordeals. If he interprets *ætheling* too narrowly by *filius regis de legali coniuge,* he may have thought of William ætheling (1102-20).[5]

The earliest manuscript of the 'Instituta' cannot be dated later than about A.D. 1140, and traces of the author's more

[1] ii. 30, 2. 71. iii. 45, 2 sq.   [2] i. 9.
[3] iii. 57 sq.   [4] iii. 60.
[5] iii. 56, 2. Eadgar aetheling was not a king's son.

archaic orthography peep out in some other codices.[1] Lastly the 'Instituta' were used not only by the forger of the forest-constitutions who used Cnut's name, but also by the compiler of William's ten articles (*Hic intimatur*), who, while professing to state the present law, retains features more archaic than Henry I.'s reforms. I therefore assume that our tract was written under Henry I., and probably about A.D. 1110.[2]

8. The author did not consider himself a native of England. The Anglo-Saxon words which he admits into his Latin are never introduced by words like *quod vulgariter dicimus*, as we should suppose in a writer who speaks often enough of himself elsewhere,[3] if he were English. In seventy-one places he prefers to say instead: *quod Angli dicunt*, or *vocant*, or *nominant*, or *id est*, or *quod dicitur*. In the same way he replaces words like 'this land, this nation, here, home,' by *Anglia*.[4] Even the original *we hatað* (*i.e.* 'we call') is carefully altered into *Angli vocant*.[5] But a French word (with a Latin ending[6]) he introduces by *quod nos possumus dicere*. Furthermore, his Franco-Norman expressions prove that his parents or the people that educated or surrounded him spoke French. They are: *aisia*[7] glossed by *commoditas*, iii. 52; *alod* (*bocland*, i. 11. ii. 13. 77. iii. 46; *land*, ii. 15, 1); *in capite terra* (*possessa*), i. 8; *carruca* (plough); *clocarium* (bell-house), iii. 60, 1; *contrastatio* (see annot. 6); *despectus* (for *mundbrece* or *oferseenes*, ii. 15, 2, 28, 42, 66, iii. 3, 56); *dispensa*, ii. 16, 1; *divisio*, piece of land, iii. 52; *dominium*, manor-domain not let to tenants, i. 11, 1; *forisfactura*, i. 3, 2, iii. 5; *missiaticum*, iii. 61; *morthrum*, ii. 5; *perdonare*, to remit, ii. 22, 2, 78; *placitum* (*gemot*, ii. 17 f, 20, 1, 59, d, e); *vicecomes* (*gerefa*, ii. 8, officer of the ealdorman, ii. 59 f.); *villanus* (*ceorl*, ii. 15, 1, iii. 44; *tunesman*, i. 11, 1); *warantem vocare*, ii. 23 f.

---

[1] The *Instituta* occur almost everywhere by the side of lawbooks composed under Henry I.
[2] Cf. below, 16, on the hundreds.
[3] See above, 4.   [4] ii. 8. 76, 2.   [5] iii. 2.
[6] i. 12, *foresteal: contrastatio causa mali*; cf. Wace, Rou. 1692: *contrestace*.
[7] Perhaps the earliest appearance of modern *ease* in England.

9. To translate Old English into Latin was no easy task for a Norman clerk;[1] and our author, though he surpassed the scribe of 'Quadripartitus' in correctness, made more than one curious mistake. Perhaps the most comical one occurs in the passage in which he translates Alfred's law on the price of wounding a man's *lendebræde* (haunch[2]) by *assatura renum*. 'Roast loin' he can hardly have meant; probably he looked for *bræde* (broad side) in Aelfric's Glossary, where he found *assatura* for the word of the same spelling but of another gender. Another English-Latin dictionary[3] seems responsible for the confusion in the names of human teeth. For in common with 'Quadripartitus' (copied in 'Henry's Laws') he translates *wongtoð* (grinders) by *caninus*, and *tux* (tusk) by *molaris*.[4] In some cases the author is misled by the similar sound of two words. Thus he translates *mære, eðel, unmagan, butu*,[5] through a confusion with *mare, æðelo, maga, buton*, by *maior, liberalitas, non parenti, sine*, instead of 'sublime, homestead, not strong, both.' Or he chooses the wrong meaning of an ambiguous word, for instance, *cwydeleas* and *stande inne*[6] may mean indeed *obmutescit*[7] and *stet in*; but here the sense requires 'without testament' and 'remain unperformed.' Some Old English terms had changed their meaning in Norman times, and thus our author takes *thegn*, where it has the sense of 'follower, retainer,' to mean *liberalis*, and *eorl* and *ceorl*,[8] 'noble and commoner,' to mean *comes et villanus*, according to the language in use in 1100.

[1] Inst. and Quadr. retain many an Old English word beside its Latin translation, because it seems rare, *e.g. throtbolla: gurgulio*, iii. 16; Alf. 51.
[2] iii. 31; Quadripartitus gives correctly *lumbos*.
[3] In Wright-Wülcker, *Anglo-Saxon Vocabularies*, 1885.
[4] iii. 13 from Alfred 79; cp. Hn. 93, 7. Another mistake common to both may be due to a similar source: they give for *neb* in Alf. 48 *maxillam* instead of 'nose, face.'
[5] i. 4. ii. 41. 59 c. iii. 9. Another mistake, *theoden: subliberalis*, instead of 'lord,' may be explained by a confusion with *theow*, unfree.
[6] ii. 70. iii. 12.
[7] If this expression has anything to do with Lex 25, Digest. 28, tit. 2 (*Si is qui testamentum faceret, ... prius quam secundos exprimeret heredes, obmutuisset*), the author received it indirectly through an intermediate source unknown to me.
[8] iii. 60 sq.

The author seems to have spoken English fluently. He not only transfers English words unaltered from the original into his text, but he adds Anglo-Saxon inflections, prepositions, pronouns,[1] technical terms,[2] and other words[3] of his own. When he replaces the old words of the laws by English synonyms, he probably feels instinctively which expressions were fast dying out, and which were destined to live on. Thus he alters *Romfeoh* into *Romescot*, *searwe* into *swice*, *hættian* into *behættian*, *cierlisc man* into *ceorlman vel ceorlboren*, *thegnriht* into *thegnscip*, and *medeme thegn* into *lesse thegn*.[4] One of his scribes continues this modernising tendency and puts *ofræce* instead of *ofga*.[5] Altogether the original words when retained appear in a partly Middle-English garb,[6] but these trifling changes of sounds or inflections may be to some extent due to the copyists and not to the author.

10. The 'Instituta' were doubtless written in England. Their material and their form prove this sufficiently, and it was only here that they were excerpted and copied during the Middle Ages.[7] Let us try to localise the author. In eight places[8] he puts *XL solidos* instead of the original '120 shillings,' and in two more *II* and *I libr.* instead of '120' and '60 shillings,' which his first draft had retained. Now such a small shilling as that of fourpence, which he supposes to have been current in Cnut's time, had existed in Mercia, and is called

[1] ii. 22; *be* ii. 16; *hyre* ii. 52.
[2] *Kadcniht*, ii. 59, 1; *gecydne utlaga*, ii. 113; *be weres mæðe*, iii. 8; *sace et socn*, ii. 30, 6.
[3] *Oðres mannes*, i. 7. In iii. 25 the scribe of Textus Roffensis glossed *in ilio* by *grin*, perhaps the earliest example of modern *groin* [Prof. Zupitza kindly confirms that *groin* may be derived from *grin*].
[4] i. 9. ii. 26. 30, 5. 59 a. iii. 60, 1. ii. 71, 2.   [5] Codex H, ii. 30, 3.
[6] *Maibot* instead of *mægbot*, i. 2, 4.
[7] Ch once belonged to England, and its Copenhagen transcript is modern.
[8] i. 11; ii. 15, 1; 25, 1; 33, 2; 59, d, e; 65; i. 3, 2. One might think that he wanted, with an anti-royalistic tendency, to lower the high amounts of the amends and fees due to the king; but some of these payments belong to the earl, and some to the church, which an author full of clerical aspirations would not be likely to diminish to their third part. But in two cases I am unable to explain the alteration of the amounts: he puts *XL sol.* instead of *CL*, and *XX* instead of *C* in ii. 59 a, translated from Alfred 15.

in the 'Leis Willelme,'[1] the Anglian one. On the other hand, he nowhere notices, as 'Quadripartitus'[2] and 'Leges Henrici' often do, the West-Saxon shilling of fivepence. Secondly, he betrays a decided predilection for the Denalagu. Among the heriots of a king's thane he discards the West-Saxon one and admits the Danish one, without saying that Cnut restricted it to the Danes alone. Again, among the mulcts for withholding church-dues he omits the English one and mentions the Danish one.[3] After translating Cnut's law,[4] that the violation of privileged church-peace costs in English law as much as breach of king's *mund*, viz. 5*l.*, he adds: 'secundum certe legem Danorum viii libr.' He imagines the common Saxon word *healsfang*[5] to be Danish, an error into which a man living in Wessex or Kent could hardly have fallen. Lastly, he assigns[6] to the earl the third penny of towns and of pleas in his county, which before the Conquest seems to have been a general rule only in the Denalagu; and one of his insertions reveals an intimate knowledge of the different fines for *lahslit* (breach of law) among the Danes. This, indeed, is nearly akin to three articles of 'the Northumbrian priests.'[7] Now, if our author had read and excerpted their law with a distinctly Northern colouring we should not feel inclined to look for his home in Southern England. The striking Danish tendency of the 'Instituta,' or the limited district where they perhaps exercised some practical influence, may have induced a rubricator,[8] already about the year 1200, to call them *Danelage*, a blunder repeated by the majority of our codices. On the other hand, not the slightest trace exists that this tract originated in the province of York. East Anglia, too, will perhaps have to be excluded from the different possible claims, because the author must have lived surrounded by a class of 'radknights,' a title which he inserts more than once instead of men of *sixhynde*-rank. This class occurs in Berk-

---

[1] I. Wl. 11. [2] P. 29. About the modern shilling see above, 7.
[3] ii. 71. 48. [4] i. 3, 2. [5] ii. 37.
[6] See below, 21. [7] See above, 6.
[8] In the lost archetype of the interpolated Huntingdon.

shire, Hampshire, and in the three counties of Worcester, Gloucester, and Hereford, which belonged to Mercia, but not to the Denalagu. Perhaps the Dano-Mercian region nearest to these, viz. Northamptonshire or Staffordshire, is the most likely home of the author. If so, he must have had access to an Anglo-Saxon legal library elsewhere, as we know that one then existed at Worcester.[1] The long[2] connection of this see with the archbishopric of York would allow us to assume that the laws of Northumbrian priests were to be found there.

11. No writer in England under Henry I. was a layman. That our author was an ecclesiastic appears from many points of the 'Instituta.' He knows the technicalities of catholic rites and discipline,[3] and dilates on laws ordaining religious education and matrimonial fidelity as well as on the prohibitions of heathenish superstition.[4] Cnut's spiritual admonition, addressed to churchmen only, he extends to nuns as well, and the protection of strangers to pilgrims.[5] He replaces Cnut's enactment concerning St. Peter's pence by the much more severe and then no doubt obsolete one of Eadgar. For the inviolability of the church and for clerical privileges and dues[6] he shows a strong bias; nor will he recognise any monk's lord but the prelate, nor the full dignity of a priest unless he be unmarried.[7] How is it, then, to be explained that the majority of the articles he skips are ecclesiastical ones?[8] If this is not due to mere chance or to his wish to shorten his labour, this contemporary of St. Anselm probably felt convinced that spiritual admonitions, fasting

[1] We gave our reasons for excluding Canterbury, Rochester, and Winchester. If the author was a mere translator and not a collector at the same time, if in other words an Anglo-Saxon compilation once existed containing all these features, our attempt to grasp the man's individuality would apply, of course, to this shadowy predecessor.

[2] A. 972-1016; 1040; 1061.   [3] i. 16, 1. ii. 4. iii. 45, 2.
[4] i. 22. i. 7. ii. 6. ii. 5.   [5] i. 6. ii. 35.   [6] i. 11, 1. 13.
[7] i. 5, 2 a (the same alteration from Alfred 20 is in Leg. Henr. 23, 3. 45, 2). i. 4. 5. iii. 45. 63.
[8] i. 18; 19, 1; 20 f.; ii. 10 1.; 29, 1; 38; 46, 1; 49; 65; 67 f.; 76 1; 79; 81; 51; 54.

enactments, church repair and wills belonged rather to canon law than to a royal statute. Or did the fine of ten shillings for injuring a clerk appear too slight? Did the warning to avoid crimes on holidays as a twofold sin[1] seem superseded by the 'Treuga Dei'?

The author does not betray any monkish tendency; he rather accentuates the parson's right to get tithes and soul-scot from all his parishioners. Nobody is to be buried outside the parish without the curate's permission:[2] an interpolation which seems to aim at the monastic encroachments on the parishes. He reminds the clergy of their pastoral duty besides that of prayer, and it is the poor, instead of the convent,[3] to whom he assigns a share of the fines for injuries offered to a man in holy orders. He likes to enhance the bishop's power; and altogether his views and his legal knowledge might well befit an archdeacon or a clerk of a court Christian.

12. The literary merits of a writer who simply aims at collecting a few legal documents and at translating them honestly can but be small. Still he deserves some modest praise. He succeeds in laying hold of about the fourth part of all the Anglo-Saxon laws now preserved and of two fragments otherwise unknown. In completeness, therefore, he surpasses almost all the collections of his age which pretend to expound the 'Laga Eadwardi,' the unwritten constitution of the last Saxon king, viz. 'Leis Willelme,' 'Leges Henrici,' 'Leges Edwardi Confessoris' and 'Consiliatio Cnuti.' 'Quadripartitus' indeed, embodying about three-fourths of what has come down to us, remains the most successful collection of all, but our author is the only mediæval translator of 'Grith,' and perhaps of 'Northumbre.' With 'Consiliatio, 'Cnut's Forest-law,' 'Quadripartitus' and the 'Leis' he shares the opinion that among old English laws then still valid the first place belonged to Cnut's code, and like the two latter works he assigns the second place to Alfred's. Here, there-

[1] ii. 38.   [2] i. 12 b. 13.   [3] i. 6; iii. 45.

fore, he helps to confirm the probability that no English king between Alfred and Henry, except Cnut, ever published a larger code, though plenty of single ordinances of the witan and many private notes of customary law seem to have been irretrievably lost to us.

The author's Latin flows with ease and clearness. He keeps himself equally free from the pedantic pseudo-classicism of the 'Consiliatio' as from the obscure bombast of the 'Quadripartitus.' His accidence is generally right ; his syntax mediæval throughout, and his vocabulary, tinged with some Northern-French colouring, happily retains a quantity of English technical terms. Altogether it would not surprise us to find that he came from a school of Lanfranc's creation. In a few places we may perhaps detect some vanity in the choice of rare Latin words or a weak attempt to enliven a little the dry language of the originals.[1]

In the main he translates exactly. His tendency is indeed to shorten his labour by omissions,[2] and he commits not a few faults, sometimes owing to want of knowledge,[3] more rarely to inattention.[4] But how conscientiously he generally works, appears from the glosses which exhibit, either between the lines or in the margin, a more faithful rendering, or a more Latin expression, found during the process of the translation,[5] in place of the former faulty one.[6] In their original place they still occur in earlier manuscripts, while other scribes[7]

---

[1] iii. 21 sq. 38. 61.   [2] See above, 11 ; cf. ii. 5. 30 ; iii. 28.

[3] Above, 9.

[4] He puts 'above' instead of 'beneath' (ii. 217. 29, 1), 'kills' instead of 'bites,' and leaves out *be*, iii. 41.

[5] In ii. 59 g the author at first retained from Alfred 39 *ceorlman* ; but he put dots under *man* and wrote in the margin *boren*. We find this in Cb, while Di has *ceorlman vel ceorlboren*, and H *ceorlboren*. Cf. *commoditatem* for *airiam*, iii. 52. The position of words is also often altered ; *vocant* preferred to *dicunt*, etc. These trifling changes occur so often, that they cannot be due to the scribes ; they prove that the author retouched his work.

[6] For *thearf* the MSS. read variously, *necessitas, profectus, utilitas*, i. Pr. 4 ; cf. iii. 13.

[7] See iii. 38, 1, *delicatiores* and *i. minores* above it in H and Di, while Cb has only *del.*, and S only *min*. Cf. ii. 46 ; 75. H retains *bocland* in several places above *alodium*.

either omit them or the correction,[1] or else retain both of them in their text.

13. Sometimes our author ventures to leave the humbler task of a mere translator purposely and to take some timid steps on the way leading to juristic literature of original value. Now and then he alters the order of his materials,[2] in favour of a more logical system. He suppresses obsolete matter, he inserts views or customs of his own age among the ancient ordinances, and amalgamates ancient and modern law, or compares them historically. If he had followed up those laudable beginnings energetically, he would have risen above the modest ideal of 'Quadripartitus' and 'Consiliatio,' and have approached the standard of a work like the 'Leges Henrici'; but abandoning them only too soon, he merely produces that inorganic mixture of antiquities and valid law which characterises the private law-books of the century before Glanville, especially the 'Leges Edwardi Confessoris.'

But though he names his book (assuming that he is the author of the 'Incipit') 'Cnut's laws,' still the insertions and the continuation which do not belong to Cnut must not induce us to call him a forger, such for instance as was certainly the fabricator of the Forest-law who speaks under Cnut's mask. He simply follows the mediæval practice of naming a compilation after its opening clause, just as the Worcester monks call their chronicle 'Marianus,' because they have continued his work, and not because they want to make him responsible for their own additions. Besides, all the interpolations in the Instituta,' as well as the whole third part, may be due to an afterthought, since unsystematic collections are among all literary productions the most liable to have appendices subjoined which had not been comprised in the original plan.

14. An intelligent translator will not cling too literally to

---

[1] Other glosses belong to a Kentish copyist who puts *suling* over *hida*, i. 12; cf. above, 9, annot. In Battle and in Canterbury deeds *swulinga* (*swolling*) is explained by *hida*, *terra aratri*; cf. Taylor, *Domesday Studies*, i. 161.

[2] He arranges i. 12 before 11; 11, 1 before 10; ii. 66, 1 before 66; 71, 3 before 71, 2, and ii. 43 behind i. 5.

his original. Our author judiciously helps his reader by references to former chapters,[1] by the substitution of substantives [2] for ambiguous pronouns, by the selection of more characteristic expressions,[3] and by the expansion of the too succinct or elliptical Anglo-Saxon into an easier and clearer style. Thus he says, *quod a latrone exegit* for *ceapgeld*; and to *homo sine calumnia* he adds *de terra aut alia re*.[4] He studies the text in hand until he has grasped its innermost meaning, and then proceeds to enliven the sketchy original by some colouring of his own. Where the law exempts the monk from paying or receiving any 'wergeld,' he adds *licet sit parens occisoris vel occisi*, and in a picture from life he describes the *flemen* as *latrones latitantes in silvis qui spoliant et occidunt alios homines*.[5]

Unlike the 'Consiliatio' and 'Quadripartitus,' the 'Instituta' do not present us with an interesting prologue disclosing the writer's own mind. Here we can only casually recognise the author's individual knowledge and personal opinions by his short insertions, or unintentional deviations from the original. Unconsciously he reveals some new facts to us when he is aiming only at a clearer expression than his text offered him. He replaces, for instance, *CC manc.* by *L marc.*,[6] because the *mancus* had gone out of use. While in these cases we clearly perceive that he is talking of things still current in 1100, we must be cautious against ascribing to his age all those ideas which he translates without any change, because we know for certain that some of the institutions he treats of had disappeared long before his time. There is, however, another criterion which, if used *cum grano salis*, may

[1] ii. 45 refers to i. 5; cf. above, 4, ann.
[2] ii. 75, 1. iii. 41; *vir post acceptus* for *he*, ii. 73, 1.
[3] *Domino* for 'receiver of fines,' ii. 73, 4; *latro* for 'forfeited,' ii. 44 sq. The place is repeated instead of 'there,' ii. 75, 1.
[4] ii. 30, 6. 72.
[5] i. 5, 2. iii. 48. cf. *in villis pleniter arent et seminent* for *tilian*, ii. 69, 1.
[6] ii. 71. About the shilling of fourpence, see above, 10. The knowledge of ores, ii. 15, 1, may come from the Northumbrian priests or from Danish custom. Suffolk people reckoned after the ore still in 1253; Ellis, *Introd. to Domesday*, i. 167.

assure us that he is dealing with customs still in practice, viz. the addition of the English technical term. It is hardly from a mere antiquarian or philological interest that a Norman jurist introduces a Saxon word with the explanation *quod Angli dicunt* in addition to the Latin equivalent. These articles of the 'Instituta' where this criterion or some alteration by the translator is found will, therefore, serve to illustrate English law under Henry I.

15. It is a characteristic sign of the strong Anglo-Norman monarchy, that he considers seignorial jurisdiction and the baronial share of legal fines as royal privileges.[1] He restricts the title of *ætheling*,[2] once pertaining to all the princes of the blood royal, to the king's legitimate son. Instead of 'England,' or 'this country,' he makes the king say *regnum meum*;[3] he alters the royal style from the singular into the plural *nos*.[4] It is perhaps from a reminiscence of William II.'s abuses that he expands Cnut's prohibition addressed to the royal reeves against extortions for the royal household.[5]

16. As all the land was then feudalised, 'the lord of the land' here becomes a tenant *in capite*, and *alodium*, used for *bocland*, stands in contradistinction to land given by a mesne lord, not to fief.[6] Instead of 'entitled to receive' the mulct, our author employs the technical *saca et socn*, and instead of *socn, consuetudines suas*.[7] Where Ini dictates the fines for taking the law into one's own hands against wrong-doers[8] and for riotous gangs, he is anxious to assign them to the lord of the territory if he possesses *consuetudines*, and to him he allows the wergeld of the private revenger.[9] For the harbouring of an outlaw, or of a retainer who left his lord without licence, he demands, besides the mulct due to the

[1] ii. 12. 15.
[2] Above, 7. In ii. 58, however, *regulus* may mean 'prince of the blood.'
[3] i. 17, 1. [4] ii. 82 ; cf. Quadrip. p. 48.
[5] ii. 69, 1. Cf. on the royal prerogative below, 20.
[6] i. 8. ii. 77. In Domesday *alodium* designates also other tenures ; Ellis, *Introd.* i. 54.
[7] ii. 30, 6. 71, 3 ; iii. 3.
[8] The 'Instituta' call this violent self-help *nam*.   [9] iii. 1. 3.

government, a *despectus*, which is equivalent to the English *oferseones*, for the judge who proscribed the criminal and for the lord.[1] The legal distinction between the possessor of a household and a landless 'follower,' and between the thane's domain and the land let to peasants, i.e. *tunm[e]n*, is still in full force.[2] The hundreds (*popularia placita*) are to be appealed to three times before the suit is brought into the shire. *Constituantur*, adds our author, *sicut ante hoc factum est*,[3] an insertion which also points to the time when Henry I. restored the hundreds, i.e. about A.D. 1110. *Teonscip* is translated by *plegium*, because frankpledge[4] constitutes its main object. These *fideiussores* are to pay the *ceapgeld*, i.e. the amount claimed, if the defendant escapes before the fulfilment of the sentence, and either to bring him to trial or to pay his wergeld to the king (and in a privileged territory to its lord). A lord keeps his men in his own pledge, and he is to get his money back from the fisc if he brings the man to justice in a year and a day.[5]

Instead of the wergeld, 'William I.'[6] asks in such a case 'wite' and twenty shillings; but he and 'Edward the Confessor' enact also the repayment to the surety or to the village, if the accused is found in a year and a day.

Where the author speaks of different ranks he distinguishes, to use his own words, first the *ceorlboren* (*twyhynde man* or *villanus*), who is perhaps not yet unfree, but ranges in the social scale below the owner of *alodium*;[7] secondly, the *sixhynde* (which name, unusual in the author's age or province, he prefers to replace by *radcniht*[8]); and lastly, the *twelfhynde*, thane or *liberalis*.[9] *Liber(alis)* meant in the language of the day more than free—perhaps, a gentleman. 'Quadripartitus'[10] has *plene nobilis* instead. Among the thanes the *kinges thegn qui habet consuetudines suas* stands

---

[1] ii. 15, 2. 28. 66. [2] ii. 20; i. 11, 1; ii. 19. [3] ii. 17.
[4] Cf. 'Consiliatio,' Einl. 15. [5] ii. 25, 1. 30, 6. 31, 1.
[6] 'Leis,' 3, 4; 'Ed. Conf.' 15, 5. [7] ii. 15, 1.
[8] ii. 59 i. iii. 5. 43. 60 sq.
[9] Only once the word means legally free, ii. 20. [10] P. 48.

above the *lesse thegn*. This term is hardly a mere outcome of Cnut's *thegn læsse maga*, as the expression is used also by the forger of Cnut's forest-law.[1] The appreciation of earl and bishop at the value of a double thane belongs to a past age;[2] but the Anglo-Saxon designation of rank is not yet replaced by a Norman one.[3] Nor is heriot, *debitum post mortem*,[4] confounded with relief.[5]

17. As to criminal law, our author abhors capital punishment for *latrocinium aut talia*; nevertheless *locus latronum* means, according to him, the unconsecrated burial-place of criminals.[6] But the fines he is inclined to expand according to the various receivers; in addition to Ini's punishments in case of riotous assault by a gang of seven to thirty-five men, which he still calls *hloth*, he assigns *despectus* (mundbryce) to the injured party, and 2*l.* to the owner of 'saca and socn'; and in case of manslaughter the gang is to pay *forisfacturas*, i.e. wite to the judge, beside the 'wer' to the dead man's relations.[7] The non-judicial taking of *nam*, or self-help in civil obligations, is confounded with *wrace* or revenge for criminal offences and threatened, more severely than in the original, by the mulct of 'wergeld'[8] payable to the lord. Furthermore, the amount due to the king (or to the owner of saca and socn) is raised from thirty shillings to forty. The technical terms *wergeld, wer and wite (pretium et forisfactura), be healve were, be weres maðe, mægbot and manbot (emendatio parentibus et domino occisi), ægylde (impersolutus)*, are well understood;[9] *lahslit* is recognised as Danish, and used convertibly with *X sol*, or *healsfang*, to which the author

---

[1] ii. 71, 2 sq.
[2] iii. 55. 57. Such as the rising of the ceorl to thaneship, where already the Anglo-Saxon original uses the past tense, iii. 60.
[3] See above, 7.   [4] ii. 70 sq. 73, 4. 78.
[5] As in Domesday, Quadripartitus, and William's Laws.   [6] ii. 2, 1. 33.
[7] iii. 1–4. 8. Ini demands the purgation oath or the 'wer' according to the value of the rioter, our author according to the value of the assailed party.
[8] ii. 19. iii. 1; intentionally, as iii. 3 has *duas libras*.
[9] i. 2, 4. ii. 16. 20. 30, 8. 48 sq. 52. 59 d. 60. 62. 66. 69, 1. iii. 6 sqq. 44 sq. 56, 2.

erroneously assigns a Danish origin.[1] The names of the offences *grithbrece, weofodbot, foresteal, fleman fermian, hlafordswice*,[2] are retained; *hamsocn* is freely explained as *invasio domus aut curiæ*, and *ferdwite* as *dimissio belli*;[3] *despectus* does duty for *mundbrece* and *oferhyrnes*, which in the author's view was replaced by the more modern *oferseones*. Instead of *feohtwite* he once [4] puts *violatio monetæ*, apparently because he, or the scribe whose manuscript he used, misread *feohwite*, but we need not assume that such a term ever existed in practical life. *Behætian* [5] is explained as *auferatur corium capitis cum capillis*. *Gecydne utlaga* he calls, as it seems technically, the *friðleas man*, i.e. the criminal proscribed by the judge.[6]

18. The procedure retains its Anglo-Saxon features,[7] and the author is careful to note the old terms *ath, forath, werelade, anfealde spæce, corsnæd*, and so on. A man with whom stolen chattels are found is allowed *warantem nominare* (*vocare*) only if he has two [8] eye- and ear-witnesses for his lawful acquisition. Only two previous possessors are permitted to vouch to warranty, while the third previous warrantor must *suum facere*, i.e. prove that the object belonged originally to him,[9] or give it up.

The oath is delivered on relics [10] or the gospel. Instead of the 'purgation by 120 hides,' our author demands correctly eleven compurgators and the defendant to be the twelfth.[11] The accuser's *praeiuramentum* is sworn with two *consacramentales*, if simple, or with five, if threefold; the defendant is

[1] ii. 3. 37 sq. 45 sq. 48. 60. 71, 2.
[2] ii. 15. 61. 42. 12 sq. 26; iii. 49.
[3] ii. 12. 15. 61; *forisfactura belli*, iii. 46.   [4] ii. 15.
[5] ii. 30, 5; *decapilletur* Quadrip.; *piletur* Consil.; *dæalvare* elsewhere.
[6] ii. 15.
[7] The author adds for instance *et ipse sit duodecimus*, where the original mentioned the eleven compurgators, ii. 65.
[8] This number is the author's addition, ii. 23. 24, 2.
[9] Kolderup remarked that there must be a lapsus in *vocatus vocet alium et tertius tertium*, and proposes: *secundus t.* I prefer to read *t. quartum*, as ii. Cnut 24, 2, i. Wil. 45, and their Latin versions read 'the fourth time.'
[10] So *haligaom* is rightly translated.
[11] Ine 19. 46; cf. Quadripartitus: *iurare pro LX hidis, i.e. pro hominibus VI*.

obliged by it to undergo a simple or triple purgation respectively.[1] The gaining of such a processual claim (*conquirere, adquirere*) is called *ofgan* in the original, which a glossator about A.D. 1140 replaces by *ofrœcan*.[2] A man to whom *ne bærst ne ath ne ordel* enjoys *legalitas*, i.e. he is *athes (lade) wurðe*.[3] The *ordal* is explained as *iudicium ferri aut aquæ;* but *ignitum ferrum*, still[4] applied to the serf as well, constitutes a threefold ordeal,[5] without the old aggravations being mentioned.

19. In ecclesiastical law[6] the author demands most anxiously that emendations for bloodshed in churches, and trials against priests accused of crimes, *fiant secundum iudicium episcopi*,[7] without, however, altering the old compurgation or the ancient social scale, according to which the celibate priest ranks above the *popularis (vulgaris)*, i.e. married one. Not only Sundays but all festivals are to be undisturbed by executions of criminals.[8] The church dues are mentioned by their old names light-, church-, soul- and Romescot.[9] The author explains *lignum frondosum, lignum viride aut aridum adorare*,[10] as heathenish tree-worship, which therefore seems to have lingered on in his own age.

He betrays a decided interest in matrimonial law. Being aware of the Teutonic reckoning of relationship according to knees, he translates *sibfæc* by *genu*,[11] an error he shares with 'Consiliatio.' *Raptus*, complete only *si cum ea coitus factus sit*, is to be paid by the woman's wergeld.[12] The prohibition of a widow's marriage (*othres mannes ælæte*) before a twelvemonth has elapsed after the husband's death, is expressed in stronger language. Adultery[13] is to be punished according to the

[1] i. 5, 2. ii. 8. 22, 1 sq. 30, 3. iii. 61.
[2] MS. H over ii. 30, 3.
[3] ii. 20. 22. 36 sq. 39.
[4] See Glanville, 14, 1.
[5] i. 17. ii. 8. 22. 30, 3. 32. 35.
[6] See above, 11.
[7] i. 2, 4. 5 ; ii. 41 ; iii. 45.
[8] ii. 45.
[9] i. 9 sq. 12 sq.
[10] ii. 5.
[11] i. 7, while Æthelred vi. 12 gives 6 *manna sibfæc binnan tham* 4. *cneowe*. Cf. Amira, in Paul's *Grundriss German. Philol.* ii, 2, 137.
[12] Cnut demands in one MS. the man's wergeld, ii. 52.
[13] As a violation of marriage he mentions *iacendo sub coniuge*, ii. 50.

Penitential. The husband must preserve matrimonial fidelity, though the wife be *infirma*; if he keeps a concubine he forfeits the religious attentions not only of the priest but of everybody besides.[1]

20. But apart from the translator's alterations, explanations, and interpolations there are in the middle of the third part two pieces, separated from one another by a version from a well-known source, which are unique in form and partly so in contents. The language unmistakably bears our author's stamp;[2] but even here he is not an original writer; he rather follows a lost Anglo-Saxon treatise, composed in the middle of the eleventh century. This appears from the quantity of English words retained, not all of which are technical;[3] and still more clearly from two oblique cases[4] one of which makes bad grammar in the Latin text, because the word on which it depended[5] in Anglo-Saxon has disappeared. The rubric *Istæ sunt consuetudines regum inter Anglos* prepares the reader for the author's passing to a new document; perhaps even it is a verbal translation of its title. Chapters 46-55 deal, indeed, only with the royal prerogative. It appears to be further developed than in Cnut's law, which may have been the source of that tract, and less extended than in the 'Leges Henrici'; also it is free from Norman influences. Once, however, we seem to perceive the translator's own interpolation: 'Qui divisionem habet iuxta terram regis, claudat contra regem aut custodiat aut dilectione aut pretio adquirat, si voluerit aliquam in terra illa aisiam habere.' This advice would answer to our author's hatred of the encroaching royal reeves;[6] it harmonises well with the greed of the Conqueror and his sons.

21. The document assigns to the king, besides *multas alias consuetudines quae sibi conveniunt*, and which it does not

---

[1] i. 8. ii. 50. 54. 73.
[2] *Alod*, iii. 46; in *ferd* he sees *bellum*, in *ham*, *curia*, as above, 17, ann.; *quod Angli dicunt* occurs very often.
[3] *Punderes*, 59.   [4] *Bebodenes*, 47.   [5] *Beo weorth* (?)
[6] See above, 15, ann.

specify, the *rectitudines civitatum* (just as Eadgar demands, for every *byrig* kingship's *gerihta*), *pastus* (i.e. 'feorm') and *carta allodii ad aeternam hereditatem* (the right to create 'bocland' and the fee payable for it). All the following cases agree with Cnut's claims[1]: *forisfactura alodii, pretium allodi*[*arii*],[2] *ferdwite, pastio bebodenes utlage, pastio flemen, riht*[3] *hamsocn* and *grithbrece ex parte regis*[4]; while *emendatio fracti pontis in via regia* is perhaps a combination of Cnut's *bricgbot*[5] with *stretbrece*.[6] *Vita aut pretium publici latronis* seems to mean that the life or wergeld of an 'æbære'[7] thief is forfeited to the king, as, indeed, is well known from other Anglo-Saxon laws.[8] *Latro extra proclamatus* may signify criminal pleas outside a district of jurisdiction exempted and privileged with 'infangenetheof.' A division of the mulcts between king and bishop, which we know[9] to have existed in England during the tenth and eleventh centuries in the cases of injury to the secular right of the church or of opposition to the bishop's power, is here ordained in case of *fractae pacis ecclesiae*, i.e. 'ciricgrithbrece.' But when the author continues: 'Antiqua consuetudo fuit ut omnis ecclesiastica et secularis emendatio communis erat regi et episcopo,' he either grossly exaggerates a legal custom locally restricted and valid for a few offences only, or possibly he wants to point out the mixed cases of ecclesiastical and civil transgression as one notion, for instance the violation of church-peace just mentioned. The bishop's income arising from sums paid in atonement for ecclesiastical offences is to go to the churches and to the poor. As to the *comes* (ealdorman or earl?) the author states, *secundum Anglos* (which most likely means out of an English document) that he possesses, as *rectitudines com-*

[1] Bocland forworht, flymena fyrmð, utlages [fyrmð], etc., ii. Cn. 12 sq. 15.
[2] Cf. i. Æthelred, 1, 14.
[3] *I.e.* 'perfect'; cf Bosworth-Toller riht-handdæda.
[4] *I.e. cyninges handgri*ð; *pax data manu regis*; Domesday, Chester.
[5] ii. Cnut, 10. 65. [6] Henr. 10, 1. 12. 35, 2.
[7] This word is translated *publicus latro*, ii. Cnut, 26.
[8] Schmid, p. 556.
[9] Edw. Guthrum Pr. 2; viii. Æthelred, 8. 15. 36.

munes cum rege, the *tertius denarius* from market towns and from the emoluments arising from *castigatio latronum*, and lastly the *comitales villas*, i.e. townships or manors officially belonging to the earldom.[1] Domesday notices several city rents of which *duæ partes erant regis et tertia comitis*.[2] But no fixed rule on this point occurs elsewhere, nor was it ever applicable to the whole country. In exact confirmation of the distinction ably drawn the other day by Mr. Round,[3] the earl's third penny arises, not from all the sums paid by the shire to the government, but only from 'redditus burgi,' and from crown pleas; for 'theofes steore' (as most likely our author's original read) means criminal justice generally. The system where, according to Domesday, this latter share belonged to the earl 'was confined to the Danish district.'

22. The four remaining entries,[4] chiefly concerning the earl and the bishop, are, indeed, not to be expected under the above rubric *Consuetudines regis*. But they also are drawn from an Anglo-Saxon source, and our author in no way separates them from the preceding piece; possibly he found them as its appendix.

To the *comes* he assigns a privileged rank double as high as the thane's in every respect, for instance in *mund*, *manbot*, *forisfactura* [i.e. 'wite'] and *wer*. In this general form the statement finds no exact parallel anywhere; nay, it directly contradicts 'Northleod,' a late Anglo-Saxon document, partly used by our author. It is true that the earl could ask double as many sureties from the party whom he accused as the thane could: and Cnut had enacted that the earl's heriot should cost double as much as the thane's.[5] Possibly our author himself generalised from a few theoretical relations between the earl's and the thane's value. 'From olden times,' he continues, 'bishop and earl enjoy equal secular rank in many

---

[1] Cf. *ealdormannes land* apud Schmid, p. 560; cf. Eyton, Domesday of Somerset, i. 78.
[2] So Chester; Lincoln, *reddebat regi XX l.., comiti X*.
[3] Geoffrey of Mandeville, 287. 289; Edw. Conf. 27.
[4] End of c. 55; 57 sqq. [5] III. Æthelred, 12; ii. Cnut, 71.

respects.' That their 'wergeld, mundbryce, fihtwite' and the surety to be given by the defendant whom they accused were the same, is said by Anglo-Saxon documents [1] which our author partly availed himself of elsewhere and perhaps here too. But equality of civil rank in every respect was again most likely a mere assumption of some writer.

The bishop possesses *ecclesiasticam correctionem et christianam dominationem super omnes* (his diocesans). Though this line means canonical jurisdiction, its untechnical form harmonises more with Ælfric's age than with the time of the developed court Christian; and the spiritual admonition which follows it is, in fact, a mere translation from Cnut.[2] *Secundum iusticiam*, i.e. in civil polity, *multis locis*, i.e. not as a rule, the bishop possesses *in sua propria terra et in suis villis*, i.e. in the barony appurtenant to the bishopric (besides *varias consuetudines quas statuerunt qui Dei honorem amaverunt*), *monetarios et punderes (vel[3] ponderatores) et loca iudiciorum ferri aut aquæ, proprias mensuras et pondera*. The supervision of coinage, weights, and measures belongs to the bishop according to 'Polity[4];' and we know from Æthelstan's law and from coins still preserved, that several prelates[5] kept their own mint. The ordeal by boiling water and hot iron was performed in church. Our author cannot mean to assign to the bishop all the churches under the name of *loca iudiciorum*. He either thinks of the cold water ordeal,[6] which possibly was restricted to certain waters possessed by the bishop, or he merely wants to say that while an ordeal is going on, the place stands under the bishop's 'grith. But what comes next agrees only with the very last generation of Anglo-

[1] iii. Æthelred, 12; Grith, 11 sq.; Northleod, 3.

[2] ii. Cnut, 84, 1.

[3] This gloss stands in its correct place in H, but after *aquae* in Cb, which then repeats *aquae*. This nonsense is followed in the edited texts.

[4] Ch. 7: *Episcopus*.

[5] St. Edmund's, York, later on Durham, besides Canterbury mentioned in Æthelstan, 14.

[6] Its existence is attested by late Anglo-Saxon rituals and Quadripartitus, p. 48, accepted by Brunner, *Deutsche Rechtsgesch.* ii. 410.

Saxon rule. *Tol et team* are indeed ceded to bishops by many charters. *Pretium latronum infra terminos eorum proclamatorum* seems to be a translation of 'infangenetheof.'[1] All this and *unworthe hamsocn* may apply to fines only.[2] But it is clearly secular criminal jurisdiction that is meant by *correctionem latronum quousque sint condemnati ad mortem*; to condemn to death was canonically forbidden to churchmen.[3] Lastly, the bishop has in the lands of his bishopric *hundredsetene*, 'constitutionem hundredi.'[4] Charters of Edward the Confessor granting hundreds to churches exist. But the laws of Anglo-Saxon times are silent on these franchises, which came in late and, as our author himself says, not everywhere.

23. The 'Instituta' were often read in the Middle Ages. In the twelfth century excerpts were made from them by the compiler of William I.'s articles 'Hic intimatur,'[6] and by the forger of forest-law who calls himself Cnut. They were copied at least sixteen times,[7] and twelve manuscripts still exist. One class ending with iii. 44 may belong to Middle or Northern England, while the other is derived, as it seems, from an archetype glossed by a Kentishman.[8] The autograph is lost. If we are right in ascribing to it those graphic features of our codices which went out of use by the end of the twelfth

---

[1] Vgl. ii. Cnut, 61 : *gif hwa griðbryce fulwyrce*, . . . *gif he samwyrce*.

[2] Cf. Henr. 20, 2 : *Episcopi in terris propriae potestatis suae sacam et socnam habent, tol et theam et infongentheof et super alterius homines, si in forisfaciendo retenti vel gravati fuerint, emendationem*.

[3] Cf. Kemble, *Saxons*, ii. 393 ; Dove, *Jurisd. eccles. progres*. 116.

[4] Corrupted from *setenes* or *settan*?

[5] Cf. Stubbs, *Constit. Hist*. i. 106.

[6] III. Wl. 1 and 8 come from the 'Instituta,' i. Cn. Pr. and ii. Cn. 20, while iii. Wl. 5. 8 a. 9. 10 are only materially akin to ii. Cn. 24. 17. 3. 30, 5, and iii. Wl. 6 comes from William's ordinance on procedure.

[7] Including those lost MSS., the existence of which must be assumed for the sake of classification. A copyist of the author's own lifetime adds *abbatiae* behind the churches privileged with royal *mund*; the word is in H T Di S, but not in Cb. The variations printed by Kolderup from B, and after Thorkelin's notes from D, do not at all belong to the 'Instituta,' but to the Quadripartitus MSS. Br and Dm, partly however to R, though D is quoted ; see Quadr. p. ix.

[8] See above, 12.

century, and therefore cannot have been introduced by the scribes, it very often placed *e* or *æ* for *ae*, and in Anglo-Saxon words the letters p, ð, þ, ʒ, and ꝑ for *w*, *th*, *g*, and *r*.

24. H, the celebrated 'Textus Roffensis'[1] contains the 'Instituta' at the commencement of what was formerly a separate part of the MS., where they are followed by William's 'Hic intimatur.' The scribe, writing about A.D. 1140, introduces many accents and retains the original rubrics, paragraphs, and *e* for *æ*.[2] He prefers, however, to substitute the Gallican *w*, *g*, and *th* for the Anglo-Saxon letters, and he is not free from Kenticisms, prefixing *h* to short vowels at the beginning of words and expressing *è* in the middle of syllables by *æ*.[3] He betrays a Latinising tendency, introduces some valuable glosses of his own,[4] and alters the old *ofga* (*adquirat*) into the Middle English *ofræce*.[5] As a whole he offers the best text; but there are some trifling deviations from the original in places where the other manuscripts faithfully follow Cnut.[6] He therefore was neither identical with the author nor the source of any other codex, though he is earlier than all the rest. From a transcript of H, Hearne printed part iii.[7]

Rl, the Rawlinson MS. C. 641, f. 30-43, of about A.D. 1200, is nearly akin to H.[8] Here the 'Instituta' follow after the 'Leges Edwardi Confessoris' (in the first form) and after some assizes of the twelfth century. Henry I.'s coronation charter and 'Hic intimatur' are subjoined to the 'Instituta.'[9] The form of both these latter pieces is also like H.

---

[1] The Very Rev. the Dean and Chapter of Rochester kindly allowed me to inspect it at Rochester, and in 1890 sent it for my use to the British Museum. I herewith beg to offer them my most respectful thanks.

[2] Fol. 58-118; the preceding part, containing Anglo-Saxon laws, seems to be somewhat earlier. On fol. 119 the Rochester Chartulary begins.

[3] *His* for *ii*, iii. 63; *hundræd*, *pundæres*, iii. 58 sq.

[4] *Nocere ordinato* instead of *-tum*, which answers to the Anglo-Saxon original; see above, 9, ann. 8.

[5] ii. 30, 3.

[6] i. 17, 1, which the other MSS. place after 17, occurs after 19; *etiam* is left out in i. 15.

[7] See above, 2. [8] After iii. 44 both add *sex villanorum*.

[9] Cf. Stubbs, *Hoveden*, ii. xxiij.

T, MS. Titus A 27, in the Cottonian collection contains the 'Instituta' on fol. 159*v*-173*v*,[1] in a hand of about A.D. 1225, after the 'Quadripartitus,' where 'Hic intimatur' had been inserted.[2] In some respects T stands in nearer relation to Cb than to the other MSS.[3]

25. Cb, Colbert's MS. 3,860, now in the Parisian Bibliothèque Nationale,[4] Fonds Latin 4771, was written about A.D. 1150, and certainly before 1172. It was read about A.D. 1200 by a South-Englishman who glossed *wapentagiis* with *lestis*. Before the fifteenth century the MS. wandered into France. In place of the first two chapters of the 'Instituta' it contains, on fol. 1, the prologue and the commencement of the 'Consiliatio Cnuti.' From the conclusion of that work it subjoins on f. 35 four lines to the 'Instituta,' before going on with a third legal collection [5] which consists of 'Hic intimatur,' 'Leges Edwardi Confessoris,' [6] and 'Genealogia Normannica.' This strange blending with another translation from Cnut is sufficient to prove that Cb cannot have been the source of any other manuscript.[7] Nor can it have been derived thence, because its readings often cling more slavishly to the original, and therefore seem to represent a former recension of the work.[8] In other places, indeed, Cb's peculiarities are clearly the afterthoughts,[9] either of a scribe or of the author retouching his work. In the latter case the only explanation is that one autograph showed the original reading

[1] The end of this last page of the MS. is blank.
[2] Quadr. p. 64, 145. T is not the only MS. where two different translations of Cnut occur; also Hk exhibits *Consiliatio Cnuti* after *Quadripartitus*.
[3] See *ecclesiarum*, i. 22, and an insertion, i. 4.
[4] Its Administrateur-général, M. Léopold Delisle, with his usual kindness, informed me about the MS. in a long letter, and sent the codex to the Berlin library in 1892. Cf. *Consiliatio Cnuti*, Einl. 20 sqq.
[5] Copied, not without gross errors, by Roger de Hoveden, s. a. 1180.
[6] In their second form.
[7] *In sura* in Cb, where the other MSS. read correctly *infixa*, iii. 31 proves the same.
[8] In i. 3, 2 Cb has *XXX. sol.* like Cnut (while H Di T give *octoginta denar.*) and in ii. 60 the word *hominem* left out by H Di S; cf. i. 6, 2. 8, and see above, 12.
[9] In i. 13 a whole sentence is in Cb alone, not drawn from Cnut.

as well as the later alteration. This manuscript offers a complete system of rubrics composed most likely after 1163, the year when Edward the Confessor was canonised, as the rubric mentioning Saint Eadward adds *martyris*, apparently in order to distinguish the latter from the Confessor. Though written in the hand of the scribe of Cb, these rubrics were not composed by him,[1] but by the predecessor whom he merely followed, an intelligent man, who, for instance, once introduces the technical term *nam*, not from the chapter he is going to rubricate, but in accordance with the author's sentiments.[2] Cb's scribe softens the Anglo-Saxon *c* before *e* and *i* into Middle-English *ch*, uses *t* instead of *c* before *i*, and sometimes drops his *h*.[3] He was ignorant of Old English.[4] Probably for this reason the Anglo-Saxon words are entered either after some hesitation with fresh ink or by a contemporary corrector, who faithfully preserves the Anglo-Saxon letters for *w, th, g, r, s,* and *e*.[5] He did not merely guess the right reading,[6] but, filling in [7] words omitted by the scribe, must have worked with Cb's source at his elbow. He corrected in addition to the 'Instituta' also the remaining pieces [8] of the volume, all of which are in one hand.

Cb was copied at Paris for F. Rostgaard, who died in 1745. He collated the transcript, now Codex Arne-Magnæanus at Copenhagen, with Cb. This transcript was printed by Kolderup-Rosenvinge [9]; but a great many mistakes are due to the modern copyist or to the printer, and not to Cb.[10]

[1] This appears from Cb's text erroneously exhibiting *detractione* (in H this same mistake is still visible under a later correction), while the rubric correctly reads *De traditione*, ii. 57. Secondly, the commencement of ii. 15 is written in red ink, as if it were a rubric.   [2] iii. 1; cf. ii. 19.
[3] *Breche, cherl, cherche*, iii. 56, 42; i. 3, 2; *sotiis, untie,* i. 5, 2; iii. 10; *idas* for 'hydas,' iii. 61.
[4] *i porte* instead of *un porhte*, iii. 58; *lihtgescotter* for *lihtgescot, ter*, i. 12.
[5] We shall use this archaic orthography in the future text.
[6] *Decreto* for *secreto*, i. 2, 4.
[7] Sometimes in the margin, i. 8; ii. 74, 9–78.
[8] *Ælfgiua* is in Anglo-Saxon characters; *Geneal. Normann.* S.
[9] See above, 2.
[10] E.g. *id est* for *et, quod* for *quia, tantum* for *tamen, multae* for *inultae, parvulus* for *per vulnus*.

26. All the remaining manuscripts end with iii. 44.

Di, the Bodleian MS. Digby 13, contains the 'Instituta' on f. 41[1] in a hand of about 1170. It preserves generally þ, ð, p and sometimes *e*. As one quire is missing from the middle, the piece i Cnut 13 to ii. 15, 1 is wanting. Di alters the mulct of 40 shillings several times into *X sol.*[2] It cannot have been the source of the other manuscripts,[3] but it sometimes shows archaic features obliterated elsewhere, even in H.[4]

Lastly there are six or eight manuscripts of Henry of Huntingdon,[5] which insert in his sixth book, after Cnut's history, the 'Instituta,' calling them *Danelage*, and subjoin to the chronicle the appendix exhibited by Cb as well, viz. William's 'Hic intimatur,' Edward the Confessor, and 'Genealogia Normannica.'[6]

Lb, the oldest of these MSS. containing the interpolated Huntingdon,[7] is n. 118 at Lambeth, written about A.D. 1200.

Pa, the Paris MS. in the Bibliothèque Nationale nr. 6044, of the sixteenth century, 'exactly resembles Lb.'[8]

Va, the Vatican MS., once Queen Christina's, nr. 587, written in the sixteenth century, shows the same arrangement and, judging from some portions collated, the same readings as Lb.

The five following codices date from the fourteenth century. Two of them are in Cambridge colleges, viz. Ct, Trinity R 5, 42, 'arranged as Lb,'[8] and Jo, St. John's, G 16.

---

[1] The other parts of the volume are written in different hands, and deal with other subjects. After the 'Instituta' the rest of the page is left vacant.

[2] ii. 15, 1. 33, 2. 59e. 65. [3] It skips one line, ii. 30, 3.

[4] See above, 12. 24.

[5] In Henry's edition of 1145. William of Malmesbury is another chronicler of the twelfth century into whose history contemporary laws were interpolated ; and Roger of Howden embodied such in his chronicle himself.

[6] In those MSS. where the whole of the three pieces do not occur together, I assume that the copyist left out something rather than that he is more original than the fuller MSS.

[7] Cp. my paper 'Heinrich v. Huntingdon,' *Forschungen Deutsch. Gesch.* 18, 294. La[mbeth 179], written in the fourteenth century, has only *Hic intimatur* and *Genealogia*. It is said 'to be a transcript, with abridgments, of Lb.' Arnold, *Huntingdon*, p. xl–xliii, 188. I have not yet examined Arnold's MSS. 28 sqq., 'arranged as Lb.' They are modern. [8] Arnold.

The MSS. Va, Ct, and Jo have faults of their own [1]; they therefore do not depend on each other.

(Ph, No. 8079 in the collection of the late Sir Thomas Phillipps at Cheltenham, which formerly belonged to St. Mary's, Dublin, then to Twysden, and afterwards to Heber, probably belongs to this class, as 'Hic intimatur,' Edward and 'Genealogia' follow Huntingdon.)

Pl, Phillipps nr. 8078, also bought from Heber, is closely akin to S, the Harleian nr. 746 of the British Museum.[2] They retain only one paragraph of Huntingdon, but just that on Cnut's death which follows the 'Instituta' also in Lb, Pa, Va, Ct, and Jo. They subjoin to the 'Instituta' 'Hic intimatur' and 'Genealogia,' leaving out 'Leges Confessoris.' (The reason for this omission probably was that they had copied these 'Leges'[3] before the 'Instituta.') As Pl does not depend on S, nor S on Pl,[4] they go back to a lost manuscript.

The interpolator of Huntingdon has many readings in common [5] with Di, in contradistinction to the rest of the manuscripts. But he neither used Di [6] nor was the source of that MS., as his erroneous rubric sufficiently proves. They both followed one scribe, whose copy, in other words the archetype of the shorter class, is lost.

27. Those features, which the interpolator shares with the majority and the earliest MSS. of the longer class, most likely represent the authentic shape of the lost autograph. I therefore suppose that William I.'s 'Hic intimatur,' though not found in T and Di, was appended to the autograph of the 'Instituta,' before they had been published. As the 'Instituta'

[1] Ct omits *Anglorum* in the rubric ; Jo reads *it* for *hoc*, iii. 43, 3, and Va *perfectum* for *profectum*, i. Prol.

[2] Thorkelin's transcript of S preserved at Copenhagen was collated by Kolderup-Rosenvinge under the sigla H.

[3] In their more original shape, as in Rl, and followed by the London *Libertas civitatum*.

[4] In Cn. iii. 44 Pl has *chelfende* for 'twelfhynde.'

[5] iii. 22. 24 *unguis* ; iii. 27 *fuerit*. The end of ii. 59 a is wanting.

[6] H and S read *plegium*, Di sets wrongly *inditium*, and Cb omits the word, ii. 58. Again Jo, Pl, and S insert, together with the longer MSS. and the source (Merce 3), a line wanting in Di iii. 43, 3.

are excerpted by the jurist who wrote 'Hic intimatur,' the authors of these works seem to have exchanged their productions.

As to 'Leges Edwardi Confessoris' in the second form with the appended 'Genealogia,' I should prefer not to decide yet whether they were added to 'Hic intimatur' by the author of the 'Instituta' or the publisher of a later edition or by Cb[1] and the Huntingdon interpolator independently one from another. In a collection professing to exhibit William's complete laws, 'Hic intimatur' might have appeared as an unfinished treatise; and this might have induced both those scribes to add the two remaining parts as well.

[1] Rl presents 'Leges Ed. Conf.' in their more original form, without the 'Genealogia.'

THE LAWS OF THE MERCERS COMPANY OF LICHFIELD

COMMUNICATED AND TRANSCRIBED FROM THE ORIGINAL MS.
BY W. H. RUSSELL
WITH AN INTRODUCTION BY THE REV. PROFESSOR CUNNINGHAM, D.D.

THE Laws of the Mercers of Lichfield which have been transcribed by Mr. Russell and will, I trust, find a place in our next volume of Transactions, seem to me to have very special interest. They are typical of the ordinances which were made for industrial regulation in the seventeenth century. Throughout this century there was an extraordinary development of industrial and commercial companies, many of which were formed by statute and others by letters patent. The wisdom of granting such patents for commercial purposes was the subject of long-continued discussion—this centred round the action of the East India Company. But, if we except some special cases in the time of Charles I., there seems to have been comparatively little dispute about the industrial companies, and a great many were formed or were reconstituted during this period. Of these the Cutlers Company of Sheffield is the most celebrated.

With regard to many of these companies the question arises how far they were the survivals of earlier institutions, and merely carried on the work of the fourteenth-century gilds. But in the case of Lichfield there is no such question, so far as my information goes. The Mercers Company appears to be a new institution. Lichfield had been controlled by a gild in earlier times, but this was not, as appears from Dr. Gross's researches, a *Gilda Mercatoria*; and the various crafts of Lichfield seem to have been destitute of coercive powers of regulating the industries carried on within the city. Hence in the Lichfield ordinances we do not need to exercise criticism, and try to discriminate ancient ordinances which were incorporated among new ones from the new regulations.[1] We have to deal with a code that was newly enacted as a complete whole, and that may be supposed to contain what was thought to be of primary importance for the time, without admixture of ordinances which were mere survivals.

The Mercers Company was instituted by the town authorities immediately after receiving a charter which gave them special powers for taking a step of the kind. It may therefore, I think, be argued that the town could not have taken such action unless they had been specially empowered.[2] In this we have a striking contrast with what went on in the fourteenth century. The formation of new industrial gilds *with coercive powers* was a perfectly ordinary occurrence in most English towns at the earlier date. The municipalities were not inclined to look to outside authority for interference in this matter ; they were ready to complain of charters which instituted companies, and which *set aside* the municipal control. But in the seventeenth century the town of Lichfield did not attempt to confer this authority until they were empowered by royal charter : and this may be taken as typical of the seventeenth century. The crown or parliament was the source of coercive jurisdiction in matters of industry : it was no longer an ordinary function of municipal government.

This point is of some importance with regard to the much-disputed question as to the precise position of the surviving gilds in the later years of Edward VI. and the reign of Elizabeth. That gilds might be formed for charitable and social purposes is obvious enough ; that they might continue to exist for such purposes—for education or the display of

[1] Mr. Russell informs me that the oldest company appears to be that of the Bakers which was formed in 1576.

[2] Mr. Russell informs me that the Bakers (1576), Tailors (1576), Saddlers (1594), Smiths (1601), and Dyers (1601) had their laws sanctioned by the Justices in accordance with the Act of 1503 ; but subsequently to 1625 they were renewed by the City.

pageants—need not be discussed; but did they continue as *craft gilds*, that is as bodies with coercive powers for the regulation of any special trade? To my mind it remains to be proved that the old gilds, on a *municipal* basis, retained such powers after the reign of Edward VI., except in so far as they were reconstituted by the crown or by parliament.[1]

Again in the laws of the fourteenth-century gilds we find constant reference to the conditions of work, and the supervision of the quality of materials; we have brought before us the actual ways in which industry was carried on and the actual mischiefs which occurred in the industrial process. But the laws of this seventeenth-century company in Lichfield have quite a different tone: they have to do, not with the making of goods, but with the condition of goods as sold. The right of search has an entirely different significance from that which it formerly had; it is much more nearly akin to the Scotch 'trades' than to the fourteenth-century English gilds. It has to do with the examination of goods as offered for sale, and hardly at all with the supervision of the *processes* of manufacture themselves. This is a broad contrast in character.

Once more in the accounts of the formation of the earlier craft gilds we find an extreme subdivision, and an attempt to form a separate organisation for each branch. Weavers, shearmen, fullers, dyers, all were working at the production of cloth: but in the earlier days they were organised as separate trades, as they had to do with separate *processes*, involving distinct kinds of skill. There were plenty of ordinances passed with the view of insisting that the same man should not exercise two callings. But the Mercers Company of Lichfield embraced a most heterogeneous group of trades and there seems to have been no effort made to prevent men from passing from one trade to another.

[1] In York the coercive powers of the searchers of different occupations had been re-assumed by the mayor in 1519 (Drake, *Eboracum*, 215), though in 1581 the Mercers secured exemption from his jurisdiction by charter. So too did the Drapers and Linen Weavers.

From this it seems to follow that the motive which is almost explicitly alleged for the institution of the company is different from the alleged motive of earlier times. Then the gild was formed in the supposed interest of the public, and as a security for good work; now the company was instituted deliberately with the view of excluding strangers and foreigners. The monopolist character of the institution is much more pronounced in the seventeenth than it had been in the fourteenth century.

These four points, (1) the source of *coercive* power, (2) the commercial rather than industrial character, (3) the combination of many callings in one company, and (4) the avowed intention of securing a monopoly as against strangers, serve to point the contrast between a company formed in the sixteenth and a gild formed in the fourteenth century.

The differences can to some extent be easily accounted for: the great law of apprenticeship had made the supervision of the processes of working less necessary, while it had greatly limited the possibility of changing from one trade to another. Many of the old gild functions had been taken over by the legislature.

On the other hand, the seventeenth-century company also shows us the culmination of the aims which had been observable in the history of the earlier gilds. As Professor Ashley has pointed out with great clearness in his recent volume, the objection to strangers and the desire to obtain exclusive powers had become increasingly prominent in the gild legislation during the fifteenth century. This tendency was fostered by the incursion of aliens under Elizabeth and of Scots under James I. We need not be surprised that it is so pronounced in the characteristic specimen of seventeenth-century trade regulation which Mr. Russell has brought before us to-night. The few remarks I have ventured to make may, I trust, serve to show how much the Society is indebted to him for bringing such an interesting set of rules to light.

To all Christian people vnto whome this present writing shall come, John Allington and William Burnes the now Bayliffs of the Cittie of Lichfeild and one and twenty Bretheren of the Incorporaçõn of the said Cittie send greeting in our Lord God everlasting. Wheras it hath pleased our Soveraigne Lord King James, by his highnes letters pattents vnder the greate Seale of England bearing date at Westmonastre the fowre and twentieth daie of May in the one and twentieth yeare of his highnes raigne of England Fraunce and Ireland and of Scotland the six and fyftieth, to graunt vnto the Bayliffs and the Cittizens of the said Cittie of Lichfeild and their Successors (emongest diuerse and sundriȩ other things) that the Bayliffs and the one and twentie Bretheren of the said Bayliffs of the aforsaid Cittie for the tyme being or the major parte of them should for ever from hencforth haue full power facultie and aucthoritie at their pleasures to make ordeyne constitute and appoint Lawes, Statutes, Constituçõns, Orders and Ordinances in Writing vnder the Common Seale of the said Cittie for the good governing ordering and disposing of the said Cittie and of all and singuler the Cittizens, officers and ministers, Trades and Tradesmen, Fraternities and severall Companies or Societies of any Misterie or occupaçõn whatsoever within the aforsaid Cittie, the liberties and precinctes of the same; and how and in what manner and forme all and singuler the Cittizens, Artificers, Tradesmen, Fraternities and all and euerie the severall Companies or Societies of any Misterie or occupaçõn within the said Cittie for the tyme being in their seuerall Trades, Misteries and occupaçõns shall vse, governe and behaue themselues within the said Cittie, the liberties and precinctes of the same And if any p̃son or p̃sons within the said Cittie, the precinctes and liberties of the same shall offend breake or neglecte any of the Lawes, Statutes, Orders and

Ordinances soe to be made by vs the said Bayliffs and Bretheren of the said Cittie for the tyme being, that then wee shall and may punish everie p̃son which shall offend or breake any of the orders and ordinances which wee shall make by imprisonment, fyne or amerciament of everie p̃son soe offending, as to vs the said Bayliffs and Bretheren for the tyme being shall seeme most fitt. And wheras alsoe by the said Letters Pattents it is graunted vnto the Bayliffs and Cittizens of the said Cittie of Lichfeild and their Successors that no p̃son or p̃sons, not being a freeman of the said Cittie, vnlesse he hath served seaven yeares apprentishipp within the said Cittie, shall sell or put to sale by retayle any wares or merchandizes within the said Cittie but victualls, vnless it be in tyme of Faires there, nor shall keepe any shopp, boothe or stall here to that purpose or vse any trade, misterie or manuall arte within the said Cittie, the liberties and precinctes of the same Cittie, without the speciall lycence of vs the Bayliffs and Bretheren of the Incorporacõn of the said Cittie for the tyme being first had in writing vnder our Common Seal, vppon payne to pay vnto our vse such fyne or amerciament as we shall taxe and assesse vppon him or them soe offending, as by the said letters pattents more plainlie it doth and may appeare And wheras also vppon good consideracõn had and taken by vs the said Bayliffs and the one and twentie Bretheren of this Incorporacõn it manifestlie appeareth that the estate of the Mercers, Grocers, Lynnen Drapers, Woollen Drapers, Silke men, Hosiers, Salters, Appothecaries and Haberdashers of small wares is mightilie decayed within the said Cittie, aswell for want of good orders and ordinances emongest them for the better governing and ordering of the said Trades and Tradesmen, as also for that many strangers and yong men which haue not served their apprentishipps within the said Cittie, and manie other which haue shifted abroad in the Countrie and haue not orderlie served any apprentishipp in any one place, haue hither repaired and sett vpp all or some of the aforsaid Trades, by meanes wherof the Freemen of the said Trades within the said Cittie are verie much hindred and impoverished; soe that they cann not mayntaine and haue such choise of wares and comodities as heretofore they haue had; which tendeth to the generall discreditt of the whole Cittie For the reforming and amending of which abuses and inconveniencies, knowe yowe that wee the said Bayliffs and one and twentie Bretheren of the Incorporacōn of this Cittie with one consent and agreement according to the power and aucthoritie given vnto vs by the said letters patents have devised, made, ordayned, and appoynted, and by theise presents doe devise, make, ordayne, and appoynt all and singuler theise Lawes Statutes Orders and Ordinances for the good and prosprous estate of the said Trades and Misteries and for the ordering ruling and governing of all and everie of the Tradesmen of the said Trades within the said Cittie of Lichfeild, the liberties and precincts of the same.

First, wee ordeyne and order that the Mercers, Grossers, Woollen Drapers, Lynnen Drapers, Silkmen, Hosiers, Salters, Appothecaries and Haberdashers of small Wares which now are Freemen of the said Trades within the said Cittie or hereafter shall be Freemen, and hath or shall have served seaven yeares apprentishipp vnto any Freeman of any of the said Trades within the said Cittie of Lichfeild, or shall compound for his Freedome in manner following, shall from hencforth be a Brotherhood or Companie called by the name of the Master, Wardens and Company of Mercers of the Cittie of Lichfeild.

Item, it is ordayned and ordered that everie yeare, vppon the Wensdaie next after the feast of Saint James the Apostle, there shall be chosen and elected by the major part of the said Companie then present three good and sufficient men of the same Companie, the one of them to be the Master and the other two to be the Wardens of the said Companie for the yeare next following for the ruling and governing of the same Companie and for the redressing of all disorders therin and for the execūtion of all ordinances and orders herin mencōned And if any such Master and Wardens or any of them soe to be elected shall refuse to take vppon him his said office or place of Mastershipp or Wardenshipp, or shall after that he hath taken vppon him the said place be willfullie negligent and remisse in the due execuc͠on of his said office (and he be therof soe judged) by the major part of the same Companie, vppon due examinac͠on therof, he shall forfeit to the vse of the said Companie for everie such refusall or willfull neglect and remissnes, 5£ And that everie one of the said Companie which hath not leaue of the Master of the said Companie to be absent, shall yearlie vppon the said daie of elecc͠on attend in their gownes or cloakes vppon the Master and Wardens of the same Companie vntill the said elecc͠on be fullie ended : And shall also vppon that day trewlie pay vnto the Wardens of the said Companie two shillings a peece in the name of their quartridge, to be imployed at the discrec͠on of the said Master and Wardens then newlie elected vppon payne of everie one that shall faile or offend therin or in any part of this order shall forfeit to the vse of the said Companie for everie tyme that he soe faileth or offendeth tenn shillings.

Item, it is ordeyned and ordered that the two Wardens oi the said Companie shall yearlie within seaven daies next after ther elecc͠on into their said offices becom bound joyntlie or seuerallie by sufficient obligac͠on vnto three of the most Auncyentes of the said Companie, not being Master or Wardens, in the summe of fortie poundes of lawfull money of England with condic͠on for their trew accompt making to the next Master and Wardens vppon the day of their elecc͠ons or within tenn daies of all such money and other things as shall come to their handes during their yeare by reason of their Wardenshipp and for the payment of their arrerage, vppon paine that everie man soe fayling and refusing soe to enter into bond shall forfeit tenn poundes to the vse of the said Companie.

Item, it is ordeyned and ordered that the old Master and Wardens of the said Companie shall vppon the daie that a new Master and Wardens shalbe elected or within tenn daies after not onelie make and deliuer vpp vnto the new Master and Wardens a trew and just accompt in writing vnder their handes of all such money, writings and other things whatsoever which by reason of their offices or places shall haue come to their handes, but alsoe shall then trewlie paie and deliver to the said new Wardens the Arrerags which shalbe due vppon their accompt to the vse of the said Companie, vppon payne that everie one that shall offend or faile therin shall forfeit to the vse of the said Companie three poundes. But if it fall out and vppon their accompt it trewlie appeare that the said Companie shalbe indebted to the Accomptants, then the Master and Wardens of the same Companie for that tyme being shall trewlie pay out of the common stocke of the said Companie vnto the said Accomptants their said debt, arreare and due vnto them by the said Companie vppon their accompt And if there be not stocke sufficient to satisfie the same, then such debt arreare to be raised by collection or contribuc̃on emongest the rest of the said Companie.

Item, it is ordeyned and ordered that everie one of the said Companie shall conceale and keepe the Counsells of the said Companie (which are to be concealed and kept) and not disclose the same to any other not being of the said Companie: And that everie one of the said Companie shall, vppon reasonable warning given vnto him, appeare before the Master of the Companie for the tyme being at such place within the said Cittie where the said Master shall appoint for or about any business of the said Companie or for or about any p̃rson or p̃rsons of the same Companie: And also that everie p̃rson of the said Companie shall duelie and respectiuelie carrie and behaue himself towards the Master and Wardens of the said Companie for the tyme being without giving them or any of them evill or vnseemlie wordes or behauiors, vppon payne that everie one that shall doe any thing contrarie to this Ordinance and Order or any part therof shall for euerie such offence or neglect forfeit to the vse of the said Companie, six shillings eight pence ; and for not coming vppon warning, twelue pence.

Item, it is ordeyned and ordered that no p̃son that shall herafter serue his Apprentishipp seauen yeares to any of the aforsaid trades in the said Cittie shalbe a Freeman of the said Companie or admitted to keepe open shopp or vse his trade in the said Cittie before he shall haue first binn approved by the Master and Wardens or the major part of the said Companie for his due service and apprentishipp; and vppon their approbac̃on shall take his Corporall Oath before the Bayliffs of this Cittie, or one of them, well and faithfullie to p̃forme and keepe all and everie of theise ordinancs and orders; and shall haue subscribed his name for the p̃formance of theise Ordinancs.

Item, it is ordeyned and ordered that no p̃son or p̃sons not having served an Apprentishipp in some of the trades aforsaid dulie and trulie to one of the said Companis in the said Cittie by the space of seauen yeares at the least shalbe made a Freeman of the said Companie without the consent of the Master and Wardens of the said Companie for the tyme being and of the major part of the other freemen of the said Companie; nor shall keepe open shopp nor vse the said trade of a Mercer nor any other of the said trades appertayning to the said Companie within the said Cittie, vppon payne that everie such p̃son that shall doe contrarie to this Ordinance and Order or any p̃te therof shall forfeit for everie moneth that he shall so offend to the vse of the said Companie, tenn poundes   And that no man of the said Companie shall colourablie in or vnder his name suffer any p̃son not being free of the said Companie to vse the said Trades or any of them belonging to the said Companie within the said Cittie, vppon payne that everie p̃son soe offending shall forfeit to the vse of the said Company five poundes for everie moneth that he shall soe suffer or p̃mitt the same.

Item, it is ordeyned and ordered that it shall be lawful to and for the Master and Wardens of the said Companie for the tyme being or any two of them to enter from tyme to tyme into any howse or howses shopp or shoppes of any of the said offenders and ther to the vse of the said Companie to take and carrie away any goodes or chattells of everie such

THE LAWS OF THE MERCERS COMPANY OF LICHFIELD 119

offender and the same to detayne and keepe to the vse of the said Companie vntill the forfeiture and forfeitures for which they or any of them shalbe so taken shalbe trewlie paid to the Master or Wardens of the said Companie for the tyme being to the vse of the said Company; or to sue or implead any of the said offenders in the Court of Record within this Cittie vppon an accōn of Debt for any of the said forfeitures herin conteyned, at their discretion, or in any other Court of Record.

Item, it is ordeyned and ordered that if the partie offending whose goodes are so taken doe not redeeme them within tenn daies next after the taking therof by paying the forfeitures for which they were taken vnto the Wardens of the said Companie or one of them, that then and all tymes after it shalbe lawfull to the said Master or Wardens of the said Companie to cause the said goodes to be appriced in the Portmote Court of the said Cittie by the Burgesses of the Mannor of Lichfeild, according to the Custom there, for Pawnes; and if within fourteen daies after they be appriced the partie offending doe not satisfie vnto the said Wardens or to one of them the seuerall forfeitures for which the said goodes shalbe taken, that then and att all tymes after it shalbe lawfull for the Master and Wardens of the said Companie for the tyme being to sell the said goodes to any p̄son or p̄sons at that price they were appriced att, rendring to the p̄tie onelie the overplus if any be.

Item, it is ordeyned and ordered that the two Wardens for the tyme being shall yearlie before the Nativitie of Christ make diligent search and viewe thorough the whole Companie of all such weights and measures as are vsed by any of the said Companie, and the same to trie by the King's standard: And all such weights and measures as they shall find faultie to take and to carrie away and to bring them in before the Master and Companie at there next meeting. And if the said weightes or measures so brought before the said Master and Companie be judged by the Master and the greater parte of the Companie that shall be ther present to differ from the standard, or that any such p̄son or p̄sons shalbe found and adjudged to haue sold by any false or vntrue weight or measure, that then everie p̃rson so offending with such false weightes or measures shall forfeit to the said Companie for the vse of the Poore of the said Cittie of Lichfeild for everie weight or measure that soe shalbe adjudged false, fortie shillings. And everie Warden neglecting and not pr̃forming his dutie shall forfeit for everie such neglect tenn shillings to the vse of the said Companie.

Item, it is ordeyned and ordered that no p̃rson being free and belonging to this Companie shall receiue or take into his service any p̃rson or p̃rsons to be bound as an Apprentice and to be instructed in any of the said Misteries or Trades belonging to the said Companie vnder the tearme of nyne yeares fullie to be compleat, and everie Master that taketh an Apprentice shall cause the Indentures of the said Apprentice to be read and sealed in the presence of the Master or Wardens for the tyme being, and there to pay vnto the said Wardens for entering the same into their booke, twelve pence. And whosoeuer shall take or bynd any Apprentice contrarie to this ordinance shall forfeit and paie for every Apprentice so taken and bound, five poundes to the vse of the said Companie.

Item, it is ordeyned and ordered that what p̃rson soever of this Companie which shall take a servant to be an Apprentice, he shall cause him to be bound and his Indentures to be sealed in manner and forme before mencõned within one moneth or six weekes at the farthest after his coming vnto him, or else he shall forfeit and paie to the vse of the said Companie for everie moneth that he so keepeth him longer vnbound, contrarie to this Ordinance, six shillings eight pence.

Item, it is ordeyned and ordered that whatsoever p̃rson being a Freeman of this Companie which shall take any Apprentice according to the Ordinance aforesaid, and shall suffer any such his Apprentice to depart from him vnder any pretence and collour whatsoever before he haue fullie accomplished the tearme of nyne yeares according to his Indentures, to the intent he should sett vpp or clayme any freedom to vse any of the said Trades in this Cittie ; everie such Master soe suffering his Apprentice to depart from him, without consent of the Master and Wardens of the said Companie for the tyme being, shall forfeit and paie for everie Apprentice which shall soe depart from him contrarie to this ordinance five poundes to the vse of the said Companie.

And it is alsoe ordeyned and ordered that if the Master of any Apprentice of this Companie happen to die before his Apprentice hath served out his yeares, then the said Apprentice or Apprentices shalbe putt over at the discrecōn of the Master of the said Companie: And if it happen the Master to be dead, then at the discrecōn of the Wardens to serue out the rest of the said tearme of his Indentures with some other freeman of the Companie, and not to be suffered to sett vpp or vse any of the said trades belonging to this Companie vntill he or they haue fullie served forth the whole tearme of his Indentures, or else shall agree and submite himself to abide such Order and to pay such fyne as shalbe appointed and determined by the Master and Wardens or the greater prte of the said Companie. And that the executors or administrators of such Master as shall so die shall pay to such p̄son or p̄sons to whome such Apprentice or Apprenticers shalbe so putt over so much of such summe or summes of money which such Master that soe dieth hath received or is to receive with such Apprentice as the said Master and Wardens or the greater parte of the said Companie shall appoint ; and if such executors or administrators shall not within fourteen daies after such appointment made and notice therof given vnto them pay such summe or summes of money as shalbe so appointed, that then such executors or administrators shall loose double the value of such summe so appointed.

Item, it is ordeyned and ordered that no Milliner, Pedler, or Pettie Chapman or any other p̄son whatsoever which doth not now dwell and inhabitt within the said Cittie (except he hath served seaven yeares Apprentishipp dulie to some of this Company within this Cittie) shall not at any tyme heraſter keepe any shopp booth or stall within this Cittie, but onelie in tyme of Faires heare, without the consent of the Master and Wardens or greater parte of the said Companie, nor shall sell or putt to sale within this Cittie (but onelie in tyme of Faires heare) any kind of Wares and Merchandizes belonging to any of the Trades of this Company, vnless everie such forren Milliner, Pedler, or Pettie Chapman do well and trewlie pay vnto the Wardens of this Companie to the vse of the said Companie three pence for everie markett day that he or shee shall keep any such shopp booth or stall within this Cittie or offer to sell any such Wares or Merchandizes here the same to be paid vppon the opening of his or her Wares within everie of the Marketts here, vppon paine to forfeit to the vse of this Companie tenn shillings for everie day that he or shee shall so offend. And that no Milliner, Pedler, or Pettie Chapman which now doth inhabitt or dwell within the said Cittie (except he hath served seaven years Apprentishipp dulie to som of this Companie within this Cittie) shall not at any tyme herafter keepe any shopp booth or stall within this Cittie, but onlie in tyme of Faires here, without the Consent of the Master and Wardens or greater part of the said Company, nor shall sell or putt to sale within this Cittie (but onelie in tyme of Faires heare) any kind of Wares and Merchandizes belonging to any of the Trades of this Companie vnless everie such Milliner, Pedler, or Pettie Chapman now inhabiting within the said Cittie doe well and trewlie pay vnto the Wardens of this Companie, to the vse of the said Companie, one penny for everie Markett day that he or shee shall keepe any such shopp booth or Stall within this Cittie or offer to sell any such Wares or Merchandizes here the same to be paid vppon the opening of his or her Wares within everie of the Marketts here vppon paine to forfeit to the vse of this Companie tenn shillings for everie day that he or shee shall so offend And that no Milliner, Pedler, or Pettie Chapman, either forrenner or now inhabiting within this said Cittie, (except he hath dulie served seaven yeares Apprentishipp to some of this Company within this Cittie) shall at any tyme herafter sell or putt to sale at any tyme within this Cittie but onelie in tyme of Faires and Markett daies here, and there according to this ordinance, any kind of Wares and Merchandizes belonging to any of the Trades of this Companie without the consent of the Master and Wardens or the greater part of the said Companie, vppon paine to forfeit to the vse of this Companie fortie shillings for everie tyme that hee or shee shall so offend.

Provided alwaies, that it shalbe lawfull to and for everie p̄son and p̄sons that shall make any huswiefes cloath either Lynnen or Woollen to sell the same here vppon the Markett Daies either by themselues their children or servants any thing in theise ordinances conteyned to the contrarie therof notwithstanding.

Item, it is ordeyned and ordered that the Master and Wardens of the said Companie for the tyme being at any tyme herafter shall and may enter into any warehowse, shopp, booth or stall either of freeman or forrenner within this Cittie to view and search and trie Fruit and all manner of Grosserie whether it be sweet wholsome and merchantable or not. And if the said Master and Wardens of the said Companie shall directlie know or vnderstand that either any freeman or forrenner att any tyme herafter shall vtter or putt to sale any such fruit and grosserie within this Cittie which shalbe adjudged by the Master and Wardens or the major p̄rte of the said Companie to be vnwholsom not sweet and merchantable ; That then everie such p̄son that shall so offend contrarie to this ordinance shall forfeit for everie tyme he so offendeth to the vse of the poore inhabitants of this Cittie, twenty shillings.

Item, it is ordayned and ordered that everie p̄son and p̄sons that shalbe made a Freeman of this Companie according to the ordinances abouewritten shall, before the taking of his Oath for his freedom before the Bayliffs of this Cittie or the one of them, well and trewlie pay vnto the Wardens of the said Companie or to one of them to the vse of the said Companie twentie shillings, to the Bayliffs of this Cittie for the tyme being, for giving the oathe, three shillings foure pence ; and to the Towne Clerke of this Cittie, for inrolling his name, three shillings foure pence. Provided alwaies ; And it is further ordained and ordered that George Dawes sonne of Thomas Dawes of this Cittie, deceased, Thomas Burnes now sonne of John Burnes of this Cittie vpholster, Mathew Bate the yonger of Derbie, Wollen Draper Walter Mathew now sonne of Humfrey Mathew of this Cittie, Tanner, Humfrey Jasson now sonne of Symon Jasson of this Cittie, gent., Robert Dilkes now sonne of James Dilkes of this Cittie, gent., Brute Thropp now sonn of William Thropp the elder of this Cittie, Mercer, Humfrey Dawes now sonn or John Dawes of this City, Tanner, William Smyth now sonne of Richard Smyth of this Cittie, Tanner, John Jotherell now sonne of John Jotherell of this Citty, Inholder, William Arrowsmyth now sonne of William Arrowsmyth of Wolluer-hampton, John Perkins now sonn of Symon Perkins of this Cittie, Tanner, Thomas Burnes now sonne of William Burnes of this Cittie, vpholster, George Ashmoale now sonne of Thomas Ashmoale of this Cittie, Corvizer, John Holmes now sonne of George Holmes of this Cittie, Felmonger, and John Shorthose now sonne of Sampson Shorthose of this Cittie, Corvizer, nor any of them, shall not be hindred or debarred by any of theise ordinances or orders; but that they and euerie of them shall and may sett vpp and vse any of the Trades of this Cittie or Companies within this Cittie, so as they haue served seaven yeares apprentishipp to the said Trade respectiuelie for the same in any other Cittie or Towne, they and everie of them that wilbe free of this Companie taking his corporall oathe and paying twentie six shillings eight pence vppon his admittance to be free of this Companie in such manner and forme as is before in the last Ordinance conteined ; theise ordinances or anything therin conteyned to the contrarie therof in any wise notwithstanding. In witnes wherof Wee the aforsaid Bayliffs and Bretheren of this Incor-poracōn haue for the better aucthoritie of all theise Ordinances herunto putt the Common Seale of the aforsaid Cittie of Lichfeild; the seaventeenth day of Julie in the yeares of his said raigne of our said Soveraigne Lord James by the grace of god of England, Fraunce and Ireland, King, defender of the Faith, &c. the one and twentieth, and of Scotland the six and fyftieth.

THE INQUISITION OF 1517. INCLOSURES AND EVICTIONS

EDITED FROM THE LANSDOWNE MS. I. 153 BY I. S. LEADAM, M.A.

PART II

PREFACE

IN the 'English Historical Review' for April (1893) Professor Ashley offers some criticisms upon the 'Introduction to the Inquisition of 1517,' contributed by me to the 'Transactions of the Royal Historical Society' for 1892. One object of that Introduction, it may be remembered, was to disprove the assertion of Professor Ashley that at the time when the evictions for inclosure began, and until 'towards the end of the period,' 'the mass of copyholders' had no legal security. In my view, the manorial records, the compilations of laws in the twelfth and thirteenth centuries, the practice of the courts, even the treatises of the jurists when critically scrutinised, led to the conclusion not merely that copyholders enjoyed protection in legal theory, but that their predecessors in title, the villeins, had done so before them. I drew no distinction in this matter between customary tenants and copyholders, as Professor Ashley appears to suppose, but showed that security extended even to villeins by blood, or 'nativi,' on customary lands.[1] Professor Ashley's proposition that 'customary tenants' and 'copyholders' were equivalent terms was never doubted by me, and is irrelevant to my argument. Indeed, it is assumed by me on the very pages to which he

[1] *Trans. R. H. S.* 1892, pp. 212, 217.

refers. 'Mr. Leadam,' he says, 'draws a sharp distinction between "copyholders" on the one side and "tenants at will" on the other—a distinction which one may doubt whether the men of the sixteenth century would have felt so keenly.' The distinction, as those who turn to the passage will see, is between 'copyholders,' used in Fitzherbert's sense as equivalent to customary tenants, who were 'tenants at will according to the custom of the manor,' and 'tenants at will at Common Law.' Professor Ashley's doubts as to the capacity of the men of the sixteenth century to apprehend the distinction will be set at rest by a reference to Littleton.[1] 'There are,' he says, 'divers diversities between tenant at will which is in by lease of his lessor by the course of common law, and tenant according to the custome of the manor in forme aforesaid. For tenant at will according to the custome may have an estate of inheritance (as is aforesaid) at the will of the lord, according to the custome and usage of the manor.'

In gleaning such evidence of the position of copyholders in the sixteenth century as was to be found in the Lansdowne MS. of the Inquisition of 1517, I drew the inference that the persons mentioned by the Herefordshire commissioners as leaving their houses because they were out of repair could not have been copyholders for lives, or they would have been themselves liable for repairs under the Statute of Gloucester (6 Ed. I.). Professor Ashley not unfairly remarks that 'this seems a somewhat narrow basis to rest upon.' He notes the proviso of Coke in a passage to which I referred, 'Wast of a copiholder is forfeiture of his copihold, if there be no custom to the contrary,' and Littleton's statement that 'the tenant by the custom in some places ought to repair and uphold his houses.' I admit that Littleton's language is such that had one or two cases only been recorded in Herefordshire, they might have chanced to be those exceptions to which he refers. But there are thirteen cases,

[1] *Tenures*, § 82; cp. § 68. I even quoted the original law French of Littleton on p. 186, *n.* 1. The English version given above is that of Coke.

and we have to ask ourselves what are the probabilities? What proportion did copyholds not subject to impeachment of waste bear to the whole number? Professor Ashley demurs to my citation of the Statute of Gloucester as conclusive that copyholders were themselves liable to repair their houses under the penalty of forfeiture on impeachment of waste, 'unless we hold that every statute succeeded in creating the conditions it aimed at.' The fact is that in resting upon the Statute of Gloucester I understated the case. In citing the Statute of Gloucester I mentioned[1] the circumstance that it was not until Coke's time that a judicial decision was given that it applied to copyholds. I ought, therefore, to have referred the liability of copyholders to repair to some more obviously operative authority. That authority I find to have been the Common Law—in other words, traditional custom; so that what the Statute of Gloucester did, so far as it affected copyholds, was not to 'create conditions,' but to declare conditions already existing. In Downingham's case, heard in 1594,[2] 'the defendant in an ejectione firmae pleaded that the lord of the manor did enter into the land of a copyholder by reason of forfeiture for waste committed in suffering the houses to be uncovered, by which the timber is become rotten, and did not allege in facto that the custom of the manor is that such waste is a forfeiture, for it was said that although other waste by the Common Law is a forfeiture, yet this permissive waste is not. Sed non allocatur; for all waste done by a copyholder is forfeitable.' So in 1597 it was held, 'si vn copiholder suffer le meason a decayer et estre wasted ceo est vnforfeiture.'[3] In his 'Complete Copy-holder' Coke expresses the rule as without exception: 'If a copyholder committeth waste voluntary or permissive, this is a forfeiture ipso facto. . . . Permissive, as if he suffereth his House to decay or fall to ground for want of necessary Re-

---

[1] *Trans. R. H. S.* 1892, p. 185, n. 3.
[2] Owen's *Reports*, T. T., 36 Eliz., in B. R. The same doctrine appears in Coke's *Rep.* Pt. IV. 24 b., M. T., 33 & 34 Eliz., Q. B.
[3] Rolle's *Abr.* I. 508, pl. 16, T. T., 39 Eliz., B. R. Rastell v. Turnor.

N.S.—VOL. VII. K

parations.[1] It is right to mention that I have discovered one case, and one case only, in which this doctrine is questioned. It was heard in 1595, but it stands by itself, and never seems to have been considered law. The report runs:[2] 'By Anderson and Walmsley, that voluntary waste is a forfeiture of the copyhold by the Common Law, but negligent waste not withoute a custom.' This is a broader statement than that of Littleton. As for the proviso of Coke, 'if there be no custom to the contrary,' I cannot but treat it, viewed in the light of his language in the 'Complete Copy-holder' and of the decisions of the time, as mere legal surplusage not improper to be introduced, since 'custom is the life of copyholds.'

Let it be supposed, however, that Littleton was acquainted with some exceptions to the Common Law of the liability of copyholders to impeachment for permissive waste. I think I have established the exceeding rarity of such exceptions.[3] Now in the case of the Herefordshire evictions there were thirteen instances in which repairs were evidently incumbent upon the landlord. These were in ten different places and in a number of different manors. After what has been said, it is quite outside probability that

[1] P. 163, ed. London, 1673. So in Eastcourt *v.* Weeks, *Salkeld Rep.* i. 186, Powell, J., treats waste as involving forfeiture at Common Law (1698). In modern text-books the law is laid down as without exception. Williams, *Law of Real Property*, 17th ed. pp. 427, 428.
[2] M. T., 37 & 38 Eliz., C. B., Noy's *Rep.* p. 51.
[3] I may cite a remarkable example in which, during the fifteenth century and under the usually indulgent administration of a wealthy abbey, copyholders were evicted 'pro defectu reparacionis,' although they could scarcely have been morally to blame. In the case of Kent *v.* Seynt John, heard by the Court of Requests in 1543-44, the history of the copyholds of the manor of Abbot's Ripton, Hunts, was carefully investigated. A witness, aged sixty-four years, deposed 'that he hathe hard hys father saye that before the batayle whiche was calleyd Ester Daye ffeld, all the tenauntes of Abbottes Rypton were copie holders & held of the abbot of Ramsey. And the Northern men laye there so long before the ffelde was ffuwghten that they impoveryshed the countrey. And the tenauntes were fayne to yeld up theyre copye holdes, for that they were not hable to repayre theym. And then came other tenauntes & occupyed them as tenauntes at wyll, & they had the Rents abatyd,' &c. This refers to the battle of Barnet, fought in 1471. MS. Record Office, Court of Requests, Mr. Hunt's Calendar, Bundle 7, No. 10.

these could all have been those exceptional cases of which the very existence is doubtful. It was, therefore, no violent inference on my part that all of them were within the rule, whether of statute or of Common Law, which laid the duty of repairs upon the copyholders, and that these tenancies were, therefore, not copyholds.

Professor Ashley has apparently supposed that I regarded as coextensive the population 'evicted' and the population 'dispossessed,' to adopt his own word, by the agricultural revolution. On the contrary, I expressly mentioned 'those who held for terms,'[1] who were compelled to leave at the expiration of their terms, and who must have largely swelled the numbers of the vagrant poor who crowded into London and other great towns. But these were not, in the legal sense of the word, 'evicted.' The way in which a tenant of this class was got rid of is graphically described by Crowley:[2] 'Yea, though he have been an honeste, true, faythfull and quiete tenant many yeres, yet *at the vacation of his copie or indentur*, he must paye welmoste as muche as would purchayse so much grounde or else voide in hast.'

Upon the subject of tenure Professor Ashley ridicules another proposition, which was not mine. 'Mr. Leadam,' he says, 'has a long argument to prove that there was a generally recognised distinction between "villani" and "nativi." The former, settled on customary land, were always protected; the latter, settled on the demesne, were never protected.' I fear that my critic has reviewed my paper without cutting the leaves. On pp. 202-204 I show how 'nativi' obtained concessions of demesne as customary land, and on pp. 214-216 I show how though nativi they yet enjoyed protection. The distinction in this matter of tenure is not so much between villani and nativi as between villani and nativi holding customary land on the one hand, and nativi on the demesne on the other.

Professor Ashley offers no evidence for his statement that

---

[1] *Trans. R. H. S.* p. 256.
[2] MS. B. M. f. 8. Furnivall's *Introd. to Ballads from MSS.* i. 24.

my account of the various classes of the manorial tenantry 'seems to rest in large measure on a misinterpretation of the term demesne,' the several meanings of which I have, on the contrary, most carefully distinguished,[1] constituting, as they do, the elementary foundation of the whole subject.

With regard to Professor Vinogradoff's proposition, 'that in legal theory servus, villanus, and nativus are equivalent terms as to personal condition,' I have no quarrel with it, as Professor Ashley imagines, if due insistence be placed upon the word 'theory.' I myself spoke[2] of the juristic identification of them (nativi), under the influence of Roman law, with villeins. This identification was, as I said in another passage, a 'confusion introduced by jurists in the endeavour to sink the distinctions of English in those of Roman law.'[3] To effect this Bracton and his fellow theorists actually copied out Titles of Justinian's 'Institutes'; and these are not usually supposed to have been the foundations of English law. On the other hand, the identification is contradicted by an early commentator on the corresponding passage in Britton, to which Professor Vinogradoff in a note refers.[4] That contradiction, I endeavoured to show, was sustained by 'Le Myrrour des Justices;' by the book of the 'Old Tenures;' by the compilation sometimes ascribed to Ranulf Flambard, usually called 'The Laws of William the Conqueror;' by the 'Laws of Henry I.;' by the formulas in Madox; by the legal privileges we see to have been in practice enjoyed by villeins, as they appear both in Bracton's treatise and in his 'Note Book' of legal cases; and by manorial records. The endeavour to Romanise English law in this respect was, on the whole, a failure. But the use of the word villanus by itself came to generally connote personal serfdom, differing, as I pointed out,[5] from its use in the Hundred Rolls, still more from that of the codes, &c. above mentioned. In the sixteenth and seventeenth centuries we find the term 'villein regardant' as equivalent to

---

[1] *Trans. R. H. S.* 1892, pp. 196-200, 256, 257, &c.   [2] *Ibid.* p. 194.
[3] *Ibid.* pp. 208, 209.   [4] *Vill. in Engl.* p. 44, n. 1.
[5] *Trans. R. H. S.* 1892, pp. 195, n. 1, 212, n. 1.

the English 'bondman,' like it a term of degraded connotation, as distinguished from 'customary tenant,' which perhaps represented its original meaning.[1] In short, I must confess that while I have been at pains to have recourse to original sources from which to draw my conclusions, I have shown myself destitute of those subjective data upon which Professor Ashley relies for the feelings of 'the men of the sixteenth century,' and which form the foundation of his dictum that in that age the mass of the copyholders were without legal security.[2]

[1] See Skeat's *Engl. Dict.* s. v.; Furnivall, in Bishop Percy's Folio MS., *Ballads and Romances*, vol. ii. pp. xxxiii ff.

[2] For a reply to some other criticisms of Professor Ashley see p. 220, *infra*; and for an account of the special tribunals which extended protection to copyholders in the fifteenth and sixteenth centuries, see an article by the author in the *English Historical Review* for October 1893, on 'The Security of Copyholders in the Fifteenth and Sixteenth Centuries.'

NORFOLK

Introduction

THE returns of inclosures in Norfolk include the entire county with the exception of the hundreds of Clacklose, Happing, and Taverham. Of no other county does the Lansdowne MS. furnish particulars so full. In the case of Norfolk, also, we have the assistance of one of the most laborious of county historians, Blomefield, and this enables us to distinguish with some degree of certainty between lay and ecclesiastical manors. To some extent this furnishes matter for judgment as to the relative parts played in the inclosing movement by laymen and ecclesiastics respectively. It must be remembered, however, that inclosures upon ecclesiastical manors do not necessarily imply the initiative of ecclesiastical lords. In the first place, although for statistical purposes the lordship of the manor has been ascertained, the freeholder of a manor would be under no restriction as to the use to which he should put his land. But copyhold tenants were subject to impeachment of waste,[1] and would, therefore, before entering upon radical changes of cultivation, take the general precaution of obtaining a licence from their lords, as we see, from the licences issued for parks, the lords themselves were compelled to do from the ultimate freeholder, the Crown. Since the superior profit of pasture farming became more evident in course of time, it is probable that such licence was seldom refused. In any case, the properties of the religious houses were scattered throughout a number of counties, and the supervision of a

[1] See Preface, *supra*, pp. 128-131.

corporation, proverbially somewhat lax, would be the less searching when the corporation was an absentee landlord. There would be a greater latitude of action on the part of an enterprising tenant than upon the manor of lay lords, whose personal consequence and political influence suffered from a depletion of population upon his estates. It is a remarkable fact that where inclosures are recorded without the name of a lay lord of the manor appearing either as such or as incloser, one or more of the manors in the parish are in such cases generally found to be ecclesiastical manors. This raises a probability that it was upon the ecclesiastical manor that the inclosure took place, a probability strengthened in one instance by the coincidence that at both Emneth and Letton one of the manors was held by the Priory of Lewes. There are indications that some of the heads of religious houses were themselves engaged in sheep-farming, a fact of which we are cognisant from contemporary sources.[1] In the Norfolk Inquisition the Prior of Castellacre [2] appears as an incloser in three places: Kempston, Wendlyng, and Bagthorp. The total of his inclosures amounted to 192 acres. The Prior of Norwich incloses in two places: Thorp Episcopi and Poswyke. The total is only 130 acres. The Prior of Walsyngham 120 acres at Walsyngham Magna, and 40 acres at Hoveton. The Prior of ffiycham makes three inclosures at Herpeley amounting to 250 acres. Of lay owners, Lady Morley is returned as incloser of 260 acres; Henry ffermer of 280 acres; Thomas Thorysby or Thurysby [3] of 151 acres, a number which there are reasons

[1] More, *Utopia*. Br. *Cal.* iv. 6043. 9. *Ibid.* 6183.

[2] This prior was an active improver. Cp. Gaird. *L. & P.* xiii. 1, 593, Norfolk to Cromwell: ' Has been at Castellacre where the lands have been by the late prior "advanced to the uttermost" and the farms let for many years' (March 25, 1538, 29 Hen. VIII.).

[3] This person is perhaps the Thomas Thorisby who was Mayor of Lynn in 1502 (Blomef.), and who is known to have been a land-jobber. See *sub* Rysyngcastell, p. 194, *infra*. He seems to have been constantly involved in litigation. In 1522 (January 21, 14 Hen. VIII.) he was sued by one Thomas Game in the Court of Requests (Appearances of Ct. Req., MS. R.O.). In 1534 he was defendant before the Star Chamber in Foster *v*. Thursby (MS. R.O., *S.C.P.* vol. xv. p. 197, 26 Hen. VIII.) :—Petition by Adam ffoster and Anne his wife against Thomas Thursby. Sets out that T. T. was seised of one third part of a tenement,

mentioned in the note upon Bawsey and Hyllyngton (pp. 192, 193, *infra*) for thinking should be put at 241 acres. The Prior of Walsingham, we are distinctly told, farmed 40 acres in pasture at Hoveton belonging to Lord Roos. A clerical member of the family of Grey farmed 30 acres upon their manor of Merton. In analysing this return, not from the point of view of ownership and tenancy, but from that of the status of the person singled out by the commissioners as immediately responsible for the inclosure, we find that out of the total of 10,454 acres inclosed in the county, 8,011 acres were inclosed by laymen and 2,443 acres by ecclesiastics, these areas bearing to the whole the respective proportions of 76·63 per cent. and 23·36 per cent. In the light of such statistics the petition of the insurgents in Kett's rebellion in Norfolk, a generation later, is not surprising: 'We pray that prests from hensforth shall purchase no londs neyther ffre nor Bondy and the lands that they farm, and lands in Gayton,* Norfolk, being tenant in common with petitioners, the other two thirds having been settled by William Cobb, father to Anne Foster, upon her at her marriage, the whole being forty acres; that petitioners had let the farm to Geoffrey Cobbe, W. Cobb's son and heir; that T. Thursby had been guilty of various vexatious proceedings against G. C., and had on April 10, 26 Hen. VIII., forcibly entered the lands with twenty persons and cut down forty-three cartloads of wood, hoping to force Geoffrey Cobb to leave the farm.

P. 198. The answer of Thomas Thurresby esquyer to the byll of compleynte of Adame ffoster and Anne hys wyff. Sets forth that John ffyncham, Esq., and another were seised, to the use of T. T. and his heirs, of one third part of the forty acres, and that he T. T. with consent of his feoffees peaceably cut down twenty-nine cartloads of wood and carried them 'to his mannor place at Geyton.' Denies alleged vexatious conduct towards Geoffrey Cobb.

In 1540 he was sued in the Court of Requests by the inhabitants of Middleton, probably for encroachments on their rights as tenants:

'viij° die Novembris a°xxxij⁴°. Eodem die.—Henricus Castell de lee Clyffordes Inne generosus nomine Thome Thorsbey personaliter comparuit coram consilio domini Regis apud Westm. virtute jniunccionis dicto Thome date per Edmond Benyngfeld et ali. in quadam causa contra eum motata ex parte inhabitanc. de Middelton et super consideracionem hostencam [*sic*] hostendamque [*sic*] conceditur commissio Johi Dedicke Humfredo Canvyle ad recipiendum responsum dicte [*sic*] Thome et ad certificandum xv° Martini proximi.' (*Court of Requests Orders and Decrees*, vol. vii., 32 Hen. VIII.–1 Ed. VI.)

---

* Hundred of Freebridge Marshland.

have in possession may be letted to temporall men as they wer in the fyrst yere of the reign of Kyng henry the viith.'[1]

The entire acreage returned in this Inquisition as having been inclosed in Norfolk is singularly small. Including all the areas of which the dimensions have been conjectured on data explained in the notes, the total amounts, as has been said, to no more than 10,454 acres inclosed or converted to pasture. This represents only ·094 of the entire area of which the Norfolk Inquisition furnishes returns. Of this inclosed acreage 1,485 acres, or 14·2 per cent., were retained as arable land, and these represent advance in the art of arable farming. The rest, being 8,969 acres, includes pasture areas inclosed and arable areas converted to pasture, the former item being of the insignificant extent of 277 acres, divided into ten areas ranging from ten to sixty acres, inclosed for landowners' parks. When contrasted with Yorkshire, the limited area reserved for the pleasures of the chase is remarkable; the more so that, as we know, Norfolk was a county distinguished for the number of its resident gentry.[2] The difference, of course, points to a greater thickness of population in Norfolk and to the superior profitableness of farming.[3]

In comparing the figures showing the uses to which the inclosures were put upon lay and ecclesiastical manors respectively, we are struck with the fact that the proportion of land inclosed but preserved as arable compared with the total area inclosed upon ecclesiastical manors was as high as 19·43 per cent., or, if the doubtful cases be included, 17·63 per

---

[1] The Act of 1529, prohibiting religious persons from farming for profit, left a loophole for evasion by the numerous class of exemptions allowed under it. There is much evidence, also, that on the eve of the Dissolution the religious houses granted many leases, and the petition of the rebels suggests the suspicion that they were frequently to clerical tenants.

[2] September 19, 1536, Norfolk to Cromwell: 'I think the organ maker deserves death, for he intended to make an insurrection, which were more difficult to do here [*i.e.* in Norfolk] than in any other shire, for "we be too many gentlemen here to suffer any such business."' Gaird. *L. & P.* xi. 470.

[3] April 28, 1537 (Disaffection in Norfolk): 'Ralph Rogerson said "the gentlemen had all the farms and cattle in the country in their hands, and poor men could have nothing."' Gaird. *L. & P.* xii. 1056.

cent. On the lay manors the arable inclosures preserved as arable amounted to no more than 12·31, or, with the doubtful, 12·13 per cent. This at first appears to show that the inclosing movement was carried out upon the ecclesiastical manors with less disregard of the tenants than was the case on the manors of lay landowners; but that this was directly due to the benevolent interposition of the ecclesiastics a closer inspection of the figures will prove an untenable conclusion. The returns give us the numbers of houses destroyed, most of these acts of destruction doubtless involving evictions In most cases they are explicit as to the status of the agents of this work of destruction or decay. The total number of houses destroyed in this county was seventy-six,[1] in addition to 'vnum integrum hamelett cum omnibus tenementis' at Castellacre. This last was the work of Thomas Thurysby, already mentioned, probably the lord of the manor. Of this number seventy-six, fifteen 'inhabitaciones' destroyed at Flytcham may have been upon the lay or upon the ecclesiastical manors belonging to that parish, and their ruin may have been the work either of laymen or of churchmen. Upon this the returns are silent, though the immediate precedence of a lay inclosure here of 394 acres raises the suspicion that the agents were the same in this case also. Excluding these, however, there remain forty-eight houses decayed, besides the hamlet mentioned, at the hands of laymen, as against thirteen at the hands of ecclesiastics. Now thirteen represents to the entire number of sixty-one undoubted cases a proportion of 21·32 per cent., always excluding the hamlet. If we take the total number of acts of inclosure returned in this Inquisition for Norfolk, we find ecclesiastics the direct authors of forty-one out of 186, which is a proportion of 22·04 per cent.

[1] This total includes five 'mansiones,' inferred upon grounds given in the notes to have been destroyed by ecclesiastics, and five similarly inferred to have been destroyed by laymen at Choysell, six inferred to be the number intended by 'diuersa tenementa' destroyed by laymen at Holkeham, and three the number intended by the same phrase as destroyed by ecclesiastics at Schadewell. If these conjectural cases be all excluded, the argument in favour of the ecclesiastics becomes strengthened.

Nor, since the average area of the ecclesiastical inclosures is 59½ acres as compared with an average area of 55¼ acres for lay inclosures, does the proportion sensibly vary if the acreage inclosed be taken as the basis. The 2,443 acres inclosed by ecclesiastics stand to the 8,011 acres inclosed by laymen as 22·36 per cent. to 76·63 per cent. of the whole. In short, the number of evictions of which ecclesiastics were the authors corresponds, whether as compared with the acts of inclosure or with the areas inclosed, with the number accompanying inclosures undertaken by laymen. What scarcely appreciable difference there is remains in favour of the ecclesiastics.

Of the total number of persons who were the victims of these acts of eviction it is easy to make an approximate calculation. Taking 5 to a tenementum,[1] the number 76 gives a total of 380 persons evicted, in addition to the inhabitants of the hamlet destroyed.[2] But no details as to evictions are given in the Norfolk return, and, indeed, the expulsion of 'inhabitantes' is only twice noticed, in the two cases at Choysell already mentioned.

The most numerous inclosures were those in the hundred of Freebridge Lynn, in the north-west of the county, amounting to 2,395 acres, or 3·03 of the area of the hundred Next comes the hundred of Launditch, contiguous to and south-east of the hundred of Freebridge Lynn, with inclosures in thirty-five areas, mostly small, of 1,447 acres, being 2·41 per cent. of the area of the hundred. After this the hundred of Smythdon, west of the hundred of Freebridge Lynn, shows inclosures of 1,036 acres, two of which, at Choysell, amount to 600 acres in all. But this only represents 2·27 per cent. of the total area of the hundred. The only other hundred that approaches this, North Greenhoe, where the percentage of inclosures is 2·47, returns no more than 892

---

[1] This is the average given in the Yorkshire return. See *sub* Southcowton and Sprotley, *infra*.
[2] If the 'putting down of a plough' is interpreted to imply the destruction of houses, though no mention is made of such destruction, the total displacement rises to 550 persons. See *infra*, pp. 163, 220.

acres as the area inclosed. This, too, is in the middle portion of the northern coast. On the whole, therefore, it may be said that the inclosing movement, such as it was, confined itself to the north-west of the county. The return from Belawe (p. 202) expressly ascribes its extension to the growth of the worsted industry in that neighbourhood, of which the effect is represented to have been to create a disinclination for the labour of the plough. Perhaps this cause, coupled with the insignificance of the movement, explains why no mention was made of inclosures as a grievance by the Norfolk rebels under Kett.[1] Indeed, Tusser, writing just forty years after the date of this Inquisition, speaks of Norfolk as 'the despair of tillage' from the disregard of inclosures exhibited by a population accustomed to the licence of 'champion fields.'[2]

[1] See *Kett's Rebellion in Norfolk.* F. W. Russell, London, 1859, pp. 48-51.
[2] 'A comparison between champion country and severall.' Ed. W. Mavor (London, 1812), 9, p. 206.

ANALYSIS OF THE INQUISITION FOR THE COUNTY OF NORFOLK

I.—AREAS INCLOSED ON LAY AND ECCLESIASTICAL MANORS.

Hundred	A Area of hundred	B Total area inclosed	C Inclosures remaining arable	D Conversions and pasture areas inclosed	Areas of inclosure on lay manors			Areas of inclosure on ecclesiastical manors		
					E Total	F Remaining arable	G Conversions and pasture areas inclosed	H Total	I Remaining arable	K Conversions and pasture areas inclosed
	acres	acres	acres	acres	acres	acres	acres	acre	acres	acres
1. Humilyard	29,620	150	—	150	150	—	150	—	—	—
2. Holte	42,290	180	—	180	—	—	140	40	—	40
3. E. and W. Flegge	31,760	56	—	56	—	—	—	56	—	56
4. Loddon and Knaveryng	55,630	110	80	110	150	40	110	40	—	—
5. Saynedon	45,660	1,036	100	946	616	30	586	430	40	360
6. Lanndyche	59,930	1,447	483	964	767 (853)	178 (220)	589 (633)	594 (680)	263 (305)	331 (375)
7. Northgreeow	34,320	893	200	692	570 (662)	200	370 (492)	200	—	200 (322)
8. Southerpynham	90,760	679	223	692	575 (583)	198	377 (391)	90	—	65 (79)
9. fryheryge iuxta Lynne	75,770	2,395	46	2,349	2,042 (2,208)	46	1,996 (2,162)	187 (353)	25	187 (353)
10. Depwade	30,950	93	—	23	23	—	23	—	—	—
11. Shropham and Gyllcroste	78,910	394	—	394	228	14	228	166	—	166
12. Tunstede	35,440	127	41	86	100 (127)	—	86 (113)	0	—	0 (27)
13. Northerpyngham	35,770	62	—	62	62	—	62	—	—	—
14. Heusted	19,770	182	72	110	182	72	110	—	—	—
15. Eynesford	49,990	180	—	180	180	—	60	120	—	120
16. Dyse	25,440	112	—	112	25 (82)	—	25 (82)	30 (87)	0 (20)	30 (87)
17. fyhrigge Marceland	57,280	20	20	—	—	—	—	30 (20)	—	—
18. Southgrennee	63,850	390	78	312	240 (106)	23	217 (106)	150 (86)	55	95 (86)
19. Metford	33,570	106	—	106	20 (157)	—	20 (127)	0 (85)	—	0 (57)
20. florowe	41,130	223	52	171	144	30	114	66	22	44
21. Blofeld and Walsham	46,990	525	40	485	395	60	395	130	—	90
22. Wayland and Grymsowe	101,950	459	60	399	429	—	369	30	—	30
23. Galowe and Brothercrosse	63,300	626	—	626	20 (346)	—	320 (346)	286 (306)	—	286 (306)
	1,100,790	10,454	1,485	8,964	7,238 (7,855)	891 (953)	6,347 (6,902)	2,599 (3,216)	905 (567)	2,121 (2,649)

NOTE.—Where two numbers are given, that in brackets is the number if the doubtful cases are included. The totals will then be obtained by adding the bracketed figures of the columns giving the ecclesiastical areas to the appropriate unbracketed figures of the columns giving the areas upon lay manors.

II.—Proportionate Analysis of Areas Inclosed on Lay and Ecclesiastical Manors.

Hundred	A. Proportion of total area inclosed to area of hundred	B. Proportion of inclosures remaining arable to total area inclosed	C. Proportion of conversions and inclosures of pasture to total area inclosed	Lay Manor D. Proportion of areas inclosed to total areas	E. Proportion of inclosures remaining arable to total areas inclosed	F. Proportion of inclosures remaining arable to total areas inclosed on lay manors	G. Proportion of conversions and inclosures of pasture to total areas inclosed	H. Proportion of conversions and inclosures of pasture to total areas inclosed on lay manor	Ecclesiastical Manors I. Proportion of areas inclosed to total areas	K. Proportion of inclosures remaining arable to total areas inclosed	L. Proportion of inclosures remaining arable to total areas inclosed on ecclesiastical manors	M. Proportion of conversions and inclosures of pasture to total areas inclosed	N. Proportion of conversions and inclosures of pasture to total areas inclosed on ecclesiastical manors
1. Humlyard	·66	—	100	100	—	—	100	100	—	—	—	—	—
2. Holte	·04	—	100	77·78	—	—	77·78	100	—	—	—	22·22	100
3. E. & W. Flegge	·18	—	100	—	—	—	—	—	22·22	—	—	100	100
Loddon and Knaveryng													
4. Smythdon	·34	42·11	57·89	78·95	21·05	26·66	57·89	73·33	21·05	21·05	100	—	—
5. Laundyche	·27	8·69	91·31	59·46	2·9	4·87	56·56	95·7	40·54	5·79	14·28	34·75	85·71
6. Northgrenow	·33	·33	77·57	53 (58·09)	12·3 (15·21)	23·2 (25·79)	40·7 (43·74)	76·70 (74·2)	41·05 (46·99)	18·17 (21·07)	44·27 (44·85)	22·87 (25·91)	55·72 (55·14)
7. S. Erpyngham	·47	24·42	67·16	35·58 (28·9)	22·42	35·58 (28·9)	41·47 (55·16)	64·91 (72·54)	22·42 (36·06)	3·65	—	22·42 (36·06)	100
8. fforbrygge iuxta Lynne	·34	32·84	62·16	84·68 (86·74)	9·15	34·4 (33·61)	55·52 (66·38)	65·56 (66·38)	13·35 (15·31)	—	27·77 (24·63)	9·57 (9·16)	72·22 (75·96)
10. Depwade	3·03	1·92	98·07	85·26 (92·19)	1·92	2·25 (2·08)	83·34 (90·27)	97·74 (97·91)	7·8 (14·78)	—	—	7·8 (14·78)	100
11. Shropham and Gyltcroste	·07	—	100	—	—	—	100	100	—	—	—	—	—
12. Tunstede	·5	67·72	100	9·87	11·02	14 (11·02)	57·87 (88·97)	67·71 (88·97)	42·13	—	—	42·13	100
13. Northarpingham	·36	—	100	78·74 (100)	—	—	78·74 (88·97)	86 (88·97)	0	0	(100)	0	0
14. Hensted	·17	—	100	—	—	—	—	—	—	—	—	—	—
15. Eynesford	·92	39·56	66·44	100	39·56	39·56	66·44	66·43	66·67	—	—	66·67	(100)
16. Dysse	·36	—	100	33·33	—	—	33·33	100	26·69 (77·67)	—	—	26·69 (77·67)	100
17. ffrybrigge Marceland	·44	—	100	22·32 (73·21)	—	—	22·32 (73·21)	100	—	—	—	—	—
18. Southgrenowe	·04	100	—	0	0	0	55·64	90·41	0	0	0	24·36	61·33
19. Metford	·61	20	80	61·54	5·9	9·58	18·87 (100)	100	38·46	14·1	36·66	0	0
20. fflorowe	·32	—	100	18·87 (100)	—	—	51·12 (56·95)	100	0	0	(81·13)	0	(100)
21. Blofeld and Walsham	·54	23·32	76·68	64·57 (70·4)	13·45	20·83 (19·1)	75·24	79·16 (80·89)	29·59 (35·42)	9·87	33·33 (97·84)	19·73 (25·36)	66·66 (72·15)
22. Waylond and Grymsowe	1·12	7·62	92·38	75·24	—	—	80·39	100	24·76	7·62	30·76	17·14	69·23
23. Galowe and Brotthercrosse	·45	13·07	86·93	93·46	13·07	13·98	51·12 (55·27)	86·01	6·54	—	—	6·54	100
	·30	—	100	51·12 (55·27)	—	—	60·71 (66·22)	87·68 (87·86)	44·73 (44·88)	4·83 (5·42)	19·43 (17·63)	44·73 (48·88)	100
	·094	14·2	85·79	69·23 (75·13)	8·52 (9·11)	12·31 (12·13)			24·86 (30·76)			20·28 (25·34)	81·16 (82·3)

NOTE.—Where two numbers are given, that in brackets is the number if the doubtful cases are included. The totals will then be obtained by adding the bracketed figures of the columns giving the ecclesiastical areas to the appropriate unbracketed figures of the columns giving the areas upon lay manors.

THE INQUISITION OF 1517   143

III.—ACTUAL INCLOSERS

LAYMEN	ECCLESIASTICS

Hundred of Humlyara

	Acres
Brakon	60
Est Carleton	30
Intewoode	30
Querarlam	30
	150

Hundred of Humlyara

Acres

Hundred of Holte

Bayffeld	60
Saxlyngham	40
Melton	40
	140

Hundred of Holte

Egefeld	22
Egefeld	18
	40

Hundred of E. & W. Flegge

Hundred of E. & W. Flegge

Martham	40
Westsomerton	16
	56

Hundred of Loddon & Knaveryng

Alby	80
Wheteacreburgh	40
Mondambrome	30
	150

Hundred of Loddon & Knaveryng

Loddon	40
	40

Hundred of Smythdon

Choysell	300
Stanowe	120
Honston	16
Snethysham	60
Stanehewe	60
Barwyk	60
	616

Hundred of Smythdon

Choysell	300
Hecham	60
Barwyk	60
	420

ACTUAL INCLOSERS—*Continued*

LAYMEN		ECCLESIASTICS	
Hundred of Laundyche	Acres	*Hundred of Laundyche*	Acres
Hoo	30		
		Betele	45
North Elynham	37		
North Elynham	26		
North Elynham	16		
North Elynham	30		
Bayselee	16		
Bayselee	26		
Gatelee	24		
		Gatelee	26
		Gatelee	30
Myleham	80		
Myleham	60		
Myleham	18		
Tytelyshale	40		
		Kempston	12
		Kempston	80
		Wendlyng	(60)
Rougham	200		
Wesenham	80		
Dunham Parva	40		
Dunham Parva	160		
ffraunsham Magna	18		
ffraunsham Magna	16		
		Skernyng	40
Skernyng	18		
Skernyng	25		
Skernyng	19		
Colkryke	26		
Colkryke	16		
Colkryke	30		
Colkryke	43		
Hornyngtoft	30		
Oxwyk	30		
	1154		293
Hundred of Northgrenow		*Hundred of Northgrenow*	
Holkeham	200		
Holkeham	100		
Holkeham	30		
Warham	30		
Warham	80		
Styfkey	20		
		Hyndryngham	100
Hyndryngham	20		
Thyrrysforth	30		
Wytton	80		
Wytton	40		
		Walsyngham Magna	60
		Walsyngham Magna	60
Walsyngham Magna	2		
		Hoveton	40
	632		260

THE INQUISITION OF 1517

ACTUAL INCLOSERS—*Continued*

LAYMEN		ECCLESIASTICS	
Hundred of Southarpynham		*Hundred of Southartynham*	
	Acres		Acres
Colteshale	25		
Bylawe	37		
Haughboys Magna	40		
Haughboys Magna	100		
Buxston	180		
Bakenthorp	19		
Calthorpe	20		
Calthorpe	24		
Calthorpe	26		
Causton	16		
Blykelyng	18		
Blykelyng	10		
Aylesham	14		
Arpyngham	30		
Arpyngham	20		
Arpyngham	(not specified)		
Arpyngham	100		
	679		
Hundred of ffrybryge iuxta Lynne		*Hundred of ffrybryge iuxta Lynn*	
		fflytcham	60
		Herpeley	250
ffiytcham	168		
ffiytcham	400		
ffiytcham (qu. ecclesiastical)	(840)		
		Harpeley	98
Massyngham Parua	16		
Massyngham Parua	16		
Castellacre	40		
Castellacre ('Vnum integrum hamelett')			
Bawsey	60		
Gaywood	19		
Rowton	10		
Wynche	35		
Hyllyngton	30		
Grymston	15		
Sandryngham	26		
Rysyngcastell	30		
North Wotton	56		
Donmer (Anmer)	100		
Lynne	40		
Brabyngle	36		
Brabyngle	30		
Brabyngle	20		
	1987		**408**
Hundred of Depwade		*Hundred of Depwade*	
Mornyngthorpe	23		

ACTUAL INCLOSERS—*Continued*

LAYMEN		ECCLESIASTICS	
Hundreds of Shropham & Gylcroste	Acres	*Hundreds of Shropham & Gylcroste*	Acres
Attyllburgh	80	Attyllburgh	30
Besthorpe	80		
		Ekkyllys	20
Shropham	48		
Lytlebrekylles	20		
		Schadewell	20
		Schadewell	80
Stalham	16		
	244		150

Hundred of Tunstede		*Hundred of Tunstede*	
Northwalsham	30		
Northwalsham	70		
Rydlyngton & Crostwyke	27		
	127		

Hundred of Northarpyngham		*Hundred of Northar yngham*	
North Barnyngham	24		
Town Barnyngham	8		
Suffeld	30		
	62		

Hundred of Henstea		*Hundred of Hensted*	
Parua Parlond	12		
Stoke	10		
Stoke	100		
Shotesham	60		
	182		

Hundred of Eynesford		*Hundred of Eynesford*	
		Brandeston	(60)
		Weston	(60)
Belawe	60		
			120

Hundred of Dysse		*Hundred of Dysse*	
Thorp Parua	30		
Tetyshale	27		
Tetyshale	30		
Wyndeferthing (' villata ')	25		
	112		

Hundred of ffybrigge Marceland		*Hundred of ffybrigge Marcesana*	
Emneth	20		

THE INQUISITION OF 1517

ACTUAL INCLOSERS—*Continued*

LAYMEN		ECCLESIASTICS	
Hundred of Southgrenowe	Acres	*Hundred of Southgrenowe*	Acres
Hale	40		
Palgraue	(120)		
Dunham	40		
		Estbradenham	80
		Scarnyng and West Bradenham	40
Pykenham	40		
Estbradeham	30		
	270		120
Hundred of Metford		*Hundred of Metford*	
Dereham	20		
Dereham	50		
Letton	36		
	106		
Hundred of fforowe		*Hundred of fforowe*	
Hyngham	40		
Morley	30		
Barnahambrome	34		
Kemerley	40		
Wyndham	13		
		Bowthorp	48
		Bowthorp	18
	157		66
Hundreds of Blofeld & Walsham		*Hundreds of Blofeld & Walsham*	
Plompsted Magna	50		
		Thorp Episcopi	80
Plomsted	15		
		Poswyke	50
Wytton	100		
Okyll	30		
Bastwyke	(120)		
Canteley	80		
	395		130
Hundreds of Waylond & Grymsowe		*Hundreds of Waylond & Grymsowe*	
Saham Tony	60		
Elyngham Parua	76		
Watton	77		
		Merton	30
		Merton	40
Asshell	26		
Asshell	60		
Asshell	60		
		Methewold	30
	359		100

L 2

ACTUAL INCLOSERS—*Continued*

LAYMEN	ECCLESIASTICS
Hundreds of Galowe & Brothercrosse	*Hundreds of Galowe & Brothercrosse*

Laymen	Acres	Ecclesiastics	Acres
Ketelston	26	Ryborow	80
Destreton	80		
Northbarsham	80	Bagthorp	40
Skulthorp	80		
Howton	80	Estrudham	80
Westrudham	40	Burnham	40
	386		240

THE INQUISITION OF 1517   149

IV.—INCLOSURES BY ECCLESIASTICS AND LAYMEN UPON ECCLESIASTICAL MANORS

Manor	Lord of Manor	Area Inclosed	Object of Inclosure			Incloser				Transcript page
			Park	Inclosure	Pasture	Lord of Manor	Clerical land-owners	Clerical tenants	Lay tenants	
Hundred of Holte		acres	acs.	acs.	acs.					
Egefeld . . .	Prior of Bynham .	40	—	—	40	—	—	1	—	2
Hundred of East Flegge										
Martham . .	Prior of Norwich	40	—	—	40	1	—	—	—	3
Hundred of West Flegge										
West Somerton .	Prior of Butley .	16	—	—	16	1	—	—	—	,,
Hundred of Loddon										
Loddon . . .	Abbot of Langley . .	40	—	40	—	—	—	1	—	,,
Hundred of Smythdon										
Choysell . .	Hospital of Burton Lazars	300	—	60	240	1	—	—	—	4
Berwyk . . .	Prior of Buckenham .	60	—	—	60	—	—	—	1	,,
Berwyk . . .	Prior of Buckenham .	60	—	—	60	1	—	—	—	,,
Hundred of Laundyche										
Hoo . . .	Bishop of Ely . .	30	—	—	30	—	—	—	1	5
Betele . . .	Bishop of Norwich .	45	—	—	45	—	—	1	—	,,
North Elynham .	Bishop of Norwich .	37	—	37	—	—	—	—	1	,,
North Elynham .	Bishop of Norwich .	26	—	20	6	—	—	—	1	,,
North Elynham .	Bishop of Norwich .	16	—	16	—	—	—	—	1	,,
North Elynham .	Bishop of Norwich .	30	—	—	30	—	—	—	1	,,
Bayselee . .	Bishop of Norwich .	16	—	16	—	—	—	—	1	,,
Bayselee . .	Bishop of Norwich .	26	—	26	—	—	—	—	1	,,
Gatelee . . .	Qu. Bishop of Norwich .	24	—	24	—	—	—	—	1	6
Gatelee . . .	Bishop of Norwich .	26	—	26	—	—	—	1	—	,,
Gatelee . . .	Bishop of Norwich .	30	—	30	—	—	—	1	—	,,
Tytelyshale . .	Prior of Coxford .	40	—	40	—	—	—	—	1	,,
Kempston . .	Prior of Castellacre .	12	—	12	—	1	—	—	—	,,
Kempston . .	Prior of Castellacre .	80	—	—	80	1	—	—	—	,,
Wendlyng . .	Prior of Castellacre .	60	—	—	60	1	—	—	—	,,
Wesenham . .	Prior of Castellacre .	80	—	—	80	—	—	—	1	7
Skernyng . .	Abbot of Wendlyng .	40	—	40	—	1	—	—	—	,,
Skernyng . .	Qu. Abbot of Wendlyng .	18	—	18	—	—	—	—	1	,,
Skernyng . .	Qu. Abbot of Wendlyng .	25	—	—	25	—	—	—	1	,,
Skernyng . .	Qu. Abbot of Wendlyng .	19	—	19	—	—	—	—	1	,,
Hundred of Northgrenow										
Holkeham . .	Bishop of Norwich .	100	—	—	100	—	—	—	1	8
Holkeham . .	Qu. Prior of Walsingham .	30	—	—	30	—	—	—	1	,,
Hyndryngham .	Prior of Norwich .	100	—	—	100	1	—	—	—	,,
Walsyngham Magna	Qu. Prior of Bynham .	60	—	—	60	—	—	1	—	9
Walsyngham Magna	Qu. Prior of Bynham .	60	—	—	60	—	—	1	—	,,
Hundred of Southgrynham										
Colteshale . .	King's College, Cambridge	25	—	25	—	—	—	1	—	,,
Bylawe . . .	Abbot of St. Bennet, Norwich	37	—	—	37	—	—	1	—	,,
Blykeling . .	Bishop of Norwich .	18	18	—	—	—	—	1	—	10
Blykeling . .	Bishop of Norwich .	10	10	—	—	—	—	1	—	,,
Aylesham . .	Qu. Abbot of Bury St. Edmund's	14	—	—	14	—	—	1	—	,,
Hundred of ffrybryge iuxta Lynne										
Mytcham . .	Prior of Walsingham .	60	—	—	60	—	—	1	—	11
Mytcham . .	Prior of Walsingham .	168	—	—	168	—	—	—	1	,,
Gaywood . .	Bishop of Norwich .	19	—	—	19	—	—	—	1	12

INCLOSURES BY ECCLESIASTICS AND LAYMEN UPON ECCLESIASTICAL MANORS—*Continued*

Manor	Lord of Manor	Area inclosed	Object of Inclosure			Incloser				Transcript page
			Park	Inclosure	Pasture	Lord of Manor	Clerical land-owners	Clerical tenants	Lay tenants	
Hundred of ffrybrygge iuxta Lynne (cont.)		acres	acs.	acs.	acs.					
Wynche	Qu. Prior of Pentney	35	—	—	35	—	—	—	1	12
Grymston	Qu. Prior of Coxford	15	—	—	15	—	—	—	1	,,
North Wotton	Qu. Prior of Windham	56	—	—	56	—	—	—	1	,,
Hundreds of Shropham and Gylcroste										
Attyllburgh	College of Holy Cross	30	—	—	30	1	—	—	—	13
Ekkyllys	Bishop of Norwich	20	—	—	20	—	—	—	—	,,
Schadewell	College of Rushworth	20	—	—	20	1	—	1	—	14
Schadewell	College of Rushworth	80	—	—	80	1	—	—	—	,,
Stalham	College of Heringby	16	—	—	16	—	—	—	1	,,
Hundred of Tunstede										
Rydlyngton and Crosswyke	Qu. Prior of Bromholm	27	—	—	27	—	—	—	1	,,
Hundred of Eynesford										
Brandeston	Magdalen College, Oxford	60	—	—	60	1	—	—	—	15
Weston	New College, Oxford	60	—	—	60	1	—	—	—	,,
Hundred of Dysse										
Thorp Parua	The rector of the parish	30	—	—	30	1	—	—	—	16
Tetyshale	Qu. Abbot of Bury St. Edmund's	57	—	—	57	—	—	—	1	,,
Hundred of ffybrigge Marceland										
Emneth	Qu. Prior of Lewes	20	—	20	—	—	—	—	1	,,
Hundred of Southgrenowe										
East Bradenham	Abbot of Bury St. Edmund's	80	—	40	40	—	1	—	—	17
Scarnyng and West Bradenham	Abbot of Wendlyng	40	—	—	40	—	—	—	—	,,
Estbradeham	Abbot of Bury St. Edmund's	30	—	15	15	—	—	—	1	,,
Hundred of Metford										
Dereham	Qu. Bishop of Ely	50	—	—	50	—	—	—	1	18
Letton	Qu. Prior of Lewes	36	—	—	36	—	—	—	1	,,
Hundred of fforowe										
Wyndham	Qu. Abbot of Wyndham	13	—	—	13	—	—	—	1	,,
Bowthorp	Dean &c. of St. Mary-in-fields, Norwich	48	—	22	26	1	—	—	—	19
Bowthorp	Dean &c. of St. Mary-in-fields, Norwich	18	—	—	18	1	—	—	—	,,
Hundred of Blofeld and Walsham										
Plompsted Magna	Prior of Norwich	50	—	—	50	—	—	—	1	,,
Thorp Episcopi	Prior of Norwich	80	—	40	40	1	—	—	—	,,
Hundreds of Wayland and Grymsowe										
Methewold	Canons of Thetford	30	—	—	30	1	—	—	—	21
Hundreds of Galowe and Brothercrosse										
Ketelston	Qu. College of Pomfret	26	—	—	26	—	—	1	—	
Ryborow	Prior of Walsingham	80	—	—	80	—	—	1	—	
Bagthorp	Prior of Castellacre	40	—	—	40	1	—	—	—	
Skulthorp	College of Pomfret	80	—	—	80	1	—	—	—	
Est Rudham	Prior of Coxford	80	—	—	80	1	—	—	—	,, 22

THE INQUISITION OF 1517

V.

ANALYSIS OF LAY AND ECCLESIASTICAL INCLOSURES

Hundred	Lay Inclosures			Ecclesiastical Inclosures		
	Total area inclosed	Inclosures remaining arable	Conversions and inclosures of pasture	Total area inclosed	Inclosures remaining arable	Conversions and inclosures of pasture
	acres	acres	acres	acres	acres	acres
Humlyard	150	—	150	—	—	—
Holte	140	—	140	40	—	40
E. and W. Flegge	—	—	—	56	—	56
Loddon and Knaveryng	150	40	110	40	40	—
Smythdon	616	30	586	420	60	360
Laundyche	1,154	394	760	293	108	185
Northgrenow	632	202	430	260	—	260
Southarpyngham	679	223	456	—	—	—
ffrybryge iuxta Lynne	1,987	46	1,941	408	—	408
Depwade	23	—	23	—	—	—
Shropham and Gylcroste	244	—	244	150	—	150
Tunstede	127	41	86	—	—	—
Northarpyngham	62	—	62	—	—	—
Hensted	182	72	110	—	—	—
Eynesford	60	—	60	120	—	120
Dysse	112	—	112	—	—	—
ffybrigge Marceland	20	20	—	—	—	—
Southgrenowe	270	38	232	120	40	80
Metford	106	—	106	—	—	—
fforowe	157	40	117	66	—	66
Blofeld and Walsham	395	—	395	130	—	130
Waylond and Grymsowe	359	60	299	100	—	100
Galowe and Brothercrosse	386	—	386	240	—	240
Total	8,011	1,206	6,805	2,443	248	2,195

VI.—Proportionate Summary of Lay and Ecclesiastical Inclosures

Hundred	Proportion of area inclosed to total area inclosed	Lay Inclosures				Ecclesiastical Inclosures			
		Proportion of inclosures remaining arable to total areas inclosed	Proportion of inclosures remaining arable to total areas inclosed	Proportion of con-versions and inclo-sures of pasture to total areas inclosed by laymen	Proportion of con-versions and inclo-sures of pasture to total areas inclosed by laymen	Proportion of area inclosed to total area inclosed	Proportion of eccle-siastical inclosures remaining arable to total areas inclosed	Proportion of eccle-siastical inclosures remaining arable to total areas inclosed by ecclesiastics	Proportion of con-versions and inclo-sures of pasture to total areas inclosed by ecclesiastics
Humlyard	100	—	—	100	100	—	—	—	—
Holte	77·77	—	—	77·77	100	—	—	—	—
E. and W. Flegge	78·94	—	—	—	—	—	—	—	—
Loddon and Knaveryng	59·45	21·05	26·66	57·89	73·33	22·22	21·05	100	100
Smythdon	79·75	2·89	4·87	56·56	95·12	100	—	—	—
Laundyche	70·85	27·22	34·14	52·52	65·85	21·05	5·79	14·28	85·71
Northgrenow	100	22·64	31·96	48·2	68·03	40·54	7·46	36·86	63·13
Southarpynham	82·96	32·84	32·84	67·15	67·15	20·24	—	—	100
ffrybryge iuxta Lynne	100	1·92	2·31	81·04	97·68	29·14	—	—	—
Depwade	61·92	—	—	61·92	100	—	—	—	—
Shropham and Gylcroste	100	—	—	67·71	67·71	17·03	—	—	100
Tunstede	100	32·25	32·25	100	100	—	—	—	—
Northarpyngham	100	—	—	60·43	60·43	38·07	—	—	100
Hemsted	39·5	39·5	39·5	33·33	100	—	—	—	—
Eynesford	33·33	—	—	100	100	—	—	—	—
Dysse	100	—	—	—	—	66·66	—	—	—
ffybrigge Marceland	100	100	100	—	—	—	—	—	—
Southgrenowe	69·23	9·74	14·07	59·48	85·92	30·76	10·25	33·33	100
Metford	100	—	—	100	100	—	—	—	—
fforowe	70·4	17·93	25·47	52·46	74·52	29·59	—	—	66·66
Blofeld and Walsham	75·23	—	—	75·23	100	24·76	—	—	100
Wayland and Grymsowe	78·21	13·07	16·71	65·14	83·28	21·78	—	—	100
Galowe and Brothercrosse	61·66	—	—	61·66	100	38·33	—	—	100
	76·63	11·53	15·05	65·08	84·97	23·36	2·37	10·15	20·99	89·84

NOTE.—The words 'total area' refer to the area of the respective hundreds.

THE INQUISITION OF 1517   153

VII.—INCLOSURES BY CLERICS NOT ON ECCLESIASTICAL MANORS

Parish	Incloser's Name	Area	Ecclesiastical Land	Laymen's Land
		acres		
Heacham	Johannes Wyngfeld, clericus	60	. . .	The Wingfields' manors
Hoveton	Prior of Walsyngham	40	. . .	Lord Roos's land and manor
Harpeley	Prior of Castellacre	250	Qu. Priory of Castellacre	—
Poswyke	Prior of Norwich	50	.. . .	The Boleyns' manor
Merton .	Thomas Grey, clericus	30	. . .	The Greys' manor
Merton .	John Pory, clericus	40	Qu. Rector's land	—

VIII.—INCLOSURES BY LAYMEN ON ECCLESIASTICAL LANDS NOT BEING IN ECCLESIASTICAL MANORS

Parish	Incloser's Name	Area	Ecclesiastical Land	Laymen's Land
Harpeley	Magister Strange .	98	Christ's Coll., Cambridge	—

IX.—SELECTED INCLOSURES, &C. BY LAYMEN

Name	Place	Area inclosed	Object of inclosure		Lay Lords of Manors	Landowners'	Tenants	Transcript page
			Incl.	Pasture				
		acres		acres				
Thomas Thorysby .	Barwyk . .	60	—	60	—	1	—	4
Roger Martyn .	North Elynham	16	16	—	—	1	—	5
Roger Martyn .	North Elynham	30	30	—	—	1	—	"
Roger Martyn .	Gatelee . .	24	24	—	—	1	—	6
Henry ffermour	Tytelyshale .	40	40	—	—	—	1	"
Robert Merkaunt .	Bayselee . .	16	16	—	—	1	..	5
Robert Merkaunt .	Hornyngtoft .	30	30	—	—	1	—	8
Henry ffermer .	Hyndryngham .	20	—	20	1	—	—	9
Henry ffermer .	Wytton . .	40	—	40	—	1	—	11
Lady Morley .	Alby . .	80	40	40	1	--	—	3
Lady Morley .	Buxston .	180	90	90	1	--	—	9
Henry ffermer .	Arpyngham .	100	—	100	—	—	1	10
Thomas Thurysby, sen. .	Holt . .	vnum integrum hamelett	—	—	—	—	—	11
Thomas Thurysby, sen.(?)	Bawsey .	60	—	60	1	—	--	12
Thomas Thurysby .	Wypche .	35	—	35	—	1	—	"
Thomas Thurysby, sen.(?)	Hyllyngton .	30	—	30	1	—	—	"
Thomas Thurysby .	North Wotton .	56	—	56	—	1	—	"
Henry ffermer .	Skulthorp .	80	—	—	—	1	-- ..	21

¹ *I.e.* in the sense that they are not described as tenants.

X.—SELECTED INCLOSURES BY ECCLESIASTICS

Prior of ffytcham's Inclosures

	Area inclosed	Inclosure	Pasture
Herpeley	250	—	250

Prior of Castellacre's Inclosures

	Area inclosed	Inclosure	Pasture
Kempston	92	12	80
Wendlyng	60	—	60
Bagthorp	40	—	40

Prior of Norwich's Inclosures

	Area inclosed	Inclosure	Pasture
Thorp Episcopi	80	40	40
Poswyke	50	—	50

Prior of Walsyngham's Inclosures

	Area inclosed	Inclosure	Pasture
Walsyngham Magna	120	—	120
Hoveton	40	—	40

SUMMARY

Name	Area inclosed	Object of inclosure	
		Inclosure	Pasture
Thomas Thurysby	151 (? 241)	—	151 (? 241)
Henry ffermer	280	—	16
Roger Martyn	70	70	—
Lady Morley	260	130	130
Robert Merkaunt	46	46	—
Prior of ffytcham	250	—	250
Prior of Castellacre	192	12	430
Prior of Walsyngham	160	—	160
Prior of Norwich	130	40	90

THE INQUISITION OF 1517   155

XI.—Houses Decayed

Place	Lay or Ecclesiastical Manor	Destroyed by	Designation of Houses	Number of Houses
Choysell	Lay	Layman	mansiones	Qu. 5 [1]
Choysell	Ecclesiastical	Ecclesiastic	mansiones	Qu. 5 [1]
Barwyk	Ecclesiastical	Layman	messuagium	1
Hoo	Ecclesiastical	Layman	messuagium	1
Myleham	Lay	Layman	mansio	1
Wendlyng	Ecclesiastical	Ecclesiastic	messuagia	(2)
Dunham Parva	Lay	Layman	tenementum	1
Styfkey	Lay	Layman	tenementum	1
Holkeham	Lay	Layman	diuersa tenementa	Qu. 6
Colteshale	Ecclesiastical	Layman	{ messuagium tenementum }	1
Haughboys Magna	Lay	Layman	tenementum	1
Haughhoys Magna	Lay	Layman	manerium	1
Buxston	Lay	Layman	manerium	1
Calthorpe	Lay	Layman	tenementum	1
Causton	Lay	Layman	tenementum	1
Aylesham	Qu.	Layman	messuagium	1
Blykelyng	Ecclesiastical	Layman	tenementum	1
Arpyngham	Lay	Layman	tenementum	1
fflytcham	Ecclesiastical	Qu.	inhabitaciones	15
Harpeley	Ecclesiastical	Layman	tenementum	1
Castellacre	Lay	Layman	vnum integrum hamelett cum omnibus tenementis	Qu.
Gaywood	Ecclesiastical	Layman	tenementum	1
Hyllyngton	Lay	Layman	tenementum	1
Rysyngcastell	Lay	Layman	tenementum	1
Anmer	Lay	Layman	manerium	1
Lynne	Lay	Layman	tenementum	1
Brabyngle	Lay	Layman	messuagium	1
Besthorpe	Lay	Layman	tenementum	1
Shropham	Lay	Layman	tenementum	1
Schadewell	Ecclesiastical	Ecclesiastic	diuersa tenementa	Qu. 3
Stalham	Ecclesiastical	Layman	tenementum	1
North Walsham	Lay	Layman	tenementum	1
North Walsham	Lay	Layman	tenementum	1
Suffeld	Lay	Layman	tenementum	1
Stoke	Lay	Layman	placea	1
Hale	Lay	Layman	messuagium	1
Palgraue	Lay	Layman	manerium	1
Thorp Parua	Ecclesiastical	Ecclesiastic	mansio manerii	1
Tetyshale	Lay	Layman	tenementum	1
Wyndeferthing	Lay	Layman	tenementum	1
Emneth	Qu.	Layman	messuagium	1
Dunham	Lay	Layman	messuagium	1
Dereham	Lay	Layman	manerium	1
Hyngham	Lay	Layman	messuagium	1
Morley	Lay	Layman	messuagium	1
Bowthorp	Ecclesiastical	Ecclesiastic	tenementum	1
Bowthorp	Ecclesiastical	Ecclesiastic	tenementum	1

[1] *I.e.* at sixty acres to an aratrum (see *sub* Wendlyng, p. 176, *infra*).

Summary

Total Number of Houses Decayed	By Laymen	By Ecclesiastics	Uncertain
76	48 (and a hamlet)	13	15

XII.—AREAS OF INCLOSURES

I. Above 200 acres = 4

Place	Acres	Hundred
ffiytcham .	840	ffrybryge
ffiytcham .	400	iuxta Lynne
Choysell .	300	Smythdon
Choysell .	300	

II. 200–98 acres = 18

Place	Acres	Hundred
Rougham .	200	Laundyche
Holkeham .	200	Northgrenow
Buxston .	180	Southarpynham
ffiytcham .	168	ffrybryge iuxta Lynne
Dunham Parva .	160	Laundyche
Stanowe .	120	Smythdon
Palgraue .	(120)	Southgrenowe
Bastwyke .	(120)	Walsham
Holkeham .	100	Northgrenow
Hyndryngham .	100	
Haughboys Magna .	100	Southarpynham
Arpyngham .	100	
Donmer (Anmer)	100	ffrybryge iuxta Lynne
Herpeley .	100	
Herpeley .	100	
Stoke .	100	Hensted
Wytton .	100	Walsham
Harpeley .	98	ffrybryge iuxta Lynne

III. 80 acres = 18

Place	Acres	Hundred
Alby .	80	Knaveryng
Kempston .	80	Laundyche
Myleham .	80	
Wesenham .	80	

III. 80 acres.—cont.

Place	Acres	Hundred
Warham .	80	Northgrenow
Wytton .	80	
Attyllburgh .	80	Shropham and Gylcroste
Besthorpe .	80	
Schadewell .	80	
E. Bradenham .	80	Southgrenowe
Thorp Episcopi .	80	Blofeld
Canteley .	80	
Ryborow .	80	Galowe and Brothercrosse
Destreton .	80	
North Barsham .	80	
Skulthorp .	80	
Howton .	80	
Est Rudham .	80	

IV. 80–70 acres = 3

Place	Acres	Hundred
Watton .	77	Waylond
Elyngham Parva .	76	
North Walsham .	70	Tunstede

V. 60 acres = 20

Place	Acres	Hundred
Brakon .	60	Humlyard
Bayffeld .	60	Holte
Hecham .	60	Smythdon
Snethysham .	60	
Stanehewe .	60	
Barwyk .	60	
Barwyk .	60	
Myleham .	60	Laundyche
Wendlyng .	(60)	
Walsyngham Magna .	60	Northgrenow
Walsyngham Magna .	60	
ffiytcham .	60	ffrybryge iuxta Lynne
Bawsey .	60	

THE INQUISITION OF 1517

AREAS OF INCLOSURES—Continued

V. 60 acres.—cont.

Place	Acres	Hundred
Shotesham	60	Hensted
Brandeston	(60)	
Weston	(60)	Eynesford
Belawe	(60)	
Saham Tony	60	
Asshell	60	Waylond
Asshell	60	

VI. 60–40 acres = 9

Place	Acres	Hundred
North Wotton	56	ffrybryge
Herpeley	50	iuxta Lynne
Plompsted Magna	50	Blofeld
Poswyke	50	
Dereham	50	Metford
Shropham	48	Shropham and Gylcroste
Bowthorp	48	fforowe
Betele	45	Laundyche
Colkryke	43	

VII. 40 acres = 23

Place	Acres	Hundred
Saxlyngham	40	Holte
Melton	40	
Martham	40	Flegge
Loddon	40	Loddon
Wheteacreburgh	40	Knaveryng
Tytelyshale	40	
Dunham Parva	40	Laundyche
Skernyng	40	
Wytton	40	Northgrenow
Hoveton	40	
Haughboys Magna	40	Southarpynham
Castellacre	40	ffrybryge
Lynne	40	iuxta Lynne
Hale	40	
Dunham	40	
Scarnyng and W. Bradenham	40	Southgrenowe
Pykenham	40	
Hyngham	40	fforowe
Kemerley	40	
Merton	40	Waylond
Bagthorp	40	Galowe and Brothercrosse
West Rudham	40	
Burnham	40	

VIII. 40–30 acres = 6

Place	Acres	Hundred
North Elynham	37	Laundyche
Bylawe	37	Southarpynham
Brabyngle	36	ffrybryge iuxta Lynne
Letton	36	Metford
Wynche	35	ffrybryge iuxta Lynne
Barnahambrome	34	fforowe

IX. 30 acres = 27

Place	Acres	Hundred
Est Carleton	30	
Intewoode	30	Humlyard
Querarlam	30	
Mondambrome	30	Loddon
Hoo	30	
N. Elynham	30	
Gatelee	30	Laundyche
Colkryke	30	
Hornyngtoft	30	
Oxwyk	30	
Holkeham	30	
Warham	30	Northgrenow
Thyrysforth	30	
Arpyngham	30	Southarpynham
Hyllyngton	30	ffrybryge iuxta Lynne
Rysyngcastell	30	
Brabyngle	30	
Attyllburgh	30	Shropham and Gylcroste
N. Walsham	30	Tunstede
Suffeld	30	Northarpyngham
Thorp Parva	30	Dysse
Tetyshale	30	
E. Bradeham	30	Southgrenowe
Morley	30	fforowe
Okyll	30	Walsham
Merton	30	Waylond
Methewold	30	Grymsowe

X. 30–20 acres = 28

Place	Acres	Hundred
Rydlyngton and Crostwyke		Tunstede

AREAS OF INCLOSURES—*Continued*

X. 30–20 *acres—cont.*

Place	Acres	Hundred
Tetyshale	27	Dysse
N. Elynham	26	
Bayselee	26	
Gatelee	26	Laundyche
Colkryke	26	
Calthorpe	26	Southarpynham
Sandryngham	26	ffrybryge iuxta Lynne
Asshell	26	Waylond
Ketelston	26	Galowe and Brothercrosse
Skernyng	25	Laundyche
Colteshale	25	Southarpynham
Wyndeferthing ('villata')	25	Dysse
Gatelee	24	Laundyche
Calthorpe	24	Southarpynham
N. Barnyngham	24	Northarpyngham
Mornyngthorpe	23	Depwade
Egefeld	22	Holte
Styfkey	20	Northgrenow
Hyndryngham	20	
Calthorpe	20	Southarpynham
Arpyngham	20	
Brabyngle	20	ffrybryge iuxta Lynne
Emneth	20	ffrybryge Marceland
Dereham	20	Metford
Ekkyllys	20	
Lytlebrekylles	20	Shropham and Gylcroste
Schadewell	20	

XI. 20–2 *acres* = 30

Place	Acres	Hundred
Skernyng	19	Laundyche
Bakenthorpe	19	Southarpynham

XI. 20–1 *acres—cont.*

Place	Acres	Hundred
Gaywood	19	ffrybryge iuxta Lynne
Egefeld	18	Holte
Myleham	18	
ffraunsham Magna	18	Laundyche
Skernyng	18	
Blykelyng	18	Southarpynham
Bowthorp	18	fforowe
West Somerton	16	Flegge
Honston	16	Smythdon
N. Elynham	16	
Bayselee	16	
ffraunsham Magna	16	Laundyche
Colkryke	16	
Causton	16	Southarpynham
Massyngham Parva	16	ffrybryge iuxta Lynne
Massyngham Parva	16	
Stalham	16	Shropham and Gylcroste
Grymston	15	ffrybryge iuxta Lynne
Plomsted	15	Blofeld
Aylesham	14	Southarpynham
Wyndham	13	fforowe
Kempston	12	Laundyche
Parva Parlond	12	Hensted
Blykelyng	10	Southarpynham
Rowton	10	ffrybryge iuxta Lynne
Stoke	10	Hensted
Town Barnyngham	8	Northarpyngham
Walsyngham Magna	2	Northgrenow

XIII.

Cases where Area is not Specified, but Inferred

Place	Area mentioned	Area inferred to be acres
Querarlam	aratrum	30
Wendlyng	aratrum	60
fflytcham	aratrum	60
Brandeston	aratrum	60
Weston	aratrum	60
Belawe	aratrum	60
Palgraue	manerium	120
Bastwyke	manerium	120
Harpeley	tenementum	98

XIV.

Areas Assigned to an 'Aratrum' in the Inquisition for Norfolk

—	Acres	The 'aratrum' associated with	Transcript page	Textual data
1. Rysyngcastell	30	tenementum	12	
(2. Dereham	20	manerium	18)	
3. Morley	30	messuagium	,,	
4. Plompsted Magna	50	manerium	19	
5. Poswyke	50	nil	,,	
6. Wytton	100	nil	,,	
7. Ketelston	52	nil	21	(26 ac. = dimidium aratrum)
8. Destreton	80	nil	,,	
9. North Barsham	80	nil	,,	
10. Bagthorpe	40	nil	,,	
11. Skulthorp	80	nil	,,	
12. Howton	80	nil	,,	
13. Estrudham	40	nil	22	(80 ac. = 2 aratra)
14. Westrudham	40	nil	,,	
15. Burnham	80	nil	,,	(40 ac. = dimidium aratrum)

Average area assigned to an aratrum, 56¾; or, omitting the case of Dereham (see p. 208, infra), 59¼ (vide sub Wendlyng, p. 176, infra).

XV.

The Number of Acres apparently appurtenant to a

Placea	Mansio	Man-erium	Messua-gium	Tene-mentum	Inhabi-tacio	Cota-gium	Parishes	Transcript page
acres	acres	acres	acres	acres	acres			
—	—	—	(30)	—	—	—	Querarlam . .	2
—	? 60	—	—	—	—	—	Choysell . .	4
—	—	—	60	—	—	—	Berwyk . .	,,
—	—	—	30	—	—	—	Hoo . . .	5
—	60	—	—	—	—	—	Myleham . .	6
—	—	—	(30)	—	—	—	Wendlyng . .	,,
—	—	—	—	40	—	—	Dunham Parva .	7
—	—	—	—	(30)	—	—	Holkeham . .	8
—	—	—	—	20	—	—	Styfkey . .	,,
—	—	—	—	37	—	—	Bylawe . .	9·
—	—	—	—	40	—	—	Haughboys Magna	,,
—	—	100	—	—	—	—	Haughboys Magna	,,
—	—	180	—	—	—	—	Buxston . .	,,
—	—	—	—	24	—	—	Calthorpe . .	10
—	—	—	16	16 [1]	—	—	Causton . .	,,
—	—	—	—	7	—	—	Blykelyng . .	,,
—	—	—	14	—	—	—	Aylesham . .	,,
—	—	—	—	30	—	—	Arpyngham .	,,
—	—	—	—	—	56	—	fflytcham . .	11
—	—	—	—	19	—	—	Gaywood . .	12
—	—	—	—	30	—	—	Hyllyngton .	,,
—	—	? 100	—	—	—	—	Donmer (Anmer) .	,,
—	—	—	—	40	—	—	Lynne . .	,,
—	—	—	20	—	—	—	Brabyngle . .	,,
—	—	—	—	80	—	—	Besthorpe . .	13
—	—	—	—	—[2]	—	—	Shropham . .	,,
—	—	—	—	(26)	—	—	Schadewell . .	14
—	—	—	—	16	—	—	Stalham . .	,,
—	—	—	—	30	—	—	North Walsham .	,,
—	—	—	—	70	—	—	North Walsham .	,,
120	—	—	—	—	—	—	Stoke . .	15
—	—	? 30	—	—	—	—	Thorp Parua .	16
—	—	—	27	—	—	—	Tetyshale . .	16
—	—	—	—	30	—	—	Tetyshale . .	,,
—	—	—	20	—	—	—	Emneth . .	,,
—	—	—	40	—	—	—	Hale . . .	17
—	—	—	40	—	—	—	Dunham . .	,,
—	—	—	—	—	—	—	Dereham . .	18
—	—	—	40	—	—	—	Hyngham . .	,,
—	—	—	30	—	—	—	Morley . .	,,
—	—	—	—	48	—	—	Bowthorp . .	19
—	—	—	—	18	—	—	Bowthorp . .	,,
—	—	50	—	—	—	—	Plompsted Magna	,,
—	—	20)	—	—	—	—	Bastwyke . .	20

[1] Also called messuagium.
[2] I purposely omit Shropham, where the MS. is plainly corrupt ; see p. 197

THE INQUISITION OF 1517

Summary

Average acreage assigned to a messuagium, $30\frac{7}{11}$ acres.
Average acreage assigned to a tenementum, $33\frac{33}{35}$ „
Average acreage assigned to a manerium 140 acres.

N.B.—This excludes the cases of Holkeham, Harpeley and Schadewell, (pp. 180, 190, 198) in the case of tenementa, and Anmer, Thorp Parua, Dereham, Plompsted Magna and Bastwyke in that of maneria (pp. 194, 203, 208, 211, 213).

XVI.—CASES IN WHICH MENTION IS MADE OF PLOUGHS PUT DOWN, BUT NOT OF HOUSES DECAYED OR PERSONS EVICTED

FOLIO		PLOUGHS	ACRES
15.	Brandeston	1	(60)
15.	Weston	1	(60)
15.	Belawe	1	(60)
19.	Plompsted Magna	1	50
19.	Poswyke	1	50
19.	Wytton	1	100
20.	Bastwyke	1	(120)
21.	Ketelston	$\frac{1}{2}$	26
21.	Ryborow	1	80
21.	Destreton	1	80
21.	Northbarsham	1	80
21.	Bagthorp	1	40
21.	Skulthorp	1	80
21.	Howton	1	80
22.	Estrudham	2	80
22.	Westrudham	1	40
22.	Burnham	$\frac{1}{2}$	40

As the Norfolk Return repeatedly gives, together with the number of ploughs put down, the number of houses decayed, the inference is that these cases of conversion really were unaccompanied by the destruction of houses or by evictions. The bracketed figures are areas inferred, on grounds given in the notes.

The average area assigned to an aratrum by the Norfolk Inquisition being, roughly, sixty acres, and to a messuagium or tenementum, thirty to thirty-three acres, the conversion of the above 1,126 acres of land into pasture would, upon this basis, imply the decay or ruin of about thirty-four houses. The number of ploughs returned as having been put down upon these 1,126 acres is seventeen. If, however, the average of sixty acres the aratrum, as given in the Norfolk Inquisition, be applied, the number of ploughs put down would be eighteen. This is evidence of the closeness of my inferences as to area to the actual facts.

At five persons to a messuagium or tenementum, which is slightly above the average in the Yorkshire Inquisition (p. 232, *infra*), this would give, supposing the destruction of the houses to have actually accompanied the putting down of the ploughs, a further displacement of population, in addition to the 380 already reckoned, of 170 persons. I think it most probable that in these cases the houses were not pulled down, nor the population evicted, because the Act 4 Hen. VII. c. 19 expressly provided that owners of houses let to farm with more than twenty acres of land should maintain houses and buildings necessary for tillage. Cp. *sub* ffienton, Yorks, p. 251, *infra*. The commission specially enjoined the commissioners to make return 'quot domus et edificia prosternuntur.' Introd. *Trans.* R.H.S., 1892, p. 174.

THE INQUISITION FOR NORFOLK [1]

(Lansd. MS. I. fo. 153–166.)

Fo. 153.
(Indorsed) Norff. } Inclausur.
Com.

'Norff.   ) Inquisicio capta apud Norwicum die lune ante
hundred de } ffestum sancti martini Episcopi in yeme Anno
humlyerde) Regni Regis henrici octaui nono coram domino
Johanne Abbate monasterii sancti Benedicti de hulmo Roberto
Clere milite & Willelmo Elys iurisperitore [sic] commissionariis
per comissionem domini Regis in comitatu Norffolk eis
directam constitutis ad capiendam Inquisicionem super villas
hamelettas & alia loca vastata & euacuata aut campos & terram
nuper in cultura & in pasturam ad greges ouium & aliorum
animalium mutatam racione aliquorum clausorum aut aliquorum
parcorum aut elargacionum aliquorum parcorum in comitatu
predicto citra ffestum sancti michaelis archangeli anno iiij^{to}
Regis henrici vij^{mi} nuper Regis Anglie vsque in hunc diem
factorum & erectorum per quod icominea [sic] & agricultura
totaliter omittuntur &c. per sacramenta Thome Germyn gent.
Thome alen gent. Thome appleyerd gent. willelmi Sheres
Roberti Manuell Johannis heruy senioris Johannis heruy
junioris Roberti Galered Roberti Kyng Johannis Nesshe
Walteri palmer Willelmi Webster Thome hubberd humfridi
Randolff Thome Rose & Johannis hemyng.

vt sequitur, videlicet.'

[1] The volume Lansd. i. has been more than once paginated. The first leaf, on which is the above indorsement, is numbered 124, and also 153, both in modern handwriting, and 'No. 54' apparently in contemporary script. It is generally cited as Lansd. i. 153, but I have given at the head of each entry the pagination of my transcript, to which references were made in the Introduction (*Trans. R.H.S.* 1892). In the notes to the text I have, for the convenience of the reader, made my references to the pagination of this volume.

The commission for Norfolk (Br. 'Cal.' ii. 3297) was composed of one ecclesiastic, one lawyer, and one knight : the last presumably representing the lay landowners. The commissioner described as the 'Abbas monasterii sancti Benedicti de Hulmo' was John Redinge, abbot (1510-1530) of St. Benet's in the Holm, or Hulme, in the city of Norwich (Blomefield's 'Hist. Norfolk,' iii. 548 ; Dugdale, 'Monast.' iii. 65).

Sir Robert Clere was an influential Norfolk landowner, whose name frequently recurs in Blomefield's History. Elys was at this time Recorder of Norwich (Br. 'Cal.' ii. 3829), and also a Norfolk landowner (Foss, v. 159). Cp. p. 182, *infra*, n. 2.

1517. INQUISITION INTO INCLOSURES

B. M. MS. Lansd. I. 154.

P. 2.—HUNDRED DE HUMLYARD. (HUMILIART, *Domesday*. *Now* HUMBLEYARD.)

P. 2.—*Brakon*. (*Braconash*, Blomef. Now *Bracon Ash*.)

'Quod Nicholaus Appulyard miles fecit vnum novum parcum in villa de Brakon in quo posuit lx acras terre in pastura que fuerunt in cultura post datum commissionis.'

The sixty acres represent an arable carucate in a three-field system.

'Item predictus Nicholaus inclusit & posuit in pasturam xxx^{ta} acras terre infra villam Est Carleton que fuerunt in cultura post datum commissionis.'

A virgate or villan holding.

Sir Nicholas Appulyard had been lord of the manor of Bracon Ash from 1473 to 1511 (Blomef. v. 84) ; also of East Carleton (*ibid.* 101). The inclosures were, therefore, not very recent.

In the MS. Brakon is placed in the margin against the Est Carleton inclosure, evidently by an error of the transcriber.

P. 2.—*Intewood.*
'Item Willelmus Jeny posuit in pastura in villa de Intewoode xxx^(tie) acras terre que fuerunt in cultura post datum commissionis.'
William Jeny, or Jenney, was lord of this manor from 1497 to 1512 (*ibid.* 40).

P. 2.—*Querarlam.* (Qu. *Ketteringham.*)
'Item in villa de Querarlam est vnum messuagium in decasu vocatum Syngere cum occupacione terre vnius aratri conuerse in pasturam que erat in cultura post tempus commissionis.'
I have failed to identify this place.
The point of departure here is the decay of the messuage.
I have taken the 'aratrum' here as equivalent to a virgate, or thirty acres. In this Inquisition upon Norfolk there are two cases in which an 'aratrum' is associated with a messuagium or tenementum, which appear to be convertible terms. In the first of these, Rysyngcastell, p. 194, the tenementum has an 'aratrum' of thirty acres attached. In the second, Morley, p. 209, the messuagium has the same.

P. 2.—HUNDRED DE HOLTE. (HOLT, *Domesday and modern spelling.*)

'Per Inquisicionem captam die veneris proximo post festum sancti Martini in yeme anno nono Regis Henrici VIII^(ui) coram prefatis commissionariis, videlicet.'

P. 2.—*Bayffeld.* (Now *Bayfield.*)
'Quod magister Tounesend armiger cepit ad firmam de magistro Yeluerton integrum manerium suum de Bayffeld & posuit in pasturam lx acras de terra manerii predicti que fuerunt in cultura post tempus commissionis.'
This appears to have been a case of consolidation of farms, of which the inclosure was an incident.
The Yelvertons were lords of the manor (Blomef. ix. 359).

P. 2.—*Egefeld.* (Now *Edgefield.*)
'Item Henricus Bakon clericus inclusit & posuit ad pas-

turam xxij acras terre in villa de Egefeld que fuerunt in cultura post tempus commissionis. Item ad clausum illum cepit quandam viam communem.'

'Item predictus Henricus Bakon posuit ad pasturam in villa predicta per estimacionem xviij acras terre que fuerunt in cultura post tempus commissionis.'

Two manors existed at Edgefield: one in the hands of the Willoughbys, the other Bynham Priory Manor, 'now called Edgefield Bacon's' (Blomef. ix. 384). It does not, however, appear that this manor became the property of the Bacon family till 1611, and then only by the accident of marriage. It may be conjectured that this was a case of farming by ecclesiastics upon Church lands, against which the Act 21 Hen. VIII. c. 13 was passed.

P. 2.—*Saxlyngham.* (*Saxelinghaham*, Domesday. Now *Saxlingham.*)

'Thomas fflete generosus posuit ad pasturam iuxta communiam in villa de Saxlyngham per estimacionem xl acras terre quas habet ad firmam de spryng de lanaham que fuerunt in pastura post tempus commissionis.'

'Lanaham,' *i.e.* Langham, in Domesday Langaham, (Blomef. ix. 408, note).

Neither fflete nor Spryng appear to have been lords of the manor here, which belonged to the Lynakers or Heydons (*ibid.* 434).

P. 3.—*Melton.* (I.e. *Melton Constable.*)

'Item Thomas Asseley habet ad firmam de magistro Wyndeham milite vnum le foldecourse iacens in villa de Melton cui posuit ad pasturam xl acras terre que fuerunt in cultura post tempus commissionis.'

The 'foldcourse' or 'foldage' was the right of lords of manors to set up pens in fields for the tenants' sheep, in order to gain the benefit of the manure. Apparently the tenant rented the right in respect of a certain field, and to this he added half an arable carucate in a two-field course.

Thomas Astley was lord of one of the manors here,

and Thomas Wyndham of another (Blomef. ix. 419, 422).

P. 3.—HUNDRED DE ESTEFLEGGE & WESTFLEGGE.

'Per Inquisicionem captam quinto die Novembris anno Regis Henrici VIII^{ui} nono coram prefatis commissionariis: videlicet.'

P. 3.—*Martham.*

'Quod prior de Norwic inclusit xl acras terre arrabilis in Martham que arate fuerunt infra tempus commissionis & nunc iacent in pasturam [*sic*].'

The manor of Martham passed into the hands of the Priors of Norwich in the 33 H. III. (Blomef. xi. 169). Note the inclosure of forty acres as before.

P. 3.—*West Somerton.*

'Item prior de Butley inclusit xvj acras terre arrabilis in Westsomerton que arate fuerunt infra tempus commissionis et nunc iacent in pasturam.'

This was part of the barony of Richmond held by the Prior of Butley since *temp.* Richard I. (Blomef. xi. 189).

'Prior de Butley inclusit xvj acras terre arrabilis in Westsomerton.' An explanation of the area of sixteen acres is given by Canon Isaac Taylor in 'Notes and Queries,' 7th ser. vol. ii. p. 481. He is of opinion that it indicates that a change has taken place from a two-field to a three-field course. A two-field carucate[1] was, fallow included, 160 acres. By the Anglicus numerus, or long hundred of six score to the hundred, this would be 192 acres. The division of 192 acres into three fields, instead of two,' would give a carucate of sixty-four acres in each field.' The sixteen acres here inclosed would be a bovate from each of the tillage carucates of sixty-four acres.

[1] It must be borne in mind that the word 'carucate' was used in two senses, sometimes for the ancient term 'hide,' normally of 120 acres, all of which in turn came under the plough, sometimes of the actual tillage areas. Cf. p. 190, *infra.*

P. 3.—HUNDRED DE LODDON & KNAVERYNG. (*Domesday*, LOTHINGA, LOTHNINGA, LOTNINGA, LODDINGA. *Now* LODDON. — *Domesday*, CLAVELINGA, CLAVERNICA, GNAVERINGA. *Now* CLAVERING.)

'Per Inquisicionem captam quinto die Novembris anno nono Regis Henrici VIII^{ui} coram prefatis commissionariis, videlicet.'

'Quod infra villam de Loddon Doctor Hare fecit vnum clausum de xl acris infra tempus commissionis que diu antea fuerunt in pastura & non arate, quodquidem clausum dictus doctor habet ad firmam de abbate de langley.'

This is probably another case of clerical farming. Observe that it is an inclosure for the sake of several pasture, not for conversion from arable to pasture. See *sub* Bowthorp, p. 210, *infra*.

P. 3.—*Alby*. (*Aldeburei*, Domesday. *Aldby* or *Aldeburgh*, Blomef. Now *Aldby*.)

'Item Domina Morley fecit vnum clausum continens iiij^{xx} acras in Alby quarum xl acre arantur & quadraginta acre iacent in pastura.'

Inclosure of a whole arable carucate in a two-field manor.

The manor was at this time in the hands of the Morleys (Blomef. viii. 4). For another inclosure by Lady Morley see Buxston, p. 185, *infra*.

P. 3.—*Wheteacreburgh*. (*Wateaker*, Domesday. *Whetacre*, Blomef. Now *Wheatacre*.)

'Item in Wheteacreburgh Willelmus Dominus Wylloughby fecit vnum clausum de xl acris infra tempus commissionis que arate fuerunt infra dictum tempus & iam ponuntur in pasturam.'

Inclosure of forty acres, as before.

The Willoughbys were lords of the manor (Blomef. viii. 65).

P. 3.—*Mondambrome*. (*Mundaham*, Domesday. Now *Mundham*.)

'Item in Mondambrome Ricardus Sponer fecit vnum

clausum de xxx acris infra tempus commissionis infra quod tempus arate fuerunt et nunc iacent in pastura.'

Note the inclosure of a virgate or villan holding. This was a recent inclosure, as Richard Sponer, who was lord of the manor, did not come into the property till 1514 (Blomef. x. 169).

P. 4.—HUNDRED DE SMYTHDON. (SMETHEDUNA, *Domesday. Now* SMITHDON.)

' Per Inquisicionem captam quinto die Novembris anno nono Regis Henrici VIII^{ui} coram prefatis commissionariis, videlicet.'

P. 4.—*Choysell.* (Now *Choseley.*)

' Quod infra villam de Choysell mansiones quondam Johannis Wyllyers deuastantur & inhabitantes in eisdem recesserunt & pertinentes ad easdem mansiones ccc acre terre quarum xxx^{ta} acre sunt arabiles et residue in pastura.'

There were two manors here, one still called Willy's Manor, the other Burton Lazars Manor. John Willy, here mentioned, sold this manor with 543 acres of land to Sir Thomas Lovell, K.G., in 1513 (Blomef. x. 349).

' Item mansiones de Burton Lazar in villa predicta deuastantur, et inhabitantes ibidem recesserunt et spectant ad easdem mansiones ccc acre terre quarum lx arantur; residue vero sunt in pastura et per decasum predictum ecclesia ibidem decidit.'

The hospital of Burton Lazar in Leicestershire held the lordship of this manor (Blomef. x. 348). It does not appear for what purpose these 'mansiones' were maintained.

In the only other case in the Norfolk Inquisition in which 'mansio' by itself occurs it is associated with sixty acres, *i.e.* an 'aratrum;' see *sub* Wendlyng, p. 176, *infra*. I therefore infer that ten houses in all were pulled down in this place.

The word 'mansiones' is noticeable. The word 'mansio' was specially used of a priest's house, as in Scotland to-day the word 'manse.' See the case of Parva Cockern, Herefordshire. But Digby ('Hist. of Law of Real Property,' 4th edit. p. 44) identifies it with manerium (cf. *sub* Thorp Parua, p. 203, *infra*). See Du Cange, ed. Favre, *s. v.* The 300 acres might suggest ten virgates, or villans' holdings, of thirty acres. The total number of mansiones then destroyed would be twenty. But the connexion of one of these manors with a hospital seems to point in another direction. At Myleham (p. 174, *infra*) sixty acres were attached to a 'mansio.'

'Ecclesia ibidem decidit;' and remains ruined (Blomef. *ibid.*).

P. 4.—*Hecham.* (So in Domesday. In Blomefield, *Hitcham.* Now *Heacham.*)

'Item Johannes Wyngfeld clericus inclusit lx acras terre quondam arrabilis & iam in pastura infra villam de Hecham.

The Wyngfelds were lords of the manor. This John was not incumbent of the parish, but apparently a younger son. (See Blomef. x. 309, ix. 482.) It was not, therefore, properly a case of ecclesiastical inclosure.

P. 4.—*Stanowe.* (*Stanho*, Domesday. In Blomefield, *Stanhow.* Now *Stanhoe.*)

'Rogerus Tounesend armiger convertit cxx acras terre arabilis in pasturam ouium infra villam de Stanowe post tempus commissionis.'

There were two manors here, one called Marshe's, or the King's Manor, the other Calthorp's Manor. Blomefield (x. 384) states that the Townsends did not become lords of Calthorp's Manor till 1583. R. T. must therefore have been a freeholder or a tenant.

P. 4.—*Honston.* (*Hunestanestuna*, Domesday. Now *Hunstanton.*)

'Rogerus Strange miles elargauit parcum suum et cepit vnam peciam terre arrabilis continentem xvj acras et iam in manibus Thome Strange Armigeri infra villam de honston.'

The family of Strange or Lestrange were lords of the manor. This incloser had died in 1506 (Blomef. x. 318). This is indicated by the 'iam in manibus Thome Strange,' nephew of Roger (*ibid.*).

For an explanation of the xvj acres see *sub* West Somerton, p. 166, *supra*.

P. 4.—*Snethysham*. (In Blomefield, *Snettesham*. Now *Snettisham*.)

'Item lx acre terre arabilis iam in manibus Edwardi Bedyngfeld armigeri infra villam de Snethysham ponuntur in pasturam per ingrossamentum Warren Regis.'

Qu. Edmundi. In 1510 Henry VIII. demised to Edmund Bedingfeld of Oxburgh the site of this manor, with all the houses, sheepcotes, and profits of the conies, &c., for seven years, the property belonging to the duchy of Lancaster (Blomef. x. 372). The phrase 'iam in manibus' indicates a lessee.

Rabbits, which had been scarce in the middle ages, were now beginning to multiply to such an extent as to be a nuisance (Rogers, 'Hist. Ag.' iv. 717, and 2 & 3 Phil. & Mary, c. 2, § 3; cf. Russell's 'Kett's Rebellion,' p. 54).

P. 4.—*Stanehewe*. (I.e. *Stanowe*, vide supra.)

'Item Rogerus Tounesend armiger conuertit lx acras terre arrabilis in Stanehewe in pasturam ouium que arate fuerunt infra tempus commissionis.'

The same Roger Townesend converts sixty acres. This entry is misplaced.

P. 4.—*Berwyk*. (In Blomefield, *Berwick Magna*. Now *Great Barwick*.)

'Item Thomas Thorysby decidere permisit vnum messuagium in Barwyk & lx acras terre que arate fuerunt iam ponuntur in pasturam.'

As to T. T. see *supra*, pp. 135, 136, 153, 154, and *infra*, p. 192, from which last entry it appears that there were two of the name, presumably father and son.

P. 4.—*Bekenham*. (In Blomefield, *New Bukenham*. Now *New Buckenham*.)

'Item prior de Bekenham posuit ad pasturam lx acras terre que arate fuerunt.'

Bekenham in the margin is really a clerical error. The reference is still to Berwyk, of which the manor was called Buckenham Priory Manor (Blomef. x. 296). This explains

'Item prior de Bekenham,' that priory holding the lordship of the manor till the Dissolution.

P. 5.—HUNDRED DE LAUNDYCHE. (LAWENDIC, *Domesday*. LAUNDITCH, *Blomefield*.)

'Per Inquisicionem captam die Jouis proximo post festum sancti Martini in yeme anno nono Regis Henrici VIII^{ui} coram prefatis commissionariis, videlicet.'

P. 5.—*Hoo*. (In Blomefield, *How*.)

'Quod Johannes Pygeon posuit ad pasturam ouium xxx^{ta} acras terre in hoo que nuper arate fuerunt racione cuius messuagium suum ibidem decidit.'

I.e. a villan holding, one-fourth of the hide of 120 acres. The lord of the manor was the Bishop of Ely (Blomef. x. 49).

P. 5.—*Betele*. (*Betely*, Blomefield. Now *Beetley*.)

'Item Willelmus Soper clericus posuit ad pasturam ouium xlv acras terre in Betele que nuper arate fuerunt infra tempus commissionis.'

This manor at that time belonged to the see of Norwich. The living was a rectory. It does not appear who was rector at this time, but the incloser was described as 'clericus.' It looks as though he were a tenant of the Bishop, and that this was a case of ecclesiastical farming.

P. 5.—*North Elynham*. (*Elmenham*, Domesday. Now *Elmham*.)

'Item Simon Dykman fecit inclausuras continentes xxxvij acras terre in North Elynham infra tempus huius commissionis & tempore inclausure erant in cultura.'

This is a variation from the common form. It indicates either that the inclosures remained in cultivation or that there is no evidence of the present condition of the ground: probably the former (see *sub* R. Martyn, *infra*). The inclosures were evidently of separate strips. In the case of Bylawe, p. 185, *infra*, it will be seen that a 'tenementum' accompanies 37 acres.

P. 5.—*North Elynham*.

'Johannes Soham fecit de nouo vnum clausum continentem xxvj acras terre in North Elynham infra tempus huius commissionis & tempore inclausure illius xx^{ti} acre inde fuerunt in cultura.'

This phrase 'fecit de nouo' suggests that the Act of 1515 (see Introduction in 'Trans. R.H.S.' 1892, p. 192) had been enforced against him. As to this area, see Ketelston, p. 216, *infra*.

Qu. John Soham of Beetley. See Carthew's 'Hundred of Launditch,' iii. 61.

'Item Rogerus Martyn gentylman fecit vnum clausum continentem xvj acras terre in North Elynham infra tempus commissionis & tempore inclausure fuerunt in cultura.'

Sixteen acres. See note on West Somerton, p. 166, *supra*.

'Item dictus Rogerus posuit ad pasturam ouium xxx^{ta} acras terre que fuerunt in cultura infra tempus commissionis.'

I.e. a virgate. This form shows that the former recitals 'tempore inclausure erant in cultura' are intended to convey that the inclosed land remains arable still. It is to be observed that as all these inclosures are in the same manor, and the last two by the same person, there could be no absence of evidence as to the existing state of the land.

The manor of North Elynham belonged to the see of Norwich (Blomef. ix. 487–8). This does not, however, appear from the Inquisition.[1] Roger Martyn was a tenant of the manor (Carthew's 'Hundred of Launditch', 1879, iii. 101).

P. 5.—*Bayselee*. (Qu. *Brisley*.)

'Item Robertus Markaunt inclusit xvj acras terre infra

[1] Gaird. *L. & P.* XIII. i. 1519, 5. Sir Thos. Crumwell, lord Crumwell, keeper of the Privy Seal. Confirmation of his estate in the manors of Northelenham alias Northelmham and Beteley, Norf., with lands in Northelmeham, Beteley, Burgrave and Brisley, Norf., which belonged to the bishopric of Norwich, and were assured to him in tail male by an Act of Parliament 28 Hen. VIII.

Also grant in fee simple of the reversion of the premises with all liberties and franchises enjoyed therein by Richard, Bp. of Norwich, and licence to alienate them to Thos. duke of Norfolk, earl marshal of England. Del. Westm., 4 July, 30, Hen. VIII.—*S. B. Pat.* p. 2, m. 16.

tempus commissionis & tempore inclausure fuerunt in cultura in Bayselee.'

For this area see *sub* West Somerton, p. 166, *supra*.

'Item Johannes att hoo inclusit xxvj acras infra tempus commissionis & tempore inclausure fuerunt in cultura.'

This area constantly occurs, and in Ketelston it is explicitly stated to be a 'dimidium aratrum;' see p. 216, *infra*.

The manor of Brisley belonged to the see of Norwich (Blomef. ix. 468).

P. 5.—*Gatelee*. (In Blomefield, *Gateley*. Now *Gately*.)

'Item Rogerus Martyn gentylman inclusit de nouo xxiiij^{or} acras in Gatele infra tempus commissionis & tempore inclausure fuerunt in cultura.'

On the phrase 'de nouo' see *sub* North Elynham, p. 172, *supra*.

Twenty-four acres would be a bovate of a two-field manor of 160 acres by the great hundred, *i.e.* 192 acres. Cp. *infra*, p. 186, *sub* Calthorpe.

P. 6.—*Gatelee*.

'Item Ricardus Euerard inclusit xxvj acras terre in Gatelee infra tempus commissionis & tempore inclausure fuerunt in cultura.'

For observations on 'de nouo' see *sub* North Elynham, p. 172, *supra*. On the area see *sub* Ketelston, p. 216, *infra*.

'Idem Ricardus firmarius domini ibidem habet & occupat xxx^{ta} acras terre in Gatelee que fuerunt in cultura per septem annos tunc preteritos.'

The significance of the addition 'per septem annos tunc preteritos' is not quite apparent. It possibly refers to the three-field course and is intended to convey that though lying fallow at the time of inclosure it had been arable in the regular rotation, so that 'per' means 'in the course of, and marks the furthest retrospective limit of time within which the inclosure must have taken place. The Act of 1515 provided that land turned to pasture since the beginning of that Parliament (*i.e.* 1515) should be reconverted to tillage.

There appear to have been three manors here, one of which belonged to the see of Norwich (Blomef. ix. 504).

The phrase 'firmarius domini' indicates that this was the Bishop's manor, and that the incloser was a cleric; see *sub* Ryborow, p. 216, *infra*.

P. 6.—*Myleham*. (*Mileham*, Blomefield.)

'Item Christoferus Crowe inclusit iiij^{xx} acras terre in Myleham in ij diversis clausuris infra tempus commissionis & tempore inclausure fuerunt in pastura.'

The family of Crowe were landowners here and at a later date lords of one of the two manors. But at this time the manors belonged to the Arundel and Capel families (Blomef. x. 21).

Here, as in the preceding entries, the language points to inclosure simply, and not to conversion to pasture. Note the following entry.

'Item Georgius Willoughby armiger posuit ad pasturam per estimacionem lx^{ta} acras terre in Milham que fuerunt in cultura per nouem annos proxime elapsos racione cuius vna mansio vocata Dabys decidit.'

As to the significance of 'per nouem annos' see preceding page, *sub* Gatelee.

Note, sixty acres to a mansio, and see *sub* Choysell, p. 168, *supra*.

'Item ffranciscus Calybutt generosus fecit vnum clausum continentem xviij acras terre in Myleham infra tempus huius commissionis & tempore inclausure fuerunt in cultura.'

The bovate of a carucate of 120 acres by the long hundred, *i.e.* 144 acres in a three-field course, would give 18 acres. It is possible that carucates by either computation coexisted in a large manor such as Myleham.

P. 6.—*Tytelyshale*. (*Titeshala*, Domesday. *Titleshale* Blomefield. Now *Tittleshall*.)

'Item Henricus ffermour generosus inclusit vnum clausum continentem xl acras terre in Tytelyshale anno preterito & tunc erant in cultura.'

This manor belonged to the priory of Coxford. 'In the

7th of Henry VIII. the prior had sixty acres of pasture lying in Pike-Hall pasture and New-Hall pasture, with common and shack thereto belonging, all demised to Henry Farmer, gent., of East Barsham' (Blomef. x. 65).

This lease of permanent pasture is quite compatible with the freehold ownership or copyhold tenancy of the enclosed forty acres. As to the respective rights of the lord and tenants of a manor to pasture see Introduction,' Trans. R.H.S.' 1892, pp. 254, 255.

P. 6.—*Kempston*. (*Kempston*, Blomefield. Now *Kempstone*.)

'Item Prior de Castellacre inclusit xij^m acras terre in Kempston infra tempus huius commissionis & tempore inclausure fuerunt in cultura.'

'Idem prior occupat iiij^{xx} acras terre in Kempston positas in pasturam ouium que fuerunt in cultura per xx^{ti} annos tunc preteritos et infra tempus huius commissionis.'

'Occupat,' *i.e.* farms. Other examples of his agricultural operations are to be found at Wendlyng and Bagthorp, *infra*.

This entry shows the meaning of the recital 'infra tempus huius commissionis' to mean since Michaelmas 4 Hen. VII., and not since the issue of the letters of commission.

The manor belonged to the Priors of Castleacre (Blomef. ix. 523).

P. 6.—*Wendlyng*.

'Item Prior de Castellacre infra spacium [blank in MS.] annorum proxime preteritorum & infra tempore [*sic*] huius commissionis posuit tantas terras in pasturam in Wendlyng quantis Thomas haye sustentauit vnum sufficiens aratrum racione cuius messuagia pro iconomia manerii de heryngesbaugh [*sic*] sunt multum ruinosa.'

There are fifteen cases in the Norfolk Inquisition in which areas are specifically mentioned as equivalent to an 'aratrum.' Of these the lowest is twenty acres at Dereham (p. 208). It is doubtful, however, whether the twenty acres there mentioned are represented to constitute the entire acreage of the manerium. The average of the fifteen cases gives a little short of fifty-seven acres to an 'aratrum.' Omitting the Dereham case, the fourteen remaining give rather more than $59\frac{3}{4}$ acres, *i.e.* practically sixty acres to an 'aratrum.'

On the other hand, there are twelve cases in which areas of land are assigned to a messuagium. These give an average of $30\frac{7}{11}$ acres; in short, as nearly as possible, thirty acres or a virgate. In this case, then, the messuagia to maintain the average aratrum of fifty-seven or sixty acres would be two in number, and I have taken the 'aratrum' therefore as equivalent to two virgates, and in round figures as sixty acres.

Note the phrase 'messuagia pro iconomia manerii de heryngeshaugh.' In the Norfolk Inquisition there are five cases of maneria associated with specific areas: see p. 161, *supra*. One of these cases, Dereham, has been already mentioned, and may be struck out for this purpose. In the three cases, Anmer, Thorp Parva and Plompsted Magna, the 100 acres, the thirty and the fifty acres appear to be only part of the land belonging to the manerium. The remaining two cases give 280 acres in all, or an average of 140 acres to a manerium. We shall not be far wrong, then, in taking the average area of a manerium as the 120 acres of a three-course carucate or hide. In the case of Wendlyng the 'messuagia pro iconomia manerii' would not be likely to have appurtenant to them the whole land of a manerium. The estimate of sixty acres, therefore, to the aratrum is from this point of view not improbable.

Herringshaugh was the name of the manor here belonging to the Priory of Castleacre (Blomef. x. 88 ; Carthew, iv. 470).

P. 7.—*Rougham.*

'Item Willelmus Yelverton generosus posuit ad pasturam ouium cc acras terre in Rougham que fuerunt in cultura infra tempus commissionis.'

The Yelvertons were lords of the manor (Blomef. x. 31). This incloser appears to have been Sir William Yelverton. K.B., Judge of the King's Bench, who lived until 1518 ; unless his grandson, William Yelverton, who succeeded to the property in that year, managed it as heir; which is the more probable. This W. Y., it is to be observed, was also a learned lawyer (see Carthew, ii. 494).

P. 7.—*Wesenham.*

'Item Ricardus Southwell armiger posuit ad pasturam ouium iiij^{xx} acras terre in Wesenham que fuerunt in cultura citra tempus commissionis.'

This manor belonged to the Priory of Castleacre, and came to the Southwells at the Dissolution (Blomef. x. 77).

P. 7.—*Dunham Parua.*

'Item Ricardus Kokatt posuit xl acras terre in pasturam ouium racione cuius tenementum suum in Dunham parua prorsus destruitur et decidit.'

I.e. forty acres to a tenementum. According to Digby, tenementum generally implied a freehold ('Hist. of Law of Real Property,' 4th ed. p. 72, n. 5; *sed qu.* unless 'liberum' is expressed.

'Item Thomas Cokett gent. posuit & occupat clx acras terre in pasturam.'

Thomas Coket was lord of this manor in 1571 (Blomef. ix. 479).

'Posuit & occupat,' *i.e.* laid them down in pasture as lord of the manor, and now farms them himself (*occupat*).

P. 7.—*ffraunsham Magna.*

'Item Willelmus Stede fecit vnum clausum in ffraunsham magna continentem xviij acras.'

On this number see *sub* Myleham, *supra.*

'Item Henricus Toly fecit vnum clausum in ffraunsham magna continentem xvj acras terre que fuerunt in cultura infra tempus commissionis.'

On this area see *sub* West Somerton. Both this and the area of eighteen acres indicate a three-field manor.

Neither of the inclosers' names appears in Blomefield as lord of the manors here, which were in lay hands (ix. 496-7).

P. 7.—*Skernyng.* (Now *Scarning.*)

'Item Abbas de Wendlyng fecit vnum clausum in Skernyng continentem xl acras terre circa vj annos preteritos &

infra tempus huius commissionis & tempore facture clausi predicti dicte terre fuerunt in cultura.'

The Abbey had the lordship of one of the manors of this place. Cf. p. 208, *infra*.

'Thomas hay fecit vnum clausum in Skernyng continentem xviij acras sex annos preteritos & tunc erant in cultura.'

As to this number see above, p. 174, *sub* Myleham. The name of the incloser occurs as that of a displaced tenant at Wendlyng, p. 175, *supra*.

'Item Johannes Bullok inclusit xxv acras terre in diuersis clausis in Skernyng que fuerunt in cultura circa xij annos preteritos et iam in pastura.'

'Item Thomas Cony de Est Derham inclusit xix acras terre in Skernyng circa xvj annos preteritos & tunc erant in cultura.'

It must be remembered that there were three manors in Scarning, viz. Wendlyng Abbey manor, Waltham Abbey manor, and Drayton Hall manor.

Bullok's case is the only case of conversion to pasture.

P. 7.—*Colkryke*. (*Colechircha*, Domesday. Now *Colkirk*.)

'Item Robertus Dorrant posuit in pasturam ouium xxvj acras terre in Colkryke que nuper fuerunt in cultura.'

For this area see *sub* Ketelston, p. 216, *infra*.

'Item idem Robertus inclusit xvj acras terre in Colkryke vij annos preteritos que tunc erant in cultura.'

As to this number see *sub* West Somerton, p. 166, *supra*.

This last is not a case of inclosing for pasture.

'Item Thomas holland posuit ad pasturam ouium xxx acras terre in Colkrik que nuper fuerunt in cultura.'

I.e. a virgate: see *sub* Hoo, p. 171, *supra*; indicative of a three-field system.

By an Inquisition of 4 Ed. III. it appears that the manor had 160 acres of arable land, which would indicate at that time a two-field system (Blomef. ix. 473).

Neither of the above names appears to have been the name of lords of the manor, which belonged to the Bourchiers (*ibid.*).

P. 8.—*Colkryk*.

'Item Nicholas Barsham posuit ad pasturam ouium xliij acras terre in Colkryk que nuper fuerunt in cultura.'

This number has not occurred before.

P. 8.—*Hornyngtoft*. (Now *Horningtoft*.)

'Item Robertus Markaunt inclusit xxx acras terre in hornyngtofte infra tempus huius commissionis que tempore inclausure fuerunt in cultura.'

I.e. a virgate in a three-field manor.

This manor belonged to the family of Castell (Blomef. ix. 521).

P. 8.—*Oxwyk*. (Now *Oxwick*.)

'Item Johannes heydon miles posuit ad pasturam ouium xxx^{ta} acras terre in Oxwyk que citra decem annos fuerunt in cultura.'

This is a case of inclosure and conversion to pasture by the lord of the manor. (See Blomef. ix. 507.)

P. 8.—HUNDRED DE NORTHGRENOW. (GRENEHOW, *Domesday*. GREENHOW, *Blomef.* Now GREENHOE NORTH HUNDRED.)

'Per Inquisicionem captam die Martis proximo post festum sancti Martini Episcopi in yeme anno nono Regis henrici VIII^{ui} coram prefatis commissionariis, videlicet.'

P. 8.—*Holkeham*. (Now *Holkham.*)

'Quod Thomas Sedeney & Johannes Smyth habent ad firmam de Thoma Bolen milite cc acras terre in villa de holkeham que fuerunt in cultura citra tempus huius commissionis & diuersa tenementa eisdem terris pertinentia occasione predicta sunt in decasu.'

This is not a case of conversion to pasture, as is evident from the next entry, but of consolidation of holdings. It was, in fact, an infraction of the statute of 1488 (see Introduction, 'Trans. R. H. S.' 1892, pp. 172, 173); hence a subject for the commission's inquiry.

The Boleyns were lords of one of the manors here (Blomef. ix. 232).

'Item Avereyus Grykys posuit ad pasturam ouium c acras que fuerunt in cultura citra tempus commissionis.'

In 1538 Avery Gryggs, Esq., was returned to have held lately the quarter of a fee of the Bishop of Norwich (*ibid.* 235).

'Item Johannes Newgate posuit ad pasturam ouium xxx acras terre que fuerunt in cultura citra tempus commissionis.'

I.e. a virgate.

The Priories of Peterstone and Walsingham also owned land here, and as this case of inclosure is not coupled with the first, I infer it to be on ecclesiastical land. (See Blomef. ix. 234–5.)

It will be observed that though the first entry of 200 acres gives no indication of the system of cultivation, the total of these inclosures is 330 acres or eleven villans' holdings on a three-field manor. I therefore reckon the 'diuersa tenementa' of the first entry at six, which would account for 180 acres of the consolidated holding. The number of six may also be arrived at by another process. In the Norfolk Inquisition eighteen cases occur (Harpeley, Holkeham and Schadewell being excluded) of areas specifically mentioned as appurtenant to a tenementum : see p. 161, *supra*. The average area from these cases is a fraction over thirty-three acres. The 200 acres divided by thirty-three give six as the number of tenementa destroyed by the inclosure.

P. 8.—*Warham*.

'Item Willelmus Newby posuit ad pasturam ouium xxx^{ta} acras terre in villa de Warham que fuerunt in cultura citra tempus commissionis.'

I.e. a virgate.

'Item Johannes Stede posuit ad pasturam ouium iiij^{xx}acras terre in dicta villa de Warham que fuerunt in cultura citra tempus commissionis.'

The lord of this manor of Warham-Hales in the 3rd and 4th Philip & Mary, John Appleyard, Esq., conveyed it as containing 400 acres of land, 40 of pasture, 200 of moor, 200 of marsh, 20 of wood and 200 of heath (Blomef. ix. 264).

THE INQUISITION OF 1517   181

P. 8.—*Styfkey.* (*Stuiceai*, Domesday. *Stiockey*, Blomefield. Now *Stiffkey*.)

'Item Christoferus [blank in MS.] habet in villa de Styfkey vnum tenementum cum xx^{ti} acris terre que fuerunt in cultura citra tempus commissionis & iam tenementum illud decidit & terra conuertitur in pasturam ouium.'

Note, twenty acres to a tenementum.

The twenty acres, an area that has not occurred before, indicates a virgate, or villan holding, of the fourth of a hide in a two-field manor.

It is to be observed that by the statute of 4 Hen. VII. c. 19 all houses let to farm with twenty acres of land or more were to be maintained. (See Introduction, 'Trans. R. H. S.' 1892, pp. 172, 173.)

The two manors at Styfkey belonged to the Winter and Boleyn families (Blomef. ix. 251-2).

P. 8.—*Hyndryngham.* (Now *Hindringham*.)

'Item prior de Norwich posuit ad pasturam ouium c acras terre iuxta latus communie in hyndringham que fuerunt in cultura citra tempus commissionis.'

The Chapter of Norwich were lords of one of the manors here.

'Item Henricus ffermer & Thomas Wylby posuerunt ad pasturam ouium xx^{ti} acras terre.'

Besides the Chapter of Norwich's manor there was another manor here called Wilby's Manor, of which the family of Wilby held a part (Blomef. ix. 228). Henry Fermor was a landlord of the neighbourhood, and probably joint lord of this manor (see Blomef. vii. 55 &c.). At a later date (1520) we find 'Henry Fermor, gent.' encroaching upon the 'inhabitants' of Fakenham (MS. R. O. Star Ch. Proc. vol. xv. 11-13).

Complaint against Henry Fermor, gent., by the tenants of the lordship of Fakenham.

    1. He purchased lands[1] from R. Trynne, including a foldcourse of 300 sheep, and inclosed them and stopped up 'comen weyn,' all at Tharpland,

Quantity torn out.

within the lordship. He also let down the houses.

2. Has erected within the towns of Therplond and Fakenham aforesaid a foldcourse of 1,000 ewes, 'ther pasturying the shak and the comen of the seid town of Fakenham to the somme of c acres of lond bettyr werth in value than cc acres of pasture within the seid townes ... by the space of xiij yeres last past.'

3. He has pastured the said sheep 'in shake tyme fro the ffest of Seynt michell vnto the ffest of the invencion of the holie crosse.'

4. He has pastured 800 sheep 'goying within a ffoldcourse ... within the town of Skulthorpe [1] annexed to the ffeldes of ffakenham,' although he only owns five acres of land there.

5. He impounds their sheep and cattle.

6. Has let houses to poor men without land, and encourages them to commit waste, saying that 'the seid londes be out of the statute of punysshment for wast, whereas thei be holden of our souereygn the kyng as ancient demesne in base and the custome is the contrarie.'

Commission issued to Sir John Heydon, William Elyce a Baron of the Exchequer,[2] Roger Townesend armiger, and John Spylman gentilman : dated 24 August anno 12 from Harlyng.

(13.) Finding of the jury.

1. That Herry ffermour hath inclosed [3] acres of lond within 2 closes and has stopped up a common way and inclosed parcel of common of the Township of Thorplond.

2. Has stopped up a highway.

---

[1] Cp. *sub* Skulthorp, p. 217, *infra*.
[2] The mention of Elyce as a Baron of the Exchequer in 1520 clears up a point of difficulty in his biography. 'Dugdale,' says Foss ('Judges of England,' v. 159) 'defers his appointment till Michaelmas, 1527, but positive evidence exists of his holding the office four years before.' It can now be antedated three years further.   [3] Left blank in MS.

3. 'Doth occupie with his fflok of shepe the comen of ffakenham called the heth to the gret hurt of the seid Township of ffakenham.'
4. Keeps enclosed a common which he bought, and stops a common way.
5. He also takes shak within the fields of Fakenham with his flock there and in the fields of Skulthorp with another flock there.
6. Has kept the king's tenants' sheep out of the pastures or charged them 4*d*.
7. Has allowed a number of houses to decay.
8. Has sold a number of houses 'without eny lond with the seid plowes wherefor those men that hath bowght the seid plowes [*sic*] shall not be able to kepe up the seid plowes to the destruccion of the said town.' [1]

P. 8.—*Thyrysforth*. (Now *Thursford*.)

'Item Johannes Shelton miles posuit ad pasturam xxx acras terre in Thyrysforth que fuerunt in cultura citra tempus commissionis.'

I.e. an ordinary virgate. This was an inclosure by the lord of the manor. (See Blomef. ix. 258.)

P. 9.—*Wytton*. (Now *Wighton*.)

'Item Cristoferus Gyggs posuit ad pasturam ouium iiij^{xx} acras terre in Wyton que fuerunt in cultura citra tempus commissionis.'

'Item Henricus ffermer posuit ad pasturam ouium xl acras terre in Wytton que fuerunt in cultura citra tempus commissionis.'

As both these areas are recited to have been 'in cultura, the entries point to a two-field manor.

C. G. was lord of the manor (Blomef. ix. 206).

As to Henry Fermor see note to Hyndryngham.

P. 9.—*Walsyngham Magna*. (*Great* or *Old Walsingham*, Blomefield.)

'Item Prior de Walsyngham posuit ad pasturam ouium lx

[1] The judgments of the Court of Star Chamber for this period have perished.

acras terre in le Westfeld de Walsyngham Magna que fuerunt in cultura citra tempus commissionis.'

'Idem prior posuit ad pasturam in le Estfeld lx acras terre que fuerunt in cultura citra tempus commissionis.'

'Item Jacobus Gresham inclusit duas acras de communia de Walsyngham quod ville est magna [sic !] nocumento.'

For James Gresham of Little Walsingham see Burgon, 'Life and Times of Gresham,' i. 460.

The lords of the two manors here were the Prior of Bynham and the Crown (Blomef. lx. 267·9). The probability is that the Prior of Walsingham was tenant of the ecclesiastical lordship.

P. 9.—*Hoveton.* (Now *Houghton.*)

'Item Prior de Walsyngham posuit ad pasturam iuxta communiam in hoveton xl acras terre quas habet ad firmam de domino Roos.'

Another case of ecclesiastical farming (see *sub* Egefield, p. 165, *supra*).

This Prior of Walsingham was evidently a farmer on a considerable scale (see last entry).

One of the manors was called Ross's Manor (Blomef. ix. 245).

P. 9.—HUNDRED DE SOUTHARPYNHAM. (ERPINCHAM SUD, *Domesday.* Now SOUTH ERPINGHAM.)

'Per Inquisicionem captam die Martis proximo post ffestum sancti Martini anno nono Regis henrici viij^{ul} coram prefatis commissionaris, videlicet.'

P. 9.—*Colteshale.* (*Cokershala*, Domesday. *Colteshall*, Blomefield. Now *Coltishall.*)

'Quod Stephanus Bolte habet vnum messuagium cum xxv acris terre in Colsale que fuerunt in cultura citra tempus commissionis & tenementum illud decidit.'

It does not appear that this was a case of inclosure for pasture or otherwise. It was, in accordance with the tenour of the commission, a return of a decayed house with more than twenty acres of land. I have taken the twenty-five acres as inclosed simply. The inhabitants of this village were enfranchised by Henry III. in 1231. (See Blomef. vi. 303.)

The lordship of the manor belonged to King's College, Cambridge (*ibid.* 304).

P. 9.—*Bylawe.* (*Belaga*, Domesday. *Belagh*, Blomefield. Now *Belaugh.*)

'Item Alicia pope vidua habet tenementum cum xxxvij acris terre in Bylawe que ponebantur ad pasturam per Robertum Harryson citra tempus commissionis.'

The lordship of the manor was in the Abbey of St. Bennet at Holm, in the city of Norwich (Blomef. vi. 311).

P. 9.—*Haughboys Magna.* (*Great Hautbois*, Blomefield. Now *Great Hautboys.*)

'Item Stephanus Bolte habet vnum tenementum cum xl acris terre in haughboys magna de quibus quidem xl acris inclusit & posuit ad pasturam xij^m acras que fuerunt in cultura citra tempus commissionis & tenementum illud decidit.'

I interpret this entry as intended to convey that the forty acres were inclosed and twelve of them converted to pasture.

'Item Dominus Dacre habet in dicta villa vnum manerium & c acras terre quodquidem manerium deuastatum fuit ante datum commissionis & citra tempus commissionis xx^{li} acre de predictis c acris ponebantur in pasturam.'

Thomas Fynes, Lord Dacres, died seised of this manor in 1511 (Blomef. vi. 302).

The destruction of the manor house had taken place before Michaelmas 1488, the 'tempus commissionis.'

P. 9.—*Buxston.* (*Bukestuna*, Domesday. Now *Buxton.*)

'Item in Buxston domina Morley habet vnum manerium cum ciiij^{xx} acris terre quodquidem manerium deuastatum fuit ante datum commissionis & dimidium terre predicte fuit in cultura citra tempus commissionis & iam in pastura.'

Cp. last entry.

The Morleys were lords of this manor. For Lady Morley's previously recorded inclosure, see *sub* Alby, p. 167, *supra.*

P. 9.—*Bakenthorp.* (*Baconsthorp*, Blomefield. Now *Baconsthorpe*.)

'Item Johannes plumsted habet vnum clausum in villa de Bakenthorp quod continet xix acras terre & fuerunt in cultura citra tempus commissionis & iam est in pastura.'

The manor belonged to the family of Heydon (Blomef. vi. 506). For Sir John Heydon, see p. 182, *supra*.

P. 10.—*Calthorpe.* (*Caletorp*, Domesday. *Calthorp*, Blomefield. Now *Calthorpe*.)

'Item Thomas Drake inclusit & posuit ad pasturam xx^{ti} acras terre in Calthorpe que fuerunt in cultura citra tempus commissionis.'

'Item Robertus Kyttys habet vnum tenementum cum $xxiiij^{or}$ acris terre in villa predicta quodquidem tenementum decidit & terre ponuntur ad pasturam & fuit in cultura citra tempus commissionis.'

On the area of twenty-four acres see *sub* Gatelee, p. 44, *supra*.

'Item Willelmus Bolen miles inclusit et posuit ad pasturam xxvj acras terre que fuerunt in cultura citra tempus commissionis.'

For the area see *sub* Ketelston, *infra*.

The manors belonged to the Boleyns and Cathorpes Blomef. vi. 518, 519).

P. 10.—*Causton.* (*Cawston*, Blomefield.)

'Item Johannes Rytywyse habet vnum messuagium cum xvj acris terre in Causton que fuerunt in cultura citra tempus commissionis & iam fiunt pasture & tenementum decidit.'

For the area of sixteen acres see *sub* West Somerton, p. 166, *supra*.

'Iam fiunt pasture' is a new variation and apparently indicates that the change was being then made.

The manor was in the hands of the Crown (Blomef. vi. 258).

Note the convertibility of the terms 'messuagium' and 'tenementum.'

P. 10.—*Blykelyng.* (Now *Blickling*.)

'Item Willelmus Bolen miles elargauit parcum suum apud Blykelyng cum $xviij^{m}$ acris terre que fuerunt in cultura citra tempus commissionis et eciam cepit in parcum illum suum vnam viam communem quod multum nocet inhabitantes ville predicte.'

Sir William Boleyn was father of Sir Thomas Boleyn, the father of Queen Anne Boleyn. He held the manor under the Bishop of Norwich (Blomef. vi. 388). He had died in 1505.

This return proves that the Inquisition was honestly conducted without respect to persons, Sir Thomas Boleyn being already in high favour at Court. See Introduction 'Trans. R. H. S.' 1892, p. 179.

'Item dictus Willelmus Bolen elargauit parcum suum cum iij acris & eciam annexuit eidem parco vij acras cum tenemento quod decidit & terre ponuntur ad pasturam.'

The seven acres with a house would be the holding of a cottier (bordarius) (Seebohm, 'Engl. Vill. Comm.' 2nd ed. 1883, p. 97).

P. 10.—*Aylesham.* (*Elesham*, Domesday.)

'Item Johannes Rytwyse habet vnum messuagium cum xiiij acris que fuerunt in cultura citra tempus commissionis & iam sunt in pastura & messuagium predictum decidit.'

Follows the form under Causton as to the same owner.

The name of the incloser does not appear to have been that of any of the lords of the manors here. The four manors belonged to the Duchy of Lancaster, the Abbey of Bury St. Edmunds, the Miltons, and the Vicar of the parish (Blomf. vi. 272–4.)

P. 10.—*Arpyngham.* (*Erpincham*, Domesday. Now *Erpingham*.)

'Item Thomas Mortoft habet vnum tenementum cum xxx^{ta} acris terre quodquidem tenementum decidit & terra que tunc in cultura erat iam includitur & ponitur ad pasturam.'

'Idem Thomas fecit vnum clausum de xx^{ti} acris terre quas posuit ad pasturam et que in cultura erant citra tempus commissionis.'

As to twenty acres see *sub* Styfkey, p. 181, *supra*. No conclusion can be derived from these entries as to the character of the cultivation.

'Item Johannes Mortofte inclusit & posuit ad pasturam [blank in MS.] acras terre que fuerunt in cultura citra tempus commissionis.'

'Item Thomas Bettes dimisit ad firmam henrico ffermer c acras terre que fuerunt in cultura citra tempus commissionis et iam dictus henricus ffermer posuit predictas c acras terre ad pasturam ouium.'

As to Henry Fermer or Fermor see pp. 154, 182, 183, 217. The manor was at this time in the Crown (Blomef. vi. 419).

P. 11.—HUNDRED DE FFRYBRYGE IUXTA LYNNE. (FREDE-BRUGE, FREDEBURGE, *Domesday*. Now FREEBRIDGE HUNDRED.)

'Per Inquisicionem captam die Martis proximo post ffestum sancti martini Episcopi in yeme anno nono Regis henrici viij coram prefatis commissionariis, videlicet.'

P. 11.—*fflytcham*. (*Plicham*, Domesday. Now *Flitcham*.)

'Quod prior de fflytcham posuit ad pasturam lx acras que fuerunt in cultura citra tempus commissionis.'

'Idem prior posuit ad pasturam ouium in parte orientali de herpeley c acras terre in vna pecia & in le Northfeld eiusdem ville l acras terre & in parte australi versus eandem villam de terris suis propriis & aliorum hominum c acras per estimacionem que quidem terre fuerunt in cultura citra tempus commissionis & iam in pasturam conuertuntur.'

This 'prior de fflytcham' was John Martin (cf. C. Parkin, 'Hundred of Freebridge,' p. 67). Qu. any relation of the incloser Roger Martyn (see *sub* N. Elynham and Gatelee, pp. 173-4, *supra*).

The entry of the Herpeley inclosure under fflytcham which is not the regular mode of entry, would seem to show a design on the part of the commissioners to call attention to the Prior's action. He was, it will be observed, not lord of any of the manors here. The two manors at Herpeley belonged to the Calthorps and the Gurnays. But the Prior of Castellacre held land here (Blomef. viii. 453-7).

'Item Prior de Walsingham dimisit ad firmam in villa predicta Ricardo Migh [blank in MS.] acras terre unde posuit ad pasturam ouium clx acras & eciam inclusit & posuit ad pasturam viij^{to} acras in dicta villa que fuerunt in cultura citra tempus commissionis.'

'Villa predicta,' *i.e.* fflytcham; see below.

The Priory of Walsingham had the lordship of two of the manors in fflytcham called Sackvill's and Snoring manors (Blomef. viii. 413 -14).

The Prior of Walsingham was himself a farmer and had inclosed 160 acres (see *sub* Walsingham Magna and Hoveton, 183-4, *supra*).

'Item Magistra Wodhous habet in fflytcham vocatum le [*sic*] xx^{xx} acras quarum ccc iiij^{xx} xiiij ponuntur ad pasturam que fuerunt in cultura citra tempus commissionis.'

The Wodehouse family were lords of the manor called Poining's Manor, in fflytcham.

'Item infra dictam villam deciderunt citra tempus commissionis xv^m inhabitaciones & xiiij aratra delentur per conuersionem terre a cultura in pasturam.'

Presumably by the lords of the manors.

According to Du Cange (ed. Henschel, 1840) 'aratrum' is equivalent to 'carrucata.'

This is, on the average, correct for this Inquisition, it 'carucate' be understood in its most limited sense, *i.e.* one of the arable fields in a three-field manor.[1] In this Norfolk Inquisition, as has been mentioned under Wendlyng, p. 46, *supra*, the cases in which the area of an 'aratrum' is specified do give it approximately sixty acres; see p. 160, *supra*. The fourteen aratra put down make, upon this standard, 840 acres. If these 840 acres are divided between fifteen 'inhabitaciones' (a generic term evidently implying variety of size, and therefore substituted for the more ordinary messuagia' or ' tenementa ') the quotient is fifty-six acres. According to the ' Parliamentary Gazetteer' the total area of the parish is 3906 acres, so that two-fifths of it had been laid down to grass since 1488.

[1] Cp. pp. 166, 167, *supra*.

P. 11.—*Herpeley.* (*Harpley*, Blomefield.)

'Item Magister Strange armiger habet ad firmam in harpeley terram quondam ad abbatiam de Creke & iam ad collegium Christi in Cantebrigia pertinentem cum tenemento quod decidit et terre predicte ponuntur ad pasturam ouium citra tempus commissionis.'

The Abbey of Creke was a house of Augustinian canons, dissolved for the purpose of founding Christ's College, Cambridge.

The MS. omits to give the area of the land transferred. It is not in Blomef.; but the Bursar of Christ's College, Mr. J. A. Sharkey, obligingly informs me that the acreage held by the College at Harpley is 98a. 2r. 26p., and that he is not aware of any additions having been made to it. As the alienation of land by colleges was, until recent years, a matter of great difficulty, it may be inferred that this was the area originally conveyed to Christ's. Mr. Sharkey further mentions that this land has, in his belief, been uniformly occupied together with the land at Massingham belonging to the College, for the last 250 years, and suggests that Strange might also have held land at Massingham of the College; *sed qu.* The manors in Harpley belonged to the families of Calthorp and Gurnay (Blomef. viii. 493–5). The entry does not specifically assign the whole area to the tenementum, and I have, therefore, thought it best to exclude it from the computations of pp. 160–1.

P. 11.—*Massyngham Parua.* (*Massingham Parva*, Blomefield. Now *Little Massingham.*)

'Item Johannes le Strange inclusit & posuit ad pasturam xvj acras de communia de Massyngham parua.'

This John le Strange was reader and treasurer of Lincoln's Inn, and is said by Blomefield, though with some appearance of uncertainty, to have been a judge (Blomef. ix. 17, 18), and his name does not appear in Foss's 'Lives of the Judges.' He was lord of the manor. His inclosure of common was doubtless founded upon the Statute of Merton 20 H. III. c. 4), and it is to be noted that there is no allegation that it was 'magno nocumento' of the inhabitants, as we have had elsewhere (cp. Digby, 'Hist. of Law of Real Property,' 4th ed. p. 192). This, of course, was only a case of inclosure, not of conversion.

'Item Robertus Warcope inclusit & posuit ad pasturam xvj acras terre que fuerunt in cultura citra tempus commissionis.'

Probably a freeholder, as tenancy is not recited.

As to the area of sixteen acres, see *sub* West Somerton, p. 166, *supra*.

P. 11.—*Castellacre*. (*Acre*, Domesday. *Castleacre*, Blomefield.)

'Item ffranciscus Calybutt inclusit xl acras terre in Castelacre que fuerunt in cultura citra tempus commissionis.'

Not a case of laying to pasture.

The Calybutts were lords of one of the manors here (Blomef. viii. 361).

'Item Thomas Thurysby senior qui nuper obiit destruxit vnum integrum hamelett cum omnibus tenementis vocatum holte hamelett & posuit terram ad pasturam ouium que fuerunt in cultura infra datum commissionis.'

A Thomas Thuresby was probably lord of the manor of Ash Wicken (see Blomef. viii. 338 ; and C. Parkin, 'Hundred of Freebridge,' p. 9).

Thomas Thurysby became lord of the third part of the manor of Glosthorpe—the manor belonging to the three co-heiresses of Jeffrey Ratclyffe (C. Parkin, p. 13)—in the 28th Henry VIII., with lands in Holt (Blomef. viii. 338).

'Holt,' says Blomefield, 'is now esteemed as part of the parish of Lesiate. The church of Lesiate is in ruins. The parish was annexed to Ash Wicken in 1474' (*ibid.* 340). This suggests the destruction of Holt as belonging to that date. It is true no mention is made of the church, but its decay would be gradual ; or, if it was destroyed in 1474, the date is prior to that to which the inquiry was limited.

The 'hamelett' probably consisted of no more than four or five tenements, for we know from this Inquisition (p. 231, *infra*) that a 'villa' or town only comprised four messuages and four cottages. Further on this point, see the article by the writer in the 'Eng. Hist. Rev.' for October, 1893.

On this incloser see *supra*, p. 170. This is the only entry which specifies T. T. senior, though probably all the inclosures were by him, as tenant in possession.

For further particulars of T. T. see Cambridgeshire, *sub* Hundred de Chelterton, Cotenham.

P. 12.—*Bawsey*.

'Item apud Bawsey lx acre terre diuersorum hominum ponuntur ad pasturam que fuerunt in cultura citra tempus commissionis.'

The omission of the names of the inclosers is unusual. Bawsey is in the manor of Glosthorpe (see under last entry), and circumstances attaching to the inclosure of Hillington (see below) make it not unlikely that the incloser here and there was the same Thomas Thuresby. The manor was at this time in the hands of the Ratclyf family (Parkin, p. 13).

P. 12.—*Gaywood*.

'Item apud Gaywood Willelmus Beteryng habet vnum tenementum cum xix acris terre que fuerunt in cultura citra tempus commissionis & iam sunt in pastura et tenementum illud decidit.'

This manor belonged to the see of Norwich (Blomef viii. 420).

Qu. whether this William Beteryng was the William Betrynge who was lord of the manor of Hanworth after 1490 (see Blomef. viii. 131).

P. 12.—*Rowton* (probably by copyist's mistake for *Ronton. Rynghetona*, Domesday. *North Rungton*, Blomefield. Now *North Runcton*.)

'Item apud Rowton Johannes Burdy inclusit & posuit ad pasturam x acras que fuerunt in cultura citra tempus commissionis.'

The manor was in the Crown (Blomef. ix. 63).

The area of ten acres has not occurred before. Seebohm ('Engl. Vill. Comm.' 2nd ed. 1883, p. 97) says that cottiers (bordarii) sometimes held so much.

P. 12.—*Wynche.* (*East* or *West Winch.*)

'Item apud Wynche Thomas Thursby posuit ad pasturam ouium xxxv acras terre que fuerunt in cultura citra tempus commissionis.'

East Winch would probably adjoin land already the property of T. T. at Ash Wicken (see *sub* Castellacre, p. 191, *supra*).

The Wingfields were lords of one of the manors here; the Prior of Pentney of another. I have taken this to be the ecclesiastical manor, with a qu. (see Blomef. ix. 150-1).

P. 12. *Hyllyngton.* (Now *Hillington.*)

'Apud Hyllyngton vnum tenementum decidit cum xxx acris terre eidem tenemento pertinentibus que ponuntur ad pasturam & que fuerunt in cultura citra tempus commissionis.'

It is notable that no name is mentioned here as that ot the incloser; but it appears that one of the manors of Hillington was at this time in the Thoresby family (Blomef. viii. 464), and it adjoins Congham, the lordship of one of the manors of which belonged to them also (*ibid.* 385).

These facts awaken the suspicion that the incloser was Thomas Thoresby, and that his interest with the person who reported on Hillington was sufficient to procure the suppression of his name. See *sub* Bawsey and Castellacre, pp. 191-2, *supra*.

P. 12.—*Grymston.* (Now *Grimston.*)

'Item apud Brymston [*sic!*] Thomas Rolff inclusit & posuit ad pasturam xv acras que fuerunt in cultura citra tempus commissionis.'

This was the normal bovate in the arable of a three-field manor.

The area has not occurred previously.

There appear to have been nine manors in this place, of which four belonged to Coxford Priory, Castleacre Priory, Blackborough Priory, and Westacre Priory respectively. The others were in the hands of the family of Wodehouse. I have assumed, with a qu., that this inclosure was on one of the ecclesiastical manors. See Blomef. viii. 441-450.

P. 12.—*Sandryngham.* (Now *Sandringham.*)
'Item apud Sandryngham Galfridus Cobbe inclusit & posuit ad pasturam xxvj acras terre que fuerunt in cultura citra tempus commissionis.'
For the area see *sub* Ketelston, p. 216, *infra.*
Geoffrey Cobbe succeeded William Cobbe as son and heir and lord of this manor some time after 1492 (Blomef. ix. 68).

P. 12.—*Rysyngcastell.* (Now *Rising.*)
'Item apud Rysyng castell Johannes Dobyns habet vnum tenementum cum xxx acris terre quodquidem tenementum decidit & terre ponuntur ad pasturam per quod vnum aratrum deletur.'
A normal virgate. The entry shows that in this Inquisition 'aratrum' is not to be taken as always equivalent to 'carrucata,' although Du Cange (Henschel, ed. 1840) says distinctly, 'Aratrum idem quod carrucata terræ, quantum terræ uno aratro arari potest.' See above, *sub* fflytcham, p. 189.
The manor of Rysyng was in the hands of the Crown as part of the duchy of Cornwall, but had been let in 1516 for twenty-one years to Thomas Thursby, of Bishop's Lynne, for 50*l.* (Brewer, 'Cal.' ii. 2625). Cp. p. 135, *supra.*

P. 12.—*North Wotton.* (Now *North Wootton.*)
'Item apud Northwotton Thomas Thurisby posuit ad pasturam de terris diuersorum hominum lvj acras que fuerunt in cultura citra tempus commissionis.'
The two manors here belonged to the family of Salter and the Priory of Windham. I have taken this inclosure to be on the ecclesiastical manor, with a qu. See Blomef. ix. 201, 202.
The land was adjacent to Thursby's other property at Bawsey, etc. (see above, *sub* Barwyk, Castellacre, Bawsey Wynche, Hyllyngton).

P. 12.—*Donmer*: i.e. *Anmer* (a clerical error).
'Item M[r] Thomas le Strange dimisit manerium suum in Donmer ad firmam Edwardo Hartyng cum omnibus terris in eadem villa, et idem Edwardus posuit ad pasturam ouium c acras de terra manerii illius que fuerunt in cultura citra tempus commissionis et manerium predictum decidit.'

The family of L'Estrange were lords of this manor from 1496 to 1538 (Blomef. viii. 334).

The wording suggests that this was only part of the total area appurtenant. Cp. *sub* Thorp parua, p. 203, *infra*.

P. 12.—*Lynne*. (Now *King's Lynn*.)

'Item in Lynne est vna Guilda ad quam pertinet vnum tenementum cum xl acris terre que fuerunt in cultura citra tempus commissionis & iam sunt in pastura & tenementum illud decidit.'

For the various gilds of Lynn see Blomef. vii. 501-504.

P. 12.—*Brabyngle*. (Now *Babingley*.)

'Item Apud Brabyngle Galfridus Cobbys posuit ad pasturam xxxvj acras terre que fuerunt in cultura citra tempus commissionis.'

The manor was at this time in the hands of the Countess of Oxford and Sir W. Tyndall. Some years later the Cobbes of Sandringham became lords of the manor (Blomef. viii. 349; Parkin, p. 18). See *sub* Sandryngham, *supra*, p. 194.

'Item Thomas lewes habet ad firmam de diversis hominibus ad summam xxx acrarum quas inclusit & posuit ad pasturam & que fuerunt in cultura citra tempus commissionis.'

'Idem Thomas lawys habet ad firmam de terra magistri Cokkes xx^{ti} acras cum vno messuagio quod decidit & terre predicte includuntur & ad pasturam ponuntur.'

For the area of twenty acres see note to Styfkey, p. 181, *supra*.

P. 13.—HUNDRED DE DEPWADE. (DEPWADE, *Domesday* Now DEPEWADE.)

'Per Inquisicionem captam die Veneris proximo post ffestum sancti Martini in yeme anno ix^{no} Regis Henrici viij^{ui} coram prefatis commissionariis: videlicet.'

P. 13.—*Mornyngthorp*. (*Torp*, Domesday. *Moringthorp*, Blomefield. Now *Mourningthorpe*.)

'Quod Johannes Gambyll inclusit xxiij acras terre infra villam de Mornyngthorp unde xx^{ti} acre infra datum commissionis fuerunt in cultura & iam in pasturam conuertuntur

& tres acre residue sunt de communia ville predicte vocata Thornysgreve comyn.'

On the area of twenty acres see *sub* Styfkey, p. 181, *supra*. 'Thornysgreve comyn.' It is suggestive that Torn the Dane owned the manor of 'Bayland Hall in Morningthorp' in the time of Edward the Confessor (Blomef. v. 291).

The two manors were in the hands of the families of Gurneys and Hoe (Blomef. v. 292-4).

P. 13.—HUNDRED DE STROPHAM & GYLCROSTE. (SCREPHAM & GILLECROSS, *Domesday*. Now SHROPHAM & GILTCROSS.)

Per Inquisicionem captam die Veneris proximo post ffestum sancti martini Episcopi in yeme anno ix^{no} Regis Henrici viij^{ul} : videlicet.'

P. 13.—*Attyllburgh*. (*Atleburgh*, Blomefield. Now *Attleborough*.)

'Quod magister petrus ffoston fecit vnum clausum in villa Attylburgh continentem xxx^{ta} acras que fuerunt in cultura post tempus dicte commissionis & modo in pastura existunt.'

Peter ffoston was master of the College or Chantry of Holy Cross here, 1486-1519. The college owned seventy acres of land, four of meadow, and two of pasture here (Blomef. i. 538).

'Item in eadem villa de Attyllburgh est quoddam dominium vocatum a seuery vocatum plasshyng hall & terre fuerunt post tempus commissionis in cultura & dicte terre eidem dominio pertinentes sunt iiij^{xx} acre & posite fuerunt in pastura per Willelmum Knyvett militem & tempore capcionis Inquisicionis predicte fuerunt in manu Thome Wyndham & Roberti Drury militis.'

Plassing Hall Manor was one of the manors of Attyllburgh. Sir William Knyvett was a lord of one moiety of it (Blomef. i. 496). The Drurys were lords of a neighbouring manor in Besthorp (*ibid*. 498, 499).

'Severy,' a division or compartment of a vaulted ceiling (Halliwell).

The name plassing, plasset, or plasshyng was derived from the plashes or swampy places there (Blomef. *ibid.*).

It was at Attleborough that Kett's rebellion broke out (see F. W. Russell's 'Kett's Rebellion in Norfolk,' p. 21).

P. 13.—*Besthorpe.*

'Item Walterus hubberd gent. habet in villa de Bestthorp vnum tenementum cum iiij^{xx} acris terre que fuerunt in cultura post tempus dicte commissionis & iam in pastura & tenementum totaliter in decasu per Jacobum hubbert militem.'

Walter Hubberd, son and heir of Sir James Hubberd or Hobart (Blomef. x. 123).

The manors here were owned by the Knevets and the Drurys (*ibid.* i. 496-9).

P. 13.—*Ekkyllys.* (Now *Eccles.*)

'Item Prior de Bukkenham posuit in pastura & inclusit xx^{d} acras terre in villa de Eckylles que fuerunt in cultura post tempus dicte commissionis.'

For a previous inclosure by the same Prior see *sub* Bekenham, *supra*, p. 170.

For the area twenty acres *see* sub Styfkey, p. 181, *supra*.

The manor belonged to the see of Norwich. It included all New Buckenham and part of Old Buckenham. (Blomef. i. 405-6.)

P. 13.—*Stropham.* (Clerical error for *Shropham.*)

'Item Ricardus Dade habet vnum tenementum cum xij^{m} acris terre in villa de Stropham que fuerunt in cultura post tempus dicte commissionis & xlviij acre inde ponuntur in pasturam & tenementum in decasu.'

There is evidently a mistake here, but the MS. is clear.

The Dades were lords of the manor (Blomef. i. 459).

P. 13.—*Lytlebrekylles.* (Now *Breccles.*)

'Item Henricus Spylman gent. inclusit in pasturam in villa de lytle brekylles xx^{ti} acras terre que fuerunt in cultura post tempus dicte commissionis.'

Apparently part of Great Breccles.

The Spylman or Spelman family were connected by marriage with that of Woodhouse, who were the lords of the manor (Blomef. ii. 276).

For the area of twenty acres see *sub* Styfkey, p. 181, *supra*.

P. 14.—*Schadewell*. (Now *Shadwell*.)

'Item Dominus Johannes purpete de collegio de Russheford posuit in pasturam xx^{ti} acras terre in villa de Schadewell que fuerunt in cultura post tempus commissionis predicte.'

For the area of twenty acres see *sub* Styfkey, p. 180, *supra*.

Shadwell appears to have been part of the manor of Brettenham, and was a hamlet in the parish of Rushworth (Blomef. i. 287)—sometimes, as appears in Blomef. i. 445, called Rushford, though erroneously. Rushworth was made a collegiate church about 1326 by Sir Edmund Gonvile, priest, and founder of Gonville Hall in Cambridge. The lordship of the manor was in the hands of the College, of which John Purpete or Purpett was at this time master. (*Ibid.* 289.)

'Item magister dicti collegii habet in eadem villa diuersa tenementa cum iiij^{xx} acris terre eidem pertinentibus que fuerunt in cultura post tempus dicte commissionis & dicte terre conuertuntur in pasturam ouium & tenementa in decasu existunt.'

Presumably at least three tenements; see *sub* Holkeham, pp. 179–80, and cf. pp. 161–2, *supra*. Upon the computation there adopted sixty-six acres would go to two 'tenementa.' But the word is 'diuersa,' which clearly implies more than two. I therefore venture to estimate a minimum of three.

P. 14.—*Stalham*.

'Item Willelmus Burges inclusit & posuit in pasturam xvj acras terre in villa de [blank in MS.] que fuerunt in cultura post tempus dicte commissionis & tenementum ad easdem spectans in decasu existit.'

For the area of sixteen acres see *sub* West Somerton p. 166, *supra*.

The manors belonged to the see of Norwich and the College of Heringby (Blomef. ix. 342–3).

P. 14.—HUNDRED DE [*blank in MS.*], *i.e.* TUNSTEAD.
(TQNSTEDA, *Domesday.*)

'Per Inquisicionem captam die Martis proximo post ffestum sancti martini anno ix^{no} Regis henrici viij^{ul} coram prefatis commissionariis : videlicet.'

P. 14.—*Northwalsham.*

'Quod Robertus Brampton habuit vnum tenementum vocatum Scroopskens cum xxx^{ta} acris terre in villa de North Walsham quodquidem tenementum est in decasu & xvj acre que fuerunt in cultura post tempus dicte commissionis ponuntur in pasturam per Johannem Braton.'

A virgate.

Robert Brampton was lord of the manor (Blomef. xi. 76). Braton evidently a tenant.

'Item Johannes parker habet in eadem villa vnum tenementum vocatum Spregis cum lxx acris que fuerunt in cultura post tempus dicte commissionis & iam includuntur & in pasturam ponuntur & tenementa in decasu existunt.'

There is no previous example of this area.

P. 14.—*Rydlyngton & Crostwyk.*

'Item Robertus Brandon miles inclusit xxvij acras communis le gresyng de Rydlyngton & Crostwyke post tempus commissionis quod est magnum preiudicium predicte ville.'

The area twenty-seven acres has not occurred before. It belongs to a messuagium at Tetyshale, p. 203, *infra*.

Sir R. Brandon was probably not lord of either of the manors. The manor of Crostwick appears to have been owned by Sir Edmund Jenney (Blomef. xi. 9); that of Rydlyngton by the Priory of Bromholm (*ibid.* 62).

P. 14.—HUNDRED DE NORTHARPYNGHAM. (ERPINCHAM N., *Domesday*. Now NORTH ERPINGHAM.)

'Per Inquisicionem captam die Veneris proximo post ffestum sancti Martini anno ix^{no} Regis henrici viij^{ul} coram prefatis commissionariis : videlicet.'

P. 14.—*North Barnyngham*. (*Berningham Northwood*, Blomefield. Now *North Barningham*.)

'Quod magister henricus palgrave inclusit & posuit in pasturam in Northbarnyngham xxiiij⁰ʳ acras terre que fuerunt in cultura post tempus dicte commissionis.'

On the area of twenty-four acres see *sub* Gatelee, p. 173, *supra*.

Henry Palgrave was lord of the manor (Blomef. viii. 94).

P. 14.—*Town Barnyngham*. (*Berningham Winter* or *Ton Berningham*, Blomefield. Now *Town Barningham*.)

'Item Willelmus hawe inclusit et posuit in pasturam in Townebarnyngham viij^to acras terre que fuerunt in cultura post tempus dicte commissionis.'

A cottier's holding. Qu. a bovate of a converted manor (see *sub* West Somerton, p. 166, *supra*). The manor was the property of the family of Winter (Blomef. viii. 98).

P. 14.—*Suffeld*. Now *Suffield*.

'Item Robertus long habet vnum tenementum in villa de Suffeld cum xxx^ta acris terre que fuerunt in cultura post tempus commissionis & iam dicte terre sunt in pastura et tenementum in decasu.'

The manor belonged to the family of Herward (Blomef. ii. 165).

P. 15.—HUNDRED DE HENSTED.

'Per Inquisicionem captam die Jouis proximo post ffestum sancti martini Episcopi anno ix^no Regis henrici viij^ui coram prefatis commissionariis : videlicet.'

P. 15.—*Parua Parlond*. (*Little Poringland*, Blomefield.)

'Quod Thomas Sparhows et Willelmus Goldsmyth incluserunt in villa de parva parlondes xij acras terre que vtuntur in cultura sed dicta inclausura est magnum detrimentum dicte ville pro eo quod non habetur ibi le shakke leke ut ab antiquo habebatur ibidem.'

The manor belonged to the Norfolk family (Blomef. v. 444).

'In the county of Norfolk there is a special manner of

common called "shack," which is to be taken in arable land after harvest until this land be sowed again, etc. : & it began in ancient time in this manner: the fields of arable land in this country consist of the lands of many & divers several persons, lying intermixed in many & several small parcels, so that it is not possible that any, without trespass to the others, can feed their cattle in their own land, & therefore every one doth put in their cattle to feed promiscuè in the open field.' (Sir Miles Corbet's case, Coke's Reports, part vii. 5, a, ed. 1826; cp. Marshall's 'Rural Economy of Norfolk,' 1787, ii. 287.)

The above inclosure by two persons may have been legal under one of the resolutions in the above case : ' But if in the town of S. the custom & usage hath been that every' ('chescun' in original, *i.e.* each separately) 'owner in the same town hath inclosed their own lands from time to time, & so hath held it in severalty, there this usage proves that it was but in the nature of shack originally for the cause of vicinage & so it continues ; & therefore there he may inclose & hold in severalty & exclude himself to have shack with the others' (original, '& secluder luy mesme dauer shacke *oue* les auters.')

'Leke,' qu. meaning.

P. 15.—*Stoke*. (*Stokes*, Domesday. Now *Stoke Holy Cross*.)

'Item Willelmus Harman inclusit & posuit ad pasturam in villa de Stoke x acras terre que fuerunt in cultura post tempus dicte commissionis.'

For the area of ten acres see *sub* Rowton, p. 192, *supra*.

The manor belonged to the Billingfords (Blomef. v. 523).

'Item magister Yeluerton habet in villa de Stoke vnam placeam vocatam Nether hall ad quam pertinent cxx acre terre que fuerunt in cultura post tempus dicte commissionis & dicta placea in ruinam deducitur & c acre inde ponuntur ad pasturam.'

The word 'placea' indicates a fortified house (see Du Cange, ed. Favre, *s.v.*).

P. 15.—*Shotesham.* (*Scotessa*, Domesday. *Shotesham*, Blomefield. Now *Shottesham St. Mary.*)

'Item Stephanus Vttyng inclusit lx acras in villa de Shotesham que vtuntur in cultura sed racione dicte inclausure dicta villa omisit le shakke que [*sic*] solebat habere.'

The name Utting, though belonging to Shottesham, was not that of the lords of the manor, who were the Whites (Blomef. v. 506, 515).

There is a blank in the MS. after 'acras,' as though the word were not the familiar 'terræ,' but some word the copyist could not read.

P. 15.—HUNDRED DE EYNESFORD. (EYNSFORD, *Domesday.* EYNFORD, *Blomefield. Now* EYNSFORD.)

'Per Inquisicionem captam die Jouis proximo post ffestum sancti Martini anno ix^{no} Regis henrici viij^{ui} coram prefatis commissionariis : videlicet.'

P. 15.—*Brandeston.* (Now *Brandiston.*)

'Quod in villa de Brandeston vnum aratrum deponitur.'

The manor belonged to Magdalen College, Oxford (Blomef. viii. 196).

P. 15.—*Weston.*

'Item in villa de Weston vnum aratrum deponitur.'

I.e. sixty acres (see *sub* Wendlyng, p. 175, cf. p. 161, *supra*).

The manors of Weston belonged to New College, Oxford, and the Sulyard family ; but no fewer than five religious houses had lands in the parish, viz. West Derham Abbey, Norwich Priory, Ely Priory, Hickling, and St. Faith's (Blomef. viii. 286–7, 291).

P. 15.—*Belawe.* (*Belaga*, Domesday. Now *Belaugh.*)

'Item in villa de Belawe vnum aratrum deponitur.'

'Item in diuersis aliis villis infra dictum hundredum diuerse terre ponuntur ad pasturam que fuerunt in cultura post tempus commissionis et causa est quod sui infra idem hundredum occupant misteram siue facturam de le worsted & paruipendunt iconomiam ad detrimentum dicti hundredi.'

This manor belonged to the family of FitzLewis (Blomef. viii. 188).

P. 16.—HUNDRED DE DYSSE. (DICE, *Domesday*. Now DISS.)

'Per Inquisicionem captam die Veneris proximo post ffestum sancti Martini anno ix^{no} henrici viij^{ul} coram prefatis commissionariis : videlicet.'

P. 16.— *Thorp Parua.* (Now *Little Thorp.*)

'Quod Henricus Wyatt miles deposuit mansionem manerii de Thorp hall & xxx acras terre arrabilis dicto manerio pertinentes inclusit & ad pasturam posuit ad decasum ecclesie ibidem.'

For the area appurtenant to a manerium (see pp. 160-1, *supra*). The above entry gives no sufficient indication of the total area appurtenant in this case.

The phrase 'mansionem manerii' is noticeable (see *sub* Choysell, p. 39, *supra*).

Sir Henry Wyatt, or Wiatt knt., was rector of the church and also a joint owner in trust of the manor (Blomef. i. 138-9).

The ruins of the church remain, and are depicted in Blomef. i. 136. Blomefield remarks that it was in use in 1469, 'and, I believe, long since.'

P. 16.—*Tetyshale.* (*Tuestashala*, Domesday. Now *Titshall.*)

'Item Robertus Woodward deposuit vnum messuagium in Tetyshale & xxvij acras terre eidem pertinentes posuit ad pasturam que fuerunt in cultura citra tempus dicte commissionis.'

The area of twenty-seven acres occurs above in Rydlyngton and Crostwyke. The soil of Titshall is stated to be 'in general, rich' (Blomef. i. 212). Qu. whether on an exceptional soil it was held equivalent to a virgate.

'Item Antonius Gryse tenet xxx acras terre in Tetyshale

que fuerunt in cultura citra tempus dicte commissionis & modo ad pasturam posite & tenementum predictum circa xviij annos preteritos negligenter combustum fuit.'

Of the manors in Tetyshale one belonged to the Abbots of Bury St. Edmunds, the other to the family of Jenney (Blomef. i. 206, 207).

P. 16.—*Wyndeferthing.* (Now *Winfarthing.*)

'Item villata de Tybenham tenet xxv acras terre in Wyndeferthing cum tenemento quod totaliter in decasu existit et terre posite ad pasturam que fuerunt in cultura citra tempus dicte commissionis.'

This is a very remarkable entry. The MS. has 'villat.' which I have extended into 'villata,' since 'villatus' would have no meaning other than that of 'rusticus' (see Du Cange). The villata, or 'village community' of Tibenham, about four miles distant, farmed land, as a body, at Wyndeferthing. Possibly they farmed the whole manor, as in the example given by Mr. Seebohm from the Boldon book of Durham (2nd ed. p. 70). This is the only entry of such a kind in the Norfolk Inquisition. A case occurs in the Shropshire Inquisition at Whitecote, where the 'villata de Whitecote' incloses forty acres.

The manor of Wyndefarthing belonged to the family of Grey (Blomef. i. 189).

P. 16.—HUNDRED DE FFYBRIGGE IN PARTE MARCELAND. (*Now* FREEBRIDGE MARSHLAND HALF HUNDRED.)

'Per Inquisicionem captam apud Norwicum die lune ante ffestum sancti martini anno ix^{no} Regis henrici viij^{ui} coram prefatis commissionariis : videlicet.'

P. 16.—*Emneth.*

'Quod Johannes Bleckes habet vnum messuagium & xx^{ti} acras terre eidem pertinentes in villa de Emneth que fuerunt in cultura citra tempus dicte commissionis et dictum messuagium in decasu existit.'

For the area of twenty acres, see *sub* Styfkey, p. 181, *supra*. The lords of the manors here appear to have been the families of Cutts and Bachcroft and the Prior of Lewes (Blomef. viii. 403, 405, 406).

P. 17.—HUNDRED DE SOUTHGRENOWE. (*Now* GREENHOE SOUTH HUNDRED.)

'Per Inquisicionem captam die lune ante ffestum sancti Martini episcopi in yeme anno ix^{mo} supradicto coram prefatis commissionariis : videlicet.'

P. 17.—*Hale.*

'Quod Robertus Drury miles habet in villa de hale vnum messuagium cum xl acris terre que fuerunt in cultura citra tempus dicte commissionis & iam xvij acre dictarum xl acrarum posite ad pasturam & messuagium in decasu existit.'

The manor belonged to the family of Jenney, though the Priories of Westacre, Sporle and Blakebergh, and the canons of Thetford all had land here (Blomef. vi. 9, 10).

P. 17.—*Palgraue.* (*Little Pagrave*, Blomefield. Now *Little Palgrave.*)

'Item filius et heres henrici palgraue habet in villa de palgraue unum manerium totaliter in decasu & tota terra eidem pertinens posita ad pasturam que fuit in cultura citra tempus commissionis predicte.'

I have ventured to estimate the land belonging to a manerium at the normal area of 120 acres (see *sub* Bastwyke, p. 213, *infra*; and cp. p. 175, *supra*, *sub* Wendlyng).

The Palgraves, or Pagraves, were lords of this manor for many centuries (Blomef. vi. 127).

P. 17.—*Dunham.* (*Dunham Magna*, Blomefield. Now *Great Dunham.*)

'Item Johannes Calybutt habet in villa de Dunham vnum messuagium cum xl acris terre que fuerunt in cultura citra tempus dicte commissionis & modo posite ad pasturam & dictum messuagium in decasu existit.'

According to Blomefield, the two Dunhams were in the Hundred of Launditch. They lie next to Palgrave.

The manors of Great Dunham were in the hands of the families of Woodhouse and Cocket (Blomef. viii. 482-3). They seem afterwards to have passed to the Wyngfelds (MS. R. O. Ct. of Req., Mr. Hunt's Cal., Bdle. 8, No. 265).[1]

P. 17.—*Est bradenham.* (*Bradeham*, Domesday. Now *East Bradenham.*)

'Item Johannes Reder Rector de Scarnyng inclusit iiij^{xx} acras terre in villa de Estbradenham que fuerunt in cultura citra tempus dicte commissionis et iam ponuntur ad pasturam xl acre terre inde.'

The two principal manors were in the hands of the Abbots of Bury. This looks like a case of clerical farming under the Abbey.

The name Reder does not occur in the list of Rectors and Vicars of Scarning given by Blomefield, x, 44, 45. But a John

[1] COURT OF REQUESTS (Mr. Hunt's Cal., Bdle. 8, No. 265). Common Rights and Inclosure.—Payne and others *v.* Goldyng and others. (No date.)

Petition of the freeholders, copyholders, and inhabitants of Great Dunham, Norfolk.

Recites former bill of complaint by same plaintiffs, showing their right of common 'for the greate cattell' in the common of Great Dunham, 'conteyning by estimacion iij hundred acres'; that Thomas Wyngfeld, Esq., lord of the manor, had a foldcourse on this common of 740 sheep in a herd, 'by the lycence and sufferaunce of your said subiectes & no otherwyse'; that T. Wyngfeld let this foldcourse to John Callybutt, Esq., who then kept 800 sheep there; that T. Wyngfeld sold part of the manor to Sir Thomas Goldyng, Knt., and the residue to him in remainder; that Sir T. G. inclosed part of the manor so bought, and excluded the beasts of the petitioners from the shack, though he continued to pasture sheep on the common; that T. Wyngfeld and Sir T. G. have 'raised another ffold course of iiij hundred shepe' on the same common in addition.

Issue of commission by y* King to 'Sir R⁴. Sowthwell, Sir Nicholas Le Strange, Sir Thomas Hollys knightes; Robert Holdyche esquier & James Downes esquier.'

Award of Commissioners.—Defendants not to pasture more than 740 sheep, to be kept in one flock together, 'and not in too flockes nor in severall partes.' The recent inclosures to be thrown open, and shack to be allowed on them to the inhabitants.

Agreement of the defendants to the award.

Sir T. Goldyng, now sole owner of the manor of Great Dunham, retains 800 sheep in the fields of Dunham; has not laid open the inclosures. Petitions for letters of Privy Seal to compel Sir T. G. to fulfil terms of award.

Reder was rector of Dunham Parva in 1541 (*ibid.* ix. 480), and a person of the same name rector of Bexwell in 1530 (*ibid.* vii. 310).

P. 17.—*Scarnyng & West Bradenham.*

' Item Abbas de Wendlyng inclusit & ad pasturam posuit in villa de Scarnyng & Westbradenham xl acras terre que fuerunt in cultura citra tempus dicte commissionis.'

Note that the other inclosure by the same Abbot in Scarning was forty acres. (See p. 178, *supra.*)

Scarning and West Bradenham are contiguous and it may have been doubtful to the informer to which manor the land inclosed belonged. It does not appear that the Abbey of Wendlyng held any lordship in West Bradenham, which belonged to the Knevets (Blomef. vi. 143). It is possible, therefore, that this inclosure is really that already recorded as having been made by the same person at Skernyng (p. 178, *supra*).

P. 17.—*Pykenham.* (*Pichenham*, Domesday. Now [qu.] *South Pickenham.*)

' Item Johannes ffermor inclusit & posuit ad pasturam in villa de pykenham xl acras que fuerunt in cultura citra tempus commissionis predicte.'

Mumford ('Analysis ot Domesday,' p. 106) identifies the Pickenham of Domesday with South Pickenham, of which the church was older than that of North Pickenham (cp. Blomef. vi. 68, 74).

The name ffermor does not occur as that of any of the lords of the manors, who at this time were the Methwolds (*ibid.* pp. 70, 71).

P. 17. — *Estbradeham.* (*Bradeham*, Domesday. Now *East Bradenham.*)

' Item Johannes Wagstaff inclusit in villa de Estbradham xxx acras terre & xv acras inde posuit in pasturam que fuerunt in cultura citra tempus commissionis predicte.'

As to the manors see Est bradenham, p. 206, *supra.*

The misplacement here and also of the Stanehewe (p. '70) and Scarnyng entries is doubtless to be ascribed to a blunder in sorting the original parchment slips from which this MS. was compiled. See 'Trans. R. H. S.' 1892, p. 175.

P. 18.—HUNDRED DE METFORD. (MITTEFORT, *Domesday. Now* MITFORD.)

'Per Inquisicionem captam die Jouis ante ffestum sancti Edwardi anno nono predicto coram prefatis commissionariis : videlicet.'

P. 18.—*Dereham.* (Now *East Dereham.*)

'Quod domina Anna Capell vidua infra spacium xx^{ti} annorum proxime elapsorum deuastauit & deposuit quoddam manerium in villa de Dereham vocatum le Olde Hall & xx^{ti} acre terre arabilis eidem pertinentes pro pastura vtuntur per quod vnum aratrum deletur.'

This was Oldhall's manor, in East Dereham, so called from a family of that name from whom it had come to Sir William Capel, who died lord in 1515 (Blomef. x. 209).

Note that the 'aratrum' here equals twenty acres. In the case of Rysyngcastell it was thirty acres. (*See* above, p. 194, and fflytcham, p. 189, and cp. p. 160, *supra.*) As to the form and significance of this entry cf. Thorp Parua, pp. 203, and Wendlyng, pp. 175–6, *supra.*

'Item Henricus palmer posuit ad pasturam in villa predicta l acras terre que fuerunt in cultura citra tempus dicte commissionis.'

The other lords of manors here were Henry Parker (qu. afterwards Lord Morley) and the Bishop of Ely. The name of Palmer does not appear (Blomef. x. 206, 207). The same name occurs as that of an incloser at Okyll, p. 212, *infra.*

P. 18.—*Letton.* (*Lettuna*, Domesday. Now *Letton.*)

'Item Christina Warner vidua inclusit & posuit in pastura in villa de letton xxxvj acras terre que fuerunt in cultura citra tempus dicte commissionis.'

Of the manors one was in the hands of the Bramptons, the other belonged to the Priory of Lewes, in Sussex (Blomef. x. 221–2).

P. 18.—HUNDREDUM DE FFOROWE. (HUNDRED OF
FOREHOE.)

'Per Inquisicionem captam apud Norwicum die Veneris proximo post festum sancti martini dicto anno nono: videlicet.'

P. 18.—*Hyngham.* (Now *Hingham.*)

'Quod Gewardus Cockyn inclusit & posuit in pastura in villa de hyngham xl acras terre que fuerunt in cultura citra tempus dicte commissionis et messuagium dicte terre pertinens in decasu existit.'

The manor belonged to the Parkers, afterwards Lords Morley (Blomef. ii. 441).

P. 18.—*Morley.*

'Item Thomas parson habet vnum messuagium cum xxx acris terre in villa de Morley que fuerunt in cultura citra tempus dicte commissionis & iam in pastura posite & messuagium in decasu existit per quod vnum aratrum deletur.'

Here, as in the case of Rysyng Castell (p. 194), the aratrum is reckoned at thirty acres. See, however, *sub* Wendlyng, pp. 175–6, *supra*, and cp. p. 160, *supra*.

The manor belonged to the Parkers, afterwards Lords Morley (Blomef. ii. 481).

P. 18.—*Barnahambrome.* (*Bernham-Broom*, Blomefield. Now *Barnham Broom.*)

'Item Edwardus Chamberleyn armiger inclusit vnum clausum in villa de Barnahambrome continentem xxxiiij acras vnde iiij^{or} acre fuerunt in cultura citra tempus dicte commissionis que iam in pastura existunt per quod dicta villa caret le shakk de dictis xxxiiij acris.'

The area of thirty-four acres has not occurred before.

For 'le shakk' see *sub* Parua Parlond, pp. 200, 201, *supra*.

The Chamberleyns were lords of the manor (Blomef. ii. 380; see also *sub* l'arua Elyngham, p. 214, *infra*).

P. 18.—*Kemerley.* (Now *Kimberley.*)

'Item Thomas Woodhouse miles elargauit parcum suum

apud Kermerley cum xl acris terre que fuerunt in cultura citra tempus dicte commissionis.'

In the heading the copyist had begun Ker—and cancelled it, substituting Kemerley.

The Woodhouses had been lords of the manor since the fourteenth century (Blomef. ii. 537).

P. 18.—*Wyndham.* (Or *Wymondham.*)

'Item Thomas Tassall inclusit & posuit ad pasturam in villa de Wyndham xiij acras que fuerunt in cultura citra tempus dicte commissionis.'

The area of thirteen acres has not occurred before.

The several manors here belonged to the families of Fitz-William, Knevet, Appleyard, Wingfield, Lamb, Woodhousel and the Abbey of Wyndham or Wymondham (Blomef. ii. 500-18.

The family of Tatsall was of some consequence here (*ibid.* 526).

P. 19.—*Bowthorp.*

'Item Thomas hare decanus collegii de chappell in campo in Norwic tenet vnum tenementum vocatum Bothonis & xlviij acras terre eidem pertinentes in villa de Bowthorp quod tenementum deuastatum existit & xxvj acre terre predicte ad pasturam posite que fuerunt in cultura citra tempus dicte commissionis.

'Item idem decanus in iure dicti collegii tenet in dicta villa vnum tenementum vocatum wellys quod totaliter deuastatur & xviij acre terre eidem pertinentes ponuntur ad pasturam que nuper arate fuerunt.'

Neither the area of forty-eight nor that of eighteen acres has appeared attached to any dwelling before.

The Dean and Canons of the chapel of St. Mary in the Fields in the city of Norwich, commonly called the Chapel in the Fields, were lords of the manor and rectors. It is to be noted that shortly after this, in 1522, they petitioned the bishop of Norwich, 'that the church was of their patronage, and *that it was destitute of parishioners*, and therefore might more properly be made a chapel rather than remain a rectory with cure of souls, there being no inhabitants in the town but the college servants who tilled their lands,' &c. (Blomef. ii. 383-6). For the incloser see *sub* Loddon, *supra*.

P. 19.—HUNDRED DE BLOFELD & WALSHAM. (BLA-FELDA & WALESSAM, *Domesday*. Now BLOFIELD AND WALSHAM.)

'Per Inquisicionem captam die Veneris proximo post ffestum omnium sanctorum dicto anno nono coram prefatis commissionariis : videlicet.'

P. 19.—*Plompsted Magna*. (*Plumstede Magna*, Blomefield. Now *Great Plumstead*.)

'Quod Willelmus hermer tenet in ffirmam de priore de crischurche in Norwico manerium de magna plomsted unde posuit ad pasturam l acras que fuerunt in cultura citra tempus dicte commissionis per quod vnum aratrum deletur.'

For the areas assigned to an aratrum in this Inquisition, see p. 161. Cp. also *sub* Wendlyng, *supra*.

'Manerium' here at first sight appears to mean the area of a manor, not a manor-house. See *sub* Bastwyke, p. 213, *infra*.

The manor belonged to the Priors of Norwich (Blomef. vii. 139).

P. 19.—*Thorp episcopi*. (*Thorp-by-Norwich*, Blomefield.)

'Item Prior de Norwico habet vnum clausum vocatum limmer close in villa de Thorp episcopi continentem iiij^{xx} acras unde xl acre vse fuerunt pro cultura citra tempus commissionis & iam in pastura ponuntur.'

I.e. apparently by the Prior.

The manors here belonged to the Bishops and Priors of Norwich (Blomef. vii. 260-2).

P. 19.—*Plomsted*. (*Plumstede parva*, Blomefield. Now *Little Plumstead*.)

'Item executores Jacobi hobard militis habent vnum clausum continens [blank in MS.] in villa de magna plumsted quod fuit inclausum ante tempus dicte commissionis vnde ponuntur in pastura xv acre que fuerunt in cultura citra tempus commissionis predicte.'

Probably 'magna' is a clerical error for 'parva.'

This shows the process to have often been one of inclosure some time before conversion.

Sir James Hobard was Attorney-General to Henry VII., and lord of the manor of Little Plumstead.

Blomefield (vii. 243) says: 'Sir James died at a great age in the thirteenth year (as I take it) of King Henry VIII.,' *i.e.* 1521, but in the same page he speaks of 'Margery, his widow, who presented to this church [Little Plumstead] in 1517, as by her will, dated September 13, 1517, proved October 24, 1517.' She was therefore also dead at the time of this inquiry From the 'Dict. Nat. Biog.' it appears that the correct date of Sir James Hobard's death is 1507.

P. 19.—*Poswyke.* (*Posswic*, Domesday. *Poswick*, Blomefield. Now *Postwick.*)

'Item prior de Norwico posuit ad pasturam ouium in villa de poswyke l acras terre que fuerunt in cultura citra tempus dicte commissionis per quod vnum aratrum deletur.'

For the various areas assigned in this Inquisition to an aratrum see p. 161, *supra*.

The manor was the property of the Boleyns (Blomef. vii. 250). As the Prior is not stated to have been a tenant, he was probably a freeholder. Apparently he was himself a farmer. See *sub* Thorp episcopi, *supra*.

P. 19.—*Wytton.*

'Item dominus Jacobus hobard inclusit c acras terre in villa de Wytton & posuit easdem in pastura que fuerunt in cultura citra tempus commissionis predicte per quod vnum aratrum deletur.'

The area of 100 acres to an aratrum is without precedent in this Inquisition. See *supra*.

Probably 'dominus' as a member of the Privy Council. See *sub* Plomsted, *supra*.

The Hobards or Hobarts were lords of the manor (Blomef. vii. 265).

P. 19.—*Okyll.* (*Acle.*)

'Item Henricus palmer inclusit & posuit ad pasturam in villa de Okyll xxx acras que fuerunt in cultura citra tempus commissionis predicte.'

Acle in the hundred of Walsham.

The manor belonged to the Howards (Blomef. xi. 91). For the name of the incloser, cp. *sub* Dereham, *supra*.

P. 20.—*Bastwyke*. (*Wood-Bastwick*, Blomefield.)

'Item Johannes [blank in MS.] miles tenet ad firmam de magistro Curson manerium suum in Bastwyke quod posuit ad pasturam ouium & quod fuit in cultura citra tempus commissionis predicte per quod vnum aratrum deletur.'

The difficulty here again presents itself in an increased degree as to the area to be assigned to this inclosure. From the two previous examples of Haughboys Magna and Buxston (p. 185) it has been seen that a manerium has 100 to 180 acres attached, and may be taken roughly at 120 or more (see *sub* Wendlyng, *supra*). But the mention of the 'aratrum' complicates the question. Reason has been shown (cp. p. 161, *supra*) for taking the average aratrum at sixty acres. It is clear, both on principle and from the cases cited from this Inquisition, that a manerium would indicate a larger area than a villan's holding. I incline to the inference that 'aratrum' is here governed by 'manerium,' and is used, as in the case of Palgrave and in the sense given by Du Cange, for a ploughland or carucate of at least 120 acres. Cp. p. 166, n. 1, *supra*.

The Cursons were lords of the manor (Blomef. xi. 95).

P. 20.—*Cantely*. (Now *Cantly*.)

'Item Dominus matrauerse habet in villa de Cantely vnum clausum continens iiij^{xx} acras que fuerunt in cultura citra tempus commissionis & iam in pasturam conuertuntur.'

Sir William Arundel, Lord Matravers, had a grant of this lordship from the Crown in 1514 (Blomef. vii. 229). The inclosure was therefore recent.

P. 20.—HUNDRED DE WAYLOND & GRYMSOWE. (WANELUND & GRIMESHOU, *Domesday*. Now WAYLAND & GRIMSHOE.)

'Per Inquisicionem captam quinto die Nouembris anno nono predicto coram prefatis commissionariis: videlicet.'

P. 20.—*Saham Tony.*
'Quod infra villam de SahamTony hugo Cooe gent. inclusit lx acras terre que sunt in cultura sed dicta villa racione dicte clausure amisit le shakk.'

For 'shakk' see *sub* Parua Parlond, *supra*.

Hugh Cooe had become lord of the manor in 1507 (Blomef. ii. 330). The inclosure was therefore recent.

P. 20.—*Parua Elyngham*. (*Little Elyngham*, Blomefield. Now *Little Ellingham*.)

'Item in Elyngham parua Edwardus Chamberleyn armiger fecit vnum clausum de lxxvj acris que antea fuerunt arabiles & iam in pasturam conuertuntur & villa ea occasione amisit le shakk.'

The area of seventy-six acres has not occured before.

For 'shakk' see last note.

(Sir) Edward Chamberleyn was lord of the manor, but did not come into possession of it till after 1505 (Blomef. ii. 218). The inclosure was therefore recent.

For another inclosure by the same landowner see *sub* Barnahambrome, *supra*.

P. 20.—*Watton*. (*Wadetuna*, Domesday. Now *Watton*.)

'Item in Watton Robertus Strange fecit vnum clausum de lxxvij acris que arate fuerunt infra tempus dicte commissionis & iam in pasturam totaliter conuertuntur et le shakk perditur & modo in tenura Willelmi [blank in MS.].'

The area seventy-seven acres has not occurred before.

Strange does not seem to have been lord of any of the manors here. If this Robertus Strange is the same as Sir Robert l'Estrange, he probably succeeded to his elder brother in 1495 and died in 1511 (see Blomef. x., pedigree of l'Estrange). The date of the inclosure can thus be approximately arrived at, being apparently before he was knighted.

The manors here belonged to the families of Lovell and Colet (Blomef. ii. 314-15).

P. 20.—*Merton*.

'Item in Merton Thomas Grey clericus fecit vnum clausum de xxx^{ta} acris que arrate fuerunt infra tempus dicte commissionis & modo iacent in pastura racione cuius dicta villa amisit le shakke.'

Thomas Grey or de Grey, though an eldest son, did not succeed to this manor, the lordship of which was, nevertheless, in his family. (See Blomef. ii. 304.)

This inclosure was probably quite recent, as T. G. only took orders in 1515; see l.c.

'Item in eadem villa Johannes pory clericus fecit vnum clausum de xl acris infra tempus dicte commissionis que antea arrate fuerunt & modo in pastura existunt.'

John Pory was Rector of Merton (*ibid.*).

P. 20.—*Asshell.* (Now *Ashill.*)

'In Asshell Johannes Bullebroke posuit xxvj acras terre arrabilis ad pasturam ouium.'

'Item Thomas Germen & Christoferus Jenny armiger posuerunt lx acras olim arabiles ad pasturam ouium.'

For the area see *sub* Ketelston, p. 216, *infra.*

This Thomas German or Jermain bought one of the manors here from the Coes in 1526 (Blomef. ii. 354).

'Item in vno clauso lx acre terre includuntur olim arrabiles & modo ponuntur ad pasturam per Thomam Boleyn militem.'

One of the manors here (Panworth Hall manor) belonged to the Boleyns (*ibid.*).

P. 21.—*Methewold.* (Now *Methwold.*)

'Item in Methewold canonici de Thetford posuere xxx acras terre arabilis ad pasturam que fuerunt in cultura.'

I.e. The Prior and Canons of the Domus Dei of Thetford (see T. Martin's 'Hist. of Thetford,' 1779, p. 94).

The church and tithe belonged to the Prior and monks of Castle Acre (Blomef. ii. 207).

P. 21.—HUNDRED DE GALOWE & BROTHERCROSSE, (GALHOU & BRODECROSS, *Domesday.* Now GALLOW & BROTHERCROSS.)

'Per Inquisicionem captam die martis proximo post ffestum sancti martini Episcopi anno xl^{mo} Regis henrici viij^{ui} coram prefatis commissionariis: videlicet.'

P. 21.—*Ketelston.* (*Kettleston*, Blomefield. Now *Kettlestone.*)

'Quod Thomas Dalahay elargauit suam ouium pasturam in Ketelston cum xxvj acris terre que fuerunt in cultura citra tempus dicte commissionis, per quod dimidium aratrum deponitur.'

This explains the frequent recurrence of this area, though in no system of reckoning that I am acquainted with have fifty-two acres been taken as a carucate.

The two manors here belonged, one to the hospital or college at Pomfret, the other to the Welbys (Blomef. vii. 112, 113).

P. 21.—*Ryborow.* (*Ryburgh Magna*, Blomefield. Now *Great Ryburgh.*)

'Item Willelmus Coke ffirmarius prioris de Walsyngham elargauit pasturam ouium in Ryborowe cum iiij^{xx} acris terre que fuerunt in cultura citra tempus dicte commissionis, per quod vnum aratrum deletur.'

'ffirmar' in MS. The word 'firmarius' is defined by Du Cange (edit. Favre, 1885, *s.v.*) as 'vicarius seu presbyter cui ecclesia deservienda committitur.' In this Inquisition it is used solely of a farmer dependent on a religious house (cp. on p. 264, *infra*, the 'firmarius domus llantoni,' at Walford, Herefordshire). I am disposed to believe that it indicates a clerical farmer, and this appears more clearly from the case of Yarpole, Herefordshire, p. 267, *infra*). If it had simply meant a lessee (see Digby, 'Hist. of Law of Real Property,' 4th edit. p. 29, n. 1) the word would have occurred before, and in relation to lay landlords; whereas we have 'habet ad firmam,' as at Brabyngle, *supra*, and 'occupator, as at Taunestorn in Yorkshire, p. 247, *infra*. An explanation of the appropriateness of the term 'firmarius' to the agricultural furnisher of a religious house is given in Hale's Introduction to the Domesday of St. Paul's, Camden Soc. 1858, xxxviii., whence it appears that the original meaning of the Anglo-Saxon word was 'one who supplies with food.'

The Prior and convent of Walsingham were lords of the manor (Blomef. vii. 164).

P. 21.—*Destreton.* (*Testerton.*)
'Item Robertus Wolby elargauit pasturam ouium in Destreton cum iiij^{xx} acris terre que fuerunt in cultura citra tempus dicte commissionis per quod vnum aratrum deletur.'

Note eighty acres equal one aratrum. So in four other cases in this Hundred, cp. p. 159, *supra.*

The manor belonged to the Appleyards (Blomef. vii. 199).

P. 21.—*Northbarsham.* (*Barscham,* Domesday. Now *North Barsham.*)

'Item Thomas Seyfowle elargauit pasturam ouium in Northe Barsham cum iiij^{xx} acris terre que fuerunt in cultura citra tempus dicte commissionis per quod vnum aratrum deletur.'

Note, the 'aratrum' as before.

The Sefoule family were lords of the manor (*ibid.* 49).

P. 21.—*Bagthorp.* (*Bagthorpe,* Blomefield.)

'Item prior de Castellacre elargauit suam ouium pasturam apud Bagthorp cum xl acris terre que fuerunt in cultura citra tempus dicte commissionis, per quod vnum aratrum deletur.'

Note, forty acres to one aratrum.

The manor belonged to the Priory of Castleacre (*ibid.* 41).

For other inclosures by this Prior see p. 153, *supra.*

P. 21.—*Skulthorp.* (*Sculetorpa,* Domesday. *Sculthorp,* Blomefield. Now *Sculthorpe.*)

'Item henricus ffermer elargauit suam ouium pasturam apud Skulthorp cum iiij^{xx} acris terre que fuerunt in cultura citra tempus dicte commissionis per quod vnum aratrum deletur.'

Note, eighty acres to one aratrum.

The lordship of this manor belonged to the college of the Holy Trinity, called Knolles Almshouses, in Pontefract. Upon the Dissolution it passed to the family of the Fermers (*ibid.* 176). For Henry ffermer or Fermor see pp. 154, 181, *supra.* From the latter of these references it would seem that this inclosure had been redressed by this commission.

P. 21.—*Howton.* (*Houghton.*)

'Item Edwardus Walpole & henricus Walpole elargauit suam ouium pasturam apud howton cum iiij^{xx} acris terre que fuerunt in cultura citra tempus dicte commissionis per quod vnum aratrum deletur.'

As before in this Hundred, eighty acres to one aratrum.

These were the two sons of Thomas Walpole who died in 1512. The inclosure was therefore recent.

The manor had belonged to the Walpoles since the time of Edward III. (*ibid.* 106).

P. 22.—*Estrudham.* (*Rudeham,* Domesday. Now *East Rudham.*)

'Item prior de Cokysford elargauit suam ouium pasturam in Estrudham cum iiij^{xx} acris terre que fuerunt in cultura citra tempus dicte commissionis per quod duo aratra delentur.'

Note, forty acres to an aratrum.

The manor belonged to the Priory of Coxford (Blomef. vii. 155).

P. 22.—*Westrudham.* (*West Rudham.*)

'Item henricus Russell elargauit suam ouium pasturam in Westrudham cum xl acris terre que fuerunt in cultura citra tempus dicte commissionis per quod vnum aratrum deletur.'

Note, forty acres to an aratrum.

The Russells were the lords of the manor (*ibid.* 159).

P. 22.—*Burnham.*

'Item magister doctor Dussyng elargauit suam ouium pasturam in Burnham cum xl acris terre que fuerunt in cultura citra tempus dicte commissionis per quod dimidium aratrum deletur.'

Here eighty acres to an aratrum.

Robert Dussyng was rector from 1510 to 1540, so that this is a case of clerical farming, perhaps of glebe land.

The manor belonged to the Calthorpe family. (See Blomef. *ibid.* 12, 15).

YORKSHIRE

INTRODUCTION

THE statistical character of the Inquisition for Yorkshire resembles that of Norfolk in the smallness of the area returned as inclosed. In proportion to the whole area surveyed by the commissioners, the extent of inclosure is absolutely insignificant. For the three Ridings together it amounts to no more than 6,678½ acres, or nearly 4,000 fewer than the number inclosed in the county of Norfolk. As compared with Norfolk there are other indications of the backward state of agriculture. With the exception of a doubtful fifteen acres at fflenton, East Riding, none of the areas inclosed was inclosed with the object of improved arable farming. While in Norfolk only 277 acres were inclosed as parks, in Yorkshire the inclosures in the North Riding for the purposes of the chase were 628 acres, or 23·19 per cent. of the whole area returned as inclosed; in the West Riding 1,812 acres, or no less than 77·27 per cent. of the whole; in the East Riding 230 acres, being 14·15 per cent. of the whole area of inclosures returned. These parks were naturally inclosed by the lords out of the wastes of the manors. None of them occurs upon the ecclesiastical manors in which inclosures took place.

In the North Riding the proportion of land inclosed upon ecclesiastical manors is remarkably close to that in Norfolk. It stands at 20·6 per cent., or 24·29 per cent. if certain doubtful cases are included, as compared with 24·86 per cent. or 30·76 per cent. in Norfolk. In the West Riding it is insignificant. In the East Riding it amounts to 15·38 per cent. of the whole area inclosed.

If, on the other hand, we compare the area of the inclosures actually effected by ecclesiastics and laymen respectively, while in the North Riding the proportion is somewhat higher than in Norfolk, amounting to 27·69 per cent. inclosed by ecclesiastics, as against 72·3 per cent. by laymen, in the East Riding the share of the ecclesiastics falls to 7·56 per cent. as contrasted with that of laymen, which is 92·43 per cent.

In Norfolk we hear nothing of wood. In the North Riding no mention of it occurs. It frequently appears among the inclosures of the West Riding, and more seldom among those of the East Riding. But its acreage is rarely stated with precision, it being generally returned along with an inclosure of pasture. The conjunction of the two again points to inclosures of the wastes of manors.

The returns for Yorkshire are far more explicit than those for Norfolk as to the displacement of population. The three heads under which this is registered are: ploughs put down, houses decayed or destroyed, and actual evictions. It has been seen in the case of Norfolk[1] that it is not safe to infer from the mention of the putting down of ploughs the eviction of a proportionate number of persons, unless such is expressly recorded. On the other hand, we have such returns in the Yorkshire Inquisition as of houses destroyed, while no mention is made of persons evicted. Such a case is at Est Tanfeld, in the North Riding, where eight houses are returned as having been thrown down, but nothing is said as to their inhabitants. At Temple Newsome, in the West Riding, a whole 'villa' of four messuages and four cottages is returned as having been destroyed and four ploughs put down, but nothing is said as to evictions.[2] That such must

[1] P. 161, *supra*.
[2] This use of 'villa' disposes of Professor Ashley's contention in the *English Historical Review* for April 1893, that the putting down of a 'villa' implied a great displacement of population which must necessarily have included copyholders. For further answer to this, see an article by the writer in the *English Historical Review* for October 1893 on 'The Security of Copyholders in the Fifteenth and Sixteenth Centuries.'

THE INQUISITION OF 1517

have taken place, either at the time of or with a view to the inclosure is quite clear. It must be remembered, too, as accounting for the diversity of the returns, that the original documents were parchment slips,[1] framed according to the discretion of the jury in consonance with the general tenour of the Commission, handed in to the clerk of the Commission for transmission to the Court of Chancery. We may take it, therefore, that where houses are recorded to have been destroyed, there a displacement of the inhabitants took place, whether express mention is made of the fact or not. Whether, in cases where evictions are recorded, but no houses are said to have been pulled down, such destruction actually happened, as at fflenton, East Riding, need not concern us, the number of persons evicted, rather than the number of houses destroyed, being the principal point of interest.

That this principle of interpreting the returns is correct may be inferred from a consideration of those for the North Riding. Here forty-four evictions are specifically enumerated. The houses pulled down number twenty-nine, of which five are cottages. Now, if we are to reckon only so many evictions as are specifically recorded, without any reference to the houses stated to have been destroyed, we arrive at the incredible conclusion that the inhabitants of every house averaged one person and a half. Taking the cases in the three Ridings in which a specific number of persons is associated with a house, we find the averages to a 'messuagium' to be roughly four and a half in the North Riding and East Riding, and four persons in the West Riding. The inferred estimate of four persons evicted for each messuage and three for each cottage destroyed cannot be far from the truth, and, at least, does not err on the side of exaggeration. The displacement of population thus arrived at amounts to 128 persons in the North Riding, 94 in the West Riding, and 171 in the East Riding: in all, 393

[1] As may be seen in the Record Office. See Introd. p. 175, *Trans. R. H. S.* 1892.

persons. This is actually a larger displacement than that which occurred in Norfolk, though, as has been seen, on a considerably smaller acreage of inclosures.

In the North Riding there are signs that the ecclesiastical landowners dealt less arbitrarily with their tenants than was the case with the laity. Only two of their inclosures are marked by evictions: that at Steueton, and that at Sourbey Undercotclyff. The total number of persons evicted by them was twelve. This is no more than 9·37 per cent. of the entire number of persons evicted in this Riding, although the land inclosed upon ecclesiastical manors amounts to 20·6 per cent. or 24·29 per cent. of the whole, and the inclosures actually made by ecclesiastics form 27·69 of the whole. In the East Riding there were five ecclesiastical manors upon which evictions occurred. But in one of these, Monkewyke, we are distinctly told that a layman was the evictor; nor is it certain from the record whether at Ottringham the evictor was the ecclesiastical lord of the manor or the tenant. In this Riding the proportion of ecclesiastical land inclosed has been seen to have amounted to 15·38 per cent. Excluding the case of Monkewyke, the percentage of evictions on ecclesiastical property is as high as 18·02; but if we further exclude the case of Ottringham, in which the names of the tenants are given, as though they, and not the lord, were the agents of eviction, the percentage sinks to 10·46. On the other hand it must be remembered that this percentage, which remains the same, must be compared with 7·56 per cent. representing proportion of area inclosed by ecclesiastics themselves. From this point of view their operations were harsher towards the tenantry.

The Lansdowne MS., from which these returns are taken, had been examined by Poulson, while writing his 'History of Holderness.' See *ibid.* ii. 61.

ANALYSIS OF THE INQUISITION FOR YORKSHIRE

I.—AREAS INCLOSED ON LAY AND ECCLESIASTICAL MANORS

Riding	Area of Riding	Total area inclosed	Inclosures remaining arable	Conversions and pasture &c. areas inclosed	Areas of inclosure on lay manors			Areas of inclosure on ecclesiastical manors		
					Total	Remaining arable	Conversions and pasture areas inclosed	Total	Remaining arable	Conversions and pasture areas inclosed
	acres	acres	acres	acres	acres	acres	acres	acres	acres	acres
North	1,275,820	2,708	—	2,708	2,050 (2,150)[1]	—	2,050 (2,150)	558 (658)	—	558 (658)
West	1,648,640	2,345	—	2,345	2,252 (2,345)	—	2,252 (2,345)	0 (93)	—	0 (93)
East	711,360	1,560	15	1,545	1,376	15	1,361	249½	—	249½
Total	3,635,820	6,613	15	6,598	5,678 (5,871)	15	5,663 (5,856)	807¾ (1,000¾)[2]	—	807¾ (1,000¾)

II.—PROPORTIONATE ANALYSIS OF TOTAL AREAS INCLOSED

Riding	Proportion of total area inclosed to area of Riding	Proportion of inclosures remaining arable to total area inclosed	Proportion of conversions and inclosure of pasture &c. to total area inclosed
North	·02	—	100
West	·01	—	100
East	·02	·02	99·03
Total	·01	·02	99·77

[1] Where two numbers are given, that in brackets is the number if the doubtful cases are included. The totals will then be obtained by adding the bracketed figures of the column giving the ecclesiastical areas to the appropriate unbracketed figures of the columns giving the areas upon lay manors.
[2] Omitting the ¾.

III

PROPORTIONATE ANALYSIS OF AREAS INCLOSED ON LAY AND ECCLESIASTICAL MANORS

Riding	Lay Manors					Ecclesiastical Manors				
	Proportion of areas inclosed to total areas inclosed	Proportion of inclosures remaining arable to total areas inclosed	Proportion of inclosures remaining arable to total areas inclosed on lay manors	Proportion of conversions of pasture and inclosures to total areas inclosed	Proportion of conversions and inclosures of pasture to total areas inclosed on lay manors	Proportion of areas inclosed to total areas inclosed	Proportion of inclosures remaining arable to total areas inclosed	Proportion of inclosures remaining arable to total areas inclosed on ecclesiastical manors	Proportion of conversions and inclosures of pasture to total areas inclosed	Proportion of conversionsions and inclosures of pasture to total areas inclosed on ecclesiastical manors
North . . .	75·7 (79·3)	—	—	75·7 (79·3)	100	20·6 (24·29)[1]	—	—	20·6 (24·29)	100
West . . .	96·03 (100)	—	—	96·03 (100)	100	0 (3·96)	—	—	0 (3·96)	100
East . . .	84·67	·06	1·09	84·36	99·62	15·32 [2]	—	—	15·32	100
Total . .	85·02 (87·91)	·02	·02 (·02)	84·8 (87·69)	99·73 (99·74)	12·08 (14·97)	—	—	12·08 (14·97)	100

[1] Where two numbers are given, that in brackets is the number if the doubtful cases are included. The totals will then be obtained by adding the bracketed figures of the columns giving the ecclesiastical areas to the appropriate unbracketed figures of the columns giving the areas upon lay manors.

[2] Omitting the ⅓.

THE INQUISITION OF 1517

IV. NORTH RIDING

INCLOSURES ON ECCLESIASTICAL MANORS

Place	—	Incloser		
		Manorial lord	Layman	Ecclesiastic
Steueton	acres 200	1	—	—
Fylyng	8	—	—	—
Northottryngton	115	—	1	1
Soureby Undercotclyff	(155)	1	—	—
Marderbury	80	1	—	—
Total	558			

Add probably Dysford 40, Kyrkbywyske 24, and Mekelbargh 36. Probable total inclosures on ecclesiastical manors in North Riding = 658.

INCLOSURES ON DOUBTFUL MANORS

Place	—	Incloser	
		Layman	Ecclesiastic
Dysford	acres 40	—	1
Kyrkbywyske	24	—	1
Mekelbargh	36	—	1

WEST RIDING

INCLOSURES ON DOUBTFUL MANORS

Place	—	Incloser		Ploughs	Houses	Evicted
		Layman	Ecclesiastic			
Moretoun	acres (93)	—	1	3	3	12

EAST RIDING

INCLOSURES ON ECCLESIASTICAL MANOR

Place	—	Lord	Layman	Ploughs	Houses	Evicted
Monkewyke	acres (31)	—	1	1	1	4
Hynginge Grymston	40	1	—	2	2	8
ffraysthorp	40	1	—	—	—	—
Swyne	(31)	—	—	1	1	6
Hillom	(7½)	—	—	—	1	4
Ottringham	(100)	—	1	—	3	13

N.S.—VOL. VII.

V.

ACTUAL INCLOSERS

LAYMEN		ECCLESIASTICS	
North Riding	Acres	*North Riding*	Acres
Horneby	400		
South Cowton	120		
Harum	60		
		Steueton	200
Danby	40		
Thorntonbrige	60		
Snappe	100		
Hoton	60		
		Dysford	40
		Kyrkbywyske	24
Est Tanfeld	400		
Kylton	28		
Droton	30		
ffylyng	8		
Brieforde	20		
Thornton in lestrete	200		
		Northoteryngton	(115)
		Soureby Undercotclyff	(155)
Swalfeld	60		
		Colesby	100
		Marderbury	80
Southholme	120		
Styknam	104		
fferlyngton	40		
		Mekelbargh	36
Emslay	60		
Leuerton	40		
Lytyll Hayton	8		
	1958		750

West Riding		*West Riding*	
Temple Newsome	80		
Byrkyn	80		
Leyde	40		
Kydall	30		
		Moretoun	(93)
Calverley	20		
fferneley	100		
Bollyng & Denholme	(400)		

THE INQUISITION OF 1517

ACTUAL INCLOSERS—*Continued*

LAYMEN		ECCLESIASTICS	
West Riding—cont.	Acres	*West Riding*—cont.	Acres
Houdysworth	40		
Thornehill	60		
Cheyte	(31)		
(Kinsley)	10		
Wentworth	4		
Emssall	4		
Woley	4		
Thriber	86		
Longstroth	40		
Barden	(400)		
Houedon	(300)		
Carlton in Crayvyne	40		
Braswell	3		
Hammerton	20		
Brodeley	20		
Rymyngton	100		
Bolton	100		
Lytyll Newton	40		
Newfeld	20		
Alburgh ('parochia')	180		
	2252		93

East Riding		*East Riding*	
Brystwyke	100		
Grymston	40		
Monkewyke	(31)		
ffoytit	20		
Wharrom Percy	(124)		
Taunestorn	40		
Cayrthorp	200		
Lekenfeld	140		
Scarbrugh	80		
Holme	10		
		Hynginge Grymston	40
Estryngton	14		
		Ffraysthorp	40
Carleton	(31)		
Skarlagh Benyngholme	(31)		
		Swyne	(31)
Thurkylby	3		
ffyley	(78)		
fflenton	(52)		

Q 2

ACTUAL INCLOSERS—*Continued*

LAYMEN	ECCLESIASTICS
East Riding—cont.	*East Riding*—cont.

	Acres		Acres
fflenton	(15)		
Lylly & Dyke	(45)		
Attenwike	(78)		
Lytill Cowden	100		
Beforth	(45)		
		Hillom	(7½)
Ottringham	(100)		
ffythynge	3		
Sprotley	(62)		
	1442		118⅛

VI.—ANALYSIS OF LAY AND ECCLESIASTICAL INCLOSURES

	Lay inclosures			Ecclesiastical inclosures		
Riding	Total inclosures	Inclosures remaining arable	Conversions and inclosures of pasture	Total inclosures	Inclosures remaining arable	Conversions and inclosures of pasture
	acres	acres	acres	acres	acres	acres
North	1,958	—	1,958	750	—	750
West	2,252	—	2,252	93	—	93
East	1,442	15	1,427	118⅛	—	118⅛

VII.—PROPORTIONATE SUMMARY OF LAY AND ECCLESIASTICAL INCLOSURES

	Lay inclosures					Ecclesiastical inclosures				
Riding	Proportion of areas inclosed to total areas inclosed	Proportion of inclosures remaining arable to total areas inclosed	Proportion of inclosures remaining arable to total areas inclosed by laymen	Proportion of conversions and inclosures of pasture to total areas inclosed	Proportion of conversions and inclosures of pasture to total areas inclosed by laymen	Proportion of areas inclosed to total areas inclosed	Proportion of inclosures remaining arable to total areas inclosed	Proportion of inclosures remaining arable to total areas inclosed by ecclesiastics	Proportion of conversions of pasture to total areas inclosed	Proportion of conversions and inclosures of pasture to total areas inclosed by ecclesiastics
North	72·3	—	—	72·3	100	27·69	—	—	27·69	100
West	96·03	—	—	96·03	100	3·96	—	—	3·96	100
East	92·43	·09	10·4	92·43	100	7·56	—	—	7·56	100

THE INQUISITION OF 1517

VIII.—DECAY OF HOUSES AND DISPLACEMENT OF POPULATION, &C.

Place	Ploughs put down	Persons evicted [1]	Houses decayed	Population displaced [2]
North Riding				
South Cowton	4	20	4 mess.	20
Harum	2	—	--	—
Steueton	4	4	—	4
Est Tanfeld	—	—	8 mess.	(32)
Thornton in lestrete	6	—	5 cott.	(24) [3]
Northoteryngton	4	—	—	—
Soureby Undercotclyff	5	—	2 mess.	(8) [4]
Marderbury	2	—	—	—
Southholme	5	20	5 mess.	20
Styknam	4	—	5 { 2 mess. / 3 cott. }	(20) [5]
Emslay	1	—	—	—
Total	37	44	29	128
West Riding				
Temple Newsome	4	—	8 { 4 mess. / 4 cott. }	(32) [6]
Moretoun	3	12	3 mess.	12
Cheyte	1	4	1 mess.	4
Rymyngton	4	30	(4 mess.)	30
Bolton	4	12	3 mess.	12
Lytyll Newton	—	—	1 mess.	(4)
Total	16	58	20	94
East Riding				
Grymston	2	8	2 mess.	8
Monkewyke	1	4	1 mess.	4
Wharrom Percy	4	—	4 mess.	(16)
Cayrthorp	5	20	5 mess.	20
Hynginge Grymston	2	8	2 mess.	8
Carleton	1	6	1 mess.	6
Skarlagh Benyngholme	—	4	1 ten.	4
Swyne	1	6	1 mess.	6
Thurkylby	—	—	2 cott.	(6)
ffyley	—	10	2 mess.	10
fflenton	—	4	(1 mess.)	4
fflenton	—	3	1 mess.	3
Lylly & Dyke	—	—	1 mess.	4
Attenwike	—	17	4 { (3 mess.) / 1 cott. }	17
Lytill Cowden	4	24	(6 mess.)	24
Beforth	—	6	1 mess.	6
Hillom	—	4	1 mess.	4
Ottringham	—	13	(3 ten.)	13
Sprotley	—	8	(2 mess.)	8
Total	20	145	41	171

[1] *i.e.* actually specified. [2] *i.e.* implied or mentioned.
[3] Here I have reckoned by the number of ploughs put down, at four persons to a plough.
[4] *i.e.* at four persons to a messuagium. [5] *i.e.* at four persons to a house. See next note.
[6] This must have included a greater number than sixteen, or four to a plough. I have, therefore, given the average of five for each messuagium and three for each cotagium = 32. The exact average for the messuagium in the North Riding is 4½.

III
PROPORTIONATE ANALYSIS OF AREAS INCLOSED ON LAY AND ECCLESIASTICAL MANORS

Riding	Lay Manors				Ecclesiastical Manors			
	Proportion of areas inclosed to total areas	Proportion of inclosures remaining arable to total areas inclosed	Proportion of inclosures remaining arable to total areas inclosed on lay manors	Proportion of conversions and inclosures of pasture to total areas inclosed	Proportion of conversions and inclosures of pasture to total areas inclosed on lay manors	Proportion of areas inclosed to total areas	Proportion of inclosures remaining arable to total areas inclosed	Proportion of inclosures remaining arable to total areas inclosed on ecclesiastical manors	Proportion of conversions and inclosures of pasture to total areas inclosed	Proportion of conversions and inclosures of pasture to total areas inclosed on ecclesiastical manors
North	75·7 (79·3)	—	—	75·7 (79·3)	100	20·6 (24·29)	—	—	20·6 (24·29)	100
West	96·03 (100)	—	—	96·03 (100)	100	0 (3·96)	—	—	0 (3·96)	100
East	84·67	·06	1·09	84·36	99·62	15·32 [2]	—	—	15·32	100
Total	85·02 (87·91)	·02	·02	84·8 (87·69)	99·73 (99·74)	12·08 (14·97)	—	—	12·08 (14·97)	100

[1] Where two numbers are given, that in brackets is the number if the doubtful cases are included. The totals will then be obtained by adding the bracketed figures of the columns giving the ecclesiastical areas to the appropriate unbracketed figures of the columns giving the areas upon lay manors.
[2] Omitting the ⅔.

IV. NORTH RIDING

INCLOSURES ON ECCLESIASTICAL MANORS

Place	—	Incloser		
		Manorial lord	Layman	Ecclesiastic
	acres			
Steueton	200	1	—	—
Fylyng	8	—	—	—
Northottryngton	115	—	1	1
Soureby Undercotclyff	(155)	1	—	—
Marderbury	80	1	—	—
Total	558			

Add probably Dysford 40, Kyrkbywyske 24, and Mekelbargh 36. Probable total inclosures on ecclesiastical manors in North Riding = 658.

INCLOSURES ON DOUBTFUL MANORS

Place	—	Incloser	
		Layman	Ecclesiastic
	acres		
Dysford	40	—	1
Kyrkbywyske	24	—	1
Mekelbargh	36	—	1

WEST RIDING

INCLOSURES ON DOUBTFUL MANORS

Place	—	Incloser		Ploughs	Houses	Evicted
		Layman	Ecclesiastic			
	acres					
Moretoun	(93)	—	1	3	3	12

EAST RIDING

INCLOSURES ON ECCLESIASTICAL MANOR

Place	—	Lord	Layman	Ploughs	Houses	Evicted
	acres					
Monkewyke	(31)	—	1	1	1	4
Hynginge Grymston	40	1	—	2	2	8
ffraysthorp	40	1	—	—	—	—
Swyne	(31)	—	—	1	1	6
Hillom	(7½)	—	—	—	1	4
Ottringham	(100)	—	1	—	3	13

IX.—DISPLACEMENT OF POPULATION BY LAY AND ECCLESIASTICAL INCLOSERS

North Riding

	Ploughs put down By Laymen	By Ecclesiastics
South Cowton	4	—
Harum	2	—
Steueton	—	4
Thornton in lestrete	6	—
Northoteryngton	—	4
Soureby Undercotclyff	—	5
Marderbury	—	2
Southholme	5	—
Styknam	4	—
Emslay	1	—
Total	22	15

North Riding

	Persons evicted [1] By Laymen	By Ecclesiastics
South Cowton	20	—
Steueton	—	4
Southholme	20	—
Total	40	4

West Riding

	By Laymen	By Ecclesiastics
Temple Newsom	4	—
Moretoun	—	3
Cheyte	1	—
Rymyngton	4	—
Bolton	4	—
Total	13	3

West Riding

	By Laymen	By Ecclesiastics
Moretoun	—	12
Cheyte	4	—
Rymyngton	30	—
Bolton	12	—
Total	46	12

East Riding

	By Laymen	By Ecclesiastics
Grymston	2	—
Monkewyke	1	—
Wharrom Percy	4	—
Cayrthorp	5	—
Hynginge Grymston	—	2
Carleton	1	—
Swyne	—	1
Lytill Cowden	4	—
Total	17	3

East Riding

	By Laymen	By Ecclesiastics
Grymston	8	—
Monkewyke	4	—
Cayrthorp	20	—
Hynginge Grymston	—	8
Carleton	6	—
Skarlagh Benyngholme	4	—
Swyne	—	6
ffyley	10	—
fflenton	4	—
fflenton	3	—
Attenwike	17	—
Lytill Cowden	24	—
Beforth	6	—
Hillom	—	4
Ottringham	13	—
Sprotley	8	—
Total	127	18

[1] *i.e.* actually mentioned in the MS. as evicted.

THE INQUISITION OF 1517

X

AREAS ASSIGNED TO AN 'ARATRUM' IN THE INQUISITION FOR YORKSHIRE

No.	Place	Acres	The 'aratrum' associated with	Population	Page
1	South Cowton	30	a messuagium	5	233
2	Harum	30	—	—	234
3	Steueton	50	inhabitacio	(2)	234
4	Est Tanfeld	50	messuagium	—	235
5	Thornton in lestrete	33⅓	cotagium [1]	—	237
6	Northoteryngton	28⅔	—	—	237
7	Marderbury	40	—	—	238
8	Southholme	16	{ messuagium. } { inhabitacio. }	4	238
9	Styknam	20	messuagium	—	238
10	Emslay	60	—	—	239
11	Moretoun	—	messuagium	4	241
12	Cheyte	—	messuagium	4	242
13	Rymyngton	25	messuagium	7½	244
14	Bolton	25	messuagium [2]	3[3]	245
15	Grymston	20	messuagium	4	246
16	Cayrthorp	40	messuagium	5	247
17	Hynginge Grymston	20	messuagium	4	248
18	Carleton	—	messuagium	6	249
19	Skarlagh Benyngholme	—	tenementum	4	249
20	Swyne	—	messuagium	6	249
21	Little Cowden	25	—	6	251

[1] But 40 acres to the cotagium. See p. 237, *infra*.
[2] Three messuages and four ploughs to 100 acres. See p. 244, *infra*.
[3] *I.e.* per aratrum, 4 per messuagium, the total being 12.

XI

AREAS ASSIGNED TO HOUSES

Transcript page	—	—	Acres
23	South Cowton	messuagium	30
23	Steueton	inhabitacio	Qu.
25	Est Tanfeld	messuagium	50
25	Thornton in lestrete	cotagium	40
26	Southholme	messuagium	24
26	Styknam	—	Qu.
30	Bolton	messuagium	33⅓
30	Lytyll Newton	messuagium	40
30	Grymston	messuagium	20
31	Cayrthorp	messuagium	40
31	Hynginge Grymston	messuagium	20
32	Thurkylby	cotagium	1⅓
33	Beforth	messuagium	45
33	Hillom	messuagium	7½

This gives to the messuagium an average of 31 acres.

XII.

Averages Collected from the Yorkshire Inquisition

Aratrum . . = $30\frac{19}{171}$ acres		I take it, therefore, at thirty-one acres.
Messuagium . . = 31 ,,		It is generally associated with an aratrum.
Cotagium		There are only three examples of these. One at Thornton in Iestrete has forty acres. Two at Thurkylby have three acres between them. Perhaps three may be taken as the number of inhabitants of each.
Number of inhabitants of a messuagium . = 4		The average number of inhabitants of a messuagium is four in the W.R., $4\frac{1}{2}$ in the N.R., and $4\frac{7}{11}$ in the E.R. But as a messuagium generally signifies the dwelling-house accompanying an aratrum, I have thought it best to take it as implying four persons, where not otherwise expressed.
Number of inhabitants associated with an aratrum . . . = 4		Where an aratrum is alone mentioned with a population dependent upon it, I take the average number at four. The average is $4\frac{2}{7}$ in the E.R., $4\frac{1}{3}$ in the W.R., and in the N.R., if Steueton be included, where four persons are represented as evicted in
At Skarlagh Benyng-holme a tenementum contains . . . 4		consequence of the putting down of four ploughs, $2\frac{3}{13}$. The average based on the other cases in the N.R. is about $4\frac{1}{3}$.

The Commissioners nominated for Yorkshire were William Conyers, Lord Hornby, of Hornby Castle (see Whitaker's 'History of Richmondshire,' ii. 43, 45, 46, 51); Thomas Dalby, Archdeacon of Richmond, who, having been excepted from the general pardon at the beginning of the reign (Br. *Cal.*. i. 12), was in 1511 promoted to the office of chaplain to the king (*ibid.* 1637); Hugh Asshton, clerk, a favourite of Margaret, Countess of Richmond, mother of Henry VII. (*ibid.* 236), and one of her executors (*ibid.* 406, 5296, ii. 688), a canon of the collegiate chapel of St. Stephen's, Westminster, in 1509 (i. 107), before 1511 incumbent of Cresmere, Yorkshire (*ibid.* 1904), and in 1518 on the commission of sewers for that county (ii. 4250); Sir John Norton, a magistrate for the East and West Ridings (*ibid.* i. 3219, &c., and 1798, &c.), and William Elleson, a commissioner of sewers for Yorkshire (*ibid.* 274, ii. 4250), and a magistrate for the West Riding (i. 1995).

YORKSHIRE

(Lansd. MS. I. fo. 167-172)

P. 23.—'Per transcriptum cuiusdam Inquisicionis indentate capte apud Castrum Eboracense die sabbati proximo post ffestum sancti Michaelis archangeli Anno regni Regis Henrici viij^{ul} nono coram Thoma Dalby archideacono [*sic*] Rychmond & aliis commissionariis.'

Apparently, as in the case of Norfolk, one ecclesiastic as chairman of the Commission and to represent the interests of the Church.

(*Hornby.*)

'Willelmus Conyes miles dominus Conyes inclusit in suo parco pro feris nutriendis apud Horneby in Northriding in comitatu predicto ci[r]citer cccc acras terre quarum centum acre fuerunt tunc in cultura.'

This was William Conyers, Lord Conyers, of Hornby Castle (Whitaker's 'History of Richmondshire,' ii. 43, 44, 45, 46, 51). This record of his inclosures is an evidence of the impartiality of the Commissioners.

'Et quod Ricardus Conyes miles defunctus conuertit post ffestum sancti Michaelis archangeli anno quarto Henrici vij^{mi} apud Sowthcowton in predicto Northriding cxx acras terre in pasturam que erant in predicto ffesto sancti Michaelis anno quarto in cultura per quod quatuor messuagia & quatuor aratra prosternuntur & xx^{ti} persone ea de causa ab inhabitacionibus suis recesserunt. Et quod uxor nuper Radulphi Bowes militis est tenens liberi tenementi illius.'

It is to be noted that here the area of the 'aratrum' is a virgate or thirty acres, a normal husbandholding, the fourth part of a carucate in a three-course manor (Seebohm, p. 62), and that five persons are reckoned to the messuagium.

'Tenens liberi tenementi illius': perhaps tenant in dower (cp. *sub* Leuerton, p. 239, *infra*, and 'Old Tenures'[ed. 1525]: 'Tenir en fraunke tenaunt est a tenir a terme de sa vie demesne, ou a terme de autre vie,' p. 4). R. C. was probably lord of the manor.

'Nenianus Markynfeld miles post ffestum sancti Michaelis anno quarto Regis Henrici vij^{mi} apud Harum super Teyse in predicto Northriding conuertit lx acras terre tunc in cultura in pasturam & ea de causa duo arratra prosternuntur.'

The Markinfields were landowners at Sourton (Whitaker, ii. 68), and presumably lords of this manor.

'Abbas monasterii beate maug [*sic*] extra muros civitatis Eboraci apud Steueton in dicto Northriding post predictum ffestum sancti Michaelis inclusit & conuertit cc acras terre tunc in cultura in pasturam & quod ea causa iiij^{or} arratra prosternuntur & iiij^{or} persone ab inhabitacionibus suis recesserunt.'

The MS. has 'beate maug.' I have failed to identify this in Dugdale, Leland, Burton, or Drake. It is probably the blunder of a copyist who could not read 'Marye.' The dedication of the 'monasterium beate Marie iuxta civitatem Ebor' was to St. Mary the Virgin.

'Steueton.' No such place exists. I am inclined to take it to be a clerical error for (Great) Smeaton, or Smeton, also called Smythedon, which is in the neighbourhood (Whitaker, i. 242, 247), and of which the abbot of St. Mary's was lord. (Dugdale, 'Monast.' iii. 573.)

'Johannes Carr miles apud Danby in predicto Northriding post predictum ffestum sancti Michaelis inclusit in uno parco pro feris nutriendis xl acras terre tunc arrabilis.'

Danby: *i.e.* Danby Wiske.

As the park would naturally be formed for the most part out of the waste of the manor, I infer that Carr was lord. See Introduction in 'Trans. R.H.S.' 1892, pp. 254-6.

P. 24.—'Ricardus Nevyll armiger apud Thorntonbrige

in dicto Northriding post predictum ffestum sancti Michaelis inclusit in uno parco pro feris nutriendis lx acras terre tunc in cultura.'

Cp. last note.

'Dominus de latymer apud Snappe in dicto Northriding post predictum ffestum sancti michaelis pro elargacione parci sui de Snappe inclusit eidem parco centum acras terre tunc in cultura.'

Another of the Neville family, first husband of Queen Catherine Parr.

Snappe: *i.e.* Snape.

See note on the Danby case, p. 234, *supra.*

'Johannes mallery miles apud hoton in dicto Northriding pro elargacione parci sui ibidem inclusit eidem parco lx acras terre tunc in cultura.'

Hoton: *i.e.* Hutton.

See note as above.

P. 25.—'Abbas monasterii beate Marie de ffontibus apud dysford in dicto Northriding post predictum ffestum sancti michaelis inclusit & conuertit xl acras terre tunc in cultura in pasturam & xxiiij acras terre apud Kyrkbywyske tunc in cultura in pasturam.'

I.e. Dishforth and Kirby Wiske.

The area of forty acres indicates half an arable carucate of eighty acres in a two-field manor. The area of twenty-four acres, which has not occurred before in the Yorkshire part of this Inquisition, is a bovate or eighth part of a two-field manor by the long hundred, which gives 192 acres.

'Heredes domini Fitzhugh apud Est Tanfeld in dicto Northriding post predictum ffestum sancti michaelis incluserunt & conuerterunt cccc acras terre tunc in cultura in pasturam & ea de causa octo messuagia prosternuntur.'

The Fitzhughs were lords of the manor of Tanfield. The last of them had died *s.p.* in 1513, so that this inclosure must have been very recent. It passed at this time through a female Fitzhugh to her husband, Sir Thomas Parr, father of Queen Catherine Parr. (Whitaker, ii. 167.)

'Georgius dominus Lumney apud Kylton in dicto Northriding post predictum festum sancti michaelis in elergacionem [sic] suam ibidem inclusit eidem parco xij acras vasti & xvj acras terre tunc in cultura.'

Kylton, now Kilvington.

This entry distinguishes the two classes of inclosure which were being carried on: that of the wastes of the manor which deprived the tenants of grazing, and that of the arable, which involved actual dispossession. The inclosure of the waste sufficiently indicates that the incloser was lord of the manor. See note on the Danby case, *supra*.

'Willelmus Bolmer Balliuus de Droton apud Droton in dicto Northriding post predictum [sic] sancti michaelis inclusit & conuertit triginta acras terre tunc in cultura in pasturam.'

Qu. Droton for Brotton, in the liberty of Langbaurgh.

The bailiff was the officer of the wapentake or of the liberty, corresponding to the sheriff in the hundreds. (Cowel; Blount.) It is difficult to say in what capacity he made this inclosure, unless, as in the case of Wyndeferthing (p. 204, *supra*), it points to communal agriculture. 'Ballivus' is also used for the steward of a manor. But, as no other example has occurred of a distinction between the action of a lord and a steward of a manor, I think it more likely an official title. I am unable to identify Droton as any liberty or wapentake in the North Riding.

'Radulphus Philypp apud ffylyng in dicto Northriding post predictum ffestum sancti michaelis inclusit & conuertit octo acras terre tunc in cultura in pasturam pertinentes abbati de Whytby.'

Inclosure and conversion by a tenant.

'Thomas Pygott apud Brieforde in dicto North Riding post predictum ffestum sancti Michaelis inclusit & conuertit xx acras terre tunc in cultura in pasturam & quod Johannes Slyngesby est modo tenens liberi tenementi.'

Brieforde: qu. Brafferton.

'Tenens liberi tenementi:' see note *sub* Sowthcowton, p. 234, *supra*.

'Johannes Tueryngham miles apud Thorneton in lestrete in predicto Northriding post predictum ffestum sancti michaelis conuertit cc acras terre tunc in cultura in pasturam & ea de causa quinque cotagia & sex arratra prosternuntur.'

J. T. probably the lord of the manor.

Note, forty acres to a cotagium and $33\frac{1}{3}$ acres to an aratrum, and one plough more than the number of the cotagia.

'Dominus Conyes & magister hospitalis sancti Jacobi iuxta Northallerton apud Northoteryngton in dicto Northriding post predictum ffestum sancti michaelis conuertit centum acras terre tunc in cultura in pasturam & vnam bouatam terre pertinentem sancto Wilfrido nunc in tenura Ricardi Metcalff & ea de causa quatuor arratra prosternuntur.'

The '&' after Conyes is a mistake, since the singular 'conuertit' shows that only one person is intended. John Conyers was Master of the hospital of St. James, North Allerton, at the Dissolution. (See Ingledew's 'North Allerton,' p. 256.)

'Centum acras et unam bovatam.' The normal bovate was fifteen acres, being one-eighth of 120 acres (cp. Isaac Taylor on the Bovate, 'Notes and Queries,' 7th series, vol. ii. p. 481). A hundred and fifteen acres would neither be a carucate nor an exact number of bovates. Hence the reckoning adopted here. Each aratrum will then be $28\frac{3}{4}$ acres, approximating to the normal husbandland or virgate of thirty acres.

P. 26.—'Episcopus Dunelmensis apud Soureby Undercotclyff in dicto Northriding post predictum ffestum sancti Michaelis prosternauit duo messuagia & quinque arratra & conuertit terram in pasturam modo in tenura Radulphi Strangwyse.'

An ecclesiastical inclosure.

The area of an aratrum in this Inquisition for Yorkshire is thirty-one acres. An aratrum is generally associated with a messuagium, and the inference is that he left three messuagia standing, though he converted the entire arable.

For the statutes as to the maintenance of houses, see Introduction, p. 192, 'Trans. R.H.S.,' 1892.

'Jacobus Causon & Thomas Pyper apud Swalfeld in dicto Northriding post predictum ffestum sancti Michaelis conuerterunt lx acras terre tunc in cultura in pasturam.'

Swalefield House occurs in the county map about five miles S.W. of Northallerton.

This and the next entry look like a partnership between two farmers whose holdings were severally too small for pasture, each being a virgate.

'Persona Broue & Willelmus prestnam tenens Edwardi Burgh militis apud Colesby in Northriding predicto post predictum ffestum sancti michaelis inclusit & conuertit c acras terre tunc in cultura in pasturam.'

Broue : qu. Brough, near Richmond.

A case of ecclesiastical farming.

'Abbas de Byland apud Marderbury in predicto Northriding post predictum ffestum sancti Michaelis conuertit octoginta acras terre tunc in cultura in pasturam & ea de causa duo arratra prosternuntur.'

The manor of Matherby or Marderby in Feliskirk (see Burton's 'Monast. Eborac.' p. 334).

'Willelmus Ffayrfax nuper summus Justiciarius de Communi Banco apud Southholme in dicto Northriding post predictum ffestum sancti michaelis conuertit octoginta acras terre tunc in cultura xl acras prati in pasturam & ea de causa quinque messuagia & quinque arratra prosternuntur. Et quod Willelmus Fayrfax filius dicti Willelmi est tenens liberi & [sic] tenementi inde & xx^{ti} persone ab inhabitacionibus suis recesserunt.'

This judge, according to Foss, had died in 1514.

'Liberi & tenementi' suggests that this was taken down from dictation. I take it that the forty acres of meadow is in addition to the eighty acres of arable, but the ploughs have, of course, relation only to the eighty acres.

'Johannes Gower miles apud Styknam in dicto Northriding post predictum ffestum sancti michaelis inclusit & conuertit octoginta acras terre tunc in cultura & xxiiij acras prati & pasture in pasturam & ea de causa duo messuagia tria cotagia & quatuor aratra prosternuntur. Et quod Edwardus Gower est modo tenens liberi tenementi inde.'

Styknam, *i.e.* Stittenham; near Furlington, the next place mentioned, in N.E. Yorks.

'Brianus Stapleton de Wyghell apud fferlyngton in dicto Northriding post predictum ffestum sancti michaelis inclusit & conuertit xl acras terre tunc in cultura in pasturam.'

Possibly an inclosure by a tenant.

'Prior de Exham apud Mekelbargh in dicto Northriding post predictum ffestum sancti Michaelis inclusit & conuertit xxxvj acras terre tunc in cultura in pasturam.'

The Prior of Hexham, in Northumberland.

Mekelbargh: qu. Mickleby, in N.E. Yorks. I cannot find, however, in Dugdale that the Priory of Hexham held any land at any place with a name resembling either of these. As N.E. Yorks was too far off to be farmed from Hexham, this inclosure may have been made by the Prior as lord of the manor or, perhaps, rector.

P. 27.—'Marmaducus Thweyuy apud Emslay in dicto Northriding post predictum ffestum michaelis inclusit & conuertit lx acras terre tunc in cultura in pasturam & quod ea de causa vnum aratrum prosternitur.'

Emslay, *i.e.* Helmesley.

The highest area associated with an aratrum in the Yorkshire Inquisition. See p. 232, *supra*.

'Thomas Darell apud Leuerton in dicto Northriding post predictum ffestum sancti michaelis inclusit & conuertit xl acras terre tunc in cultura in pasturam. Et quod Guido Dawey miles in iure uxoris sue est tenens liberi tenementi inde.'

Leverton is given in the 'Nomina Villarum Eboracensium' (1778) as in the wapentake of Langbargh, Yorks, N.R. It does not appear in Hamilton's 'Gazetteer,' nor in Philips's 'County Atlas.'

'Willelmus Swanston apud Lytyll hayton in dicto North-

riding post predictum ffestum sancti michaelis inclusit & conuertit octo acras terre tunc in cultura in pasturam. Et quod Thomas Bekwyth est tenens liberi tenementi inde.'
 Lytyll-hayton, *i.e.* Little Ayton, N.E. Yorks.
 'Per transcriptum Inquisicionis capte apud castrum Eboracense die sabbati proximo post ffestum sancti michaelis archangeli anno regni Regis henrici viij nono coram Thoma Dalby Archideacono [*sic*] Rychmond & aliis commissionariis.'
 'Thomas Darcy Dominus Darcy apud Temple Newsome in Westriding in Comitatu predicto post ffestum sancti michaelis archangeli anno regni nuper Regis henrici vij^{ml} quarto inclusit in vno parco pro feris nutriendis xl acras terre in cultura & xl acras bosci. Et quod idem Thomas permisit vnam villam vocatam Skelton decaire in qua fuerunt quatuor messuagia & quatuor cotagia & ea de causa quatuor arratra prosternunt.'
 'Decaire,' a manufactured word intended to mean 'to decay.'
 The 'quatuor aratra' put down can only refer to the arable forty acres. This gives the low acreage of ten acres to the aratrum. Mention of the inclosure of wood is uncommon.
 The messuagia belong to the aratra, as at South Cowton, Est Tanfield, Styknam, etc. The cotagia are inhabited by labourers.
 Note that a 'villa' contains four messuagia, four cotagia and four ploughs.
 The 'great park' at Temple Newsom is mentioned in Gaird. 'L. and P.' xiii. i. 384, 386 (1538).
 'Johannes Eueryngham miles apud Byrkyn in dicto Westriding post predictum ffestum sancti Michaelis inclusit in vno parco pro feris nutriendis lx acras pasture & bosci & xx acras terre tunc in cultura.'
 Birkin, near Pontefract.
 'Willelmus Skekyll miles apud leyde in dicto Westriding post predictum ffestum sancti michaelis inclusit in vno parco pro feris nutriendis xl acras terre tunc in cultura.'

Leyde, *i.e.* Leede, near Pontefract ('Nomina Vill. Eborac.').

P. 28.—Willelmus Ellys apud Kydall in dicto Westriding post predictum ffestum sancti michaelis inclusit in vno parco pro feris nutriendis x acras pasture & bosci & xx acras tunnc [*sic*] in cultura.'

I cannot identify this place.

'Abbas de Kyrkstall post predictum ffestum sancti michaelis apud moretoun in dicto Westriding prostrauit tria messuagia & tria aratra & ea de causa xij persone ab inhabitacionibus suis recesserunt.'

I.e. East or West Morton. I do not, however, see property here among the possessions of Kirkstall Abbey in Dugdale, v. 551.

'Walterus Calverley post predictum ffestum sancti michaelis inclusit parco suo de Caluerley in dicto westriding in elargacionen dicti parci sui xx acras terre tunc in cultura.'

'Christoferus Danbye miles apud fferneley post predictum ffestum sancti michaelis inclusit in vno parco pro feris nutriendis centum acras terre tunc in cultura.'

'Ricardus Tempes miles post predictum ffestum sancti michaelis apud Bollyng & Denholme in dicto westriding inclusit in duobus parcis pro feris nutriendis magnam quantitatem pasture & more.'

It is difficult to hazard a conjecture as to the area intended. The largest areas inclosed in Yorkshire are those of 400 acres at Horneby and Est Tanfield—the first for sport, the second for pasture. For the purpose of arriving at some estimate of totals I take the 'magnam quantitatem' here at that figure.

'Johannes Savyle miles apud Hondysworth in dicto westriding post predictum ffestum sancti michaelis inclusit in vno parco pro feris nutriendis xl acras pasture & bosci.'

Hondysworth, *i.e.* Holdsworth, near Halifax, in the wapentake of Morley. The variation again suggests dictation.

'Et quod apud Thornehill in dicto westriding in elargacionem parci sui ibidem inclusit eidem parco lx acras terre tunc in cultura. Et quod Henricus Sayvyle filius & heres eiusdem est inde tenens.'

'Johannes Nevyle miles apud Cheyte in dicto westriding inclusit in vno parco pro feris nutriendis certas terras per quod vnum messuagium & vnum aratrum prosternuntur & iiij^{or} persone ab inhabitacionibus suis recesserunt.'

Cheet or Chevet ('Nomina Vill. Ebor.' in S.W. Yorkshire). For the family of Nevile of Chevet see Hunter's 'South Yorkshire,' ii. 393.

The average of an aratrum in the Inquisition for Yorkshire is thirty-one acres, as also of the land accompanying a messuagium. See p. 232, *supra*.

'Johannes Burton miles inclusit in vno parco adiacente domui suo in dicto westriding post predictum ffestum sancti michaelis pro feris nutriendis x acras pasture.

Qu. Sir John Burton of Kinsley, near Pontefract. (See Hunter, *ibid.* ii. 434.)

'Thomas wentworth apud wentworth in dicto westriding post predictum ffestum sancti michaelis inclusit in vno parco pro feris nutriendis domui sue adiacente iiij^{or} acras pasture.'

Lord of the manor of Wentworth. (See Hunter, *ibid.* ii. 82.)

P. 29.—'Thomas wentworth de Emsall apud Emsall in dicto westriding post predictum ffestum sancti michaelis inclusit in uno parco domui sui [*sic*] adiacente pro feris nutriendis iiij^{or} acras pasture.'

Emsall, *i.e.* North Elmsall, W.R.T.W., was Lord of the Manor. (See Hunter, *ibid.* ii. 453.)

'Ricardus woodrof miles apud woley in dicto westriding post predictum ffestum sancti michaelis in elargacionem parci sui ibidem inclusit eidem parco iiij^{or} acras pasture.'

Woley, *i.e.* Wolley or Woolley, W.R.

For the Woodruffes see Hunter, *ibid.* ii. 383-7.

'Ricardus Resby apud Thriber in dicto westriding post predictum ffestum sancti michaelis inclusit in vno parco pro feris nutriendis lx acras pasture & bosci & xxvj acras terre tunc in cultura.'

Thriber, *i.e.* Thriburgh, W.R.

Resby, *i.e.* Reresby. Qu. whether Ricardus is not a

mistake for Radulphus. Ralph Reresby was lord of the manor. (See Hunter, *ibid.* ii. 39, 40.)

'Henricus Comes Northumbrie apud Longstroth infra Chaceam suam ibidem inclusit in vno parco pro feris nutriendis post predictum ffestum sancti michaelis xl acras pasture.'

Longstroth, *i.e.* Langstorth, W.R., called in the 'Nomina Vill. Ebor.' 'Langstorth or Langstreightdale with Chase.'

'Henricus Dominus Clyfford infra forestam suam de Barden in dicto westriding post predictum ffestum sancti michaelis inclusit in vno parco pro feris nutriendis magnam quantitatem pasture & bosci.'

I.e. Barden, W.R.

'Magnam quantitatem :' qu. 400 acres. (See *sub* Bolling and Denholme, p. 241, *supra*.)

The Cliffords appear to have possessed royal forest rights in Barden. They even imprisoned trespassers during pleasure, which accounts for the inadequacy of this return. (See Whitaker's 'Craven,' pp. 306-7, and compare next note.)

'Idem dominus Clyfford in Chacea sua de Houedon in dicto westriding post predictum ffestum sancti michaelis inclusit in vno parco pro feris nutriendis certam quantitatem pasture & bosci vocatam houeden parke.'

I conjecture 'certam' to be here something short of 'magnam,' and for the purpose of obtaining an estimate of totals take it at 300 acres.

I.e. Houghton or Hawton in the wapentake of Upper Osgoldcross and the liberty of Pontefract.

'Chacea' is in area something less than a forest and greater than a park. But the legal difference between a chace and a forest was that 'a forest, as it is truly and strictly taken, cannot be in the hands of any but the king' (Cowel's Interpreter'). But the king could grant a forest, though this seems to have been uncommon. (Blount's 'Law Dict.' 1717.) The word 'suam' after 'forestam' above seems to indicate such a grant.

'Henricus Clyfford miles apud Carlton in Crayvyne in dicto westriding post predictum ffestum sancti michaelis inclusit in vno parco pro feris nutriendis xl acras pasture & bosci.'

This was Henry Clifford, afterwards first Earl of Cumberland. Whitaker's 'Craven,' p. 223. For an interesting account of his wild life see *ibid*. 327-8. He was son and heir of the Lord Clifford already mentioned (*ibid*.). The spelling Crayvyne is interesting. (See *ibid*. 9.)

'Thomas Tempes miles in elargacionem parci sui de Braswell in dicto westriding post predictum ffestum sancti michaelis inclusit eidem parco tres acras terre tunc in Cultura & quod Ricardus Tempes miles est inde tenens.'

Braswell, *i.e.* Bracewell.

For the Tempests of Bracewell see Whitaker's 'Craven,' 31, 502, 503, etc.

'Stephanus Hammerton miles in elargacionem parci sui &c. inclusit eidem parco xx acras terre tunc in cultura & quod Stephanus Hammerton est inde tenens.'

Hammerton of Hammerton. The omission of the name of the place indicates that it is already given. See Whitaker's 'Craven,' p. 152. This incloser was executed in 1537 for participation in the Pilgrimage of Grace (*ibid*.).

The manor of Hammerton or Hamerton was held of the Duchy of Lancaster.

'Galfridus Proctour apud Brodeley in dicto westriding post predictum ffestum sancti michaelis inclusit in vno parco pro feris nutriendis xx acras pasture.'

Brodeley: qu. Bradley in Craven. If so, Walter Proctour must have been a freeholder, the manor being in the hands of Sir John Carre. (Whitaker's 'Craven,' p. 221.)

P. 30.—Henricus pudesey senior apud Rymyngton in dicto westriding post predictum ffestum sancti michaelis prostrauit certa messuagia & iiij^{or} aratra & conuertit c acras terre tunc in cultura in pasturam & ea de causa xxx persone ab inhabitacionibus suis recesserunt.'

On the average of one aratrum to a messuagium this would give four messuagia. On the average of thirty-one acres to a messuagium, scarcely more than three messuagia. On the average of four and a half persons to a messuagium, rather more than six messuagia. I take four messuagia to be the number, for the purpose of obtaining a total. Cp. p. 232, *supra*.

For the Pudsay family, lords of this manor, see Whitaker's 'Craven,' p. 51.

'Idem henricus apud Bolton in Bowland in dicto westriding post predictum ffestum sancti michaelis prostrauit tria messuagia & iiij^{or} aratra & conuertit centum acras terre tunc in cultura in pasturam & ea de causa xij persone ab inhabitacionibus suis recesserunt.'

Bolton juxta Bowland or Bolland, also in the hands of the Pudsays. (*Ibid*. p. 127.)

'Idem henricus apud lytyll Newton in dicto westriding post predictum ffestum sancti michaelis prostrauit vnum messuagium & conuertit xl acras terre tunc in cultura in pasturam.'

'Animalium' after 'pasturam struck through.

Newton in Bolland.

'Rogerus Tempes apud Newfeld conuertit in dicto Westriding xx acras terre tunc in cultura in pasturam post predictum ffestum sancti michaelis.'

I cannot identify Newfeld.

'Et quod parochia de Alburgh in dicto westriding post predictum ffestum sancti michaelis inclusit & conuertit ciiij^{xx} acras terre tunc in cultura in pasturam.'

This is a remarkable entry. It apparently indicates that the inhabitants of the place, owners of the common fields, agreed to combine in co-operative pasture farming. Had they merely agreed on partition and several enclosures they would scarcely have converted the whole arable at once. For a still more striking instance of farming by a village community see under Wyndeferthing, Norfolk, p. 204, *supra*, and the references there given.

P. 30.—' Per transcriptum Inquisicionis capte apud castrum Eboracense die Sabbati proximo post ffestum sancti michaelis archangeli anno regni Regis Henrici viij^{ui} nono coram Thoma Dalby archidiacono Richemond & aliis comissionariis.'

'Dux Bukyngham apud Brystwyke in dicto Estriding conuertit c acras terre de terris suis dominicalibus tunc in cultura in pasturam & quod nulla domus nec arratrum ea de causa prosternitur.'

This is the first occasion upon which specific mention is made of the inclosure of demesne lands. The reason why, notwithstanding the inclosure of a hundred acres, neither a house nor an aratrum was put down was either that the land was let out in portions to farmers occupying other holdings, or 'cultivated by persons bound to render agricultural services for the benefit of the lord,' or that the lands were really wastes of the manor. See Introd. Trans. R.H.S. 1892, pp. 197, 198, 255, 256.

This was Edward Stafford, Duke of Buckingham, beheaded in 1521. He had lands at Burstwick. (See Brewer 'Cal.' iii. 2, 3695). Further as to him see Introd. Trans. R.H.S. 1892, pp. 189, 190.

'Margareta Grymston vidua apud Grymston in holdernes in dicto Estriding post predictum ffestum sancti michaelis conuertit xl acras terre tunc in Cultura in pasturam & quod ea de causa duo messuagia & duo aratra prosternuntur & octo persone ab inhabitacionibus suis recesserunt.'

The Grimstons of Grimston were lords of the manor (Poulson's 'Holderness,' ii. 60).

'Et quod apud monkewyke in eodem Estriding post predictum ffestum sancti michaelis vnum messuagium & vnum aratrum prosternuntur & iiij^{or} persone ea de causa ab inhabitacionibus suis recesserunt. Et quod Thomas Grymston est inde tenens liberi tenementi.'

This was the manor of Monkewyke in Tunstal, Holderness. It belonged to the Provost of Beverley at this time, passing to the Grimstons at the Dissolution. T. G. was possibly, a socage tenant. (See Digby, 'Hist. of Law of Real Property,' 4th edit. pp. 46, 47, and cp. Poulson's 'Holderness,' p. 86.)

P. 31.—'Willelmus ffoytit apud ffoytit in dicto Estriding post predictum ffestum sancti Michaelis conuertit xx acras terre tunc in cultura in pasturam.'

The Ffoytit or Footed family held land (*temp*. Ed. VI.) in Foothead or Footed Garth of the king as lord of the manor of Rise. (Poulson's ' Holderness,' ii. 413.) This, therefore, was a conversion by a copyholder or a freeholder of the manor.

'Et quod apud Wharrom percy in dicto Estriding post predictum ffestum sancti michaelis iiij^{or} messuagia & iiij^{or} aratra prosternuntur. Eo [*sic*] quod Baro de Hylton Johannes Holtby & Johannes Hansby sunt tenentes liberi tenementi inde.'

These persons were presumably trustees, seized to the use of a *cestui que use*. As such they would be feoffees to uses and legal owners.

'Alexander pudesy apud Taunestorn in dicto Estriding post predictum ffestum sancti michaelis conuertit xl acras terre tunc in cultura in pasturam. Et quod Johannes Constable est occupator inde.'

Taunestorn, *i.e.* Tanstern, a manor in the parish of Aldbrough. This record gives information as to the lordship not possessed by Poulson (see ' Hist. Holderness,' ii. 29).

Note the word ' occupator ' for farmer. For the meaning of the word 'firmarius' see *sub* Ryborow, Norfolk, p. 216, *supra*.

' Thomas ffayrefax miles apud Cayrthorp in dicto Estriding post predictum ffestum sancti michaelis conuertit x^{xx} acras terre tunc in cultura in pasturam & quod ea de causa quinque messuagia & quinque aratra prosternuntur & xx persone ab inhabitacionibus suis recesserunt & quod Willelmus Constable senior miles est tenens liberi tenementi inde.'

Cayrthorp, *i.e.* Carethorp or Cathorpe, Holderness.

As before, ffayrefax was lord of the manor, Constable socage tenant. It may be inferred from the entry that the inclosures were carried out by the lord of the manor, the existing tenants ejected, and their holdings consolidated and sold to W. Constable.

' Henricus Comes Northumbrie apud lekenfeld in dicto

Estriding post predictum ffestum sancti michaelis in elargacionem parci sui ibidem inclusit eidem parco xl acras terre tunc in cultura de dominicis terris suis & centum acras bosci & pasture.'

Note: no evictions, these being demesne lands, probably wastes of the manor. See *sub* Brystwyke, *supra*.

'Johannes Hothome miles apud Scarbrugh in dicto Estriding post predictum ffestum sancti michaelis inclusit in vno parco pro feris nutriendis octoginta acras bosci pasture & prati.'

Scarbrugh. *i.e.* Scarbrough, still belonging to the Hothams.

'Marmaducus Constable miles senior apud Holme in Spaldingmore in dicto Estriding post predictum ffestum sancti michaelis in elargacionem parci sui ibidem inclusit eidem parco x acras bosci & pasture.'

Now Holme, on Spalding Moor, near Market Weighton. The Constables were lords of the manor.

'Abbas monasterii beate marie extra muros Civitatis Eboraci apud hynginge Grymston in dicto Estriding post predictum ffestum sancti Michaelis conuertit xl acras terre tunc in cultura in pasturam & quod ea de causa duo messuagia & duo aratra prosternuntur & octo persone ab inhabitacionibus suis recesserunt.'

Hanging-Grimston.

The Abbots of St. Mary's, York, had received a gift ot lands here from William Rufus and other benefactors of his time (Dugdale, 'Monast.' iii. 534, 537).

P. 32.—'Henricus Sayvile filius & heres Johannis Sayvile in custodia Domini Regis existens apud Estryngton in dicto Estriding post predictum ffestum sancti michaelis conuertit xiiij acras terre tunc in Cultura in pasturam.'

'Prior de Bridelington apud ffraysthorpp in dicto Estriding post predictum ffestum sancti michaelis inclusit & conuertit xl acras terre tunc in Cultura in pasturam.'

Fraisthorpe is about four and a half miles from Bridlington. The Priors were lords of the manor (Dugd. 'Monast.' vi 290).

'Johannes Cute miles apud Carleton in dicto Estriding post predictum ffestum sancti michaelis prostrauit vnum messuagium & vnum aratrum & terram inde conuertit in pasturam & quod sex persone ab inhabitacionibus suis recesserunt ea de causa.'

This would be Carleton in Holderness. In 1536 it was a royal manor (Poulson's 'Holderness,' ii. 25). Sir John Cutte was Under-Treasurer of England (Br. 'Cal.' iv. 2, 2888), and possibly held land here of the king by way of salary, as no land in Yorkshire is mentioned as belonging to his son and heir (see Gaird. 'L. and P.' x. 1268).

'Idem Johannes Cutte apud Skarlagh Benyngholme in dicto Estriding post predictum ffestum sancti michaelis prostrauit vnum tenementum & quod ea de causa iiij^{or} persone ab inhabitacionibus suis recesserunt.'

As four persons are in the Inquisition for Yorkshire normally associated with an aratrum, I have here taken this as indicating a conversion of an aratrum of thirty-one acres. See p. 232, *supra*.

There are two villages, East and West Benningholme, close to North and South Skirlaugh. In 4 Ed. VI. North Skirlaugh was in the hands of the Crown as part of the manor of Rise (Poulson's 'Holderness,' i. 290, ii. 262; see note *sub* Carleton, *supra*).

For Sir John Cutte's inclosures on his own private estates in Cambridgeshire, see *sub* Cambs., Hundred of Chelterton, *infra*.

'Priorissa de Swyne prostrauit ibidem vnum messuagium & vnum aratrum & terram inde conuertit in pasturam & quod ea de causa sex persone ab inhabitacionibus recesserunt.'

The Priory of Swine held the lordship of the manor (Dugdale, 'Monast.' v. 495).

'Dominus ffitzhugh apud Thurkylby in dicto Estriding post predictum ffestum sancti michaelis conuertit tres acras terre tunc in cultura in pasturam & quod ea de causa duo cotagia prosternuntur.'

Thirkleby or Thirtleby.

Poulson, 'Holderness,' ii. 267, refers to this entry. It does not appear who was lord of the manor at this time. Lord Fitzhugh had died in 1512 (Nicolas, 'Hist. Peerage'). The inclosure was not, therefore, very recent.

'Willelmus Battom apud ffyley in dicto Estriding post predictum ffestum sancti michaelis occupat tres huseboundeholdings & quod ea de causa duo messuagia eorumdem sunt ruinosa & x persone ab inhabitacionibus suis recesserunt.'

A 'husbandholding,' called in Scotland a 'husbandland,' generally consisted on the borders and in the south of Scotland of twenty-six acres. (See Innes' 'Scotland in the Middle Ages,' pp. 138-140, 147.) I have taken it at that here, as it is evidently intended to be something other than an 'aratrum.' According to Seebohm ('Engl. Vill. Comm.' 2nd ed., 1883, p. 61), the normal husbandland at Kelso and Selkirk was two bovates, *i.e.* a virgate (cf. Skene's 'Celtic Scotland,' iii. 225 ; Burton's 'Hist. Scot.' ii. 194, *n.*).

The word ' occupat ' shows that this was a tenant farmer. See under Taunestorn, *supra*.

The word 'eorumdem' shows that there were in all three messuagia. It was a case of consolidation of holdings and conversion to pasture.

' Ricardus Harryson apud fflenton in dicto Estriding tenet ij huseboundeholdings & ea de causa sunt iiij^{or} persone minores in eadem villa quam solebant esse.'

fflenton, *i.e.* Flinton.

A farmer, but a freeholder. Note the substitution ot 'tenet' for 'occupat.' (Cp. Poulson's 'Holderness,' ii. 75.) The entry points to the pulling down of a farmhouse.

P. 33.—' Ricardus fflent tenet in eadem villa vnum messuagium & vnam bouatam terre & ponit in dicto messuagio vnus [*sic*] pauper homo & ea de causa sunt minores persone ibi inhabitantes quam solebant esse per tres.'

This was a colourable evasion of the provision of the statute 'agaynst pullyng down of townes ' (4 H. VII. c. 19), that owners of houses let to farm with more than twenty acres of land should *maintain* houses and buildings thereon necessary for tillage. See Introd. 'Trans. R.H.S.' 1892, p. 191.

fflent or fflinton appears to have been a freeholder. For the family, see Poulson's ' Holderness, ii. 75.

'Willelmus Gyrlington apud lylly & dyke in dicto Estriding post predictum ffestum sancti michaelis prostrauit vnum messuagium & conuertit tres bouatas terre tunc in cultura in pasturam. Et quod Katerina Gyrdylyngton est tenens liberi tenementi inde.'

R. O. Ebor. Placit. and Assis. 15 Henry III. (1230): 'Octo arr. terre cum pertinentiis in Lelle et Dyke.'

The ordinary bovate, or eighth part of a carucate of 120 acres, was fifteen acres, or half a virgate. Here forty five acres in all.

'Johannes Dyghton tenet in Attenwike tres huseboundeholdings & vnum cotagium & ea de causa sunt ibidem xvij persone minores quam solebant esse.'

This would probably be on a computation of five to the husbandholding and two to the cotagium, for, as we see from the case of ffyley, *supra*, a husbandholding was accompanied by a messuagium. Now the average number of inhabitants assigned to a messuagium is between four and five. See Introduction to the Yorkshire Inquisition, p. 232, *supra*.

Attenwike, *i.e.* Atwick.

J. D. was apparently a treeholder, the Ughtred family being lords of the manor (Poulson's ' Holderness,' ii. 164).

'Johannes wentworth prostrauit iiij^{or} aratra in lytill Cowden in dicto Estriding post predictum ffestum sancti michaelis & conuertit centum acras terre tunc in Cultura in pasturam & xxiiij^{or} persone ab inhabitacionibus suis recesserunt.'

This at four persons to an aratrum would give about six messuagia. See *supra*.

'Thomas Colton tenet tres bouatas terre in Beforth in dicto Estriding & ea de causa messuagium ad quod predicte iij bouate terre pertinebant & sex persone decauuntur.'

Beforth, *i.e.* Beeford.

This manor belonged to the Prior of the Hospital of St. John of Jerusalem (Poulson's 'Holderness,' i. 244).

'Abbas de Cristall prostrauit vnum messuagium in hillom in Estriding comitatus predicti Et conuertebat dimidium bouate terre ibidem adtunc in cultura in pasturam citra decimum quartum annum dicti nuper Regis qua de causa iiij^{or} persone dekauuntur ibidem contra, etc.'

The form of this entry is different from the general, though resembling that preceding and those following.

Hillom, *i.e.* Hollym.

Cristall, *i.e.* Kirkstall. Poulson was unable to discover the lord of this manor from 28 Ed. III.—3 P. & M. ('Holderness,' ii. 393.) From Dugdale, ' Monast.' (v. 552), however, it appears that at the Dissolution the Abbey of Kirkstall had here a number of 'tenentes ad voluntatem.' I take these to have been the cultivators of the terrae dominicales (cp. Digby, ' Hist. of Law of Real Property,' 4th ed., p. 25, and Introd. 'Trans. R.H.S.' 1892, pp. 255, 256), and that this is an indication that the lordship of the manor was in the hands of this abbey.

'Diuersa tenementa in Ottringham in Estriding comitatus modo occupata & in tenura Radulphi Rokeby & Sehyny fratris sui in & aliorum ibidem que citra dictum annum quartum dicti nuper [*sic*] distructi sunt & prosternantur & terre ibidem eisdem tenementis nuper pertinentes que in cultura fuerunt in pasturam conuertantur qua de causa xiij persone dekauntur ibidem.'

The only example of a tenementum that we have had was at Skarlagh Benyngholme, where it contained four persons. Four persons are the average number dependent on an aratrum of thirty-one acres. The eviction of these thirteen persons, therefore, may be taken to imply the ruin of three tenements and the conversion to pasture of about one hundred acres.

The manor of Ottringham belonged to the Abbey of Meaux (Poulson's 'Holderness,' ii. 424).

The use of the word 'occupata' indicates a lay farmer, apparently evicted. See under Taunestorne, *supra*.

Qu. Sehyny.

This entry appears to have been originally taken by an illiterate person. The MS. is in the same hand from Kydall in W.R. After 'comitatus' 'predicti' is omitted.

P. 34. —Petrus Hyllyard citra dictum annum quartum inclusit tres acras terre in ffythynge in Estriding in comitatu predicto & illas tres acras de extra cultura in pasturam conuertebat.'

ffythynge, *i.e.* Fitling.

The Hyllyards were lords of the manor (Poulson's 'Holderness,' ii. 77).

'Sunt in Sprotley in Estriding in Comitatu predicto diuersa messuagia in Decasu ac diuerse terre ibidem de extra cultura in pasturam conuersi sunt obquod viij persone ibidem decauuntur Sed dicunt quod Decasio & conversio ille facte fuerunt ante dictum quartum dicti nuper Regis & citra annum primum eiusdem nuper Regis &c.'

Sprotley, *i.e.* Sproatley, a manor of the family of Constable (Poulson's 'Holderness,' ii. 275).

It is to be noted that four persons on the average accompany an aratrum, and an aratrum is generally associated with a messuagium. See p. 232, *supra*. Hence the eviction of these eight persons indicates the putting down of two aratra, implying the conversion of sixty-two acres. The expression 'diuersa messuagia' creates a difficulty, as it seems unlikely that 'diuersa' would have been used if two were meant. Now the average number of inhabitants of a messuagium is four. I have decided to take the entry, therefore, as intending two messuagia only. In the Norfolk Inquisition 'messuagium' is sometimes used in the same entry as synonymous with 'tenementum,' *e.g.* at Cotteshale, p. 184, *supra*.

This entry, fixing the inclosures between 1485 and 1488, is exceptional in the Yorkshire Inquisition.

HEREFORDSHIRE

INTRODUCTION

THE returns for Herefordshire are scanty. Only those for the hundreds of Broxash, Greytree, Radlow or Radlode, Wolphy, and Leominster, are preserved in the Lansdowne MS. These hundreds cover an area of 217,150 acres. The areas returned as inclosed amount to 1,271 acres. Herefordshire is distinguished from Norfolk and Yorkshire by the large extent inclosed upon ecclesiastical manors—almost double that inclosed upon lay manors. It is difficult to account for this; for it is scarcely credible that in the hundreds for which returns are made the area of land possessed by the Church exceeded, and so greatly, the joint properties of the laity and of the Crown. It raises the suspicion that, as the Bishop of Hereford was active upon this commission, the religious houses entertained no hopes of concealing the extent of their operations. But this, in its turn, implies that the returns of the laity did not disclose the entire truth. As in the case of inclosures upon ecclesiastical manors in Yorkshire, no land was inclosed for parks; nor, indeed, is there any mention of parks throughout this return. Ecclesiastics were the actual inclosers of 645 acres, if we include the 'firmarii' at ffalley and Yarpole among the number, as compared with 626 inclosed by laymen.

The point of departure taken by the Herefordshire commission is the decay of the messuage, rather than the area inclosed. Though the 'inhabitantes' of the 'messuagium' are frequently mentioned, in no instance is any figure given.

I have, therefore, considered myself justified in assuming the number to be five, the normal average of a household. They are frequently represented as leaving the house 'pro defectu reparacionis,' on which I have made some observations in the general Introduction to the Inquisition.[1] The total number of messuages (including one cottage) returned as destroyed is twenty. Of one half of these the actual evictors were ecclesiastics. This implies a displacement of ninety-eight persons. Again, as in the case of Norfolk—so far as a consideration of the manors goes—we are led to the inference that the inclosures of ecclesiastics were conducted with less harshness than those of lay landowners. The total areas inclosed upon ecclesiastical manors probably amounted to 842 acres—or, discarding doubtful cases (Yarpole and Evynton), 761 acres. These figures represent respectively 66·24 per cent. and 59 per cent. of the entire area returned as inclosed. On the other hand, the return gives us the status of the persons who were the actual evictors. Of the twenty cases of evictions from destroyed messuages, ecclesiastics were only responsible for ten, *i.e.* for 50 per cent., of the total number of ninety-eight persons evicted.

When we pass from a consideration of the ownership of the manors on which inclosures took place to a consideration of the status of the persons described in the return as the actual inclosers and of the inclosures effected by them, we again observe, as in Norfolk, Hants, and elsewhere, the remarkable conformity of ecclesiastics to average. As actual inclosers the ecclesiastics were responsible for 645 out of the total of 1,271 acres inclosed. Now 645 acres represent to the whole the proportion of 50·74 per cent. And it has already been seen that the cases of eviction, and therefore of individuals evicted, for which ecclesiastics were responsible amounted to just 50 per cent. Once more the correspondence is as exact as possible, with a leaning in favour of the ecclesiastics. As landlords they were neither better nor worse than their neighbours.

[1] *Trans. R.H.S.* 1892, and cp. *supra*, pp. 128–131.

The figures given in the analytical tables are bracketed because the commissioners for Herefordshire did not make returns in acres save in three instances, but in the older terminology of virgates, which have been accordingly reduced to acres.

The figures given for the areas of the hundreds in this, as in the other counties, are, as a rule, taken from S. Lewis's 'Topographical Dictionary,' London, 1848. Where this had failed, I have had recourse to the census of 1881. But the figures given there frequently differ from those given by Lewis, either in consequence of improved methods of surveying, or perhaps more often owing to subsequent rectifications of boundaries. In this Inquisition, as in Duncumb's 'History of Herefordshire,' Leominster is included in the hundred of Wolphy.

ANALYSIS OF THE INQUISITION FOR THE COUNTY OF HEREFORD

I.—Areas Inclosed on Lay and Ecclesiastical Manors

Hundred	Area of hundred	Total area inclosed	Areas of inclosure on lay manors				Areas of inclosure on ecclesiastical manors			
			Inclosures remaining arable	Conversions and pasture areas inclosed	Total	Remaining arable	Conversions and pasture areas inclosed	Total	Remaining arable	Conversions and pasture areas inclosed
	acres	acres	acres	acres	acres	acres	acres	acres	acres	acres
Broxash	61,290	54	—	54	—	—	—	54	—	54
Greytree	43,060	600	—	600	120	—	120	480	—	480
Radlowe	52,350	252	—	252	144	—	144	108	—	108
Wolfey and Leomynstre	60,450	365	—	365	165 (246)	—	165 (246)	119 (200)	—	119 (200)
Total	217,150	1,271	—	1,271	429 (510)	—	429 (510)	761 (842)	—	761 (842)

II.—Proportionate Analysis of Areas Inclosed on Lay and Ecclesiastical Manors

Hundred	Proportion of total area inclosed of Hundred	Proportion of inclosures remaining arable to total areas inclosed	Proportion of conversions and inclosures of pasture to total areas inclosed	Lay Manors				Ecclesiastical Manors			
				Proportion of areas inclosed to total areas	Proportion of inclosures remaining arable to total areas inclosed on lay manors	Proportion of conversions and inclosures of pasture to total areas inclosed on lay manors	Proportion of inclosures to total areas inclosed on lay manors	Proportion of areas inclosed to total areas	Proportion of inclosures remaining arable to total areas inclosed on ecclesiastical manors	Proportion of conversions and inclosures of pasture to total areas inclosed on ecclesiastical manors	Proportion of conversions and inclosures of pasture to total areas inclosed on ecclesiastical manors
Broxash	·008	—	—	20	—	100	20	·008	—	100	100
Greytree	1·39	—	—	57·14	—	100	57·14	—	—	—	—
Radlowe	·04	—	—	45·2 (67·39)	—	—	45·2 (67·39)	80	—	100	100
Wolfey & Leomynstre	·06	—	—	—	—	—	—	42·85	—	—	100
Total	·05	—	—	33·75 (40·12)	—	33·75 (40·73)	33·75 (40·12)	32·63 (54·79)	—	32·63 (54·79)	100

NOTE.—Where two numbers are given, that in brackets is the number if the doubtful cases are included. The totals will then be obtained by adding the bracketed figures of the columns giving the ecclesiastical areas to the appropriate unbracketed figures of the columns giving the areas upon lay manors. Displacement of population:—19 messuagia = 93 persons; 1 conjugium = 3 persons; total, 98 persons.

III. INCLOSURES ON ECCLESIASTICAL AND LAY MANORS

INCLOSURES ON ECCLESIASTICAL MANORS		INCLOSURES ON LAY MANORS	
	Acres		Acres
? Parva Cockern	54	Walford	120
Walford	120	Spledon	36
ffalley	360	Ledburye	36
Barton Callewall	72	Esbache	72
Bosebury	36	Orleton	15
? Yarpole	30	Orleton	15
? Yarpole	36	Ouerton	30
Stoke Prior	11	Pedelleston	30
? Evynton	15	Orleton	20
Brayerley	36	Lucketon	15
Le Hida	72	Papelarns	36
		Bradfordes Brugge	4
	761 (?842)		429 (510)

I have treated Parva Cockern as an ecclesiastical manor. At any rate, an ecclesiastic was the incloser in his capacity of freeholder.

At Walford, as the MS. tells us, the incloser held both of the lay and of the ecclesiastical manors there. I have therefore divided the total inclosure between the two.

IV. ACTUAL INCLOSERS

LAYMEN		ECCLESIASTICS	
	Acres		Acres
		Parva Cockern	54
Walford	240		
		ffalley	360
Spledon	36		
		Barton Callewall	72
Ledburye	36		
Boseburye	36		
Esbache	72		
Orleton	15		
Orleton	15		
Yarpole	30		
Ouerton	30		
Pedelleston	30		
Orleton	20		
		Yarpole	36
Stoke	11		
		Evynton	15
		Brayerley	36
		Hida	72
Lucketon	15		
Papelarns	36		
Bradfordes Brugge	4		
	626		645

V. THE NUMBER OF ACRES APPARENTLY APPURTENANT TO HOUSES

Page				Acres
261	Parva Cockern	mansio		54
263	Walford	messuagium		carucate or temelande
,,	Walford	messuagium		carucate or temelande
,,	Walford	messuagium		carucate or temelande
,,	Walford	messuagium		carucate or temelande
,,	Walford	messuagium		carucate or temelande
265	Orleton	messuagium		½ virgate
,,	Orleton	messuagium		½ virgate
266	Yarpole	messuagium		1 virgate
,,	Orleton	messuagium		1 virgate
,,	Pedelleston	messuagium		1 virgate
267	Yarpole	messuagium		1 aratrum
,,	Stoke	messuagium		11 acres
,,	Evynton	messuagium		½ virgate
268	Brayerley	messuagium		1 aratrum
,,	Luckcton	messuagium		½ virgate

Average area assigned to a messuagium = 55 acres.

It is, however, to be noted that this average is made up of five cases, apparently in one place, Walford, in which 120 acres belong to the messuagium, and of ten cases where the areas appurtenant are fifteen to thirty-six acres. These ten cases taken by themselves give an average of 23¼ acres to the messuagium—rather below the Yorkshire average.

NOTE ON THE 'ARATRUM'

It is probable that an 'aratrum' is not the equivalent of a carucate which is specifically represented, as in the case of Walford, by the English 'temelande.' In the Herefordshire Inquisition the word frequently occurs, but only once is there any indication of the area assigned to it. That is in the first entry, 'Parva Cockern,' where the fifty-four acres of arable land were cultivated by a plough of six oxen. This would make the normal 'aratrum,' where eight oxen were used, equal to seventy-two acres. Now seventy-two acres was the carucate of sixty acres by the long hundred (see Taylor on the 'Bovate,' 'N. & Q.' 7th series, vol. ii. p. 481). In this place, therefore, the 'aratrum' is a carucate, *i.e.* one of the arable fields in a three-field manor. But the fact that the number of acres assigned to it here is given and the identification elsewhere of carucate make it improbable that it is elsewhere used in the same sense. It has been seen that in the case of Yorkshire the 'aratrum' slightly exceeded thirty acres. Thirty acres was a normal virgate in a three-field manor of 120 acres. This Inquisition for Herefordshire uses the word 'virgata' as well as 'aratrum,' as though they were something different. That the 'aratrum' should be a bovate is in itself highly improbable. Such an area as that of the bovate is described in this Inquisitio as 'dimidium virgate.' Now, it has been seen that in the case of some manors, as Parva Cockern, the carucate was reckoned by the long hundred. I am inclined to hold that the aratrum is to the carucate of 144 acres (*i.e.* 120 acres by the long hundred) what the virgate is to the hide of 120 acres, and that this is the difference between them. I have therefore reckoned the 'aratrum' at thirty-six acres. This area, it is to be observed, accords more nearly with the average of the areas inclosed in Herefordshire than would be the case on identification of the 'aratrum' with the carucate.

VI. AREAS OF INCLOSURES

I. 300–400 *acres* = 2

Place	Acres	Hundred
ffalley	360	} Greytree
Walford	240	

II. 100–200 *acres* = 0

III. 70–80 *acres* = 3

Barton Callewall	72	} Radlow
Esbache	72	
Hida	72	Leominster

IV. 30–60 *acres* = 9

Parva Cockern	54	Broxash
Spledon	36	} Radlow
Ledburye	36	
Boseburye	36	

IV. 30–60 *acres—cont.*

Place	Acres	Hundred
Yarpole	36	} Wolphy
Brayerley	36	
Papelarns	36	Leominster
Pedelleston	30	} Wolphy
Yarpole	30	

V. 15–30 *acres* = 5

Orleton	15	
Orleton	15	
Orleton	20	} Wolphy
Evynton	15	
Lucketon	15	

VI. 1–15 *acres* = 2

Stoke Bradfordes	11	Wolphy
Brugge	4	

In 'Domesday Studies,' i. 145, Canon Isaac Taylor remarks that the existence of the open arable fields is still shown on the Ordnance maps, particularly in the East Riding of Yorkshire. He suggests that a study of the map will frequently enable the student to distinguish between manors cultivated on the two-field and those on the three-field shift. Pursuing this hint, I have worked through the places mentioned in Herefordshire with the six-inch Ordnance map. Out of the fourteen places in which ploughlands or virgates are mentioned, rendering it desirable to know the system of cultivation, and therefore the area, I find no indication in the following seven cases : Walford, Fawley, Upleadon, Colwall, Stoke (Prior), Brierley, and Lucton. Indications of the three-field system are found at Ledbury, in the names Oldfields and Hillfield; at Pudleston, in Goldwellfield, Highfield, and Whitfield. There is here also a Barnfield. In Ivington we have Upper Hyde, Lower Hyde, and Hyde Marsh. Bosbury suggests a two-field system in Lyefield and Bosbury Southfield, Lyefield being north of Southfield. So Yarpole has Lady Meadow and Enmorefield. Evesbatch has Coldfields only. From this I conclude that no certainty can be arrived at, and that the safest course will be to take it that, as late as 1517, the three-field shift had become general. From Mr. Seebohm's investigations the three-field shift seems to have been nearly universal in the south of England.

THE INQUISITION FOR HEREFORD-SHIRE

(Lansd. MS., I. pp. 173, 174)

P. 35.—*Hereford.*

'Per transcriptum cuiusdam Inquisicionis capte apud hereford in comitatu hereford die lune proximo post festum sancti Michaelis archangeli anno regni regis henrici viij^{ui} post conquestum nono coram venerabili in Christo patre C. Episcopo hereford & Willelmo Vuedale milite comissionariis domini Regis virtute commissionis eis directe & dicte [*sic*] Inquisicio constituta per sacramentum Ricardi Vaughan militis & aliorum. Qui presentant inter alia.'

C. is for Carolus, *i.e.* Charles Booth, D.D., Bishop of Hereford, Nov. 30, 1516.

Sir W. Vuedale or Uvedale was a courtier whose name frequently occurs in the Domestic Papers of this period. He was on the commission of the peace for Herefordshire, as well as for Gloucestershire and other parts. (See Br. 'Cal.' i.) Sir R. Vaughan also appears to have been in favour at court (*ibid.*). For the rest of the commissioners see *sub* Gloucestershire, and Br. 'Cal.' ii. 3297.

'Imprimis quod fuit quedam mansio in parua Cockern infra hundred de Broxash cognita per nomen Rectorie de parua Cockern cum liiij acris terre arrabilis cum suis pertinentiis eidem mansioni pertinentibus que quidem mansio longo elapso tempore inhabitata & occupata fuit cum vno aratro sex Bovium ita quod infra viginti annos vltimo preteritos quidam Ricardus hulles vnacum vxore et familis [*sic*] eam inhabitabant & occupabant cum sex Bovibus trahentibus in aratro et ad hunc diem aula coquina & camere eiusdem mansionis prostrantur & in ruinam producuntur ac meremium cum muris asportantur [*sic*] ac inhabitantes ibidem pro defectu necessariorum edibilium abinde recesserunt necque alique Domus ibidem sunt relicte preter vnum orreum pro grano ac vnam veterem domum pro catallis ibidem pascendis vocatam a Shyppon que sunt in possessione Johannis Bele persone de Uplyngwyke & de parua Cockern. Et preterea presentant quod infra eandem villam non plures persone sunt morantes ad seruiendum Regi cum opus fuerit quam quatuor persone.'

'Parua Cockern,' *i.e.* Cowarne parva.

The mention of an aratrum or ploughgang of six oxen and fifty-four acres shows the normal ploughgang of eight oxen to have been seventy-two acres. This area is explained by Canon Isaac Taylor as being the carucate of sixty acres in one tilled field on the three-course system reckoned by the Anglicus numerus, or long hundred of 120 to the hundred. ('N. and Q.' 7th Ser. ii. 481.) As to the frequency of this reckoning, at any rate in Yorkshire, see the same writer in 'Domesday Studies,' p. 162, where he finds that out of 216 Yorkshire holdings, 170 were thus reckoned.

For the Act enforcing the maintenance of houses for tillage see Introduction.[1]

Apparently the rectory and glebe were farmed, the rector being non-resident. In 1478 the living had been united with that of Ullingswick, which is, no doubt, the Uplyngwyke mentioned in this record. It is to be observed that the ruin of the house is not attributed to the rector, John Bele, who had only been presented in 1515. (See Duncumb's 'Herefordshire,' ii. 108-9.)

Note, only four householders to a villa. It had grown since 1286, 'when a messuage and one carucate of land constituted the principal value' (*ibid.*).

The record does not in so many words state the conversion of the arable land to pasture, but it is implied in the putting down of the plough and in the expression 'inhabitantes

[1] *Trans. R.H.S.* 1892, p. 191.

ibidem pro defectu necessariorum edibilium abinde recesserunt.'

For the word 'mansio' see *sub* Choysell, p. 168, *supra*.

Walford.

'Item presentant quod Jacobus Cryll de Walford inclusit duas carucatas terre vocatas ij temelande & duo messuagia ibidem quondam edificata prosternuntur citra xiiij^{clm} annos proxime precedentes. Et tenet messuagia & terras predictas de domino Episcopo hereford ac de comite Salop.'

Temelande is a local expression. The teamland is to the oxgang as the carucate to the bovate—*i.e.* it is the land ploughed by an entire team of eight oxen in a year. As the ordinary measure of the carucate is 120 acres, this was a double carucate of 240 acres, an area of which Mr. Seebohm ('Village Community,' p. 38) explains the fiscal significance. (Cp. Canon Isaac Taylor in 'Domesday Studies,' p. 173).

James Cryll (or Kyrle) was a tenant of these manors, but lord of a third manor at Walford (Duncumb, iii. 184). He was probably, therefore, actively engaged in agriculture.

The Bishop of Hereford and the Talbots both held manors here (*ibid.* pp. 179, 183).

'Item quod David Elm de ffalley firmarius domus llantoni iuxta Gloucestriam deposuit tria messuagia & tria temeland sunt decasu racione quod conuersit terras arrabiles in pasturam ac nulla familia ibidem manutenta fuit infra xvj^{clm} annos preteritos et tenentur de domino Rege.'

'ffalley' is Fawley: like Walford, in the hundred of Greytree.

'Firmarius,' a clerical farmer. (See note to Ryborow, Norfolk, *supra*.) The house of Llanthony, near Gloucester, owned the lordship of the manor (Dugdale, 'Monast.' vi. 140). See for a further inclosure by this priory, below, *sub* Gloucestershire (Nawesley).

Hundred de Radlowe.

'Item quod Thomas leylonde de Bosyburye inclusit vnum aratrum infra dominium de Spledon & illud mutauit & conuersit in pasturam ab anno quarto regni Regis henrici vij^{mi}, ac quod dominus de seynt Jones possidet illam'

Spledon ; qu. for Super Ledon, close to Bosbury.

It is clear that here, as in the rest of the Inquisition, an aratrum is not a convertible term with a teamland or a carucate. For the grounds of my estimate of the 'aratrum' in the Herefordshire Inquisition at thirty-six acres see p. 161, *supra*.

'Item quod magister Ricardus Bromefelde canonicus de hereford inclusit duo aratra & illa occupat in pastura iacentia infra Barton Callewall & habet statum inde in feodo simplici. Tenet eandem pasturam in iure ecclesie de hereford.'

Barton Callewall, *i.e.* Colwall.

In Domesday the Cathedral of Hereford held three hides here.

'Statum inde habet in feodo simplici.' This must be a mistake. The fee simple belonged to the ecclesiastical corporation : he held a freehold estate in virtue of his canonry.

'Occupat' implies that he himself farms (see *sub* Taunstorne, Yorkshire, and Ryborow, Norfolk, *supra*). In the Introduction to the ' Domesday of St. Paul's,' p. xlii, it is mentioned that in the fourteenth century all the manors were held to farm by different canons. The mention of 'aratra' perhaps indicates, as elsewhere, land held in demesne (see *sub* Wendlyng, Norfolk, *supra*, p. 216).

P. 36.—'Item quod Ricardus Bradford de Dymmoke inclusit vnum aratrum infra forren de ledburye & illud occupat in pastura & inde statum habet in feodo simplici.'

According to Cowel ('Interp.') the 'foreign' was part of a manor with respect to which certain services were due to the king and not to the lord of the manor. This tallies with the further description, 'inde statum habet in feodo simplici.'

'Item quod Johannes ffarley de Boseburye inclusit vnum aratrum infra dominium de Boseburye & illud occupat in pastura & tenet illud de episcopo hereford secundum consuetudinem.'

In Domesday the Cathedral of Hereford held six hides at Bosbury.

'Secundum consuetudinem,' according to the custom of manor. This is the first example of this phrase. See 'Trans. R.H.S.' 1892, pp.

P. 37.—'Adhuc hundred de Radlode.

'Item presentant quod magister Roulandus Morton possidet duo aratra in Esbache & eadem occupat in pastura.'

Esbache, i.e. Evesbatch.

From the instance of Spledon it may be inferred that 'possidet' indicates ownership in fee: 'occupat' shows that he farms them himself. Probably the demesne of a manor of which he was lord.

'Hundred de Wolfey & Leomynstre.

'Item quod est quoddam messuagium decasum in Orleton & inhabitantes messuagii predicti pro defectu reparacionis eiusdem abinde recesserunt, nuper in tenura Johannis hyll de Orleton & est adherens eidem messuagio dimidium virgate terre que [*sic*] prefatus Johannes hyll nuper occupabat in manu sua propria.'

As in the case of parua Cockern, the point of departure is here the decay of the house.

'Pro defectu reparacionis ... recesserunt' points to tenancies at will or from year to year. See pp. 128-131, *supra*. The recital refers to the statute of Henry VII. for the maintenance of houses for tillage. See Introduction in 'Trans. R.H.S.' 1892, p. 191.

The virgate is here first introduced by name. The hide and virgate were old forms of measurement, giving place after the Norman Conquest to the carucate and bovate. (See J. H. Round, in 'Domesday Studies,' pp. 195-6.) Four virgates made up the hide, so that each normal virgate of thirty acres was equivalent to two normal bovates. On the relation of the virgate and hide to scutage see Seebohm, 'Engl. Vill. Com.' 2nd ed. 1883, p. 38. The virgate was the normal holding of the villanus (*ibid*. p. 94). The tenants here were practically evicted. The recital of the decay of the messuage is evidence of conversion to pasture.

'Item quod est aliud quoddam messuagium similiter

decasum cum dimidio virgate terre in Orleton predicta in tenura Thome Bromfylde.'

'Item quod est messuagium decasum in Yarpole cum vna virgata terre eidem messuagio adiacente nuper in tenura Thome Phelypps de leomynstre. Et inhabitantes eiusdem messuagii pro defectu reparacionis messuagium predictum reliquerunt.'

See note to Orleton, p. 265, *supra*.

'Item quod est messuagium decasum in Ouerton in parochia de Orleton cum vna virgata terre eidem messuagio adiacente in tenura Joannis Abrymhewe. Et inhabitantes eiusdem pro defectu reparacionis abinde recesserunt.'

See *ibid.*, *supra*.

'Item quod est messuagium decasum in Pedelleston similiter & cotagium cum vna virgata terre eidem messuagio adiacente in tenura domine Margerie Deuereux nuper uxoris Johannis Deuereux militis & inhabitantes eiusdem pro defectu reparacionis predicte abinde lacrimose recesserunt.'

Pedelleston, *i.e.* Pudleston.

The virgate is especially mentioned as belonging to the messuage. This agrees with Cowel's definition of a 'cotage' as a house without land belonging to it; though, as has been seen, *supra*, the 'cotagia' hitherto mentioned in Yorkshire appear to have been accompanied with land. The 'Extenta Manerii' (4 Ed. I. st. 1), speaks of their 'curtilagia.' An example of a cotagium without land is to be found in Staffordshire, *sub* Highe Offlye, *infra*.

'In tenura domine Margerie Deuereux,' &c. This phrase suggests that the widow was 'tenant in dower.' As such she was the evictor. The decay of the messuage and cottage indicates, as before, conversion to pasture.

The 'lacrimose' seems to indicate the report of a spectator.

'Item quod est quedam pastura in Orleton vocata Mourtymers Courte ac alia pastura vocata dynys more & xx^{ti} acre terre & plus ibidem sunt incluse que quondam fuerunt & iacuerunt in communia tenentibus Regis in tenura Willelmi pytte de Leyncall.'

It would appear from this that Orleton was a royal manor.

Qu. Leyncall.

The additional words 'in tenura' &c. seem to indicate that the Crown inclosed and then let to W. P.

'Item quod est messuagium decasum in Yarpole cum vno aratro eidem messuagio adiacente in tenura nuper Abbatis de Readyng & cuiusdam Johannis Walesale firmarii. Et inhabitantes eiusdem abinde recesserunt pro defectu reparacionis.'

For the 'firmarius' see *sub* ffalley, and Ryborow, Norfolk, p. 216, *supra*.

The Act 21 H. VIII. c. 13 (1529) forbade farming by the clergy.

It is not clear upon what terms the abbot and the firmarius held. From the Computus at the Dissolution it does not appear that the Abbey of Reading possessed land here (Dugdale, 'Monast.' iv. 49). 'Nuper' probably belongs to 'Abbatis' as may be inferred from the repetition of the phrase below, *sub* Evynton. Qu. whether the Abbot was the evictor. 'Inhabitantes' cannot refer to him, but would mean the farm servants, 'pro defectu reparacionis' marking their tenancy at will. (See *sub* Orleton, *supra*.)

'Item quod est messuagium decasum in Stoke per leomynstre cum xj acris terre eidem messuagio adiacentis in tenura Johannis hakeluytt. Et inhabitantes per defectum reparacionis predicte similiter recesserunt.'

I.e. Stoke Prior, three miles south-east of Leominster, probably, from its name, a manor of the Prior of that place.

'Item quod est messuagium cum dimidio virgate terre in Evynton eidem messuagio adiacentis in tenura nuper Abbatis de Readyng. Et inhabitantes pro defectu reparacionis predicte similiter recesserunt.'

Evyngton, *i.e.* Ivington, near Leominster.

For the farming of the Abbot of Reading see above *sub* Yarpole. The Abbot was probably not lord of the manors. (See the form of the record under Hida, p. 268, *infra*.)

'Item quod est aliud messuagium decasum in Brayerley cum vno aratro eidem messuagio adiacente in tenura Abbatis de Readyng. Et inhabitantes pro defectu reparacionis predicte similiter recesserunt.'

See last note.

P. 38.—'Adhuc hundred de Wolfey & Leomynstre.

'Item presentant quod sunt duo messuagia in decasu in le hida in ffranchiis de leomynstre vnacum duobus aratris eisdem messuagiis adiacentibus in manerio abbatis de Readyng. Et inhabitantes eiusdem pro defectu reparacionis messuagiorum predictorum abinde recesserunt.'

Le hida, now Hyde Ash.

The Abbot of Reading held the borough of Leominster as a fief from the Crown with very large privileges (see Dugdale's ' Monasticon,' iv. 40–41).

'Item quod est vnum messuagium decasum in lucketon cum dimidio virgate terre eidem messuagio adiacente in manerio Johannis Wygmore existenti. Et inhabitantes eiusdem pro defectu reparacionis messuagii predicti abinde recesserunt.'

Lucketon, now Lucton, near Leominster.

'Item quod est aliud messuagium decasum apud papelarns in leomynstre vnacum aratro eidem messuagio adiacente in manerio cuiusdam [blank in MS.] Burche. Et inhabitantes eiusdem pro defectu reparacionis messuagii predicti abinde recesserunt.'

Papelarns, i.e. Poplands, a part of Leominster (see Townsend's ' Leominster,' p. 62).

'Item quod est communis pastura inclusa apud Bradfordes Brugge continens quatuor vel quinque acras per Edwardum Croste militem ad magnum damnum & detrimentum inhabitancium ibidem.'

Qu. Bradfordes Brugge. There are ten bridges in Leominster, but none now answering to this name (Townsend, *ibid.*).

The recital 'ad magnum damnum,' &c., is perhaps introduced with reference to freeholders outside the manor with rights of common appurtenant, whose rights the lord was not empowered to prejudice under the statutes of Merton and Westminster II. (see Digby, ' Hist. of Law of Real Property,' 4th edit. p. 198, *n.* 2).

STAFFORDSHIRE

Introduction

THE returns for Staffordshire contained in the Lansdowne MS. are plainly fragmentary. They relate, indeed, to four out of the five Hundreds; but as they are transcribed in irregular sequence, the inference suggests itself that the original parchment slips had been mixed or mislaid before they reached the copyist's hands. One feature of value this return does present. In every case the year of the inclosure is recorded; in most cases the commissioners have gone so far as to assign a definite date to the operation. This is in strict accord with the prescription of the commission, which runs that the commissioners are to return 'per quos vel per quem vbi *quando* qualiter & quo modo,' the inclosures have been made. These dates, which possess an economic as well as a legal value, will be collated with those given in the returns from other counties. If the statistics of this return are a fair sample of the general state of things in this county, the most noticeable feature is the large proportion of land returned as inclosed for purposes of sport. The entire area returned as inclosed amounts to no more than $488\frac{1}{4}$ acres, representing seventeen inclosures, or an average of rather more than twenty-eight acres an inclosure. Of these $488\frac{1}{4}$ acres, twenty-eight acres are an inclosure of arable, and 148 acres are cases of the conversion of arable to pasture; so that 312 acres, or 63·93 per cent., were inclosures for sport. It is to be observed that these were, as a rule, inclosures of very small areas, being apparently additions to parks already existing. One, at

Cumberforde, was only forty perches. The rest, eight in number, give an average of thirty-nine acres an inclosure. Here, again, this commission scrupulously adhered to the tenour of its instructions. The commissioners were expressly enjoined to inquire, not only what land had been inclosed to form parks (an operation, be it remembered, which required a royal licence), but also what additions had been made to parks already formed : ' et que terre aliquibus parcis vel alicui parco qui tunc fuerint aut fuerit pro elargacione huiusmodi parcorum includuntur et per quos ' &c.

There is no case in Staffordshire of inclosure by an ecclesiastic; though there are two of inclosures by laymen upon ecclesiastical manors—viz. at Haywood and Chellyngton. Only two cases of houses decayed are mentioned. They have no land assigned them ; from which it may, perhaps, be inferred that the conversion from tillage which led to the decay had taken place before the 4th Henry VII. marked out as the retrospective limit of the Inquisition. At the previous reckoning of five persons to a normal messuagium and three to a cotagium, this represents a displacement of no more than eight persons.

I have not been able to ascertain the area of the liberty of the duchy of Lancaster in this county, which appears not to have been included in the area of the hundreds. This inevitably leads to an incompleteness in the statistical summary.

ANALYSIS OF THE INQUISITION FOR THE COUNTY OF STAFFORD

I. Areas Inclosed on Lay and Ecclesiastical Manors

Hundred	Area of Hundred	Total area inclosed	Inclosures remaining arable	Conversions and pasture areas inclosed	Lay Manors			Ecclesiastical Manors		
					Total	Remaining arable	Conversions and pasture areas inclosed	Total	Remaining arable	Conversions and pasture areas inclosed
	acres	acres	acres	acres	acres	acres	acres	acres	acres	acres
Cutlestone	105,500	118¼	28	90¼	113½	28	85	5	—	5
Duchy of Lancaster	—	160	—	160	160	—	160	—	—	—
Seisdon	81,380	26	—	26	26	—	26	—	—	—
Pyrehill	202,750	100	—	100	70	—	70	30	—	30
Offlowe	170,720	84	—	84	84	—	84	—	—	—
Total		488¼	28	460	453	28	425	35	—	35

II. Proportionate Analysis of Areas Inclosed on Lay and Ecclesiastical Manors

Hundred	Proportion of total areas inclosed to area of hundred	Proportion of inclosures remaining arable to total areas inclosed	Proportion of conversions and inclosures of pasture to total areas inclosed	Lay Manors			Ecclesiastical Manors		
				Proportion of areas inclosed to total areas	Proportion of inclosures remaining arable to total areas inclosed	Proportion of conversions and inclosures of pasture to total areas inclosed on lay manors	Proportion of inclosures remaining arable to total areas inclosed on ecclesiastical manors	Proportion of conversions and inclosures of pasture to total areas inclosed on ecclesiastical manors	Proportion of conversions and inclosures of pasture to total areas inclosed on ecclesiastical manors
Cutlestone	·11	23·72	76·27	95·76	23·72	24·77	72·03	76·1	—	4·23
Duchy of Lancaster	—	—	100	100	—	—	100	100	—	—
Seisdon	·003	—	100	100	—	—	100	100	—	—
Pyrehill	·004	—	100	70	—	—	70	100	—	30
Offlowe	·004	—	100	100	—	—	100	100	—	—
Total	—	5·73	94·26	92·82	5·73	6·18	87·04	93·81	—	7·17

Note.—In these computations the ¼ is omitted. Displacement of population :—1 cotagium = 3; 1 messuagium = 5; total 8.

STAFFORDSHIRE

(Lansd. MS. I. fo. 175 and 178)

P. 39.—HUNDRED DE JUTLESTONE. (COLVESTON, *Domesday. Now* CUDDLESTONE.) ('Jutlestone' is a transcriber's mistake for Cutlestone.)

'Thomas Cumberfforde inclusit apud Cumberforde xij acras terre & in pasturam conuertit xiij die Martii anno vij Regis Henrici viij^{ui} & similiter inclusit xxviij acras terre arrabilis ibidem vocate le conyngie & xiij acras terre ibidem in loco vocato Hilffelde in pasturam conuertit xij die Nouembris anno quinto Regis Henrici viij^{ui}.'

The Cumberfords or Comberfords of Comberford were for many centuries lords of the manor here (Erdeswick's 'Staffordshire,' ed. Harwood, p. 448).

Three acts of inclosure, amounting to fifty-three acres, of which twenty-five only are specified as cases of conversion to pasture.

'Et similiter idem Thomas Cumberfforde augmentauit parcum suum ibidem eodem anno de communiis terre per spacium xl perchiarum.'

I.e. a quarter of an acre.

'Thomas Walton primo die Martii anno xvij Henrici vij^{mi} lx acras terre arrabilis in Chedull sepibus & fossatis inclusit & in pasturam arabilem conuertit.'

It does not appear that T. W. was lord of the manor. (See Erdeswick, p. 505.)

Libertas ducatus Lancastrie.

'Georgius Mauerell xij die maii anno primo Henrici viij^{ui} lx acras terre in Throwleye imparcauit pro feris nutriendis.'

The Maverells or Meverells were lords of the manor of Throwley. (See Erdeswick, p. 483.)

'Johannes Aston miles primo die Augusti anno xij Henrici vij^{mi} centum acras terre arrabilis imparcauit pro feris nutriendis.'

Sir John Aston was lord of the manor of Tickeshall or Tixall (see Clifford's 'Hist. of Tixall,' p. 245), which is probably the place where this inclosure took place. Tixall Park is still marked on the maps of Staffordshire. (See Erdeswick, p. 67.)

'Thomas Kynnersley armiger anno xx Regis Henrici vij^{mi} xx acras terre arrabilis & tres acras bosci & more in loxley imparcauit pro fferis nutriendis.'

T. K. was lord of the manor (Erdeswick, p. 514, *n.* a). It is still in the hands of the same family, which acquired it *temp.* Henry III. (*ibid.*).

'Thomas Welles anno nono Regis Henrici vij^{mi} iiij^{or} acras terre apud Thehorecrosse in parco suo inclusit pro fferis nutriendis.'

'The Horecross' is a house in the parish of Yoxall, in which the family of Wells were lords of the manor (Erdeswick, p. 270).

'Ricardus Asteleye in anno xij Henrici vij^{mi} inclusit tres acras prati communis in patteshill & in pasturam arabilem conuertit.'

R. A. was lord of the manor (Erdeswick, p. 365).

The fact that the head of this folio (Lansd. MS., fo. 175) gives Staffordshire, headed by mistake, 'Sowthapt,' shows this to be a copy. See further as to the transcription, 'Trans. R.H.S.' 1892, pp. 175, 176.

P. 46.[1]—HUNDRED DE PYREHILL. (PIREHOLLE, *Domesday.* Now PIREHILL.)

'Symon Harcourte fuit seisitus de vno messuagio & xl acris terre arrabilis & cultui usitate & apte in Brycheford &

[1] The intervening folios of the Lansd. MS. contain Hants and London.

primo die Marcii anno tercio henrici viij^ud messuagium & terram sepibus & fossatis includit & in pasturam animalium conuertit.'

Brycheford, now Bridgford.

The Harcourts owned considerable property in the neighbourhood, and were, perhaps, lords of the manor. (See Erdeswick, p. 136, *n.* a.)

Note: it does not appear that the messuagium was allowed to fall into decay.

'Willelmus Coton eisdem die & anno vnum messuagium in highe Offleye prosterni fecit.'

Unusual instance of a 'messuagium' with no land mentioned as appurtenant.

It does not appear that the Cotons were ever lords of this manor. (See Erdeswick, p. 128, *n.* a.)

'Dominus Barneys predictis die & anno prosterni fecit vnum cotagium in highe offleye predicta.'

On the cotagium without land, see note on Pedelleston, Herefordshire, p. 266, *supra*.

The manor at this time was in the hands of the family of Bourchier (Erdeswick, pp. 128 and 490, *n.* a). This 'Dominus Barneys' was John Bourchier, 2nd Lord Berners, 1495-1529 (Nicolas, 'Hist. Peerage,' p. 58).

'Ricardus Bedulffe secundo die Aprilis anno primo Regis Henrici vij^ml xxx acras terre arrabilis imparcauit.'

Qu. at Biddulph, where they were lords of the manor (Erdeswick, pp. 8-10).[1]

Libertas Episcopi Cestriensis.

'Humfredus Stanleye tercio die Augusti anno xvj Henrici vij^ml xxx acras terre arrabilis imparcauit.'

The Bishop of Chester's fief contained four principal manors: Brewood in Culveston Hundred, Haywood and Eccleshall in Pirehill Hundred, Lichfield in Offlow Hundred (Eyton's 'Domesday Studies,' Staffordshire, p. 39).

[1] The MS. is bound out of order, a page of Staffordshire being followed by Hampshire and London, in consequence of a confusion between Staff. and Southampt. I have brought together here the separated leaves of Staffordshire.

Stanley would be a tenant, probably of the manor of Haywood or Heywood. See as to this person Erdeswick, p. 70, n.

'Johannes Gyfford anno secundo Henrici viij^{ul} quinque acras terre arrabilis in Chellyngton imparcauit pro fferis nutriendis.'

Chillington formed part of the Bishop's manor of Brewood (Eyton, pp. 3, 114). It was the seat of the Giffards (Erdeswick, p. 159, and n. b). The park is still marked on the maps.

HUNDRED DE OFFLOWE. (OFFLOW, *Domesday*.)

'ffranciscus Braddocke primo die Maii anno secundo Henrici viij^{ul} xx acras terre arrabilis in Adbaston cum quadam pala inclusit & in pasturam animalium conuertit.'

The family of Braddocke or Bradoke were lords of the manor (Erdeswick, p. 125).

'Johannes Harper decimo die ffebruarii anno vij^{mo} Henrici viij^{ul} l acras pasture & decem acras terre arrabilis in Russhall cum quadam pala inclusit pro fferis nutriendis.'

The Harpers or Harpurs were lords of the manor (Erdeswick, p. 404).

HAMPSHIRE AND THE ISLE OF WIGHT

INTRODUCTION

HAMPSHIRE was anciently divided into thirty-seven Hundreds and eight Liberties. The returns in the Lansdowne MS. only include eight of the Hundreds. The rest of the returns for the county are therefore lost. In the case of Hampshire we find a considerable proportion of the area inclosed devoted to purposes of sport—viz. 249 acres out of 559 acres, or 44·54 per cent. There is no sign of inclosure for improved arable farming, the rest of the acreage inclosed being converted to pasture. No displacement of population is explicitly recorded, though that must be inferred from the two firmae, four tenementa and one cotagium returned as ruined. By 'firma' is clearly intended a farm-house. In Norfolk, as has been seen (*vide sub* Causton, p. 186, *supra*), a messuagium and tenementum are convertible terms. Taking five persons as the normal household of a firma or messuagium, and allowing three for the cotagium, we have a total displacement of thirty-three persons. The Bishop of Bath evicts no one for his inclosure at Dogmersfeld. The only ruined house upon manors undoubtedly ecclesiastical is the cottage at Alington, and that is the work of a lay tenant. If the doubtful Erleston and Ewerst are both included among the ecclesiastical manors, the evictions from ecclesiastical land will amount to 54·54 per cent.—viz. eighteen out of thirty-three— a little in excess of the proportionate area of ecclesiastical land, which is, in that case, 270 out of 559 acres, or 48·3 per cent. But, it must be remembered, the land was perhaps farmed out to lay tenants. If we take Hampshire and the Isle of Wight together, the total number of evictions rises to thirty-eight. Excluding the doubtful Erleston and Ewerst from the area of ecclesiastical land, the total ecclesiastical property inclosed will be seventy acres in Hants and 255 in the Isle of Wight, or 325 acres in all. This represents 35·55 per cent. of the entire acreage of 914 acres inclosed in Hants and the Isle of Wight taken together. But the proportion of evictions, eight in thirty-eight, is no higher than 7·89. Add the doubtful 200 acres to the ecclesiastical land, and the evictions will number twenty-three to a total of thirty-eight, or 60·52 per cent., the proportionate area of ecclesiastical land being slightly less, viz. 57·43 per cent.

We now pass to the other test which, as in Norfolk, has been applied to the relation of ecclesiastical and lay landlords to their tenants. If we take the actual inclosers, 252 acres in Hants must be assigned to the inclosures of ecclesiastics, assuming that here, as elsewhere in these Inquisitions, the word 'firma' indicates ecclesiastical property. In this case the 'firmarius' was either actually an ecclesiastic, or sufficiently identified with the ecclesiastics to pass for one in this connexion. Now 252 acres represents to the whole 559 acres inclosed in Hampshire 43·29 per cent., while the fifteen evictions for which ecclesiastics must be held responsible at Erleston and Ewerst represent to the whole number of Hampshire evictions 45·45 per cent. In this case, therefore, as in Norfolk, there is a remarkable correspondence between the land inclosed by ecclesiastics and the land inclosed by laymen with respect to the number of evictions accompanying inclosure. In Hampshire, reversely to Norfolk, the difference is slightly against the ecclesiastics. If the area and evictions of the Isle of Wight be added to the figures for Hampshire, the outcome remains practically the same, though once more with a slight balance in favour of the ecclesiastics. Of the total area of 914 acres inclosed, ecclesiastics are responsible for just one half, or 50 per cent. The evictions accompanying their inclosures are then eighteen in number, or 47·36 per cent. of the total number of evictions. The ecclesiastics, in short, were no worse and no better than other landlords.

The inclosures returned in the Isle of Wight amount to 355 acres, as compared with 559 in the rest of the county of Hants. The area of the Isle of Wight being 86,810 acres, and that of the Hundreds of Hampshire from which returns are made being 186,548 acres, the percentage of inclosures returned for the Isle of Wight is ·04, as compared with that of ·02 for the rest of the county. It must be remembered that the Isle of Wight had long been notorious for the large area inclosed. This may account for the small progress of inclosure there since 1488, which happens also to be the year of the passing of the 'Act concerninge the Isle of Wight' (4 Hen. VII. c. 16) for checking the inclosures there. The statute recited that this 'Isle is late decayed of people, by reason that many Townes and vilages been lete downe and the feldes dyked and made pastures for bestis and catalles and also many dwelling places fermes and fermeholdes have of late tyme ben used to be taken into oon mannys hold and handes that of old tyme were wont to be in many severall persones holdes and handes.' The remedy prescribed by the Act, however, was not a prohibition of inclosures, but a prohibition of the consolidation of farms, no one person being allowed to hold more farms than one above the value of ten marks yearly rent. The fact that the entire area of 355 acres inclosed in the Isle of Wight was converted to pasture, and none of it inclosed for sport, is an indication of superior or more profitable farming than on the mainland. The inclosures on ecclesiastical land amount to no less than 255 acres, or 71·83 per cent. of the whole. No mention of ecclesiastics as among the inclosers occurs in the Act of 1488, so that it would seem as though in the Isle of Wight the ecclesiastics had rather lagged in the rear than led the inclosing movement. It is to be observed that four dates are returned for as many inclosures in Hampshire and the Isle of Wight taken together. Two of these are ecclesiastical inclosures: one, that at Hassebourne, belongs to a lay inclosure, and the last, at Erleston, is of an inclosure upon a doubtful manor.

The inclosures in the Isle of Wight are five in number. Of these the acreage of the first and second are explicitly stated in numbers as being a hundred and fifty acres respectively. In the second case this area is identified with half an aratrum. In two of the remaining cases this standard is referred to, one inclosure being of a whole, the other of half an aratrum. Though the area is large for an aratrum, as compared with the areas assigned to it in the rest of the MS., we must accept it as fixed by the former entry. With regard to the remaining case, conclusion is more difficult. The inclosure is described as being of the land belonging to a messuagium. A comparison of Herefordshire shows that this was on an average fifty-five acres in that southern county. I have therefore admitted that as the area intended in this case.

ANALYSIS OF THE INQUISITION FOR THE COUNTY OF SOUTHAMPTON

I. Areas Inclosed on Lay and Ecclesiastical Manors

Hundred	Area of Hundred	Total area inclosed	Inclosures remaining arable	Conversions and pasture areas inclosed	Lay Manors			Ecclesiastical Manors		
					Total	Remaining arable	Conversions and pasture areas inclosed	Total	Remaining arable	Conversions and pasture areas inclosed
	acres	acres	acres	acres	acres	acres	acres	acres	acres	acres
Redbridge	14,950	12	—	12	12	—	12	—	—	—
Somborne	30,090	40	—	40	40	—	40	—	—	—
Mansbrigg	24,650	18	—	18	—	—	—	18	—	18
Kingsclere	21,460	200	—	200	0 (200)	—	0 (200)	0 (200)	—	0 (200)
Crondale	28,220	13	—	13	13	—	13	—	—	—
Shutteley	10,010	80	—	80	80	—	80	—	—	—
Basingstoke	23,828	144	—	144	144	—	144	—	—	—
Odiham	33,340	52	—	52	—	—	—	52	—	52
Total	186,548	559	—	559	289 (489)	—	289 (489)	70 (270)	—	70 (270)

II. Proportionate Analysis of Areas Inclosed on Lay and Ecclesiastical Manors

Hundred	Proportion of total area inclosed to area of Hundred	Proportion of inclosures remaining arable to total areas inclosed	Proportion of conversions and inclosures of pasture to total areas inclosed	Lay Manors — Proportion of areas inclosed to total areas inclosed	Lay Manors — Proportion of inclosures remaining arable to total areas inclosed	Lay Manors — Proportion of inclosures remaining arable to total areas inclosed on lay manors	Lay Manors — Proportion of conversions and inclosures of pasture to total areas inclosed	Lay Manors — Proportion of conversions and inclosures of pasture to total areas inclosed on lay manors	Ecclesiastical Manors — Proportion of areas inclosed to total areas inclosed	Ecclesiastical Manors — Proportion of inclosures remaining arable to total areas inclosed	Ecclesiastical Manors — Proportion of inclosures remaining arable to total areas inclosed on ecclesiastical manors	Ecclesiastical Manors — Proportion of conversions and inclosures of pasture to total areas inclosed	Ecclesiastical Manors — Proportion of conversions and inclosures of pasture to total areas inclosed on ecclesiastical manors
Redbridge	·008	—	100	100	—	100	100	51·69 (87·45)	—	—	—	—	12·31 (48·3)
Somborne	·01	—	100	100	—	100	100		—	—	—	—	
Mansbrigg	·007	—	100	0 (100)	—	0 (100)	0 (100)		—	—	0 (100)	0 (100)	
Kingsclere	·09	—	100	100	—	100	100		—	—	—	—	
Crondale	·004	—	100	100	—	100	100		—	—	—	—	
Shirleley	·07	—	100	100	—	100	100		—	—	—	—	
Basingstoke	·06	—	100		—				—	—	—	—	
Odiham	·01	—	100		—				—	—	—	—	
Total	·03	—	100	51·69 (87·45)	—	51·69 (87·45)	51·69 (87·45)		—	—	12·31 (48·3)	12·31 (48·3)	12·31 (48·3)

ANALYSIS OF THE INQUISITION FOR THE ISLE OF WIGHT

III. AREAS INCLOSED ON LAY AND ECCLESIASTICAL MANORS

Place	Area of island	Total area inclosed	Inclosure remaining arable	Conversions and pasture areas inclosed	Lay Manors			Ecclesiastical Manors		
					Total	Re-maining arable	Conversions and pasture areas inclosed	Total	Re-maining arable	Conversions and pasture areas inclosed
	acres	acres	acres	acres	acres	acres	acres	acres	acres	acres
Hassebourne	86,810	100	—	100	100	—	100	—	—	—
? Esthamlode	86,810	50	—	50	—	—	—	50	—	50
Stepelhirst	86,810	(55)	—	(55)	—	—	—	(55)	—	(55)
Lytell panne	86,810	(50)	—	(50)	—	—	—	(50)	—	(50)
Chalcom	86,810	(100)	—	(100)	—	—	—	(100)	—	(100)
Total	—	355	—	355	100	—	100	255	—	255

IV. PROPORTIONATE ANALYSIS OF AREAS INCLOSED ON LAY AND ECCLESIASTICAL MANORS

Place	Proportion of total areas inclosed to area of island	Proportion of inclosures and conversions of pasture to total areas inclosed	Proportion of inclosures remaining arable to total areas inclosed	Proportion of conversions and pasture to total areas inclosed	Lay Manors			Ecclesiastical Manors		
					Proportion of areas inclosed to total areas inclosed on lay manors	Proportion of inclosures remaining arable to total areas inclosed on lay manors	Proportion of conversions and inclosures of pasture to total areas inclosed on lay manors	Proportion of areas inclosed to total areas inclosed on ecclesiastical manors	Proportion of inclosures remaining arable to total areas inclosed on ecclesiastical manors	Proportion of conversions and inclosures of pasture to total areas inclosed on ecclesiastical manors
Hassebourne	.01	100	—	100	100	—	100	—	—	—
? Esthamlode	.005	(100)	—	(100)	—	—	—	(100)	—	(100)
Stepelhirst	.006	(100)	—	(100)	—	—	—	(100)	—	(100)
Lytell panne	.005	(100)	—	(100)	—	—	—	(100)	—	(100)
Chalcom	.01	(100)	—	(100)	—	—	—	(100)	—	(100)
Total	.04	100	—	100	28·16	—	28·16	71·83	—	71·83

NOTE.—The brackets indicate that the area is not actually given in figures, but inferred upon data explained in the notes to the text. Displacement of population :—1 messuagium = 5 persons.

V. OWNERSHIP OF MANORS

Lay Manors	Doubtful	Ecclesiastical Manors
Newtonberye	Wynsore	Alington
ffarley	Erleston	Dogmersfelde
Ichill	Ewerst	—
Loke Dewer	—	—
Breche & Sockborowe	—	—
Bramsyll	—	—
Bewraper	—	—

VI. ACTUAL INCLOSERS

Hampshire

LAYMEN	Acres	ECCLESIASTICS	Acres
Newtonberye	12		
ffarley	40		
Alington	18		
		Erleston (qu.)	100
		Ewerst (qu.)	100
Ichill	13		
Loke Dewer	40		
Breche & Sockborowe	40		
Bramsyll	120		
Bewraper	24		
		Dogmersfelde	52
	307		252

Isle of Wight

	Acres		Acres
Hassebourne	100		
Lytell Panne	50		
		Esthamlode (?)	50
		Stepelhirst	55
		Chalcom	100
	150		205

THE INQUISITION FOR HAMPSHIRE AND THE ISLE OF WIGHT

(Lansd. MS. I. fo. 175, 176)

P. 40.—SOUTHAMPTON.

'Presentatum est per quandam inquisicionem captam apud Romeseye in comitatu predicto primo die Septembris anno nono Regis Henrici viij^{ui} coram domino Audeley & Johanne lysley milite commissionariis eiusdem Regis modo & forma sequente videlicet.'

John Touchet, Baron Audeley.

Sir John Lysley or Lisle was pricked sheriff of Hants Nov. 1517 (Br. 'Cal.' ii. 37, 83).

HUNDRED DE REDBRIGE.

'Quod quoddam tenementum scituatum in Wynsore infra hundred predictum vocatum Reynoldes prosternitur citra ffestum Sancti Michaelis archangeli anno quarto Regis henrici vij^{mi}.'

A place called Wynsor in the parish of Millbrook, without the bounds of the New Forest, is mentioned in 'An Abstract of all the Claims on the New Forest,' Salisbury, 1776, § 87. But according to the Census of 1831, ii. 574, the hundred of Redbridge only includes the parish of Eling, the total area of the hundred being 14,950 acres.

'Et quod vnum tenementum iacens in Newtonberye infra hundred predictum cum xij acris terre eidem tenemento adiacentis prosternuntur [*sic*] citra dictum ffestum sancti Michaelis dicto anno iiij^{to}. Et Willelmus Whight habet ius hereditatis & proficua inde.'

I cannot identify this place. But see last note.

The phrase 'habet ius hereditatis' seems to indicate that he had not yet been admitted as heir on the court roll, or he may have been the reversioner of land let for lives on lease. The record as to 'proficua' seems to point to this and that he was at least responsible as having licensed the inclosure.

HUNDRED DE SOMBORNE.

'Item presentatum fuit per quandam inquisicionem captam apud Romesey xxj die Septembris anno nono Regis Henrici viij^{ui} coram prefatis comissionariis

'Quod Johannes Ewirsbye cepit in parcum suum de ffarley xl acras terre citra iiij annum Regis Henrici vij^{mi} infra hundred predictum.'

I.e. Farley Chamberlayne, near Winchester. Presumably J. E., as owner of a park here, was lord of the manor.

HUNDRED DE MANSBRIGG.

'Et quod Johannes Warde tenet vnum cotagium & xviij acras terre in parochia de Alington infra hundred predictum quod est in decasu & ruina & predicte xviij acre terre arrabilis in pasturam posite post dictum annum quartum predicti nuper Regis Henrici vij^{mi}. Et quod dicte terre tenentur de domo sancti dionisii.'

Here the 'cotagium,' as in Yorkshire, has land assigned to it. See note on Pedelleston, Herefordshire, p. 266, *supra*.
Alington or Aldington.

The 'domus sancti dionisii' is the Priory of St. Denys near Southampton, belonging to the Austin canons. At the Dissolution their rents in Aldington were 2*l*. 14*s*. 4*d*., they being lords of the manor (Dugdale, 'Monast.' vi. 214).

SOUTHAMPTON.

'Presentatum fuit eciam per quandam inquisicionem captam apud Basingstoke xxj die Septembris anno ix^{no} Regis Henrici viij^{ui} coram Willelmo Sandes milite Willelmo pawlett armigero Thoma More gent. & aliis comissionariis in comitatibus predictis infra hundred de Kingesclere.'

Sir William Sandes or Sandys, of the Vine, Hants, was a successful courtier, to judge from the numerous grants recorded in Br. 'Cal.' i. and ii. He had been Sheriff of Hants in 1511 (Br. 'Cal.' i. 1316), was made a Baron in 1523 (Nicolas).

W. Paulet was on the list for sheriffs of Hants in 1516 (*ibid.* ii. 2533). He was afterwards first Marquis of Winchester.

This 'Thomas More, gent.,' was the famous Sir Thomas More, and Campbell's statement in his 'Lives of the Chancellors,' i. 516, that he was knighted in 1514 is incorrect. He was included in the Commission for Hants in 1515, but not as a knight (Br. 'Cal.' ii. 170, 670), and similarly in 1518 (*ibid.* 3917). In 1519, when nominated ambassador to treat with the Hanse, he is styled in the commission 'Thomae More armigeri' (Rym. 'Foed.' xiii. 722). The first mention that I find of him as a knight in the Domestic Papers is Br. 'Cal.' iii. 1437 in a letter of Pace to Wolsey dated July 24 1521. That this was the real year of his knighthood further appears by a letter of the same year from Erasmus to Budaeus (Er. 'Ep.' xvii. 16), in which Erasmus, after mentioning that More has been appointed Treasurer, adds : ' Nec hoc contentus Princeps benignissimus: equitis aurati dignitatem adjecit.' (Cp. Br. 'Cal.' iii. 1527.) There is no mention of his knighthood in Metcalfe's ' Book of Knights,' London, 1885.

KINGESCLERE.

'Quod quedam ffirma vocata Gogiens iacens infra dominium de Erleston infra hundred predictum in decasu existit fferme ad terram & Iconomia eiusdem in pasturam posita infra quinque annos.'

The word 'iconomia' is not given in Ducange in any sense appropriate to this entry. I take it to mean 'cultivation.' No acreage is given. It frequently occurs in the Record

Office MS. of these Inquisitions. See 'Trans. R.H.S.' 1892, p. 174.

As to 'firma' see *sub* Ryborow, Norfolk, *supra*. It usually denotes ecclesiastical property.

Earlston is in the parish of Burghclere.

No acreage is given. I have inferred from the next entry 100 acres as the area attached to a 'firma.'

P. 41.—ADHUC HUNDRED DE KINGESCLERE.

'Item quod quedam ffirma vocata Ewerst desolata & in decasu existit & nulla persona super eandem inhabitat. Et quod maxima eiusdem terre pars includitur & in pasturam posita pro ouibus et eciam vnum tenementum eidem pertinens in decasu existit & terra vnius aratri in pasturam posita.'

'Firma' again used for a farmhouse.

'Terra vnius aratri.' There is one indication in the Hampshire Inquisition of the area of an 'aratrum' in this county. That is given under the Isle of Wight, in the case of the inclosure, at an unnamed place, by the Abbot of Bewleye (see p. 291, *infra*). There fifty acres appear to be reckoned as half a ploughland. In Norfolk the average acreage assigned to an 'aratrum' was nearly fifty-seven acres. In Yorkshire it was thirty-one acres. Here two houses are destroyed—a 'firma' and a 'tenementum.' In Hampshire a tenementum is twice associated with a specified area : once, at Newtonberye (p. 285, *supra*) with twelve acres, again, at Bewraper, p. 290, *infra*, with twenty-four acres. This gives an average of eighteen acres to the Hampshire 'tenementum' as compared with one of thirty-three acres in Norfolk. A messuagium, which appears to be the usual designation of a farmhouse, is associated with thirty-one acres in Yorkshire, thirty acres in Norfolk, and fifty-five acres in Herefordshire. A Herefordshire messuagium and a Hampshire tenementum would give seventy-three acres, or a Herefordshire messuagium with a Norfolk tenementum eighty-eight acres. I think, though with some doubt, that in the Hampshire Inquisition the measurement given in the Isle of Wight case must be that of a normal Hampshire 'aratrum,' and that the inclosure in this case must be taken at 100 acres.

'Presentatum fuit eciam per quandam inquisicionem captam apud Basingstoke xx die Septembris anno ix^{no} Regis Henrici viij^{ui} coram prefatis Willelmo Sandes milite & aliis comissionariis &c.'

HUNDRED DE CRONDALE.

Quod Willelmus Gifford miles imparcauit post dictum annum iiij dicti domini Regis Henrici vij^{mi} xiij acras terre pro elargacione parci sui vocati Ichill quarum quinque acre tunc arrabiles existebant & viij bosci.'

This entry is perhaps an example of the impartiality of the commissioners, since this Sir William Gifford was brother-in-law to W. Pawlett, one of their number. (See Woodward's 'Hist. of Hampshire,' iii. 246.)

Ichill, *i.e.* Itchel.

HUNDRED DE SHUTTELEY, *i.e.* CHUTELY.

'Item quod Nicholaus warram inclusit xl acras terre arrabilis extra communem campum vocatum loke dewer infra hundred predictum & easdem in pasturam posuit pro ouibus.'

The Warham family, from which sprang the famous Archbishop, were landowners at Malshanger.

'Item dictus Nicholaus inclusit in pasturam post dictum iiij annum xl acras terre arrabilis extra communes agros vocatos Breche & Sockborowe.'

The recitals 'extra communem campum' and 'extra communes agros' apparently indicate that the inclosures were of the waste of the manor.

'Item presentatum fuit per quandam inquisicionem captam apud Basingstoke xxj^{mo} die Septembris anno nono Regis nunc Henrici viij^{ui} coram supranominatis Willelmo Sandes milite & aliis comissionariis supradictis.'

Hundred de Basingstoke.

'Quod Egidius nuper dominus dawbeneye inclusit in parcum suum de Bramsyll centum & viginti vel centum & quadraginta acras de communi de hasill ad damnum tenentium Regis ibidem inhabitancium post dictum annum quartum predicti nuper Regis Henrici vij^{ml}.'

Hasill, *i.e.* Hazely Heath, held of the royal manor of Basingstoke (Woodward, iii. 297-8).

An alternative computation is unusual. I have taken it at the smaller acreage of 120 acres.

Giles Daubeney, K.G., created Baron 1486, died 1507 (Nicolas).

'Item presentatum per dictam inquisicionem quod Willelmus Brocas armiger iam defunctus inclusit in parcum de Bewraper post dictum iiij annum dicti Regis Henrici vij^{ml} xxiiij acras terre pertinentes cuidam tenemento quod est in decasu racione eiusdem imparcacionis. Et quod dominus Dawbeney est inde seisitus in ffeodo.'

W. B., the last male of the family of Brocas, who were lords of the manor here (Woodward, iii. 261).

'Jam defunctus'—died 1506 (*ibid.*).

'Inde' would appear to refer to the tenement. Apparently Lord Dawbeney was owner at the time of the Inquisition.

P. 42.—Hundred de Odihum.

'Presentatum est per inquisicionem predictam quod Oliuerus Kynge nuper Episcopus Bathonensis imparcauit post dictum annum quartum dicti nuper Regis Henrici vij^{ml} lij acras terre pro elargacione parci sui de Dogmersfelde quarum xv acre tunc arrabiles existebant & v acre prati.'

In Lewis's 'Topographical Dictionary' the ruins of the palace here are said to be of that of the Archbishop ot Canterbury. This entry points to its having been the property of the Bishop of Bath.

Insula Vecta.

'Presentatum est eciam per quandam inquisicionem captam apud Suthwike xxj die Septembris anno ix^{no} dicti Regis nunc henrici viij^{ul} coram Ricardo episcopo Wintoniensi & aliis comissionariis Regis.'

As to inclosures in the Isle of Wight see Introduction, pp. 278–280, *supra*.

'Ricardo episcopo Wintoniensi,' *i.e.* Richard Fox.

'Quod centum acre terre arrabilis includuntur & in pasturam posite per vj annos tunc preteritos in hassebourne per quendam Johannem fflemynge tanner. Et quod hereditas eiusdem in quodam Willelmo Barleye existit.'

'Item quod abbas de Bewleye posuit l acras terre arrabilis in pasturam per xj annos tunc preteritos. Et quod dimidium terre vnius aratri in decasu racione eiusdem.'

The place is not mentioned. The Abbey of Beaulieu or or Bewley in the New Forest possessed land at Esthamlode in the Isle of Wight (Dugdale, 'Monast.' v. 683).

I take the entry to mean that this area of fifty acres is half a ploughland. A carucate of eighty acres by the long hundred would give the approximate area of ninety-six acres.

'Item quod est ibidem quedam ffirma vocata Stepelhirst posita in pasturam per quendam Thomam Sygons per xij annos tunc preteritos per quod quoddam messuagium ibidem est in decasu. Et quod abbas de Quarrye habet successionem eiusdem.'

The manor of Staplehurst was the property of the Abbey of Quarr or Quarreria in the Isle of Wight (Dugdale, 'Monast.' v. 320).

Here 'ffirma' is used as the area of a farm. No area is given and it can only be inferred. It has been seen (*sub* Ewerst, p. 288, *supra*) that in the southern county of Hereford the area associated with a messuagium is on the average fifty-five acres. The area in this case is clearly not fifty or a hundred acres, or it would have been described as 'dimidium aratri' or 'aratrum.' I venture, therefore, to put it at the Herefordshire area of fifty-five acres.

The phrase 'habet successionem' seems to indicate that the tenant held of the abbey for his life. Here, as elsewhere I have taken the use of the word instead of the derivatives of *occupo* and *teneo* as implying a clerical tenant.

'Item presentatum per dictam inquisicionem quod tunc quedam terre vocate lytell panne que in pasturam ponuntur racione cuius dimidium acre vnius aratri est in decasu post dictum annum quartum dicti nuper Regis Henrici vij^{mi}.'

'Tunc' apparently refers back to the last entry, the incloser and landowner being the same. But qu. whether incorrectly transcribed for 'sunt.'

'Dimidium acre vnius aratri' cannot be intended to mean that an 'acra' is equivalent to an 'aratrum.' I take it that 'acra' is used here in a sense of which I can find no instance in Du Cange, viz. for 'acreage.' The area converted will then be fifty acres. See p. 291, *supra*, under the Abbot of Bewleye's inclosure.

'Item quod quedam sunt terre in pasturam posite vocate Chalcom per Willelmum porter ffirmarium eiusdem. Et quod terra vnius aratri in decasu existit racione eiusdem. Et quod Abbas de Quarre modo seisitus existit vt in iure domus sue.'

Chalcomb, Shalcombe, or Shancomb. The Abbey owned the manor here at the Dissolution (Dugdale, 'Monast.' v. 320).

For the meaning of 'ffirmarius' see *sub* Ryborow, *supra*.

THE PROGRESS OF HISTORICAL RESEARCH DURING THE SESSION 1892-93.

THE dearth of serious literature, which has been the chief feature of the English book-market in the publishing season of 1892-3, has visited with especial vigour the domain of History. Some who are well qualified to discuss the causes of the above phenomenon have attributed the falling-off to the vast increase in the production of serial literature. In the last volume of 'Transactions' attention was called to this state of affairs, with the remark that 'it would seem as though the progress of research in this country must, for some time to come at least, be traced in the pages of periodical and serial publications.' This somewhat bold prediction is apparently in a fair way to be verified, and it may be worth while to examine more closely the nature of the crisis with which we are confronted.

It might possibly be supposed that this indisposition to engage in the production of substantial 'Histories' is due to a want of energy or of application on the part of the modern historian. This, however, is by no means the case. On the contrary, the study of historical problems is pursued with an almost feverish zeal by the younger school of writers, and with an expenditure of time and labour which is out of all proportion to the apparent results. The truth is that the science of history has become very exacting. The unremitting exertions of the national libraries and of publishing societies, in addition to the researches of foreign scholars, have made available for the first time a vast mass of authentic materials which were entirely overlooked, or at least ignored, by a former generation of writers. Moreover, the standard of historical accuracy has reached a formidable height. It is not enough to cite original authorities haphazard, or to edit the same with a pleasant, easy-going scholarship. The respective merits of the different manuscripts are now well established, and it is regarded as a criminal offence to employ an inferior version.

All these considerations have to be taken into account in estimating the progress made by the latter-day historian. His path is beset with pitfalls, and if he would avoid disaster and consequent disgrace he must walk circumspectly; therefore his progress is slow. Those who are inclined to make light of these difficulties are soon daunted by some terrible example. 'Before all things,' we are told, 'let us be accurate.' This laudable desire for accuracy is the keynote of the modern historian's method, and it sometimes manifests itself in a curious striving after realism. There is no room left for the play of the imagination, and there is very little scope for art in this new method, which strips every legend of its picturesque embellishments and exposes the truths of history in all their naked ugliness.

After all, however, this method has its drawbacks. It is too obviously a reaction from the political partisanship and the incompetent scholarship of the second quarter of the present century. Because certain historians resolutely ignored the only authentic sources of history, and because certain antiquaries were unequal to the task of editing an historical manuscript with the critical acumen that we should expect from a modern German savant, we are not compelled to execrate their literary memories. A purely destructive criticism is fatal to the progress of the work of historical reconstruction, which demands the unselfish labour of the whole body of earnest students, each of whom in his own way can contribute something for the common benefit. It is absurd to contend that the work should stand still pending the erection of a universal standard of accuracy.

During the last twelve months the great work of one of the greatest of modern historians has been exposed to the fierce light of a highly technical criticism, and the interest of the historical world has been aroused by the fierce controversy which this criticism has provoked and which is not even yet at an end. It cannot be said, however, that we are much the wiser for all this intensity of criticism, while we are certainly inconvenienced by the clouds of dust raised by some one of the combatants which for the time being have obscured all possible view of the battle of Hastings.

This is only a single instance in point; but it is notorious that there are scores of accomplished scholars who have never yet made any useful contribution to the work of historical research, simply because they are unable to satisfy a fastidious standard of accuracy. Perhaps this irresolution is preferable to the feverish energy with which some people devote their lives to finding out mistakes in other people's work. This last disease, however, is very infectious, and it may lay hold with slight warning on those who are not occupied with an appointed task. Moreover, as probably no history that was ever written does not contain a large number of mistakes, most of which yet remain to be detected and exposed, it will be evident that a good deal of moral courage would be a useful part of the equipment of the historical student in the future.

The Public Record Office is admittedly the fountain-head of English historical research, and moreover, furnishes a very considerable part of the material for Continental history. It is true that in the British Museum, the University Libraries, and in a number of public and private collections, there is preserved a vast mass of precious manuscripts; but of these the most important have already been printed, and, apart from certain vexed questions concerning their legal authority, it will be found that a very large proportion of these manuscripts are either supplementary to the main series in official custody or else later and inferior transcripts.

The work of repairing, sorting, and classifying the public records is making slow but satisfactory progress, to judge from the latest report of the Deputy Keeper. In addition to the almost daily discovery of new hoards of buried Record-treasure, which had probably lain for centuries undescribed and inaccessible to students, the existing classes of Records have been carefully arranged, classified, and described in official Indexes and Lists, and more than 60,000 damaged leaves or membranes have been carefully repaired.

The important series of official Record Calendars, founded within the last few years by Mr. Maxwell Lyte, embraces a number of works, the value of which is now fully recognised. Of these probably the most important are the Calendars of Patent and Close Rolls for the Edwardian period and the reign of Richard II. Each of these volumes is prepared on the same plan, and in all the greatest care has been bestowed upon the identification of names and places, and the preservation and adequate rendering of technical terms. The Rolls for the reign of John, which are the earliest in existence, have already been printed *in extenso*, and it is probable that Mr. Maxwell Lyte will be able to extend the same treatment to the Rolls of Henry III., while the Calendars are to be continued (as we now learn) to the reign of Henry VII. This great and truly national work will be, and indeed is already, welcomed as an inestimable boon by mediæval historians at home and abroad, though not in a few instances it will necessitate the rewriting of some page of history.

Another invaluable mediæval Calendar is that which deals with the Ancient Deeds and Charters deposited amongst the Public Records, and progress has been made with the preparation of yet another Calendar of Ancient Correspondence. The importance of this last *précis* of the Royal letters and other mediæval State Papers can scarcely be exaggerated, and the appearance of the first volume will be a great event for the mediæval student.

In addition to these elaborate Calendars, which are practically uniform with the well-known Calendars of State Papers, a number of Indexes or Catalogues have been prepared and some of these have been printed. By the aid of these official 'Lists' (as they are commonly called), the reader will be able to consult for himself such important Records as the Ministers (or Bailiffs') Accounts of the Crown lands, and the Rolls of the Manor Courts held within the same; the Inquisitions taken on the death of all who held of the Crown by military service, the Ancient Petitions of the Chancery and Exchequer, the vast series of Judicial Rolls, and the assessments made in every district for the levy of the Parliamentary Subsidy.

Less fortunate or less favoured than his brother of mediæval research, the historical student of the Tudor and Stuart periods has still to be content with the continuation of the Calendars which have been before the public for so many years, with the welcome additions that have been provided by the present Deputy Keeper in the shape of Calendars of the Venetian and Spanish State Papers, and of the Privy Council Registers. It will soon be possible, however, to include in the above list two new Calendars for the later Stuart period, the one a continuation of the Calendar of the Domestic State Papers from the year 1668, and the other a new departure from the year 1689, including that remarkable collection known as King William's Chest, of which only very partial use was made by Macintosh and Macaulay.

Several important volumes in this group have been issued during the past year. Mrs. Everett Green has completed the extensive Calendar of Royalist Composition Papers, and is at present engaged on a volume of *Addenda* to the Calendar of the regular series of State Papers, 1660–7, previously published in seven volumes. Mr. Noel Sainsbury has completed a further instalment of his Colonial Calendar, dealing with the State Papers for India and Persia, 1630–34, and is far advanced with a new volume for the American and West India plantations from the year 1675. Mr. Gairdner's new volume of the Calendar of all Letters and Papers of the reign of Henry VIII. deals with the eventful year 1538. Mr. Hamilton's latest volume completes the Calendar of the State Papers of the reign of Charles I., and a volume of *Addenda* will shortly be added to the series. The Calendar of Irish State Papers of the reign of Elizabeth is still in progress; but the most noticeable volume of the whole series is perhaps that in which 'the innermost working of the tortuous Spanish policy of the reign of Elizabeth is for the first time laid bare to English students,' from the Spanish correspondence at Simancas, edited with great learning and literary skill by Major Martin Hume, a Fellow of this Society.

It will soon be possible for students to become acquainted with the nature of the contents of every single State Paper preserved in official custody from the reign of Henry VII. to that of George I., with the striking exception of the great series of Foreign State Papers, which have only been calendared as far as the year 1577. When it is remembered that some two thousand volumes of despatches from English residents in the several capitals of Europe still remain to be calendared before the Hanoverian period, it is clear that the present loss and future gain to students are matters of some importance.

For the eighteenth century itself, there is unfortunately no immediate prospect of any concession to the requirements of a still larger circle of workers. The Calendar of Treasury Papers has stopped short early in the reign of George II., and the Home Office Calendar early in that of George III. There is absolutely no published guide to the contents of the thousands and thousands of volumes of State Papers for the Hanoverian period, and until some such guide is provided we can know very little of the true history of the period outside the works of the pioneers who have reproduced the text or the substance of these authentic documents. This is a serious deficiency, to which the Royal Historical Society has repeatedly called attention, and which it has set itself to remedy as far as its means of doing so exist. In addition to the numerous papers based on these State Archives which have appeared in its Transactions, the Society has inaugurated a series of publications of the texts of selected despatches of the eighteenth century. A volume of the despatches of Lord Whitworth has already appeared under the title of 'England and Napoleon in 1803,' edited by Mr. Oscar Browning, and two further volumes are still in the press. Even the most modest efforts in this direction are deserving of encouragement, for hitherto the contents of our own State Papers have been chiefly known to us through the investigations of foreign historians, who have long ago published all that was best worth knowing in their own archives.

On the whole, however, we must feel very grateful for the work that has been accomplished by the Record Office during the past year, especially when we remember that the regular series of Calendars has been supplemented by a number of valuable Indexes or Lists of the legal records of the sixteenth and seventeenth centuries.

Following the useful precedent of the establishment of a regular Calendar of the State Papers relating to English affairs preserved at Venice and other cities of Northern Italy, the Deputy Keeper of the Records has arranged for the preparation of a Calendar of the Papal *Regesta* relating to this country, which have hitherto been transmitted in manuscript from the Vatican.

One of the most important and instructive publications of the past year is undoubtedly the Thirteenth Report of the Historical Manuscripts Commission. Some of the appendices to the Report have already appeared in a separate form, while others yet remain to be published. Amongst the former the historical value of the collections in the possession of the Duke of Portland, Mr. J. B. Fortescue, and the Earl of Lonsdale is at least equal to that of any that have been described in previous Reports, with the exception of course of the Hatfield manuscripts, which fairly rival in volume and importance the State Papers of the Crown itself.

The Rolls Series, as surmised in the last volume of 'Transactions,' is obviously drawing to a close. Only a single volume was issued during the past year, and only nine more remained to be issued unless a further grant is made by the Treasury, a concession which naturally depends on the historical value of any edition which may be contemplated in the future.

The Colonial Governments of Canada and Australia have continued with unflagging energy the gigantic task of transcribing all the historical documents existing in this country or in Continental Archives which relate to the early history of their respective settlements. It is now a recognised fact that the authentic materials for these branches of colonial history have to be sought for in the pages of the official Blue Books issued in the Colonies.

The numerous learned societies which publish materials for the study of local or imperial history have continued their invaluable labours during the past year, but in several cases the actual publication of certain volumes has been delayed owing to accidental causes. Quite recently two new publishing societies have been founded, one of which will devote itself to the publication of Anglo-Norman Cartularies, which must necessarily rank among the most important evidences for the history of the eleventh and twelfth centuries. The second of these new societies will undertake the publication of the Naval Records which are preserved in the Public Record Office and elsewhere, beginning probably with a collection of Howard letters descriptive of the repulse of the Armada, edited by Professor Laughton.

Co-operation in the writing of history, whether popular or scientific in character, still continues to be in fashion. The number of 'epochs,' 'stories,' and other monographs of universal history, for the most part of a purely ephemeral nature, is continually increasing. Although these works have but little connection with research, they possess some distinct advantages over the ordinary school histories. In the first place, they are well written and well 'got up,' while they may be procured at a very modest price. Secondly, they are usually contributed (at the suggestion of an enterprising publisher) by the best authorities on the respective subjects, with whose views and characteristics the younger generation of scholars and the general reader can therefore make themselves acquainted at first hand. Such works, however, as Professor Tout's admirable sketch of Edward I.'s reign, and Mr. Morfill's 'Poland,' have an individuality and an importance of their own, and in this connection mention may be made of two forthcoming handbooks by Mr. Oscar Browning, the 'Guelphs and Ghibellines,' a short history of mediæval Italy, and an elementary handbook of political science, dealing with the rights and responsibilities of the English citizen.

In addition to the above series of monographs, the valuable results of co-operation in the writing of history can be seen in the recent additions to the Dictionaries of Philology, National Biography, and Economic Terms, whilst the first instalment of an exhaustive 'Social History of England,' compiled by several hands, is on the point of appearing. We hear, indeed, of several projects of this nature under discussion, and it is possible that the fashion for separate epochs may before long give place to the encyclopædic form of publication, which certainly has the advantage of providing a more permanent authority.

The most noticeable form of historical compilation in the present day is, however, that in which a number of original texts are edited for the use of students under the title of ' Select Documents.' The immense success achieved by the Bishop of Oxford's well-known volume, has, after a long interval, led to the welcome appearance of similar works. Dr. Gardiner's selection of documents illustrative of the Puritan Revolution has been still another triumph for the cause of original research, and two more notable collections of a precisely similar nature, M. Bémont's scholarly volume of charters of English liberties in the twelfth and thirteenth centuries, and Dr. Henderson's useful selections of European historical documents during the Middle Ages, have recently appeared. It is well known amongst historical workers that another collection will shortly be published by Mr. G. W. Prothero, which in some respects will mark a new departure, and we hear of other volumes of a similar kind under contemplation. All this is highly encouraging, and the only drawback is that the texts of the documents selected are in most cases derived from printed books, the authority of which has been of late years somewhat rudely shaken. Certainly we must wait for the results of Dr. Liebermann's researches, and for the publications of the Anglo-Norman

Cartulary Society, before a definite text can be accepted for the earliest of these constitutional documents, and even in later times a careful collation is advisable.

In fact the writing of mediæval history in the present day is absolutely dependent on this documentary evidence, supplemented by that of the chroniclers, and for this reason the value of a series of historical excerpts from contemporary writers, such as the one edited by Mr. York Powell, is almost as great as that of purely constitutional documents.

In this particular, however (as in so many others), we lag behind our Continental neighbours. In the above-mentioned series Mr. Jacob's 'History of the Jews in Angevin England' is, in spite of some shortcomings, a most valuable compilation.

A special feature of mediæval research during the past year has been the publication of a further instalment of the tracts which mark the progress of Dr. Liebermann's great work on the Anglo-Saxon and Anglo-Norman Laws and Institutes. These include the 'Consiliatio Cnuti' and the 'Instituta Cnuti,' the latter of which, in the author's own English, appears among the contents of the present volume. A further tract is shortly to be published dealing with that remarkable collection of early laws preserved in the Guildhall registers, in connection with the date and motive of whose interpolations our greatest historians have gone grievously astray.

The Tudor period has succeeded in attracting the attention of several new workers, and, in addition to the important labours of Mr. James Gairdner and Father Gasquet, Dr. Wilhelm Busch has completed the first volume of a history which will rank high amongst modern text-books; while the legal, economic, and maritime history of the period is to be specialised through the researches of Mr. R. G. Marsden, Mr. Leadam and M. Spont, Dr. Brugmans and Professor Logermann, not to mention recent monographs such as Mr. Page's account of the Aliens in England, 1509–1603, Baron Schickler's very important work on the same subject, and Mr. Barrett's 'History of the Trinity House' from the records of the Corporation.

In the Stuart period Dr. Gardiner holds the field during the Puritan Revolution, and after the Restoration the materials for authentic history are being only slowly collected from the State Papers and Historical Manuscripts. For all that, new editions of Dr. Wishart's 'Montrose' and Colonel Walker's narrative of the Siege of Londonderry, together with an authoritative edition of 'Pepys's Memoirs,' must be heartily welcomed. In the Hanoverian period, however, there is the wonted dearth of research in marked contrast to the numerous and important publications in other countries.

The history of Modern Europe has indeed received almost more than usual attention during the last two years, and a great deal of good work is the result. It is very noticeable that several of these works take the form of an explanation or justification of a particular episode or the policy of individual statesmen, from Cade's rebellion to the battle of Waterloo, or from Machiavelli to Moltke. Then we have works of wider interest like M. Waliszewski's 'Catherine II.,' Mr. Horatio Brown's 'Venice,' Mr. Hume Brown's 'History of Scotland,' and Mr Hodgkin's 'Italy and her Invaders;' but the special research of the year seems to centre, as usual, in the study of periods like the era of Frederick the Great, the Revolutionary and Napoleonic wars, the Greek and Turkish questions, the Peninsular war, and the like, in all of which some notable works have been published or are in active progress in different countries.

In Naval and Military history, besides the foundation of the Naval Records Society and the publication of Mr. Ropes's history of Waterloo, a most important contribution to regimental histories is found in Major Edye's 'History of the Marines,' whilst Captain Wharton, the Hydrographer of the Navy, has published an authoritative edition of Captain Cook's Journal, and Mr. Mahan, in his two histories of the influence of sea-power, has achieved one of the greatest literary successes of recent years.

In Colonial history, besides the official Calendars, Histories, or Blue Books of the Colonial Governments, we have to notice the active continuation of Mr. B. F. Steven's important series of historical Facsimiles, in addition to the volume of State Papers relating to the Secret Service (British and Colonial) under George III., which he is engaged in editing for the new series of Publications of the Royal Historical Society. Mr. Henry Adams continues his valuable, though by no means exhaustive or even impartial, history of America from 1801 to 1817.

There have also been published during the past year a number of exceptionally important works relating to Colonial history, such as Mr. Robert Chalmer's invaluable 'History of Colonial Currency,' Dr. Bourinot's 'History of Cape Breton,' Mr. Calvert's 'Discovery of Australia,' Mr. Payne's 'History of the New World,' and M. Bonnassieux's 'History of the great Trading Companies of the Seventeenth and Eighteenth Centuries.' Although a great modern authority on Colonial history has pronounced the Australasian colonies to be fortunate in not possessing any recorded history, several histories of those colonies have nevertheless been recently produced, including, besides Sir H. Parke's well-known narrative, such an important work as Hodder's 'History of South Australia.'

For Colonial history proper it may be well to refer to the admirable paper read in April last by Mr. Noel Sainsbury, the veteran editor of the Colonial State Papers, before the American Antiquarian Society. This paper probably gives the best account yet written of the progress of modern research in the department of American History. Although Mr. Parkman's histories of the French occupation of Canada are still the supreme authority, we can state with confidence that more than one forthcoming work will throw a flood of light upon the colonial relations and policy of France and England from the year 1754, and will considerably modify the received version.

In Oriental history we are naturally struck with the continued publication of numerous histories of Indian affairs and Indian statesmen. A work of some originality and research is Rogers' history of the administration of Bombay.

The fiscal history of the principality is very curious and some of the original tallies or receipts for the payment of the fee-farm rent reserved to the Crown in the reign of Charles II., are still preserved at the India Office. One of the most interesting of recent publications connected with India is the Memoir of Sir Henry Maine, the eminent jurist and Indian statesman, by Sir M. E. Grant Duff, the President of the Royal Historical Society. The same writer has contributed an Introduction to Broughton's Letters from a Mahratta camp in 1809, besides a very sympathetic memoir of another Orientalist, his friend M. Ernest Renan.

Economic History may still be classed amongst the most flourishing branches of historical science. The second volume of Professor Cunningham's great work, 'The History of Industry and Commerce,' carries the subject from the reign of Elizabeth to modern times, and somewhat later a second and revised volume of Professor Ashley's thoughtful and suggestive text-book has made its appearance. The same writer's recent lecture on the study of economic history should by no means be overlooked ; but the latest and in some respects the most remarkable work of the past year is the 'Commonweal of this Realm of England,' which Miss Lamond was engaged in editing at the time of her much regretted death. This work, which has now been completed by Professor Cunningham, will remain as a rare example of laborious and polished scholarship. Another admirable work is 'The Old English Manor' by an American historian.

The history of English law is not usually considered in connection with historical research, but reference to the Year Books edited in the Rolls Series by Mr. Owen Pike, and to the several editions under the auspices of the Selden Society (which include such works in progress as the 'Mirror for Justices') will reveal its true importance. America continues to make rapid strides to the front in the study of this same science, and Germany is still able to hold her own ; but there are whispers now of the approaching publication of a great history of the origins of English law by two of the most eminent of our own legal writers and teachers.

INDEX

ABBOT'S Ripton (Hunts.), 130
Abbott, Mr. Evelyn, 18, 19
Aberbrothwick, Abbot of. *See* Betoun
Abrymhewe, John, 266
Acle, Okyll (Norf.), 147, 157, 212
Adamnan, 69
Adbaston (Staffs.), 276
Aegean Sea, 15
Aegylde, 94
Agricola, 74
Aife, wife of Trad, 66
Albemarle, Baldwin de Betun, Earl of. *See* Betoun
Alburgh (Yorks), 227, 245
Alby. *See* Aldby
Alcibiades, 2, 13, 18
Aldby, Alby, Aldeburgh, Aldburei (Norf.), 143, 153, 156, 167
Alen, Thomas, 162
Alexander the Great, 3
Alfred the Great, 80, 89
Alington, Aldington (Hants), 277, 284, 286
Alispán, 45, 50, 52
Allington, John, 113
Almain Castle, 65
American proposals of 1856, 13
Ammianus Marcellinus, 73
Anaxagoras, 19
Andamnan, his Life of St. Columba, 74
Anglesey. *See* Mona
Anglo-Norman Cartulary Society, 300
Angus, Archibald Douglas, Earl of, 23
Anmer (Norf.), 145, 155, 156, 160, 161, 176, 194
Annandale, 28
Anne of Denmark, 31
Appleyard, John, 180
— Thomas, 162
— the family, 210, 217
Appulyard, Nicholas, 163

Arany Bulla, 49
Aratrum, meaning of the word, 288
d'Arbois de Jubainville, 56, 57, 65, 75
Archidamus, 2, 6
Aristophanes, 19
Aristotle, his acquaintance with Druidism, 63
Armagh, 'Book of Armagh,' 56
Armstrong of Liddesdale, 29
Arpingham. *See* Erpingham
Arrowsmith, William, sen., 124
— — jun., 124
Arundel, Sir William. *See* Matravers
— family mentioned, 174
Arvaszét, 48
Ashill, Asshell (Norf.), 147, 157, 158, 215
Ashley, Professor, 127 *et seq.*, 305
Ashmole, George, 124
— Thomas, 124
Ash Wicken (Norf.), 191, 193
Asia Minor, 15
Asseley, Thomas. *See* Astley
Asshell. *See* Ashill
Asshton, Hugh, 232
Asteley, Astley, Asseley, Richard, 274
— — Thomas, 165
Aston, Sir John, 274
Athenians, 5, 8, 12, 14
Athens, 11, 13, 14, 16, 19
Attenwik. *See* Atwick
Attica, 19
Attleborough, Attylburgh, Attleburgh (Norf.), 146, 150, 155, 156, 196
Atwick, Attenwike (Yorks), 227, 229, 230, 251
Audeley, John Touchet, Baron Audeley, 285
Auldwais, 28, 29, 30
Aylesham, Eleshain (Norf.), 145, 149, 155, 160, 187

x 2

BABINGLEY, Brabyngle (Norf.) 145, 155, 157, 158, 160, 195
Bachcroft family, 205
Bacon, Bakon, Henry, 165
Baconsthorpe, Bakenthorp (Norf.), 145, 158, 186
Bagthorp, Bagthorpe (Norf.), 135, 148, 150, 154, 157, 159, 161, 176, 217
Bakenthorp. *See* Baconsthorpe
Bakon. *See* Bacon
Baldwin, 22
Balfour, 35
— Balfour of, 22
— Betoun of, Bethune of. *See* Betoun
Balmuto, 32
Balwearie, 30
Barden (Yorks), 227, 243
Barnam Broom, Barnahambrome, Bernham Broom (Norf.), 147, 157, 209, 214
Barneys (Berners), John Bourchier, Lord Barneys, 275
Barnyngham. *See* Town Barnyngham, North Barnyngham
Barrett, Mr., 302
Barsham, Nicholas, 179
Barton Callewall. *See* Colwall
Barwyk. *See* Great Barwick
Basingstoke hundred (Hants), 281, 282, 289, 290
Bastwyke, Wood Bastwick (Norf.), 147, 156, 159, 160, 161, 205, 213
Bate, Matthew, 124
Bath, Bishop of, 277, 290
Battom, William, 250
Bawsey (Norf.), 136, 145, 153, 156, 192, 193, 194
Bayfield, Bayffeld (Norf.), 143, 156, 164
Bayselee. *See* Brisley
Beaton. *See* Betoun
Beaulieu, Bewley, Abbot of, 291, 292
Bedingfeld, Edmond, 170
Bedulffe, Richard, 275
Beeford, Beforth (Yorks), 227, 229, 230, 231, 251, 252
Beetly, Betele, Betely (Norf.), 144, 149, 157, 171, 172
Beforth. *See* Beeford
Behœtian, 95
Bekenham. *See* New Buckenham
Béla IV., King of Hungary, 44
Belaugh, Bylawe, Belaga, Belagh (Norf.), 140, 145, 146, 149, 157, 159, 160, 161, 171, 185, 202
Bele, John, rector of Cowarne Parva and Ullingswick, 262
Bémont, C., 301

Benningholme near Skirlaugh, Skarlagh Benyngholme (Yorks), 227, 229, 230, 231, 249, 252
Benyngfeld, Edmond, 136
Berwyk. *See* Great Barwick
Besthorp (Norf.), 146, 155, 156, 160, 196, 197
Betele, Betely. *See* Beetly
Beteryng, Betrynge, William, 192
Béthune (Artois), 21
Betoun, Beton, Betun, Bethune, Beaton, 21
— genealogy of the family, 34
— Andrew of Auchmuty, 24
— Baldwin de, Earl of Albemarle, 21
— David, of Creich, Lord High Treasurer and Comptroller of the Exchequer (of Scotland), 22, 25
— — Abbot of Aberbrothwick and Archbishop of St. Andrews, 23, 24
— James, of Creich, 21, 25, 26, 27
— — Archbishop of St. Andrews, Lord Treasurer and Chancellor of Scotland, 22, 23, 24
— John, of Auchmuty, 24, 25
— Mary, 27
— Sir Robert, 27
— Robert, of Balfour, 21, 22, 25, 27, 30, 31, 32
— Maximilian Béthune de Sully, Seigneur de Rosni, 22
Bettes, Thomas, 188
Beverley, Provost of, 246
Bewraper (Hants), 284, 288, 290
Bezirk, 51
Biddulph (Staffs), 275
Billingford family, 201
Birkin, Byrkyn (Yorks), 226, 240
Bishop's Lynne, 194
Blackborough Priory, 193, 205
Bleckes, John, 304
Blickling, Blykelyng (Norf.), 145, 149, 155, 158, 160, 186
Blofield and Walsham, Blofeld and Walsham, Hundred (Norf.), 141, 142, 147, 150, 151, 152, 156, 157, 158, 211
Blykelyng. *See* Blickling
Boleyn, Bolen, family, 153, 181, 212, 215
— Anne, wife of Henry VIII., 187
— Sir Thomas, 179, 215
— William, 186, 187
Bollyng (Yorks), 220, 241
Bolmer, William, 236
Bolte, Stephen, 184, 185
Bolton in Bolland (Yorks), 227, 229, 230, 231, 245

INDEX 309

Bonnassieux, Monsieur, 303
Booth, Charles, Bishop of Hereford, 261
Borderie, M. de la, his 'Etudes historiques Bretonnes,' 74
Bosbury, Bosebury, Bosybury (Heref.), 258, 260, 263, 264
Boswell of Balmuto, 32
Bothwell, 25, 26
— Francis Stewart, Earl of, 26
— James Hepburn, Earl of, 26
Bourchier family, 178
— John, Lord Berners, 275
Bourinot, Dr., 303
Bowthorp (Norf.), 147, 150, 155, 157, 160, 210
Brabyngle. *See* Babingley
Bracewell, Braswell (Yorks), 227, 244
Bracon Ash, Brakon (Norf.), 143, 156, 163
Braddocke, Francis, 276
Bradenham. *See* East Bradenham, West Bradenham
Bradford, Richard, 264
Bradfordes Brugge (Heref.), 258, 260, 268
Bradley in Craven (Yorks), 244
Brafferton (Yorks), 236
Brakon. *See* Bracon Ash
Brampton family, 208
— Robert, 199
Bramsill, Bramsyll (Hants), 284, 290
Brandiston, Brandeston (Norf.), 146, 150, 157, 159, 161, 202
Brandon, Sir Robert, 199
Brasidas, 12, 18
Braswell. *See* Bracewell
Braton, John, 199
Brayerley (Heref.), 258, 259, 260, 268
Breccles, Lytlebrekylles (Norf.), 146, 158, 197
Breche and Sockborow, names of fields (Hants), 284, 289
Bresal the Druid, 67, 69
Brewood Manor, 275, 276
Bridgford, Brychford (Staffs), 274
Bridlington, Prior of, 248
Brieford (Brafferton?) (Yorks), 226, 236
Brierley (Heref.), 260
Brisley, Bayselee (Norf.), 144, 149, 153, 158, 172, 173
Brocas, William, 290
Brodeley (Bradley?) (Yorks), 227, 244
Bromefeld, Richard, 264
Bromfylde, Thomas, 266
Bromholm, Priory of, 150, 199
Brothercrosse. *See* Gallow and Brothercrosse
Brottenham Manor, 198

Brotton (Yorks), 236
Broue (? Brough near Richmond, Yorks), 238
— Persona, 238
Brown, Mr. Horatio, 303
— Mr. Hume, 303
Browning, Mr. Oscar, 298, 300, 301
— Robert, 17
Broxash Hundred (Heref.), 254, 257, 260, 261
Brugmans, Dr., 302
Brychford. *See* Bridgford
Brystwyke. *See* Burstwick
Buchan, 31
Buckenham, Priory of, 149, 171, 197
Buckingham, Edward Stafford, Duke of, 246
Budæus, 287
Budapest, 41
Bullebroke, John, 215
Bullok, John, 178
Buoch, Dr. William, 302
Burdy, John, 192
Burges, William, 198
Burgh, William, 238
Burghclere (Hants), 288
Burnes, John, 124
— Thomas, 124
— William, 113
Burnham (Norf.), 148, 157, 159, 161, 218
Burstwick, Brystwick (Yorks), 227, 246, 248
Burton Lazar (Leic.), 168
— — Hospital, 149
Burton, Sir John, 242'
Burton's 'History of Scotland,' 61
Bury St. Edmunds Abbey, 149, 150, 187, 204, 206
Butley Priory, 149, 166
Buxton, Buxston, Bukestuna (Norf.), 145, 153, 155, 156, 160, 185, 213
Byland, Abbot of, 238
Bylawe. *See* Belaugh
Bynham Priory. *See* Edgefield Bacon's
Byrkyn. *See* Birkin

CÆSAR, his description of Druids, 63, 64
Cairill the Druid, 64
Calthorp, Culthorpe, Caletorp (Norf.), 145, 155, 160, 173, 186
— family, 188, 190, 218
— 's Manor, 169
Calverley (Yorks), 226, 241
— Walter, 241
Calvert, Mr., 304
Calybutt, Francis, 174, 191

Calybutt, John, 205, 206
Canteley. *See* Cantley
Canterbury, 87
— Archbishop of, 290
Cantly, Canteley (Norf.), 147, 156, 213
Capel family, 174
Capell, Anna, 208
— Sir William, 208
Carlton in Craven, Carleton in Crayvyne (Yorks), 227, 244
Carlton in Holderness (Yorks), 227, 229, 230, 231, 249
Carnbie, 30
Carr, Sir John, 234, 244
Castell, Henry, 136
Castle Acre, Castellacre (Norf.), 138, 145, 155, 157, 191, 193, 194
— priory of, 135, 149, 150, 152, 153, 175, 176, 177, 188, 193, 215, 217
Cathbad, the Druid of Ulster, 60, 63, 72
Catherine II., 303
Catherine Parr, 235
Cathorpe, Cayrthorp, Carethorp (Yorks), 227, 229, 230, 231, 247
Causon, James, 238
Causton, Cawston (Norf.), 145, 155, 158, 160, 186, 187, 277
Cayrthorp. *See* Cathorpe
Ceapgeld, 91, 93
Cellardyke, 32
Cenn-Cruaich, Crom-Cruach, 61
Chalcom, Shalcombe, Shancomb, I. W., 283, 284, 292
Chalmers, Mr. Robert, 303
Chamberleyn, Edward, 209, 214
Charles I., 109
Charles Robert, King of Hungary, 44, 45, 48
Chatsworth, 25
Chauvinism, 17
Chedull (Staffs.), 273
Cheet, Chevet (Yorks), 227, 229, 230, 231, 242
Chellyngton. *See* Chillington
Chelterton Hundred (Cambs.), 249
Chester, liberty of bishopric of, 275
Chevet, Cheyte. *See* Cheet
Chians, 14
Chillington, Chellyngton (Staffs.), 271, 276
Choseley, Choysell (Norf.), 138, 139, 143, 149, 155, 156, 160, 168, 174, 263
Christ's College, Cambridge, 153, 190
Christina, Queen, 105
Chuteley, Shutteley, Hundred (Hants), 281, 283, 289

Clacklose Hundred (Norf.), 134
Clareconstat, 35
Clavering. *See* Knavering. *See* Loddon
Cleon, 7, 8
Clere, Sir Robert, 162, 163
Clifford, Sir Henry, Earl of Cumberland, 243, 244
Clifford's Inn, 136
Closeburn, 28
Cnut, 78 *et seq.*, 302
Cobbe, Cobhys, Geoffrey, 136, 194, 195
— — William, 136, 194
Cockett family, 206
Cockyn, Gewardus, 209
Coe family, 215
Coke, William, 216
Cokershala. *See* Coltishall
Coket, Richard, 177
— Thomas, 174
Colesby (Yorks), 226
Colet family, 214
Colkirk, Colkryke, Colechircha, 144, 157, 158, 178, 179
Coltishall, Colteshale, Colteshall, Cokershala (Norf.), 145, 149, 155, 158, 184, 253
Colton, Thomas, 251
Colwall, Barton Callewell (Heref.), 258, 260, 264
Conall, 65
Conchobar, King of Ulster, 72
Congham (Norf.), 193
Conlavin of Connaught, 74
Constable, John, 247
— Sir Marmaduke, 248
— William, 247
Constantinople, taking of, 22
Cony, Thomas, of East Dereham, 178
Conyers, Richard, 233
— Sir William, Lord Hornby, 232, 233, 237
Cooe, Hugh, 214
Corcyra, 11
Corcyræans, 4
Corcyræan sedition, 8
Corinthians, 5, 6
Cormac's Glossary, 68
Cormac MacAirt, King, 70, 74
Cornwall, duchy of, 194
Coton, William, 275
Cottenham, Cotenham (Cambs.), 192
Cowarne Parva, Parva Cockern (Heref.), 168, 258, 259, 260, 261, 262, 265
Coxford Priory, 149, 160, 174
Creich. *See* Betoun

INDEX

Creke, abbey of, 190
Crichton, 28
Cristall. *See* Kirkstall
Crom-Cruach. *See* Cenn Cruaich
Cromwell, Thomas, 137
Crondale Hundred (Hants), 281, 282, 289
Croste, Edward, 268
Crostwyke. *See* Rydlyngton and Crostwyke
Crow, Christopher, 174
Crowe, O'Beirne, 56, 57, 58
Cryll, James, 263
Cuchulainn, 65, 69, 70, 72
Cuddlestone, Cutlestone, Colveston Hundred (Staffs.), 272, 273
Culdreimne, battle of, 69, 71, 75
Cumberford (Staffs.), 271, 273
— Thomas, 273
Cunningham, Rev. Professor, 109, 304
Cursing-stones, 71
Curson family, 213
Cutlestone. *See* Cuddlestone
Cuttle, Sir John, Under-Treasurer of England, 249
Cutts family, 205

DABYS (Norf.), 174
Dacre, Thomas Fynes, Lord Dacres, 185
Dade, Richard, 197
Dalan, the Druid, 69
Dalby, Thomas, Archdeacon of Richmond, 232, 233, 240, 246
Dallan, Forgdill, 56
Danby (Yorks), 226, 234
Danbye, Sir Christopher, 241
Darcy, Thomas, 240
Darell, Thomas, 239
Darius, King of the Romans, 65
Daubeney, Dawbeney, Sir Giles, 290
Dawes, George, 124
— Humphrey, 124
— John, 124
— Thomas, 124
Debateable land, 29
Dechtire, daughter of Cathbad, 72
Delahay, Thomas, 216
Denholme (Yorks), 241
Depewade, Depwade Hundred (Norf.), 141, 142, 145, 151, 152, 158, 195
Dereham. *See* East Dereham
Dergdamsa, Munster Druid, 61
Destreton. *See* Testerton
Devereux, Lady Margery, 266
— Sir John, 266
Diarmid, King of Tara, 69, 75

Dilkes, James, 124
— Robert, 154
Diodotus, 8
Dishford, Dysford (Yorks), 225, 226, 235
Disraeli, Mr. (Lord Beaconsfield), 18
Diss, Dysse, Dice Hundred (Norf.), 141, 142, 146, 150, 151, 152, 157, 158, 203
Dobyns, John, 194
Dogmersfeld (Hants), 277, 284
Donmer. *See* Anmer
Dorrant, Robert, 178
Douglas, the Douglasses, 23
— Archibald, Earl of Angus, 23
— James, Earl of Morton, 23
— of Torthorrald, 28, 29, 30
— of Drumlanrig, 28, 30
Dovaido, 75
Downes, James, 206
Downingham case, 129
Dowse, Mr. Serjeant, 18
Drade, Thomas, 186
Drayton Hall manor, 178
Droton (Yorks), 226, 236
Druidism, its origin, 57
— in Gaul, 58, 63, 64
— in Mona, 61, 63
Druids, meaning of the word, 56
— of Ireland, 55-75
— Chief, 59-60
Drummelzear, 30
Drury, Sir Robert, 196, 205
Dryffe Sands, Battle of, 29
Dubh the Druidess, 73
Dunham. *See* Great Dunham
Dunham Parva (Norf.), 144, 155, 156, 157, 160, 177
Dunnskellie, 28
Durham, Bolton Book of, 204
— Bishop of, 237
Dussing, Robert, 218
Dyghton, John, 251
Dykeman, Simon, 171
Dymmoke (Heref.), 264
Dysford. *See* Dishford

EACHAIDT, King, 71
Eadgar, 80, 86
Earlston, Erleston (Hants), 277, 278, 284, 287, 288
East Bradenham, Estbradenham, Bradeham (Norf.), 147, 150, 157, 206, 207
East Carleton, Est Carleton (Norf.), 143, 157, 163
Eastcourt v. Weekes, 130

East Dereham, Dereham (Norf.), 147, 150, 155, 157, 158, 159, 160, 161, 175, 176, 208
East Rudham, Est Rudham (Norf.), 148, 150, 156, 159, 161, 218
Eccles, Ekkylys (Norf.), 146, 150, 158, 197
Eccleshall manor, 275
Edensor, 25
Edgefield, Egefeld (Nerf.), 143, 149, 158, 164
Edgefield Bacon's manor, 149, 165
Edinburgh, 25, 26
Edward the Confessor, 77-107 *passim*
Edward VI., 110, 111
Edye, Mr., 303
Ekkylys. *See* Eccles
Elesham. *See* Aylesham
Elizabeth, Queen, 110, 112
Elleson, William, 232
Elliot of Liddesdale, 29
Ellys, William, 241
Elm, David, 263
Elmham, North Elynham, Elmenham (Norf.), 144, 149, 153, 157, 158, 171, 172, 173
Elphinstone, Mountstuart, 5
Ely, Bishop of, 149, 150, 171, 208
Ely Priory, 202
Elyce, Elys, William, 162, 182
Elyngham Parva. *See* Little Ellingham
Elynham. *See* Elmham
Emneth (Norf.), 135, 146, 150, 155, 158, 160, 204
Emsall. *See* North Emsall
Emslay. *See* Helmsley
Erasmus, 287
Erdathe, day of, 64
Erechtheum, the, 19
Erleston. *See* Earlston
Erpingham, Arpingham, Erpincham (Norf.), 145, 153, 155, 156, 157, 158, 160, 187
Errelstoun, 30
Esbache. *See* Evesbatch
Eskdale, 29
Esküll, 45
Estbradenham. *See* East Bradenham
Est Carleton (Norf.). *See* East Carleton
Est Flegge. *See* Flegge
Esthamlode (Hants), 283, 284
Est Rudham. *See* East Rudham
Estryngham (Yorks), 227, 248
Est Tanfeld (Yorks), 220, 226, 229, 231, 235, 240, 241
Etain, 67, 69
Euripides, 19
Everard, Richard, 173

Everyngham, John, 240
Evesbatch, Esbache (Heref.), 258, 260, 265
Evyngton. *See* Ivington
Ewerst (Hants), 277, 278, 284, 288, 291
Ewirshye, John, 286
Eynsford, Eynesford, Eynford, Hundred (Norf.), 141, 142, 146, 150, 151, 152, 157, 202

FAFNIR, 68
Fakenham, Lordship of, 181, 182, 183
Falley. *See* Fawley
Farley, John of Bosbury, 264
Farley Chamberlayne, Farley (Hants), 284, 286
Farmer, Fermer, Fermour, John, 207
— — —. Henry, 135, 153, 154, 175, 181, 182, 183, 188, 217
— — — John, of Kingsbarns in Fife, 30
Fawley, Falley (Heref.), 254, 258, 260, 263, 267
Fayrefax, Sir Thomas, 247
Fayrfax, William, 238
Fedelm, Princess, 66, 73
Fedelmid, the Druid, 72
Felire, 56
Ferdiad, 72
Ferdwite, 95
Ferlyngton. *See* Furlington
Fermor, Fermour. *See* Farmer
Ferneley (Yorks), 226, 241
Filé, 56
Filey, Fyley (Yorks), 227, 229, 230, 250
Finn, 67, 72
Fitling, Ffythynge (Yorks), 227, 253
Fitzhugh, Lord, 235, 249, 250
Fitzlewis family, 203
Fitzwilliam family, 210
Flanders, the Count of, 21
Fleete, Thomas, 165
Flegge, East and West, Hundred (Norf.), 141, 142, 143, 149, 151, 152, 157, 158, 166
Fleming, Lord, 30
Flemynge, John, 291
Flent, Richard, 250, 251
Flinton, Flenton (Yorks), 161, 227, 228, 229, 230, 250
Flitcham, Flytcham, Plicham (Norf.), 138, 145, 149, 156, 159, 160, 188, 189, 194, 208
— Priory of, 154, 188
Flodden, 22

INDEX 313

Flytcham. *See* Flitcham
Fóispan, 45-50
Footed, Foytit (Yorks), 227, 247
— — William, 247
Forehoe, Forowe, Hundred (Norf.), 141, 142, 147, 150, 151, 152, 157, 158, 209
Fortescue, Mr. J. B., his collection of MSS., 299
Forth, Firth of, 32
Foster, Adam, 135
— Anne, 135
— *v.* Thursby, 135
Foston, Peter, 196
Fountains Abbey, 235
Fox, Richard, Bishop of Winchester, 291
Foytit. *See* Footed
Fraisthorpe, Fraysthorpp (Yorks), 225, 227, 248
France, 13
Fraunsham Magna, 144, 158, 177
Fraysthorpp. *See* Fraisthorpe
Freebridge, Frybrigge juxta Lynne, Hundred (Norf.), 139, 141, 142, 145, 149, 150, 151, 152, 156, 157, 158, 188
Freebridge Marshland, Ffybrigge Marcelond, Hundred (Norf.), 141, 142, 146, 150, 151, 152, 158, 204
Furlington, Ferlyngton (Yorks), 226, 239
Fyley. *See* Filey
Fylyng (Yorks), 225, 226, 236
Fynes, Thomas. *See* Dacre
Fythynge. *See* Fitling

GAIRDNER, Mr. James, 297, 302
Galered, Robert, 162
Gallow and Brothercross, Galowe and Brothercrosse, Hundred (Norf.), 141, 142, 148, 150, 151, 152, 156, 157, 158, 215
Gambyll, John, 195
Game, Thomas, 135
Gardiner, Dr. S. R., 302
Gasquet, Rev. Father, 301, 302
Gately, Gatelee (Norf.), 144, 149, 153, 157, 158, 173, 186, 200
Gayton (Norf.), 136
Gaywood (Norf.), 145, 149, 155, 158, 160, 192
Geddes, Charles, of Raucleane, 30
Germen, Thomas, 215
Germyn, Thomas, 162
Gesa, 67
Gifford, John, 217

Gifford, Sir William, 289
Gight, 30
Gladstone, Mr. W. E., 18
Glam Dichinn, 68
Glanville, 90
Glasgow, Archbishop of. *See* Betoun
Glesthorpe manor (Norf.), 191, 192
Gloucester, statute of, 129
Gogiens (farmhouse), 287
Goldsmyth, William, 200
Gonville, Sir Edmund, 198
— and Caius College, Cambridge, 198
Gordoun, George, apparent of Gight, 30
— from Buchan, 31
Gortigern, British king, 61
Gower, Sir John, 238
Graeme of the Debateable Land, 29
Grange, Marie Casimir de la, 22
Grant-Duff, Sir M. E., 1, 304
Great Barwick, Berwyk, Barwyk, Berwick Magna (Norf.), 143, 149, 153, 155, 156, 160, 170, 194
Great Breccles (Norf.), 197
Great Dunham, Dunham, Dunham Magna (Norf.), 147, 155, 157, 160, 205, 206
Great Hautboys, Great Hautlois, Haughboys Magna (Norf.), 145, 155, 156, 157, 160, 185, 213
Great Plumpstead, Plomsted Magna, Plumstede Magna (Norf.), 147, 150, 157, 159, 160, 161, 176, 211
Great Ryburgh, Ryborow, Ryburgh Magna (Norf.), 148, 150, 156, 161, 174, 183, 216, 247, 264, 267, 288, 292
Great Walsingham, Old Walsingham, Walsyngham Magna (Norf.), 135, 144, 149, 154, 156, 158, 183
— Priory of, 135, 136, 149, 150, 153, 154, 180, 183, 184, 189, 216
Greece, 3, 4, 18, 19
Green, Mrs. M. A. Everett, 297
Greenhoe North, Hundred, Northgrenowe (Norf.), 139, 141, 142, 144, 149, 151, 156, 157, 158, 179
— South, Hundred, South Grenowe (Norf.), 141, 142, 147, 150, 151, 152, 156, 157, 205
Grenville, George, his proposals to the American colonists, 4
Gresham, James, 184
Grey family, 136, 204
— Thomas, 153, 214, 215
Greytree Hundred (Heref.), 254, 25 260, 263
Grierson of Lag, 28

Grimston, Grymston (Norf.), 145, 150, 158, 193
— — (Yorks), 227, 229, 230, 231, 246
— — Margaret, 246
— — Thomas, 246
Grote's 'History of Rome,' 19
Gryggs, Grykys, Avery, 180
Grymsowe. *See* Wayland and Grimshoe
Grymston. *See* Grimston
Gryse, Antony, 203
Gurney family, 188, 190, 196
Gyggs, Christopher, 183
Gylcroste. *See* Shropham and Giltcross
Gylippus, 18
Gyrlington, Katherine, 251
— William, 251

HALE (Norf.), 147, 155, 157, 160, 205
Halifax (Yorks), 241
Haliruidhous. *See* Holyrood House
Hamilton, Mr. H. C., 297
— the family of, 23
Hammerton (Yorks), 227, 244
— Sir Stephen, 244
Hamsocn, 95
Hanging Grimston, Hyngynge Grymston (Yorks), 225, 227, 229, 230, 231, 248
Hansby, John, 247
Happing Hundred (Norf.), 134
Harcourte, Simon, 274
Hare, Dr., 210
— Thomas, 167
Harlyng (Norf.), 182
Harman, William, 201
Harper, John, 276
Harpley. *See* Herpeley
Harryson, Richard, 250
— Robert, 185
Hartyng, Edward, 194
Harum (Yorks), 226, 229, 230, 231
Hassebourne (I.W.), 279, 283, 284, 291
Hatfield collection of MSS., 297
Haughboys Magna. *See* Great Hautboys
Hawe, William, 200
Hay, Thomas, 178
Haywood Manor (Staffs), 271, 275, 276
Hazeley Heath, Hazill (Hants), 290
Heacham, Hecham, Hitcham (Norf.), 143, 153, 156, 169
Healsfang, 86
Helmsley, Emslay (Yorks), 226, 229, 230, 231, 239

Heming, John, 162
Henderson, Dr., 301
Henri IV. of France, 22
Henry I., 86, 89, 92
Henry VIII., 23
Henry, son of James VI., 32
Hensted hundred (Norf.), 141, 142, 146, 151, 152, 156, 157, 158, 200
Hereford, 261
— Bishop of, 261, 263
— Cathedral, 264
Heringby College, 130, 198
Hermer, William, 211
Hermocrates, 2, 12, 18
Herodotus, 14
Herpeley, Harpeley (Norf.), 135, 145, 153, 154, 156, 159, 161, 180, 188, 190
Herringshaugh Manor, 176
Hervy, John, senior, 162
— — junior, 162
Hexham, Prior of, 239
Heydon family, 165
— Sir John, 179, 182, 186
Hickling Priory, 202
Hida. *See* Hyde Ash
High Offley (Staffs), 266, 275
Hillington, Hyllyngton (Norf.), 136, 145, 153, 155, 157, 160, 193, 194
Hillom. *See* Hollym
Hindringham, Hyndryngham (Norf.), 144, 149, 153, 156, 158, 181, 183
Hingham, Hyngham (Norf.), 147, 155, 157, 160, 209
Hitcham. *See* Heacham
Hobart. *See* Hubberd
Hoe family, 196
Holdsworth, Hondysworth (Yorks), 227, 241
Holdyche, Robert, 206
Holkham, Holkeham (Norf.), 138, 144, 149, 155, 156, 157, 160, 161, 179, 180, 198
Holland, Thomas, 178
Hollym, Hillom (Yorks), 225, 229, 230, 252
Hollys, Sir Thomas, 206
Holme (Yorks), 227, 248
Holmes, George, 124
— John, 124
Holt, Holte, hundred (Norf.), 153, 156, 157, 158, 164, 191
Holtby, John, 247
Holy Cross, College of the, 150, 196
Holyrood House, Haliruidhous, 25, 26, 27, 28, 31
Hondysworth. *See* Holdsworth.
Honston. *See* Hunstanton

INDEX 315

Hoo, How (Norf.), 143, 149, 155, 157, 160, 171, 178
— John att, 173
Horecrosse in Yoxall, 274
Hornby, Horneby (Yorks), 226, 233, 241
Horningtoft, Hornyngtoft (Norf.), 144, 153, 157, 179
Hothom (Hotham), Sir John, 248
Hoton (Yorks), 226, 235
Houghton, Hoveden, Hawton (Yorks), 227, 243
Houghton, Hoveton (Norf.), 135, 136, 144, 153. 154, 157, 184
Houghton. Howton (Norf.), 148, 156, 159, 161, 218
Howard, James, 213
Hubberd (or Hobart), Sir James, 197, 211, 212
— Thomas, 162
— Walter, 197
Hulles, Richard, 261
Humbleyard, Humlyard, Humiliart, Hundred (Norf.), 141, 142, 143, 151, 152, 156, 157, 162, 163, 164
Hume, George, 26
— Major Martin, 297
Humlyard. *See* Humbleyard
Hungary, 37-53
Hunstanton, Honston (Norf.), 143, 169
Huntingdon, Henry of, 105
Huntley, 29, 30
Hy, Island of, 62
Hyde Ash, Hida, le Hida (Heref.), 258, 260, 267, 268
Hyll, John, 265
Hyllyard, Peter, 253
Hyllyngton. *See* Hillington
Hylton, Lord, 247
Hyndryngham. *See* Hindringham
Hyngham. *See* Hingham
Hynginge Grymston. *See* Hanging Grimston

ICTINUS, 19
Illyrians, 12
India, British Rule in, 5
Inismurray, monastery of, 71
Intewoode (Norf.), 143, 157, 164
Ireland, 7
Israel, 19
Italian Republics, 3
Itchell, Ichill (Hants), 284, 289
Ivington, Evyngton (Heref.), 255, 258, 259, 260, 267

JACOBS, Mr. J., 302
Jambres, 66
James II. of Scotland, 23
James IV. of Scotland, 23
James V. of Scotland, 23
James VI. of Scotland and I. of England, 21, 31, 112, 113, 125
Jannes, 66
Járás, 47
Járások, 37
Jasson, Humphrey, 124
— Simon, 124
Jegysö, 48
Jenny or Jeny family, 204, 205
— — Christopher, 215
— — Sir Edmund, 199
— — William, 164
Jerusalem, Priory of St. John at, 252
Jingoism, 17
Johnstone of Annandale, 28, 29
— William, of Auldwais, 28, 29, 30
— William, of the Borders, 31
Jotherell, John (1), 124
— John (2), 124
Jowett, Dr., late master of Balliol, 16, 18

KASIMIR the Great, of Poland, 40
Kemerley. *See* Kimberley
Kempstone, Kempston (Norf.), 135, 144, 149, 154, 156, 158, 175
Kent *v.* Seynt John, 120
Ketteringham (Norf.), 164
Kettlestone, Ketelston (Norf.), 148, 150, 158, 159, 161, 173, 178, 186, 194, 216
'Kett's Rebellion,' 127-218 *passim*
Kilvington, Kylton (Yorks), 236
Kimberley, Kemerley (Norf.), 147, 157, 209, 210
Kilrenny (Fife), 32, 33, 35, 36
Kingsbarns (Fife), 30
Kingsclere hundred (Hants), 281, 282, 287, 288
King's College, Cambridge, 149, 185
King's Lynn, Lynne (Norf.), 135, 145, 155, 157, 160, 195
King's Manor, or Marshe's Manor, 169
Kinsley (Yorks), 227, 242
Kirby Wiske, Kyrkbywyske (Yorks), 225, 226, 235
Kirkpatrick of Closeburns, 28
Kirkstall, Crystall, Abbey of, 241, 251, 252
Knavering Hundred (Norf.), 141, 142, 143, 149, 151, 152, 156, 157. *See also* Loddon and Clavering

Knevet, Knyvett, family, 197, 207, 210
— — William, 196
Kokatt. See Coket
Kolderup-Rosenvinge, J. L. A., 78, 104
Kydall (Yorks), 226, 241, 253
Kylton. See Kilvington
Kyng, Robert, 162
Kynge, Oliver, Bishop of Bath, 290
Kynnersley, Thomas, 274
Kyrkbywyske. See Kirby Wiske
Kyrkstall. See Kirkstall
Kyttys, Robert, 186

LACEDÆMONIANS, 8, 11, 14
Lag, 28
Labslit, 86
Lamb family, 210
Lambarde, 78
Lamond, Miss, 305
Lanaham. See Langham
Lancaster, Duchy of, 187, 244, 271, 273
Langbaurgh, Liberty of (Yorks), 236
Langham, Lanaham (Norf.), 165
Langley, Abbot of, 149
Langside, 24, 25
Langstorth, Longstroth (Yorks), 227, 243
Laogaire, King of Ulster, 59, 60, 65, 70
Latymer, Lord, 235
Launditch, Laundyche, Lavendic Hundred (Norf.), 139, 141, 142, 144, 149, 151, 152, 156, 157, 158, 171, 208
Leabhar Breac, 62
— Gabhala, 63
Leadham, Mr. L. S., 127, 302
Lecky, Mr., the historian, 4
Ledbury (Heref.), 258, 260
Leede, Leyde (Yorks), 226, 240, 241
Le Hida. See Hyde Ash
Lekenfeld (Yorks), 227, 247
Leominster Hundred (Heref.), 254, 256, 257, 260, 268
Leopold I., King of Hungary, 48
Lesiate (Norf.), 191
Leslie, William, 26
L'Estrange, le Strange, family, 194, 195. See also sub Strange
Letton (Norf.), 135, 147, 150, 157, 208
Leverton (Yorks), 226, 234, 239
Lewes, Priory of, 135, 150, 205, 208
Lewes, Thomas, 195
Leyde. See Leede

Leylonde, Thomas, 263
Leyncall, 266
Lichfield, 1c9, 125
— Manor, 275
Liddesdale, 29
Liebermann, Dr. F., 77, 301, 302
Lincoln's Inn, 190
Lisle, Sir John, 285
Little Ayton, Lytyle Hayton (Yorks), 226, 240
Little Ellingham, Little Elyngham, Elyngham Parva (Norf.), 147, 156, 209, 214
Little Massingham, Massingham Parva (Norf.), 145, 158, 190
Little Plumstead, Plomsted, Plumstede Parva (Norf.), 147, 158, 211, 212
Little Poringland, Parva Parlond (Norf.), 146, 158, 200, 209, 214
Little Thorp, Thorp Parva (Norf.), 146, 150, 155, 157, 160, 161, 176, 194, 203, 208
Llanthony, near Gloucester, 263
Lochleven Castle, 24
Loddon Hundred (Norf.), 143, 149, 157, 211
— and Clavering (Norf.), 141, 142, 143, 149, 151, 152, 167, 168
Loke, Dewer, 284
Long, Robert, 200
Longstroth. See Langstorth
Lonsdale, collection of MSS., 299
Louis the Great, of Hungary, 40
Lovell family, 214
Lowe, Mr. (Viscount Sherbrooke), 1
Loxley (Staffs), 274
Lucad the Druid, 59
Lucan, his description of Gallic Druids, 58, 63, 64
Lucton, Lucketon (Heref.), 258, 259, 260, 268
Lughaidt, King of Ireland, 63
Lumney, Geoige, Lord, 236
Lylly and Dyke (Yorks), 227, 229, 251
Lynaker family, 165
Lynne. See King's Lynn
Lysley. See Lisle
Lyte, Mr. H. C. Maxwell, Deputy-Keeper of the Public Records, 295–297, 299
Lytele Panne (I. W.), 283, 284, 292
Lyttle brekylles. See Breccles
Lytyll Cowden (Yorks), 227, 229, 230, 231, 251
Lytyll Hayton. See Little Ayton
Lytyll Newton. See Newton in Bolland

INDEX

MACAULAY, Thomas Babington, Lord, 297
Macintosh, the historian, 297
Magdalen College, Oxford, 150, 202
Maghbile, 71
Magh-Tuireadh, Battle of, 69
Magyar County, 37-53
Mahan, Mr., 303
Mallery, John, 235
Malshanger (Hants), 289
Mansbrig; Hundred (Hants), 281, 282, 286
Manuel, Robert, 162
Marathon, 3
Marches, the, 29
Marderbury, Marderby. *See* Matherby
Margaret, daughter of James IV., 31, 32
Markaunt, Merkaunt, Robert, 153, 154, 172, 179
Markinfield family, 234
Marsden, Mr. R. G., 302
Marshe's Manor, or King's Manor (Norf.), 169
Martham (Norf.), 143, 149, 157, 166
Martin, John, Prior of Flitcham, 188
Martyn, Roger, 153, 154, 172, 173, 188
Mary Stewart, 23, 24
Massingham Parva, Massyngham Parva. *See* Little Massingham
Massilia: its influence on Druidism, 61, 63
Matherby, Marderbury, Marderby (Yorks), 225, 226, 229, 230, 231, 238
Mathew, Humfrey, 124
— Walter, 124
Matravers, Sir Wm. Arundel, Lord Matravers, 213
Maverell, George, 273
Maxwell of Nithsdale, 28, 29
Meath, 59
Meaux, Abbey of, 252
Medb (Queen), 66
Mekelbargh (Mickleby?) (Yorks), 225, 226, 239
Melian controversy, 12
Melton Constable, Melton (Norf.), 143, 157, 165
Melville, Sir John, of Carnbie, 30, 31, Menacles, 19
Merkaunt. *See* Markaunt
Merton (Norf.), 136, 147, 153, 157, 214, 215
Merton, statute of, 269
Metcalf, Richard, 237
Metford. *See* Mitford

Methwold, Methewold (Norf.), 147, 150, 157, 215
Methwold family, 207
Mickleby (Yorks), 239
Mider, 69
Migh, Richard, 189
Mileham, Milham, Myleham (Norf.), 144, 155, 156, 158, 160, 169, 174, 177, 178
Milton family, 187
Mind, Minn, 59
Mitford, Metford, Mittefort Hundred (Norf.), 141, 142, 147, 150, 151, 152, 157, 158, 207
Mogh-Ruith, the Druid, 69
Mog-Neid, King of Munster, 61
Mona (Anglesey), 57, 61, 63, 74
Monkewyke (Yorks), 222, 225, 227, 229, 230, 246
More, Sir Thomas, 287
Morley (Norf.), 147, 155, 157, 159, 160, 209
— Lady, 135, 154, 185
— Lord, 208, 209
— Wapentake of (Yorks), 241
Morrough O'Carthy, Arch-druid, 75
Mortoft, Thomas, 187
Morton, Moretoun (Yorks), 225, 226, 229, 230, 231, 241
— Roland, 265
— James Douglas, Earl of. *See* Douglas
Moses, 70
Mourningthorpe, Morningthorp, Moringthorp (Norf.), 145, 158, 195
Mourtymers Courte in Orleton, 266
Mund, 86
Mundbrece, 95
Mundham, Mundambrome, Mundaham (Norf.), 143, 157, 167, 168
Myleham. *See* Mileham
Mylnebank, 28, 29
Myreheid, 28, 29
Myron, 19

NAVAL Records Society, 300
Nawesley (Glouc.), 263
Nemzetsétjek, 43
Nennius, 61
Ness, Princess, 72
Nesshe, John, 162
Nether Hall, 201
Nevile of Chevet, Sir John, 242
Neville, Nevyll, family, 235
— Richard, 234
New Buckenham, Beckenham (Norf.), 170

Newby, William, 180
New College, Oxford, 150, 202
Newfeld (Yorks), 227, 245
New Hall, 175
Newtonberye (Hants), 284, 285, 288
Newton in Bolland, Lytyll Newton (Ycrks), 227, 229, 231, 245
Nicias, 2, 14
Ninnian, 73
Nithsdale, 28
North Barningham (Norf.), 146, 158, 159, 200
— Barsham (Norf.), 148, 156, 159, 161, 217
— Elmsall, Emsall (Yorks), 227, 242
— Elynham. *See* Elmham
— Erpingham, North Arpyngham, Erpincham, Hundred (Norf.), 141, 142, 146, 151, 152, 157, 158, 199
— Grenow. *See* Greenhoe
Northottryngton (Yorks), 225, 226, 229, 230, 231
North Pickenham (Norf.), 207
— Rungton, North Runcton, Rowton, Ronton (Norf.), 145, 158, 192, 201
Northumberland, Henry, Earl of, 243, 247
North Walsham (Norf.), 146, 155, 156, 157, 160, 199
— Wootton, North Wotton (Norf.), 145, 150, 151, 153, 157, 194
Norton, Sir John, 232
Norwich, Bishop of, See of, 149, 150, 172, 173, 174, 180, 181, 187, 198, 202, 211
— Prior of, 135, 149, 150, 152, 153, 154, 166, 211, 212
Nuadu the Druid, 72

ODHRAN, 62
Odihun Hundred (Hants), 281, 282, 290
Offlowe, Offlow, Hundred (Staffs.), 272, 275
Ogham writing, 64, 71
Okyll. *See* Acle
Ordeal, 100
Orleton (Heref.), 258, 259, 260, 265, 266
Oroszággyüles, 42
Ottringham (Yorks), 222, 225, 227, 229, 230, 252
Overton (Heref.), 258, 266
Oxford, Countess of, 195
— Priory, 193, 218
Oxwick, Oxwyk (Norf.), 144, 157, 179

PACE: a letter from Pace to Wolsey quoted, 287
Page, Mr., 302
Palgrave (Norf.), 147, 155, 156, 159, 206, 213
— family, 205
— Henry, 200
Palmer, Henry, 208, 212
-- Walter, 162
Palmerston, Lord, 7
Panworth Hall Manor, 215
Papelarns. *See* Poplands
Paris, Declaration of, 13
Parke, Sir H., 304
Parker family, Lords Morley, 209
— John, 199
Parkman, Mr., 304
Parlond Parva. *See* Little Poringland
Parr, Queen Catherine, 235
— Sir Thomas, 235
Parson, Thomas, 209
Parthenon, the, 19
Parva Cockern. *See* Cowarne Parva
Parva Ellynham. *See* Little Ellingham
Parva Parlond. *See* Little Poringland
Pawlett, Wm. (Marquis of Winchester), 286, 287, 289
Payne, Mr., 303
— *v.* Golding, 206
Pedelleston. *See* Pudleston
Peloponnesian War, 3, 4, 17
Pentney, Prior of, 150, 193
Pepys, Samuel, 302
Pericles, 6, 7, 17, 18
Perkins, John, 124
— Symon, 124
Pesth, 50
Peterstone Priory, 180
Pflugk-Harttung, Prof. J. von, 55
Pharaoh, 70
Phidias, 19
Phillips, Sir Thomas, 106
Philypp, Randolph, 236
Pike, Mr. Owen, 305
Pike Hall, 175
Pirehill, Pyrehill Hundred (Staffs.), 272, 274
Plassing Hall Manor, 196
Plicham. *See* Flitcham
Pliny, 71, 73
Plompsted Magna. *See* Great Plumstead
Plomsted. *See* Little Plumstead
Plumsted, John, 186
Polycleitus, 19
Pomponius Mela, 64, 72
Pontefract, Pomfret, College of, 150, 216, 217

Pope, Alicia, 185
Poplands, Papelarns (Heref.), 258, 260, 268
Poppo, 17
Porter, William, 292
Portland collection of MSS., 299
Pory, John, 153, 215
Postwick, Postwyke, Poswic (Norf.), 135, 147, 153, 154, 157, 159, 161, 212
Powell, Mr. York, 301
Presburg, 50
Prestnam, William, 238
Price, the historian, 78
Proctour, Walter, 244
Propylæa, the, 19
Prothero, Mr. G. W., 301
Prussia, development of, 38–39
Pudleston, Pedelleston (Heref.), 258, 259, 260, 266, 275, 281
Pudsay, Pudesey, family, 245
— — Alexander, 247
— — Henry, 244, 245
Purpete, John, 198
Pygeon, John, 171
Pygott, Thomas, 236
Pykenham. *See* South Pickenham
Pyper, Thomas, 238
Pyrehill. *See* Pirehill
Pytte, William, de Leyncall, 266

QUARR, Quarrye (I. W.), Abbot of, 291
Querarlam (Ketteringham?) (Norf.), 143, 157, 159, 160, 164

RACH Archail (Sligo), 62
Radlow or Radlode Hundred (Heref.), 254, 257, 260, 263, 265
Rákosmező, 41
Randolff, Humphrey, 162
Ratclyffe, Geoffrey, 191
— family, 192
Raucleane, 30
Reading, Abbot of, 267, 268
Redbridge, Redbrigge, Hundred (Hants), 281, 282, 285
Reder, John, 206
Redinge, John, Abbot of St. Benet's in the Holm, 163
Reich, Dr. Emil, 37
Renan, Ernest, 18, 304
Reresby, Resby, Richard, 242
Rhys, Professor, 57, 61
Richard I., 21, 22
Richelieu : ' Testament de Richelieu,' 8
Richmond, barony of, 166

Rising, Rysyngcastell (Norf.), 135, 145, 155, 157, 159, 164, 194, 208, 209
Rochester, 87
Rogerson, Ralph, 137
Rokeby, Randolph, 252
— Sehyny, 252
Rolff, Thomas, 193
Rome, 19
Romsey, Romeseye (Hants), 285, 286
Ronton. *See* North Rungton
Roos, Lord, 136
Ropes, Mr., 303
Rose, Thomas, 162
Rosni. *See* Betoun
Rostgoard, F., 164
Rougham (Norf.), 144, 156, 176
Rowton. *See* North Rungton
Rudham. *See* West Rudham
Rushworth, Russheford, College of, 150, 198
Ruskin, Mr. John, 3
Russell, Henry, 218
— family, 218
— Mr. W. H., 109
Russhall, Rushall (Staffs.), 276
Ryborow. *See* Great Ryburgh
Rydlyngton and Crostwyke Hundred (Norf.), 146, 150, 157, 199, 203
Rymyngton (Yorks), 227, 229, 230, 231
Rysyngcastell. *See* Rising
Rytywyse, John, 186, 187

SACKVILL's Manor, 189
Saham Tony (Norf.), 147, 157, 214
Sainsbury, Mr. Noel, 297, 304
St. Abbs Head, 36
St. Andrews. *See* Betoun
St. Bennet, Norwich, Abbey of, 149, 185
St. Boniface, 62
St. Bridget, 67
St. Ciaran, 67
St. Columba, 66, 69, 71
— Life of, by Andamnan, 74
St. Denys, Priory of, Southampton, 286
St. Faith's Priory, 202
St. Finnian of Maghbile, 71
St. Gildas, 59
St. James, Hospital of, Northallerton, 237
St. John's College, Cambridge, 105
St. Mary's, Dublin, 106
St. Mary's in the Fields, Norwich, 150, 210
St. Mary's, York, Abbot of, 246

St. Patrick, 56, 62, 67, 70, 74
— 'Life of St. Patrick,' by Fiace, 56
— 'Tripartite Life of St. Patrick,' by Todd, 59, 62, 65
— 'Hymn of St. Patrick,' 56
St. Peter's pence, 86
St. Stephen, King of Hungary, 39, 44
Salamis, 3
Silter family, 194
Sandes, Sandys, Sir William, 286, 287, 289
Sandringham, Sandryngham (Norf.), 145, 158, 194, 195
Saxlingham, Saxlyngham (Norf.), 143, 157, 165
Sayvile, Sayvyle, Henry, 241, 248
— Sir John, 241, 248
Scarborough, Scarbrugh (Yorks), 227, 248
Scarning, Scarnyng, Skernyng, 144, 149, 157, 158, 177, 178, 206, 207
— and West Bradenham, 147, 150, 157
Schadewell. *See* Shadwell
Schickler, Baron, 302
Schmid, the historian, 78
Scott, of Eskdale, 29
— of Teviotdale, 29
— James, of Balwearie, 30
Scroopskens House, North Walsham, 199
Sculthorpe, Skulthorp (Norf.), 148, 150, 153, 156, 159, 161, 182, 217
Sedeney, Thomas, 179
Sefoule, Seyfoule, family, 217
— Thomas, 217
Seisdon Hundred (Staffs.), 272
Senchus Mor, 65
Seynt John, Kent v., 130
Seytoun of Errolstoun, 30
Shadwell, Schadewell (Norf.), 138, 146, 150, 155, 156, 158, 160, 161, 198
Shalcombe, Shancombe. *See* Chalcom
Sharkey, Mr. J. H., 190
Sheffield, cutlers' company of, 109
Shelton, John, 183
Sherbrooke, Viscount, 1
Sheres, William, 162
Shilling: Mercian shilling of four pence, 85
— West Saxon shilling of five pence, 86
Shorthouse, John, 124
— Sampson, 124
Shottesham S^t. Mary, Shotesham, (Norf.), 146, 157, 202

Shrewsbury, the Earls of, 263
Shropham (Norf.), 146, 155, 157, 158, 160, 197
Shropham and Giltcross, Shropham and Gylcroste, Hundred (Norf.), 141, 142, 146, 150, 151, 152, 156, 157, 158, 196
Shutteley. *See* Chuteley
Sicilian Expedition, the, 14, 17
Sigurd, 68
Simon Magus, the Druid, 65, 69
Skarlagh Bennyngholme. *See* Benningholme
Skarning. *See* Scarning
Skekyll, William, 240
Skelton (Yorks), 240
Skerning. *See* Scarning
Skinfasthaven, 36
Skulthorp. *See* Sculthorpe
Slyngesby, John, 236
Smeaton, Smeton, Smythdon (Yorks), 234
Smithdon, Smythdon Hundred (Norf.), 139, 141, 142, 143, 149, 151, 152, 156, 158, 168
Smyth, John, 179
— Richard, 124
— William, 124
Snape, Snappe (Yorks), 226, 235
Snettisham, Snethysham, Snettesham (Norf.), 143, 156, 170
Snoring Manor (Norf.), 189
Sobieski, John, 22
Sockborowe (Hants), 289
Socrates, 18
Soham, John, 172
Somborne Hundred (Hants), 281, 282, 286
Sophocles, 19
Soureby Undercotclyff (Yorks), 222, 225, 226, 229, 230, 237
Sourton (Yorks), 234
Southampton, 285, 286
South Cowton (Yorks), 139, 226, 229, 230, 231, 236, 240
South Erpingham, Southarpyngham, Hundred (Norf.), 141, 142, 145, 149, 151, 152, 156, 157, 158, 184
South Grenowe. *See* Greenhoe
Southholme (Yorks), 226, 229, 230, 231, 238
South Pickenham, Pykenham (Norf.), 147, 157, 207
Southwell, Sir Richard, 177, 206
Sparhows, Thomas, 200
Sparta, 16
Spelman. *See* Spylman

INDEX 321

Sphacteria, 11
Spledon (Super ledon ?) (Heref.), 258, 260, 263, 264
Sponer, Richard, 167, 168
Spont, Dr., 302
Sporle Priory, 205
Spread-eagleism, 17
Spregis House, North Walsham, 199
Sproatley, Sprotley (Yorks), 139, 227, 229, 230, 253
Spryng family, 165
Spylman family, 198
— Henry, 197
— John, 182
Stalham (Norf.), 146, 150, 155, 158, 160, 198
Stanhoe, Stanow, Stanehew (Norf.), 143, 156, 169, 170, 207
Stanley, Humphrey, 275, 276
Staplehurst, Stepelhirst (I.W.), 283, 284, 291
Stapleton, Brian of Wyghell, 239
Stede, John, 180
— William, 177
Stepelhirst. *See* Staplehurst
Stevens, Mr. B. F., 303
Steveton (Yorks), 222, 225, 226, 229, 230, 231, 232, 234
Stewart, Francis, Earl of Bothwell, 21
Stiffkey, Styfkey (Norf.), 144, 155, 158, 160, 181, 187, 195, 196, 198, 205
Stirling Bridge, 36
Stittenham, Styknam (Yorks), 226, 229, 230, 231, 238, 239, 240
Stoke Holy Cross, Stoke (Norf.), 146, 155, 156, 158, 160, 201
Stoke Prior (Heref.), 258, 259, 260, 267
Strabo, 73
Strange, Thomas le, 194
— John le, 190
— Sir Nicholas le, 206
— Sir Robert le, 214
— Roger, 169
— Thomas, 169
— Magister, 153, 190
Strangwyse, Ralph, 237
Stropham. *See* Shropham
Stubbs, Rev. Dr., Bishop of Oxford, 301
Styfkey. *See* Stiffkey
Styknam. *See* Stittenham
Sualtan, King of Ulster, 60
Suetonius Paulinus, 74
Suffield, Suffeld (Norf.), 146, 155, 157, 200
Sully. *See* Betoun

Super Ledon (Heref.), 264
Swalefield, Swalfeld (Yorks), 226, 238
Swanston, William, 239
Swine, Swyne (Yorks), 225, 227, 229, 230, 231, 249
— Prior of, 249
Sygons, Thomas, 291
Szabad királyi város, 37
Szolgabiró, 45, 47

TACITUS, 15, 61, 63
Tadg, the Druid, 72
Tanstern, Taunestorn (Yorks), 227, 247, 250, 264
Tara, 59, 61
Tartománye gyülések, 50
Tassall, Thomas, 210
Taunestorn. *See* Tanstern
Taverham Hundred (Norf.), 134
Taylor, Canon Isaac, 166
Tempes (Tempest), Richard, 241
— — Roger, 245
— — Sir Thomas, 244
Tempest family of Bracewell, 244
Temple Newsome (Yorks), 220, 226, 229, 230, 240
Ternmlaegda, 67, 68
Terrible, the Druid, 65
Testerton, Destreton (Norf.), 148, 156, 159, 161, 217
Tetyshale. *See* Titshall
Teviotdale, 29
Tharpland, Therplond (Norf.), 181, 182, 183
Thetford, Canons of, 150, 205, 215
Thirkleby, Thirtleby, Thurkylby (Yorks), 227, 229, 231, 232, 249
Thorisby. *See* Thursby
Thornehill (Yorks), 241
Thorntonbrige (Yorks), 226
Thornton in Lestrete (Yorks), 226, 229, 230, 231, 232, 237, 241
Thornyngsgreve common, 196
Thorp Episcopi (Norf.), 135, 147, 150, 154, 156, 211
Thorp Parva. *See* Little Thorp
Thorpe, the historian, 78
Thriburgh, Thriber (Yorks), 227, 242
Thropp, Brute, 124
— William, 124
Throwley (Staffs.), 273, 274
Thucydides, 1–19
Thurkylby. *See* Thirkleby
Thursby, Thurisby, Thurysby, Thorsby, Thorisby, Thorysby, Thomas, senior, 153, 191, 192
— Thomas, 135, 138, 153, 154, 170, 193, 194

N.S.—VOL. VII. Y

Thursford, Thyrysforth, 144, 157, 183
Thwevy, Marmaduke, 239
Tibenham, Tybenham (Norf.), 204
Tigernach, 75
Timagenes, 73
Titleshale. *See* Tittleshall
Titshall, Tetyshale (Norf.), 146, 150, 155, 157, 158, 160, 199, 203, 204
Tittleshall, Tytelyshale (Norf.), 144, 149, 153, 157, 174
Tixal, Tickeshall (Staffs.), 274
— Park, 274
Todd, 56
Toly, Henry, 177
Torn the Dane, 196
Torthorrald, 28, 29
Town Barningham, Town Barnyngham (Norf.), 158, 200
Townesend, Roger, 169, 170, 182
Trad, 66
Trinity College, Cambridge, 105
Trynne, R., 181, 182
Tueringham, John
Tunstead, Tunstede, Hundred (Norf.), 141, 142, 146, 150, 151, 152, 156, 157, 199
Turkish Islands, 15
Tweedie, James, of Drummelzeir, 30
Twysden, 106
Tyndall, Sir W., 195
Tytelyshale. *See* Tittleshall
Tytler's 'History of Scotland,' 32

UGHTRED family, 251
Ugyész, 48
Uisnech, 59
Ullingswick, Uplyngwyke (Heref.), 262
Upleadon (Heref.), 260
Uplyngwyke. *See* Ullingswick
Utting, Stephen, 202

VÁRMEGYÉK, 37
Vaughan, Sir Richard, 261
Vinogradoff, Professor, 132
Vuedale, Uvedale, Sir William, 261

WAGSTAFF, John, 207
Walesale, John, 267
Walford (Heref.), 258, 259, 260, 263
Walitzeuski, Monsieur, 303
Walker, Colonel, 302
Walpole family, 218
— Edward, 218
— Henry, 218

Walpole, Thomas, 218
Walsham Hundred (Norf.), 156, 157, 213
Walsyngham. *See* Great Walsingham
Waltham Abbey manor, 175
Walton, Thomas, 273
Warcope, Robert, 191
Warde, John, 386
Warham (North), 144, 156, 157, 180
Warner, Christina, 208
Warram, Nicholas, 289
Watton (Norf.), 147, 156, 214
Wayland & Grimshoe, Waylond & Grymsowe Hundred (Norf.), 141, 142, 147, 150, 151, 152, 156, 157, 158, 213
Webster, William, 162
Weekes, Eastcourt v., 130
Welby family, 216
Welles, Thomas, 274
Wendlyng (Norf.), 135, 144, 149, 154, 155, 156, 159, 160, 168, 175, 176, 178, 189, 202, 205, 208, 209, 211, 213, 264
— Abbot of, 149, 150, 177, 178, 207
Wentworth (Yorks), 227, 242
— John, 251
— Thomas, 242
Werk, master of, 25, 26
Wesenham (Norf.), 144, 149, 156, 177
Westacre Priory, 193, 205
West Bradenham (Norf.), 157, 207. *See also sub* Scarning
West Dereham Abbey, 202
West Flegge. *See* Flegge
Westminster, second Statute of, 269
Weston (Norf.), 146, 150, 157, 159, 161, 202
West Rudham, Westrudham (Norf.), 148, 157, 159, 161, 218
West Somerton (Norf.), 143, 149, 166, 170, 172, 177, 178, 198, 200
Wharrom, Percy (Yorks.), 227, 229, 230, 247
Wharton Captain, Hydrographer Royal, 303
Wheatacre, Wheteacreburgh (Norf.), 143, 157, 167
Whight, William, 285
Whitby, Abbot of, 236
Whitworth, Lord, 297
Wight, Isle of, 277, 278, 279, 280, 291
Wighton, Wytton (Norf.), 144, 147, 153, 156, 157, 159, 161, 183, 212
Wilby, Wylby, Thos., 181
Wilde, Lady : her 'Ancient Legends,' 62, 71

INDEX

William I., 77-107 *passim*
William II., 92
Willoughby, Wylloughby, William, Lord, 167
— George, 174
Willy, Wyllyers, John, 168
Willy's Manor, 168
Winch, Wynche (Norf.), 145, 150, 153, 157, 193, 194
Winchester, 87
Windham Priory, 150, 194
Winfarthing, Wyndeferthing (Norf.), 146, 155, 158, 204, 236, 245
Wingfield, Wyngfield, family, 193, 206, 210
— — John, 153, 169
— — Thomas, 206
Winter family, 181
Wishart, Dr., 302
Wodehouse, Woodhouse, family, 189, 193, 198, 206, 210
— Thomas, 209
Woley, Wolley, Wooley (Yorks), 227, 242
Wolphy, Wolfey, Hundred (Heref.), 254, 256, 257, 260
— — and Leominster, 265, 268
Wolsey, Cardinal, 287

Woodhouse. *See* Wodehouse
Woodrof, Woodruff, family, 242
— Sir Richard, 242
Woodward, Robert, 203
Worcester, its library, 87
Wyatt, Sir Henry, 203
Wygmore, John, 268
Wylby. *See* Wilby
Wynch. *See* Winch
Wyndeferthing. *See* Winfarthing
Wyndham (Norf.), 147, 150, 158, 210
— Abbey, 210
— Thomas, 165, 166, 196
Wynsore (Hants), 284, 285
Wytton. *See* Wighton

YARPOLE (Heref.), 216, 254, 255, 258, 259, 260, 267
Yelverton, Magister, 201
— family, 164
— William, 176, 177
Yoxall (Staffs.), 274

ZIMMER, 68
Zupan, 43, 50

Royal Historical Society,
20 HANOVER SQUARE, LONDON :
January 19, 1893.

REPORT OF THE COUNCIL.

SESSION 1891-92.

THE Council of the Royal Historical Society present their Annual Report to the General Meeting of the Fellows at the close of a Session which will be remarkable for several important and useful administrative reforms, as well as for an increased activity in furthering the literary objects of the Society.

Several vacancies which had occurred in the body of the Council have been filled by eminent historical scholars, and as the Council meetings have been more fully attended than they have been for some time past, a great deal of business has been satisfactorily concluded, which has also been much facilitated by the investigations and Reports of the several permanent Committees, namely, the Finance Committee, the Publication Committee, and the Library Committee.

These Committees were reconstituted by a Minute of Council dated March 1892, in which their respective jurisdictions and duties were defined; and in accordance with this Minute, they have held frequent ordinary and special meetings, and have presented several important Reports and recommendations to the Council. As the result of these deliberations, the annual Publications of the Society will, in future, include a substantial volume of Transactions containing selected Papers read at the Society's Evening Meetings, together with the most valuable of the original documents which may be communicated to the Society from time to time by historical scholars, the President's Address, and a Summary of the Progress of Historical Research during the past Session. In addition to this, the Council are hopeful of being able to ensure the annual production of a volume of Publications, and a scheme will shortly be prepared for the purpose of facilitating the foundation of a uniform series of Publications dealing with the unpublished State Papers preserved in the national Archives. It has, however, been resolved that no volume of the Transactions or Publications of the Society will in future be presented to any Fellow whose subscription is in arrear at the date of publication.

The Sixth Volume of the New Series of the Transactions of the Society, recently issued, contains, in addition to Selected Papers read at the Evening Meetings, three important historical documents communicated to and edited for the Society. Of these, the English Diary of Philip Julius, Duke of Stettin-Pomerania, in the year 1602, will be found valuable for the notices which it affords of the Elizabethan society, archæology, and drama, as well as for its political allusions. The remarkable memorial of Henry Rumbold during the period of the Restoration is considerably above the ordinary historical value of the State Papers published in the Government Calendars, or in the reports of the Historical MSS. Commission, while the first instalment of Mr. Leadam's exhaustive edition of the famous Lansdowne MS., containing the text of the Inquisition of 1517, promises to throw a flood of light upon one of the chief historical phenomena of the Tudor period, and has already been heartily welcomed by students of Economic History.

A volume of the Society's Publications, edited by Mr. Oscar Browning, and containing selections from the hitherto unpublished and highly interesting despatches of British diplomatists on the Continent during the period of the Third Coalition against Napoleon, and of the battles of Austerlitz and Jena (which are described by eye-witnesses), is still in the press, and, it is hoped will be issued to Fellows during the ensuing Session.

The following Papers were read during the past Session:

1890.
Nov. 20. 'Some Notes on the Πολιτεία τῶν 'Αθηναίων.' By C. W. C. Oman, M.A.
Dec. 18. 'John Robinson, and the Secret Service under George III.' By B. S. Stevens, F.R.Hist.S.
1891.
Jan. 26. 'The Evolution of the Family.' By Oscar Browning, M.A., V.-P.R.Hist.S.
Mar. 19. 'The Roumanian Language.' By the Rev. Robinson Thornton, D.D., F.R.Hist.S.
Apr. 16. 'The Perversion of Economic History.' By the Rev. Prof. W. Cunningham, D.D., F.R.Hist.S.
May 14. 'The Publication of the Gascon Rolls by the British and French Governments, considered as a new element in English History.' By Prof. Montagu Burrows, M.A., V.-P.R.Hist.S.
June 18. 'Diary of Philip Julius, Duke of Stettin-Pomerania, through England in the year 1602.' Communicated by Dr. Gottfried von Bülow, Keeper of the Archives in Stettin, and Wilfrid Powell, H.B.M. Consul in Stettin.

Of the above, the last-mentioned communication was subsequently edited and translated for the Society's Transactions. The Paper for April 1892 was not printed, and Mr. Stevens's most important and original investigations into the mysterious disposition of the Secret Service, chiefly between the years 1770 and 1783, are still engaging the attention of the Publication Committee of the Council, in order that the remarkable revelations which are contained in the Paper (which was partly read before the Society in December 1891) may be published in a suitable form.

In connection with the literary work of the Society during the past Session, special mention should be made of the Inaugural Address delivered by the President at the Annual Meeting of the Society on February 18, 1892, which excited considerable attention in historical circles from its clear and forcible criticism of the methods at present employed for the teaching of history in our schools and universities, and particularly of the great deficiency that exists in the historical literature of this country for the study of Universal History, a matter which is still engaging the attention of the Council.

The removal of the Society's Library to 115 St. Martin's Lane has been successfully carried out. The books are now displayed to the best possible advantage in a separate bay of the Reference Room of the Free Library, and Mr. Thomas Mason has been appointed Librarian with an *honorarium* of £10. 10s. *per annum*. The work of cataloguing, &c., will be rapidly completed, and donations of books, &c., will be duly acknowledged. A private room, adjoining the Reference Library, has been placed at the entire disposal of the Council, and has proved very useful for the meetings of the Library and other Committees.

The Council append to their Report a Prospectus of the Objects of the Society, with the necessary information respecting Subscriptions, Legacies, Donations to the Library, and Literary Contributions.

During the Session twenty-seven Fellows have been elected, seventeen have died, and twenty-three have resigned.

The following list shows the number of Fellows on the Roll as compared with that of last year :

	Oct. 31, 1891.	Oct. 31, 1892.
Ordinary Fellows	481	468
Life do.	94	94
Ex-officio do.	1	1
Honorary do.	55	55
Corresponding do.	25	25
Total	656	643

The Fellows who died during the past Session were : W. Aldain, W. B. Barbour, Dr. Bickersteth, C. A. Fyffe, Lt. W. Hawley, W. Heggerty, H. I. Jenkinson, Lt.-Col. Loyd, T. Morgan, Rev. W. L. Nicols, J. S. Noldwritt, J. Brinsley-Richards, Mrs. Johnstone Robertson, Josiah Rose, A. Whitcher, G. G. Zerffi, and Sir Wm. Arthur White, H.B.M. Ambassador at Constantinople.

The Council have referred to the loss sustained by the Society through the death of Dr. Zerffi in their previous Report, and they have on this occasion to deplore a still graver loss to the cause of Historical Research through the untimely death of Mr. C. A. Fyffe, some of whose most valuable work made its first appearance in the pages of the Transactions.

The recent elections to the Fellowship of the Society include the names of the Hon. G. C. Brodrick, Warden of Merton College, Prof. H. F. Pelham, Mr. C. W. Oman, Lord Edmond Fitzmaurice, His Excellency Sir Horace Rumbold, Bart., and Sir Donald Mackenzie Wallace.

Professor J. A. Froude has accepted the invitation of the Council to join the Society as a Life-Fellow.

The Council append a statement of the financial position of the Society from November 1, 1891, to October 31, 1892.

TREASURER'S ACCOUNT OF RECEIPTS AND PAYMENTS.

A Summary of all Moneys Received and Paid by him on behalf of the Society from November 1, 1891, to October 31, 1892.

	£	s.	d.			£	s.	d.
Balance	195	2	4	Rent		81	5	0
Annual Subscriptions	687	17	6	Costs of abandoned Lease:				
One Life Composition	21	0	0	Lake, Beaumont & Lake	£10 10 0			
Publishers' Account: Publications sold	10	1	3	Harrison & Co.	8 10 4	19	0	4
				Director		75	0	0
				" (Copyists)		15	0	0
				Librarian		2	12	6
				Secretary		150	0	0
				Clerk		25	0	0
				Spottiswoode & Co.		233	4	5
				F. Algar		9	14	6
				Whitehead & Co.		2	6	6
				Societies		4	1	6
				J. G. W. MacAlister (refreshments)		22	11	6
				Petty Expenditure		18	15	9
				Bank Charges and Postages		5	14	0
				Proportion of Life Composition transferred to Capital Acct.		14	0	0
				Subscriptions (twice paid) refunded		7	7	0
				Prince & Haugh		4	6	0
				Miss E. Salisbury		3	3	0
				Fire Insurance		4	10	0
				G. Higginbotham		3	6	6
				W. Drewitt		3	18	0
				W. H. Dalleymore		4	0	0
				W. Bell		2	12	6
				Hampton & Sons		3	6	5
				Mitchell & Co.		1	7	0
				Balance		197	19	8
	£914	1	1			£914	1	1

Examined and found correct. (Signed) R. HOVENDEN } Auditors.
B. F. STEVENS

November 12, 1892.

CAPITAL ACCOUNT.

Oct. 31, 1890.	£	s.	d.	Oct. 31, 1891.	£	s.	d.
Balance . . .	310	5	5	Balance . .	328	9	3
Two-thirds of One Life Composition . .	14	0	0				
Interest	4	3	10				
	£328	9	3		£328	9	3

We certify that the Bankers' Deposit Ledger was produced to us, showing £328. 9s. 3d. to the credit of the Royal Historical Society.

       (Signed) R. HOVENDEN } *Auditors.*
November 12, 1892.   B. F. STEVENS

The Auditors appointed to examine the Society's Accounts report :

We have compared the entries in the books with the vouchers from November 1, 1891, to October 31, 1892, and find them correct, showing the receipts to have been £914. 1s. 1d., and the payments (including £14 transferred to the Capital Account) £716. 1s. 5d., leaving a balance on October 31, 1892, of £197. 19s. 8d. in favour of the Society.

       (Signed) R. HOVENDEN } *Auditors.*
           B. F. STEVENS
November 12, 1892.

Lastly, the Council append the Secretary's Financial Statement of the Assets and Liabilities of the Society on October 31, 1892.

FINANCIAL STATEMENT OF ASSETS AND LIABILITIES
ON OCTOBER 31, 1892.

Oct. 31, 1892.	£	s.	d.	Oct. 31, 1892.	£	s.	d.
Balance on Revenue Account . . .	197	19	8	Miss Schmitz . . .	3	3	0
Outstanding Subscriptions:				Mr. MacAlister (refreshments) . . .	13	0	0
Estimated recoverable .	105	0	0	Balance in favour of the Society . . .	299	16	4
Balance of Publishers' Account . . .	13	19	8				
	£315	19	4		£315	19	4

November 12, 1892.   P. EDWARD DOVE,
                  Secretary.

    By Order of the Council.

      (Signed) M. E. GRANT DUFF, *President.*
           OSCAR BROWNING, *Chairman.*
           P. EDWARD DOVE, *Secretary.*

Royal Historical Society

(INCORPORATED BY ROYAL CHARTER).

PATRON:
HER MAJESTY THE QUEEN.

PRESIDENT:
THE RIGHT HON. SIR M. E. GRANT DUFF, G.C.S.I.

I. The Historical Society was founded in 1868, by the then Archbishop of York, the late Earl Russell, the late George Grote, the late Dean of Westminster, Sir John Lubbock, Bart., the Earl of Selborne (then Sir Roundell Palmer), and other eminent men of the day, its main objects being to promote and foster the study of History, by assisting in the publication of rare and valuable documents, and by the publication from time to time of volumes of Transactions and Publications.

II. In 1872 the Society, through the Secretary of State (The Right Hon. H. A. Bruce, now Lord Aberdare, G.C.B., for many years President of the Society), received the official permission of Her Majesty the Queen to adopt the title Royal Historical Society; and in 1889 Her Majesty was pleased to cause Letters Patent, dated July 31, to be passed under the Great Seal, granting to the Society Her Majesty's Royal Charter of Incorporation.

III. The Society consists of Fellows and Honorary Fellows and Corresponding Members, forming together a body, at the present time, of over six hundred Members.

The principal States of Europe and America, British India, and the Colonies are represented by Honorary or Corresponding Fellows.

IV. The Annual Subscription to the Society is *Two Guineas;* and at present there is no entrance fee. Fellows may, on joining the Society, or afterwards, compound for all future subscriptions upon the payment of *Twenty Guineas.*

V. The Fellows of the Society receive gratuitously a copy of each of the Society's Transactions and Publications during the period of their subscription.

The annual Publications of the Society will, in future, include a substantial volume of Transactions containing selected Papers read at the Society's Evening Meetings, together with the most valuable of the original documents which may be communicated to the Society from time to time by historical scholars, the President's Address, and a brief Summary of the Progress of Historical Research during the past Session. In addition to this, the Council are hopeful of being able to ensure the regular production of a uniform series of Publications dealing with the unpublished State Papers preserved in the national Archives.

The Society is now engaged in the publication of two important volumes dealing with the domestic, colonial, and foreign State Papers of the Reign of George III., which will shortly be issued to the Fellows.

VI. The Rooms of the Society are at 20 Hanover Square, where Meetings for the reading of Papers and discussions thereon are held from November to June, on the *third* Thursday in each month, at 8.30 P.M.

VII. The Library of the Society is deposited at 115 St. Martin's Lane, W.C. Donations of Historical books and documents will be received and acknowledged by the Librarian. All parcels should be marked "Royal Historical Society." It is hoped that all Fellows of the Society who publish Historical works will present copies to the Library.

VIII. The Royal Historical Society, being incorporated, is now in a position to receive and benefit by legacies. The means of usefulness of many corporations has been largely increased by the generous bequests of its members; and it is hoped that the income of the Society may eventually be supplemented from this source.

IX. All literary communications, proposals for Papers to be read before the Society, or Historical documents or relics to be exhibited at the ordinary Meetings, should be addressed to the Director,

HUBERT HALL,
3 Staple Inn, W.C.

All communications respecting the Library should be addressed to the Librarian,

THOMAS MASON,
115 St. Martin's Lane, W.C.

All subscriptions, unless paid by Banker's Order, should be sent to the Treasurer,

R. HOVENDEN, F.S.A.
Heathcote,
Park Hill Road,
Croydon.

Communications on all other subjects should be addressed to the Secretary,

P. EDWARD DOVE,
11 Stone Buildings,
Lincoln's Inn, W.C.

Royal Historical Society.

(INCORPORATED BY ROYAL CHARTER.)

OFFICERS AND COUNCIL—NOVEMBER 1893.

PATRON.
HER MAJESTY THE QUEEN.

PRESIDENT.
THE RT. HON. SIR M. E. GRANT DUFF, G.C.S.I.

VICE-PRESIDENTS.
THE LORD ACTON.
OSCAR BROWNING, M.A., *Chairman.*
PROFESSOR MONTAGU BURROWS, M.A., F.S.A.
HYDE CLARKE, V.P.A.S.
JAMES HEYWOOD, F.R.S.
W. E. H. LECKY, M.A.
SIR JOHN LUBBOCK, BART., M.P.
PROFESSOR MAX MÜLLER, M.A., LL.D.
PROFESSOR H. F. PELHAM, M.A.
THE EARL OF ROSEBERY.
PROFESSOR J. R. SEELEY, M.A.
SIR DONALD MACKENZIE WALLACE.

COUNCIL.
REV. J. FRANCK BRIGHT, D.D.
THE HON. G. C. BRODRICK, D.C.L.
REV. W. PROFESSOR CUNNINGHAM, B.D.
PROFESSOR T. W. RHYS DAVIDS, LL.D.
THE LORD EDMOND FITZMAURICE.
HUBERT HALL, F.S.A., *Director.*
GEORGE HURST, J.P.
I. S. LEADAM, M.A.
H. E. MALDEN, M.A., *Vice-Chairman.*
COLONEL G. B. MALLESON, C.S.I.
C. W. C. OMAN, M.A.
T. PAGLIARDINI.
CHARLES H. PEARSON, M.A.
B. F. STEVENS.
REV. R. THORNTON, D.D.
PROFESSOR T. F. TOUT, M.A.

TREASURER.
R. HOVENDEN, F.S.A., Heathcote, Park Hill Road, Croydon.

LIBRARIAN.
THOMAS MASON, 115 St. Martin's Lane, W.C.

SECRETARY.
P. EDWARD DOVE, F.R.A.S., 11 Stone Buildings, Lincoln's Inn, W.C.

Spottiswoode & Co. Printers, New-street Square, London.

Royal Historical Society.
(INCORPORATED BY ROYAL CHARTER.)

OFFICERS AND COUNCIL—OCTOBER, 1893.

Patron.
HER MAJESTY THE QUEEN.

President.
THE RT. HON. SIR MOUNTSTUART E. GRANT DUFF, G.C.S.I.

Vice-Presidents.
THE LORD ACTON.
OSCAR BROWNING, M.A., *Chairman.*
PROFESSOR MONTAGU BURROWS, M.A., F.S.A.
HYDE CLARKE, V.P.A.I.
JAMES HEYWOOD, F.R.S.
W. E. H. LECKY, M.A.
SIR JOHN LUBBOCK, BART., M.P., D.C.L.
PROFESSOR MAX MÜLLER, M.A., LL.D.
PROFESSOR H. F. PELHAM, M.A.
THE EARL OF ROSEBERY.
PROFESSOR J. R. SEELEY, M.A.
SIR DONALD MACKENZIE WALLACE.

Council.
REV. J. FRANCK BRIGHT, D.D.
HON. G. C. BRODRICK, D.C.L.
REV. PROFESSOR W. CUNNINGHAM, D.D.
PROFESSOR T. W. RHYS DAVIDS, LL.D.
LORD EDMOND FITZMAURICE.
HUBERT HALL, F.S.A., *Director.*
GEORGE HURST, J.P.
I. S. LEADAM, M.A.
H. E. MALDEN, M.A., *Vice-Chairman.*
COLONEL G. B. MALLESON, C.S.I.
C. W. C. OMAN, M.A.
TITO PAGLIARDINI.
CHARLES H. PEARSON.
B. F. STEVENS.
REV. ROBINSON THORNTON, D.D.
PROFESSOR T. F. TOUT.

Treasurer.
R. HOVENDEN, F.S.A., Heathcote, Park Hill Road, Croydon.

Librarian.
THOMAS MASON, 115 St. Martin's Lane, W.C.

Secretary.
P. EDWARD DOVE, F.R.A.S., 11 Stone Buildings, Lincoln's Inn, W.C.

Royal Historical Society.

Finance Committee.

HYDE CLARKE, V.P.A.I.
PROFESSOR T. W. RHYS DAVIDS, LL.D.
HUBERT HALL, F.S.A.
R. HOVENDEN, F.S.A.
B. F. STEVENS.
P. EDWARD DOVE, F.R.A.S., *Secretary*.

Library Committee.

OSCAR BROWNING, M.A.
HUBERT HALL, F.S.A.
TITO PAGLIARDINI.
B. F. STEVENS.
REV. ROBINSON THORNTON, D.D.
P. EDWARD DOVE, F.R.A.S., *Secretary*.

Publication Committee.

OSCAR BROWNING, M.A.
HON. G. C. BRODRICK, D.C.L.
PROFESSOR T. W. RHYS DAVIDS.
HUBERT HALL, F.S.A.
R. HOVENDEN, F.S.A.
H. E. MALDEN, M.A.
PROFESSOR H. F. PELHAM, M.A.

CAMBRIDGE BRANCH.

Committee.

PROFESSOR J. R. SEELEY, M.A. (Caius), *Chairman*.
OSCAR BROWNING, M.A. (King's), *Vice-Chairman*.
REV. W. CUNNINGHAM, D.D. (Trinity).

Honorary Secretary.

OSCAR BROWNING, M.A., King's College.

LIST OF FELLOWS.

Names of Members of Council are printed in SMALL CAPITALS.
*Those marked * have compounded for their Annual Subscriptions.*

Abbott, Richard, Forcett, near Darlington.
ABERDARE, The Lord, G.C.B., F.R.S., Duffryn, Mountain Ash, South Wales.
Aburrow, Charles, Commercial Buildings, Commissioner Street, Johannesburg, Transvaal, S. Africa.
* Ackers, B. St. John, Huntley Manor, Gloucester.
* ACTON, The Lord, 72 Princes Gate, S.W.
Adams, William Bateman, Head Master of the Fleet Road Board Schools, 10 Willow Road, Hampstead.
Alexander, Rev. J. F., Ralph House, Russell Road, Ipswich.
* Alexander, L. C., Holly Lodge, Upper Park Field, Putney.
Altschul, Dr., F.R.G.S., F.R.S.L., M.C.P., M. Philolog. Soc., 9 Old Bond Street, W.
Andrews, William, 2 Park Row, Hull.
Aiya, V. Nagam, B.A., Settlement Dewan Peishcar, Travancore, S. India.
Anthony, Charles, 166 Rosendale Road, West Dulwich, S.E.
Arnold, Arthur Claude, B.A., Whitehouse School, Thornton Heath, Surrey.
Ashbee, H. S., F.S.A., F.R.G.S., 53 Bedford Square, W.C.
Ashe, Rev. Robert Pickering, F.R.G.S., Wareham, Dorset.
Aspden, Thomas, *England* office, 291 Strand, W.C.

Backhouse, Jonathan E., Bank, Darlington.
* Baguley, Henry, 150 Leathwaite Road, Clapham Junction, S.W.
Bailie, Alexander Cumming, Rand Club, Johannesburg, Transvaal, S. Africa.
* Barnard, John, Spring Hall, Sawbridgeworth, Herts.
Barrett, F. T., Mitchell Library, Ingram Street East, Glasgow.
* Barrett, T. Squire, M.A.I., F.Z.S., Wisteria House, High Street, Berkhamsted.
Bates, Octavius I., San Rafael, California, U.S.A.
Bates, Rev. J. Chadwick, M.A., F.R.A.S., Castleton Vicarage, near Manchester.
Bayard, Robert Valentine Campbell, B.A., Cambridge House, Seabank Road, Liscard, Cheshire.
Beck, Rev. Canon Walter, Cherry Linton, Cambridge.
Bellingham, Sir Alan Henry, Bart., M.A. Oxon, Castle Bellingham, co. Louth, Ireland.
Benson, Arthur Christopher, B.A., Eton College.
Berry, William Thomas, Head Master, Winchester Street Board School, 15 Fulham Place, Maida Vale, W.
Bethune, Alexander Mackenzie, F.R.G.S., Otterburn, Hamlet Road, Upper Norwood, S.E., and 122 Leadenhall Street, E.C.
* Bevington, Colonel S. R., Neckinger Mills, Bermondsey, S.E.
* Biden, Lewis, 1, The Elms, Allison Road, Acton, W.
Billing, Rev. F.A., D.D., LL.D., F.R.S.L., 7 St. Donatt's Road, New Cross, S.E.
Binns, Richard William, F.S.A., Diglis House, Worcester.
Bird, Rev. A. F. Ryder, Forest Hill House, Honor Oak, S.E.

LIST OF FELLOWS.

Blott, Walter, Manningdale, South Norwood, S.E.
* Bogoushevsky, Baron Nicholas Casimir de, Pskow, Russia.
Booker, William Henry, Short Hill, Hollow Stone, Nottingham.
Borrow, W. S., B.A., Colet House, Talgarth Road, West Kensington.
Bowen, E. E., Harrow School.
Bowers, Robert Woodger, 89 Blackfriars Road, S.E.
Boyle, Miss Cecilia, 48 Queen's Gate Terrace, S.W.
Boynton, Thomas, Norman House, Bridlington Quay.
* Brackenridge, George Washington, San Antonia, Texas, U.S.A.
Braithwaite, Isaac.
Bramwell, Sir F. J., F.R.S., 5 Great George Street, Westminster, S.W.
Brent, Francis, F.S.A., 6 Tothill Avenue, Plymouth.
BRIGHT, Rev. JAMES FRANCK, D.D., Master of University College, Oxford.
Briscoe, John Potter, 2 Forest Grove, Colville Street, Nottingham.
Britten, Lieut.-Col. John, R.L.M., 106 Cambridge Gardens, North Kensington, W.
* Brocklehurst, Septimus, F.R.G.S., Fern Hill, Edge Lane, Liverpool.
BRODRICK, The Hon. GEORGE C., D.C.L., Warden of Merton College, Oxford.
Brooks, Ernest W., M.A., 28 Great Ormond Street, W.C.
* Broomhead, Barnard P., Bank Chambers, George Street, Sheffield.
Brough, William S., Fowlchurch, Leek, Staffordshire.
Brown, Thomas Forster, Guildhall Chambers, Cardiff.
Browne, Harold C. G., 61 Carey Street, Lincoln's Inn, W.C.
Browning, Miss M.A., The Beehive, Windsor.
BROWNING, OSCAR, M.A., King's College, Cambridge.
Buchanan, William Frederick, F.R.G.S., Union Club, Sydney, New South Wales.
Buck, J. H. Watson, Homecroft, Nantwich Road, Crewe.
* Burdett-Coutts, The Baroness, 1 Stratton Street, W.
Burroughes, Wm. Henry, Montpellier, Brecknock Road, N.
BURROWS, MONTAGU, M.A., F.S.A., Chichele Professor of Modern History, Oxford, 9 Norham Gardens, Oxford.
Butler, Rev. Charles Wesley.
* Butt, Arthur N., London Institution, Finsbury Circus, E.C.

Cadley, Edward Samuel, 17 Horder Road, Fulham, S.W.
* Carillon, J. Wilson, F.S.A., The Chimes, Richmond, Surrey.
Carnell, George Frederick, Sevenoaks.
Cartlidge S. J., School of Art, Hanley, Staffordshire.
* Catlett, William Henry, F.L.S., Burwood, Sydney, N.S.W.
* Chance, James Frederick, M.A., 51 Prince's Gate, Kensington, W.
Chancellor, E. Beresford, Ashburton House, Richmond, Surrey.
* Chase, George B., A.M., Boston, Mass., U.S.A.
Chorlton, Thomas, 32 Brazenose Street, Manchester.
* Church, George Earl, F.R.G.S., F.A.G.S., 216 CromwellRoad, S. Kensington.
* CLARKE, HYDE, V.P.A.S., F.R.S.S., M.R.A.S., 32 St. George's Square, S.W.
Clayson, Christopher William, B.A., 20 Upham Park Road, Chiswick.
Clements, George Menzies, 7 The Terrace, Camden Square, N.W.
Cleminson, James, F.R.G.S., Dashwood House, 9 New Broad Street, E.C.
* Cliff, John, F.G.S., Nisbet, Fulneck, near Leeds.
Coate, James, Lyme Road, Axminster.
Cobb, Cyril Stephen, B.C.L., M.A., F.R.G.S., 1 Dr. Johnson's Buildings, Temple, E.C., and Hughenden Berrylands, Surbiton.
Cock, Alfred, Q.C., 3 Elm Court, Temple, E.C.
Cockle, George, 9 Bolton Gardens, S.W.
Coleman, Everard Home, F.R.A.S., F.R.G.S., 71 Brecknock Road, N.
Congress Library, Washington, United States, per E. G. Allen, 28 Henrietta Street, Covent Garden.

LIST OF FELLOWS.

Cook, Alexander, F.R.G.S., 58 James Street, Docks, Cardiff.
Cooke-Taylor, R. W., 8 Spencer Road, Coventry.
Coop, James Ogden, B.A., Albemarle, Ashton-under-Lyne : present address—126 Hyde Park Road, Leeds.
Corbett, John, M.P., Imprey, Droitwich.
* Corbett, William, B.A., 44 Roland Gardens, Kensington.
Corbould, Alfred, 8 Pembroke Road, S.W.
Cornish, James Frederic, F.R.G.S., 1 Beaufort Club, Dover Street.
Cotgreave, Alfred, Rokeby House, Broadway, Stratford, E.
Cottam, Samuel, F.R.A.S., F.C.A., 49 Spring Gardens, Manchester.
Courtauld, George, M.P., Cut Hedge, near Halstead, Essex.
Cowell, Peter, Free Public Library, Liverpool.
Crake, Rev. Edward E., Jevington Rectory, Polegate, Sussex.
* Crawford, J. W., East Street Mills, Leeds.
Crawhall, Joseph, 21 Castle Bar Road, Ealing, W.
Crawley, William John Chetwode, LL.D., D.C.L., F.R.G.S., F.G.S., 3 and 4 Ely Place, Dublin.
Crockford, Frederick, Silverdale, Sydenham.
* Crofton, Henry M., F.R.A.S., M.R.I.A., Inchmappa, Ashford, county Wicklow.
* Cunningham, Major-General Sir Alexander, K.C.I.E., C.S.I., Crawley Mansions, 96 Gloucester Road, S.W.
* CUNNINGHAM, Rev. Professor W., M.A., D.D., Trinity College, Cambridge.
Currie, John Lang, Eildon, Grey Street, St. Kilda, Victoria, Australia.

* DAVIDS, Professor T. W. RHYS, LL.D., 3 Brick Court, Temple, E.C.
Davies, Sir R. Henry, Bart., K.C.S.I., C.I.E., F.R.G.S., 20 Hyde Park Gate, S.W.
Davis, Lt.-Colonel John, F.S.A., Bifrons, Farnborough, Hants.
Davison, Jonathan, 33 South Castle Street, Liverpool.
Dawson, Rev. W., M.A., St. John's Rectory, Clerkenwell, E.C.
* Dees, Robert Richardson, The Hall, Wallsend, Newcastle-on-Tyne.
Denham, Edward, 384 Acushnet Avenue, New Bedford, Mass., U.S.A.
Devereux, William Cope, R.N., F.R.G.S., c/o Messrs. Henry S. King & Co., 65 Cornhill, E.C.
* Dimelow, John Gartside, Landsmere, Palatine Road, Didsbury.
Ditchfield, Rev. P. H., Barkham Rectory, Wokingham, Berks.
Dothie, Rev. Elvery.
DOVE, P. EDWARD, F.R.A.S., 11 Stone Buildings, Lincoln's Inn.
Drummond, Major Francis Henry Rutherford, c/o Messrs. H. S. King & Co., 45 Pall Mall, S.W.
Dubbs, Professor Joseph Henry, D.D., Franklin and Marshall College, Lancaster, Pennsylvania, U.S.A.
Duthie, Rev. Wallace.

Eckersley, James Carlton, M.A., F.R.G.S., F.S.S., Ashfield, Wigan, Lancashire.
Edmunds, Wilfred Hawksley, Jersey House, Chesterfield.
Edwards, Frank, Holywell, North Wales.
* Edwin-Cole, James, Swineshead Hall, near Boston, Lincolnshire.
* Elliot, John, Free Library, Wolverhampton.
* Evans, E. Bickerton, Whitbourne Hall, near Worcester.
* Evans, Patrick F., 54 Longridge Road, S.W.
Evans, T. M., College School, Lampeter.
* Evans, W., The Spring, Kenilworth.

Fellows, James I., Saxon Hall, Palace Court, Bayswater Hill, W.
Feret, C. J., 49 Edith Road, West Kensington, S.W.
* Ferguson, Professor John, M.A., University, Glasgow.
Ferguson, Robert, M.P., Morton, Carlisle.
* Ferrers, The Earl, Staunton Harrold, Melbourne, Derby.
Field, Rev. Edmund, M.A., Lancing College, Shoreham.
Figgis, J. N., St. Catharine's College, Cambridge.
Finch, G. B., M.A., St. Peter's Terrace, Cambridge.
* Finnemore, Robert Isaac, J.P., Durban, Natal, South Africa.
Firth, Solomon, 21 Upper Tichbourne Street, Leicester.
Fitch, Edwin F., 66 Bishopsgate Street, E.C.
Fitzgerald, Gerald Beresford, F.S.A., 63 Eaton Square, S.W.
* Fitzgerald, Major William George.
FITZMAURICE, Lord EDMOND GEORGE, Leigh House, Bradford-on-Avon, Wilts.
Fleming, Sandford, C.E., C.M.G., LL.D., Ottawa, Canada.
Fletcher, Rev. G. R., B.A., Alvechurch, Redditch.
* Fletcher, John S., Treherne House, Hampstead, N.W.
Fooks, William, M.A., LL.B., 2 Brick Court, Temple, E.C.
Ford, John Rawlinson, Quarrydene, Weetwood, Leeds.
Fraser, Alexander William, Queen Street, Melbourne, Victoria.
* Freake, Lady, 11 Cranley Place, S.W.
* Froude, Professor J. Anthony, LL.D., Oxford.
Fryer, Alfred C., Ph.D., M.A., F.C.S., Cornwallis Lodge, Clifton, Bristol.

Gaikwad, Sampatras K., National Liberal Club, S.W.
Galbraith, Rev. Matthew, M.A., F.R.G.S., Ferryhill, Aberdeen, N.B.
Gannon, John.
Gardiner, Professor Samuel Rawson, South View, Widmore Road, Bromley, Kent.
Garrett, J. P., 3 Great James Street, Bedford Row, W.C.
* Garstin, John Ribton, M.A., F.S.A., M.R.I.A., Braganstown, Castle Bellingham, co. Louth.
Gill, John, Penryn, Cornwall.
Giuseppi, M.S., Public Record Office, Fetter Lane, E.C.
Gladstone Library, National Liberal Club, Whitehall Place, S.W.
Godfrey, John Thomas, Radcliffe-on-Trent, Nottingham.
Goodenough, Major-General William Howley, R.A., C.B., F.R.G.S., Blomefield House, Shooter's Hill, S.E.
Gotch, H. G., 103 Lady Margaret Road, Tufnell Park, N.
Gower, Lord Ronald, Stafford House, St. James's, London.
Graham, James.
Graham, James Henry Stuart, M.A., F.R.G.S., 179 The Grove, Hammersmith, W.
* GRANT DUFF, The Right Hon. Sir MOUNTSTUART ELPHINSTONE, G.C.S.I., York House, Twickenham, Middlesex.
Granville, Joseph Henry, F.R.G.S., Altrincham High School, Altrincham.
Graves, Rev. Michael, F.R.G.S., Sir W. Borlase's School, Great Marlow.
Grazebrook, H. Sydney, Middleton Villa, Grove Park, Chiswick.
Green, Rev. Edward Dyer M.A. Bromborough Rectory, Birkenhead, Cheshire.
Green, Samuel S., Free Public Library, Worcester, Mass., United States.
* Grey, Sir George, K.C.B., Auckland, New Zealand.
Grimsey, B. P., Stoke Lodge, Ipswich.
Guilding, Rev. J. M., St. Lawrence's Vicarage, Reading.
Gwynne, Francis Anthony, F.R.G.S., 36 Brunswick Gardens, Kensington.
Gwynne-Griffith, J. St. A. Mansel, Hendre Owen, Bedford Park, Chiswick.

Hackwood, Frederick W., 66 Bridge Street, Wednesbury.
* Hailstone, Edward, 9 Rue de Tocqueville, Paris.

LIST OF FELLOWS. 7

Hale, Surgeon-Major Thomas Egerton, B.A., M.D., V.C., Faddiley Lodge, near Nantwich, Cheshire.
Hall, Rev. Enoch, Glensdale, Poole, Dorset.
HALL, HUBERT, F.S.A., *Director*, 3 Staple Inn, E.C.
Hall, William Robert, Broxbourne, Herts.
Hamilton, Walter, Ellarbee, Elms Road, Clapham Common.
Hamilton, Walter Bernard, M.A., F.R.G.S., "Elmhurst," Cottenham Park Road, Wimbledon.
Hammond, Alfred de Lisle, M.A., Samarès, Yarra, near Goulburn, New South Wales.
Harben, Henry, Seaford Lodge, Fellows Road, N.W.
Harker, Rev. Bailey John, 1 Ducie Avenue, Gilnow Park, Bolton, Lancashire.
Harris, James Howard, Porthleven, Helston, Cornwall.
Harvard University Library, c/o Kegan Paul, Trübner & Co., Paternoster House, Charing Cross Road, W.C.
* Harvey, William Marsh, Goldington Hall, Bedford.
Hawkins-Ambler, George Arthur, 30 Royal Park, Clifton, Bristol.
Hay, James A. C., M.I.M.E., A.M.I.C.E., Royal Arsenal, Woolwich.
Headlam, J. W., King's College, Cambridge.
Healey, Edward Charles, Wyphurst, near Guildford.
Heaviside, Rev. George, B.A., F.R.G.S., 7 Grosvenor Street, Coventry.
Herries, The Lord, Everingham Park, York.
* Herz, Dr. Cornelius, F.R.G.S., 31 Boulevard des Italiens, Paris.
HEYWOOD, JAMES, F.R.S., 26 Kensington Palace Gardens, W.
Hill, Rev. H. Ernest, Abbey School, Beckenham.
Hill, Samuel Thomas, F.R.G.S., Commercial Schools, Stepney Green, E.
Hill, W. E., Estate Office, Croxteth, near Liverpool.
* Hinmers, William, Cleveland House, Lancaster Road, Eccles, Manchester.
Hoare, Rev. John V., The Parsonage, Keswick, Cumberland.
Hocking, Rev. Silas K., 21 Scarisbrick New Road, Southport.
* Hockley, Thomas, c/o The Numismatic and Antiquarian Society of Philadelphia, Philadelphia, U.S.A.
Hodgson, Shadworth Hollway, 45 Conduit Street, W.
Hodson, William Walter, Station Villa, Sudbury, Suffolk.
Holmes, Emra, H. M. Customs, Newhaven, Sussex.
Hooper, George N., Elmleigh, Hayne Road, Beckenham, S.E.
Hopkins, J. Satchell, Jesmond Grove, Edgbaston, Birmingham.
Hornby, Rev. James John, D.D., F.R.G.S., Provost of Eton, Eton College, Windsor.
* Horniman, F. J., Surrey Mount, Forest Hill, S.E.
* Hovenden, Frederick, Glenlea, Thurlow Park Road, West Dulwich, S.E.
HOVENDEN, ROBERT, *Treasurer*, Heathcote, Park Hill Road, Croydon.
Howarth, W., 102 Malpas Road, Brockley, S.E.
Hughes, Rev. Meredith Jones, Brymbo, N. Wales.
Hughes, Richard Deeton, 12 Bedford Row, W.C.
Hume, Major Martin Andrew Sharp, 14 Cavendish Mansions, Portland Place, W.
Humphrey, George Richard, 16 St. Donatt's Road, New Cross, S.E.
HURST, GEORGE, J.P., Kingsbrook House, St. Mary's, Bedford.
Hutton, Rev. William Holden, St. John's College, Oxford.

Ireland, National Library of, Dublin.

Jackson, Richard Charles, Bowyer Park, Camberwell, S.E.
Jago-Trelawny, Major-General John, F.R.G.S., Coldrenick, Liskeard, Cornwall.
Jamieson, George Auldjo, M.A., F.S.A., 37 Drumsheugh Gardens, Edinburgh.

LIST OF FELLOWS.

Jefferson, Rev. John, Lime Grove, Rawtenstall.
Jonas, Alfred C., Poundfold, nr. Penclawdd, Swansea.
Jonas, Rev. Edward James, St. John's Parsonage, Coatbridge, N.B.
Jones, Charles Edwin, Foljambe Road, Chesterfield.
Jones, Rev. T. O.
Joyce, Rev. George William, Wellington, Somerset.
Judd, James, J.P., East Knoll, Upper Norwood, S.E.

Kelly, William, F.S.A., Ivy Lodge, Alexandra Road, Stoneygate, Leicester.
Kenyon, Robert, High School, Blackpool.
Kerr, Robert, 23 Milton Place, Halifax.
Ketchley, Rev. Harry Ernest, Devon Lodge, Malvern.
Kirkpatrick, Robert, 1 Queen Square, Strathbungo, Glasgow.
Klein, Julius, M.A., Ph.D., Heath Cottage, Sydenham Road, Croydon.
Knapp, William Thomas Reeve, 68 Fernhead Road, St. Peter's Park, W.
Knibbs, Rev. Charles, Heatherdon, Tor Vale, Torquay.

Lach-Szyrma, Rev. W. S Barkingside Vicarage, Ilford.
L'Aker, Major John, F.R.G.S., Florence Villa, Boscombe, Bournemouth.
de Lamarre, Louis Bert, Bridgetown, Barbados, B.W.I.
Lane, Rev. C. Arthur, Riversdale, Wood Green, N.
* Larkin, Matthew, J.P., F.R.G.S., 438 Collins Street, Melbourne.
Lawson, Rev. John Sharpe, M.A., Ll.M., St. George's Vicarage, Barnsley, Yorks.
Lawton, William, Nunthorpe, York.
LEADAM, ISAAC SAUNDERS, M.A., 117 St. George's Square, S.W.
* LECKY, W. E. H., M.A., 38 Onslow Gardens, S.W.
Lees, William, 10 Norfolk Street, Manchester.
Leggott, J. H., Bury Street, Stowmarket.
Lewis, Rev. Thomas Curling.
* Liberty, Arthur Lasenby, F.R.S.S., F.Z.S., 13 Cornwall Terrace, N.W.
Liebmann, Professor James Alexander, F.R.S.L., F.R.G.S., Diocesan College, Rondebosch, Cape Town.
Lindsley, Dr. J. Berrien, Nashville, Tennessee, U.S.A.
* Lloyd, Rev. John, M.A., Llanvapley Rectory, Abergavenny
Lloyd, J. A., The Studio, Marlborough, Wilts.
Lloyd, Richard, 2 Addison Crescent, Kensington, W.
* Lobb, John, F.R.G.S., *Christian Age* Office, St. Bride Street, E.C.
* Lodge, R., M.A., Brasenose College, Oxford.
LUBBOCK, Sir JOHN, Bart., P.C., M.P., D.C.L., F.R.S., F.L.S., High Elms, Farnborough, Kent.
*Lydall, John French, 37 John Street, Bedford Row, W.C.
* Lyle, Thomas, M.A., Grove House, Shacklewell Lane, E.

MacAlister, J. Y. W., 20 Hanover Square, W.
* Macandrew, W., Westwood House, near Colchester.
Macartney, John Arthur, F.R.G.S., Waverley, Rockhampton, Queensland.
McCarthy, Justin, M.P., 73 Eaton Terrace, S.W.
Macdonald, Alexander Cameron, F.R.G.S., Collins Street West, Melbourne.
* Mackeson, Edward, F.S.A., 13 Hyde Park Square, W.
Maclean, William, F.R.G.S., 31 Camperdown Place, Great Yarmouth.
Maguire, Thomas Miller, M.A., LL.D., Earl's Court Square, S.W.
Maitland, Professor F. W., M.A., Downing College, Cambridge.
MALDEN, HENRY ELLIOT, M.A., Kitlands, Holmwood, Surrey.
MALLESON, Col. G. B., C.S.I., 27 West Cromwell Road, S.W.
Malleson, J. P., B.A.
Manchester Free Library.

LIST OF FELLOWS.

Margetts, William George, A.I.C.E., F.R.G.S., King's Lodge, near Rochester.
* Marsden, Mrs., 129 Chesterton Road, Kensington, W.
Marten, C. Rous, The Terrace, Wellington, New Zealand.
Maw, James, Blenheim House, Margery Park Road, Upton, Forest Gate, E.
Maybank, John Thomas, High Street, Dorking.
Mesney, General William, F.R.G.S., 22 Swatow Road, Shanghai, China.
* Metcalfe, Rev. James, M.A., Vicarage, West Teignmouth.
* Miggs, John Gilbert, 123 Cromwell Road, South Kensington, S.W.
Miles, Colonel S. B., c/o Messrs. H. S. King & Co., 45 Pall Mall, S.W.
Millais, Lady, 2 Palace Gate, Kensington, S.W.
Miller, M. H., *Leek Times*, Staffordshire.
Milman, Rev. W. H., M.A., Sion College, Victoria Embankment, E.C.
* Milward, R. H., 41 Waterloo Street, Birmingham.
Moloney, Sir Cornelius Alfred, K.C.M.G., Government House, Lagos.
Molyneux, Lt.-Colonel Edmund, F.R.G.S, Warren Lodge, Wokingham, Berks.
Money-Coutts, Francis Burdett, Walsingham House, Piccadilly.
Monk, James Henry, 5 Buckingham Gate, S.W.
Montefiore, A., 135 Finchley Road, Hampstead.
Moore, William, B.A., 56 Springfield Road, N.W.
Morrison, Hew, Librarian, Edinburgh Public Library, Edinburgh.
Mosley, George, F.G.S., The Commercial College, York.
* MÜLLER, Professor F. MAX, M.A., LL.D., 7 Norham Gardens, Oxford.
Mullins, J. D., Birmingham Free Library, Birmingham.
Munns, Henry, 55 Warner Street, Derby.

Naylor, Robert Anderton, F.R.G.S., Cuerden Hall, Thelwall, Cheshire. (*Post town*, Warrington.)

* O'Donnavan, William, LL.D., 15 Belgrave Road, Rathmines, Dublin.
OMAN, CHARLES WILLIAM CHADWICK, M.A., All Souls College, Oxford.
Ord, M. Clement, B.A., 6 Hughendon Road, Clifton, Bristol.
Orsbach, Rev. Engelbert Baron von, F.R.G.S., Mottingham House, near Eltham, Kent.
Owen, Edward Humphrey, F.S.A., Ty Coch, Carnarvon.

Pacy, Frank, Vestry Hall, Mount Street, W.
PAGLIARDINI, TITO, 21 Alexander Street, Westbourne Park, W.
Palmer, James Foster, L.R.C.P., M.R.C.S.E., 8 Royal Avenue, Chelsea College, S.W.
Parker, Henry, C.E., Irrigation Officer, P.W.D., Ceylon.
* Parr, J. Charlton, Grappenhall Heyes, Warrington.
Parrish, Rev. Henry, 3631 Wallace Street, Philadelphia, Pa., U.S.A.
Patterson, James K., Ph.D., President of the Agricultural College, Lexington, Kentucky, United States.
Paul, Alexander, 10 Guilford Place, W.C.
Payne, John Augustus Otonba, Chief Registrar, Supreme Court, Lagos, West Africa.
PEARSON, CHARLES H., Victoria Office, 15 Victoria Street, S.W.
PELHAM, Professor H. F., M.A., Oxford.
Pembroke, The Earl of, F.R.G.S., Wilton House, Salisbury, Wilts.
Penny, Arthur Paul, 18 Bedford Place, W.C.
* Perry, Captain Ottley, F.R.G.S., F.S.A., 7 Bedford Street, Bolton, Lancashire.
* Peyster, General John Watts de, 59 East 21st Street, New York.
Pflugk-Harttung, Professor Dr. Julius von, 14, York Strasse, Berlin.

LIST OF FELLOWS.

Philip, George, 32 Fleet Street, E.C.
Phillipps, Henry M.
* Pickering, J., F.R.G.S., 86 Thicket Road, Anerley.
Pierce, Francis Dormer, Monmouth Grammar School, Monmouth.
Pooley, Frank, 18 Hacken's Hey, Liverpool.
* Porges, Theodore, F.R.G.S., 11 Rue Montalivet, Paris.
Potts, Lewis W., St. Martin's House, Stamford Hill, N.
Powell, Rev. Arthur Herbert, M.A., LL.B., 23 Morella Road, Wandsworth Common, S.W.
Price, Cormell, M.A., B.C.L., F.R.G.S., Westward Ho! N. Devon.
Pullee, Miss Mary, St. Martin's Middle School, Charing Cross Road, W.C.
Purvis, Gilbert, F.R.C.I., F.R.S.S., Ingle Neuk, Beckenham, Kent.

Raikes, Lt.-Colonel G. A., F.S.A., 63 Belsize Park, Hampstead, N.W.
Raju, P. V. Ramaswami, B.A., High Court, Madras, c/o Messrs. Grindlay & Co., Parliament Street, S.W.
Rama Krishna, T., B.A., 97 Auddiappah Naick Street, Black Town, Madras.
Ranger, Henry.
Rannie, David Watson, Conheath, Dumfries, N.B.
* Read, His Excellency the Hon. General John Meredith, LL.B., M.R.I.A., United States Minister, Athens, c/o Messrs. J. Munroe & Co., 7 Rue Scribe, Paris.
Read, Rev. Philip Chesshyre.
Reich, Dr. Emil, 40 Great Russell Street, Bloomsbury.
Richardson, Captain J. G. F., Ph.D., J.P., Elmfield, Knighton, Leicester.
Ridge, Samuel Hartshorne, B.A., F.R.G.S., 257 Victoria Parade, East Melbourne, Victoria, Australia.
Ridgway, W. J. P., M.A., Barrow Hill, Chesterfield.
Rodocanachi, Emmanuel P., 54 Rue de Lisbonne, Paris.
Rodway, A. J., 22 Great Colmore Street, Birmingham.
Rolfe, Rev. Frederick William.
Rome, William, F.S.A., Oxford Lodge, Wimbledon Common.
Ropes, Arthur Reed, M.A., The Ferns, Sunnyside Road, Hornsey Rise, N.
* Ropes, J. C., 99 Mount Vernon, Boston, Mass., U.S.A.
Rose, John Holland, M.A.
* ROSEBERY, The Earl of, Lansdowne House, W.
Rumbold, His Excellency Sir Horace, Bart., British Legation, The Hague.
Rusden, George William, F.R.G.S., c/o C. P. Willan, Esq., Solicitor, 7 St. James's Buildings, William Street, Melbourne.
* Russel, Hon. Rollo, Pembroke Lodge, Richmond, Surrey.
* Ryder, Charles, The Brewery, Leeds.
Rymer, Samuel Lee, J.P., Pevensey, Wellesley Road, Croydon.

Sabel, Ernest, F.R.G.S., Lynton House, South Side, Clapham Common, S.W.
* Safford, John Burham, F.G.S., Parkshot House, Richmond, Surrey.
Samuel, Harry Sylvester, 80 Onslow Gardens, S.W.
Sanders, Samuel, 7 De Vere Gardens, Kensington Palace, W.
Saunders, C. T., 20 Temple Row, Birmingham.
Score, H. Berkeley, Lathom Park, Ormskirk.
Searelle, Luscombe, c/o William Luscombe, Esq., J.P., Clarham, Plymouth.
Seath, Thomas B., Sunnyoaks, Langbank, Renfrewshire.
SEELEY, Professor J. R., M.A., 7 St. Peter's Terrace, Cambridge.
Shannon, John Strangman, Principal of St. Martin's School, York.
Sharp, J. Fox, The Park, Hull.
Sharples, George, Waterloo Road Board School, Manchester.
Sherren, John Angel, Helmsley, Stavordale Road, Weymouth.
Shettle, Rev. George T., L.A.
Shyamal Dâss, Kavi Raja, M.R.A.S., Poet Laureate and Member of the Mahad Raj Sabha of Meywar, Oodeypore, India.

Sibbald, John Gordon Edward, Admiralty, Spring Gardens, and 3 Townshend Villas, Richmond, Surrey.
Sikes, Rev. Thomas B., M.A., Warbleton Rectory, Heathfield, Sussex.
Simmonds, Rev. Charles, B.A., Olive House, Olive Mount, Tranmore, Birkenhead.
* Simson, Alfred, 4 Fairlie Place, Calcutta ; London address, c/o Messrs. Kilburn, Brown & Co., 28 St. Mary Axe, E.C.
Simpson, Percy, F.R.G.S., F.Z.S., Fernholme, Eastbourne, Sussex; temporary address: St. George's Club, Hanover Square.
Skrine, Henry Duncan, Claverton Manor, near Bath.
Smith, E. Cozens, F.S.S., 1 Old Broad Street, E.C.
* Smith, The Hon. Sir Donald A., LL.D., 1157 Dorchester Street, Montreal, Canada.
Smith, Hubert, Hobarton, Dover Street, Ryde, Isle of Wight.
Smith, Thomas Charles, Green Nook, Longridge, near Preston.
* Smith, W. Bickford, Trevarno, Helston, Cornwall.
Smyth, Francis Lea Stourbridge, B.A.Oxon, M.A.Sydney, F.R.G.S., Union Club, Sydney, N.S.W.
Smyth, George J., *Librarian*, Linen Hall Library, Belfast.
Spencer, Augustus, Woodbine Cottage, Barkby, Leicester.
Spry, William James Joseph, R.N., F.R.G.S., Therapia, St. Andrew's Road, Southsea.
Stack, G. A., Professor of History, Presidency College, Calcutta ; Editor of the *Calcutta Review*, Calcutta, India.
* Stanley, Walmsley, F.R.G.S., The Knowle, Leigham Court Rd., Streatham, S.W.
Stapley, Sir Harry, Bart., 15 Savile Row, W.
Stead, Richard, Grammar School, Folkestone.
Stead, Thomas Ballan.
Steele, Joseph, M.D., c/o Mr. Alderman Rymer, Wellesley Road, Croydon.
Steer, Henry, M.L.L.S., 1 Irongate, Derby.
STEVENS, B. F., 4 Trafalgar Square, W.C.
Stevens, George Richard, Greenmount, Hong Kong.
* Stewart, General Alexander P., LL.D., Oxford, Miss., U.S.A.
Stewart, Rev. John, Penryn, Cornwall.
Stockdale, Thomas, Spring Lea, Leeds.
Stone, J. H., Principal, Kumbakonan College, Tanjore District, India.
Stryker, General William S., Adjutant-General of New Jersey, Trenton, New Jersey, U.S.A.
Stuart, Lieut.-Col. W., Tempsford Hall, Sandy, Bedfordshire.
Sulley, Philip, Parkhurst, Dumfries.
Surr, Watson, 28 Threadneedle Street, E.C.
Syms, Richard, Melbourne House, Barking Road, E.

Taylor, Charles Edwin, M.D., F.R.G.S., St. Thomas, Danish West Indies.
* Taylor, Miss Helen, Avignon, France.
* Teele, Rev. Albert K., D.D., Milton, Mass., U.S.A.
Tempany, Thomas William, Sheen Park, Richmond, Surrey.
Terry, Rev. George Frederick, St. Saviour's, Nottingham.
THORNTON, Rev. Prebendary ROBINSON, D.D. (Oxon), Vicar of St. John's, Notting Hill ; Boyle Lecturer ; Vice-President of the Victoria Institute ; 63 Ladbroke Grove, Notting Hill, W.
Thorpe, Lieut. Patrick Joseph, Royal Irish Rifles, Fermoy, co. Cork.
Todhunter, Charles George, Kingsmoor House, near Harlow, Essex.
Toplis, Miss Sophia Grace, 63 Bartholomew Road, N.W.
Torr, Herbert James, Riseholme Hall, near Lincoln.
TOUT, Professor T. F., 33 Mauldeth Road, Fallowfield, Manchester.
Travis-Cook, John, 14 Parliament Street, Hull.

LIST OF FELLOWS.

Tregear, Edward, F.R.G.S., Park Street, Wellington, New Zealand.
* Turton, Robert Bell, 24 Old Square, Lincoln's Inn, and 7c Lower Belgrave Street, S.W.

Udal, The Hon. John Symonds, Attorney-General of Fiji, Suva, Fiji.
Urwick, Rev. W., M.A., 49 Belsize Park Gardens, N.W.

Ventura, M., 18 Coleman Street, E.C.
Villavicencio, R., M.D., Consulate of Venezuela, 18 Broadway, New York.
Vincent, J. A., Needham Market, Suffolk.
Vos-per-Thomas, Rev. Samuel.

Wadling, Henry, Lamb Buildings, Temple, E.C.
* Wagner, Henry, F.S.A., 13 Half Moon Street, Piccadilly, W.
Wakefield, Rev. Henry Russell, The Vicarage, Sandgate, Kent.
Wakefield, Rev. Thomas, F.R.G.S., 10 Melbourne Terrace, Bradford.
Walford, John Edward, C.C., Knightrider Street, E.C.
Walker, J. Maddocks, "Mancunium," Anerley, Surrey, S.E.
* Walker, Philip F., F.R.G.S., 36 Princes Gardens, S.W.
* Walker, Robert, F.R.G.S., Woodside, Leicester.
* WALLACE, Sir DONALD MACKENZIE, St. Ermin's Mansions, Caxton St., S.W.
Wallis, John E. P., M.A., 3 Pump Court, Temple, E.C.
Ward, John Edward, F.R.G.S., 114 Grosvenor Road, S.W., and Woolmer Hill, Haslemere.
Warre, General Sir Henry J., K.C.B., F.R.G.S., 35 Cadogan Place, S.W.
Warren, Colonel Sir Charles, R.E., 44 St. George's Road, S.W.
Warner, G. Townsend, B.A.
* Watson, Rev. Albert, M.A., Brasenose College, and 20 Norham Gardens, Oxford.
* Watts, Rev. Herbert C., Milton, Sittingbourne, Kent.
Webb, H. G., "Caradoc," Blandford Road, Bedford Park, W.
Welch, Charles, Corporation Library, Guildhall, E.C.
Wellwood, Rev. Nathaniel, Danforth, near Toronto, Ontario, Canada.
West, James, Storrington, Sussex.
West, William Nowell, F.R.G.S., 30 Montague Street, Russell Square, W.C.
* Westminster, The Duke of, K.G., Grosvenor House, W.
*Whatton, J. S., 18 Hyde Park Street, W.
Wheeler, Frederic Elijah, 55 Lordship Park, N.
Whitehead, Sir James, Bart., 9 Cambridge Gate, Regent's Park, N.W.
*Whitehead, Rev. J. H., M.A., The Poplars, Alsager, Stoke-on-Trent.
Whitehead, Rowland, 14 Old Square, Lincoln's Inn, W.C.
Whitworth, Rev. Richard H., Vicar of Blidworth, Mansfield.
Wild, William I., 130 Shaw Heath, Stockport.
Wilkinson, Alfred, 23 The Terrace, Kennington Park, S.E.
Wilkinson, R. J., Singapore, Straits Settlements.
Williams, Major E. Calvin, LL.B., F.R.G.S., 1302 St. Paul Street, Baltimore, Maryland, U.S.A.
Williams, E. P., Elmhurst, Westcombe Park Road, Blackheath, S.E.
* Williams, Rev. J. D., M.A., The Vicarage, Bottisham, Cambridge.
Williams, Miss Margaret Elizabeth, 63 Shaw Street, Liverpool.
Williams, Richard, Celynog, Newtown, North Wales.
Williamson, George Charles, Ph.D., The Mount, Guildford, Surrey.
Williamson, John M., Melville House, Overhill Road, Dulwich, S.E.
Wilson, Rev. Edwin William, 73 Cadogan Terrace, Victoria Park, N.E.
Winters, William, Churchyard, Waltham Abbey, Essex.

LIST OF FELLOWS.

Wonnacott, J., F.G.S., F.R.G.S., Wadham House, Liskeard, Cornwall.
Wood, Alexander, M.A., 3 St. Peter's Square, Ravenscourt Park, W.
Wood, William, 173 Choumert Road, East Dulwich, S.E.
Woodhouse, Alderman S., 50 High Street, Hull.
Woodroffe, Prof. Latham James, M.A., 81 Waterloo Road, Dublin.
Wright, W. H. K., Free Library, Plymouth.
Wurtzburg, John Henry, Clavering House, 2 De Gray Road, Leeds.
Wyatt-Davies, Ernest, B.A., Trinity College, Cambridge.
Wyles, Thomas, F.G.S., The College, Buxton.

Yates, James, Public Library, Leeds.
York, The Archbishop of, Bishopthorpe, York.
Young, Miss Ernestine C., High School for Girls, 5 Portland Place, Bath.
Young, Herbert Edward, White Hart Street, High Wycombe, Bucks.

Zerffi, Henry Charles, 14 Randolph Crescent, Maida Vale, W.

The Council request that any inaccuracy in the foregoing list may be pointed out to the Secretary, and that all changes of address may be notified to him, so that delay in forwarding communications and the Publications of the Society may be avoided.

FOREIGN ASSOCIATIONS
WHICH EXCHANGE TRANSACTIONS WITH THE SOCIETY.

AUSTRALIA.
The Royal Society of New South Wales.

AUSTRIA.
The Imperial Academy of Sciences, Vienna.

BELGIUM.
Académie royale des Sciences des Lettres et des Beaux-Arts, Palais des Académies, Brussels.
Société d'Archéologie de Bruxelles, rue des Palais 63, Bruxelles.

BOHEMIA.
The Royal Society of Bohemia, Prague.

CANADA.
L'Institut Canadien-français d'Ottawa.
Geological and Natural History Survey Museum, Ottawa.
The Literary and Historical Society, Quebec.

DENMARK.
The Royal Society of Northern Antiquaries, Copenhagen.

FRANCE.
Société d'Ethnographie, 28 Rue Mazarine, Paris.

GERMANY.
The Historical Society of Berlin.

ITALY.
The State Archives of Tuscany.
British and American Archæological Society of Rome, 20 Via S. Basilio, Rome.

PORTUGAL.
The Royal Academy of Sciences, Lisbon.

RUSSIA.
The Imperial Archæological Society, St. Petersburg.

SPAIN.
The Royal Historical Society, Madrid.
The National Archæological Society, Madrid.

SWEDEN.
The Royal Society of Antiquaries of Sweden, Stockholm.
The Royal Academy of Belles-Lettres, History, and Antiquities, Stockholm.

TASMANIA.
The Royal Society of Tasmania.

UNITED STATES.
The Smithsonian Institution, Washington.
The Johns Hopkins University, Baltimore.
New England Historic-Genealogical Society, Boston, Mass.
The Historical Society of New York, 170 Second Avenue, New York.
The Historical Society of Pennsylvania, Philadelphia.
The Academy of Arts and Sciences, New Haven, Connecticut.
The Georgia Historical Society, Savannah, Georgia.
The Massachusetts Historical Society, Boston.
The Historical Society of Rhode Island, Providence, R.I.
The Historical Society of Virginia, Richmond.
The Historical Society of Maryland, Baltimore.
The Historical Society of Missouri, St. Louis, Mo.
The Historical Society of Minnesota, St. Paul, Minnesota.
The Historical Society of South Carolina.
The Historical Society of Vermont.
The Historical Society of Michigan.
The Historical Society of New Jersey.
The Historical Society of Maine.
Peabody Institute, Baltimore, U.S.A., care of E. G. Allen,
    28 Henrietta Street, Covent Garden.

LIBRARIES TO WHICH THE SOCIETY'S TRANSACTIONS ARE PRESENTED.
Mason Science College, Birmingham.
South Kensington Museum.
Royal Institution, Albemarle Street, W.
Historical School, Cambridge, c/o O. Browning, King's College,
    Cambridge.
Chetham's Library, Hunt's Bank, Manchester.
Imperial Institute, Imperial Institute Road, S.W.

www.ingramcontent.com/pod-product-compliance
Lightning Source LLC
Chambersburg PA
CBHW020326240426

43673CB00039B/928